£27

The Decision to Disarm Germany

The Decision to Disarm Germany

British Policy towards Postwar
German Disarmament, 1914–1919

LORNA S. JAFFE

Boston
ALLEN & UNWIN
London   Sydney

Allen & Unwin, Inc.,
Fifty Cross Street, Winchester, Mass. 01890, USA

George Allen & Unwin (Publishers) Ltd,
40 Museum Street, London WC1A 1LU, UK

George Allen & Unwin (Publishers) Ltd,
Park Lane, Hemel Hempstead, Herts HP2 4TE, UK

George Allen & Unwin Australia Pty Ltd,
8 Napier Street, North Sydney, NSW 2060, Australia

First published in 1985

Library of Congress Cataloging in Publication Data

Jaffe, Lorna S.
　　The decision to disarm Germany.
Bibliography: p.
Includes index.
1. Great Britain—Military policy.　2. Great Britain—Military
relations—Germany.　3. Germany—Military relations—Great
Britain.　4. World War, 1914–1918—Great Britain.　5. World War,
1914–1918—Germany.　I. Title.
UA647.J34　1984　　　355′.0335′41　　　84–12351
ISBN 0-04-943034-3 (alk. paper)

British Library Cataloguing in Publication Data

Jaffe, Lorna S.
　　The decision to disarm Germany.
1. World War, 1914–1918—Peace　2. Germany—History—Allied
occupation, 1918–1930　3. Great Britain—Foreign
relations—Germany　4. Germany—Foreign relations—Great Britain
I. Title
327.1′74　　　D650.D5
ISBN 0-04-943034-3

Set in 10 on 12 Plantin by
Phoenix Photosetting, Chatham
Printed in Great Britain by
Billing and Sons Ltd, London and Worcester

Contents

To My Parents

Preface

Although Britain's 1914–19 war aims and Peace Conference policy
have received considerable scholarly attention, British policy on the
question of German military disarmament has remained a neglected
area. Many historians have made assumptions about the origins of
the disarmament provisions of the Treaty of Versailles without,
however, having carefully examined the evidence. This book seeks
to fill the gap in scholarship about British policy and about the
disarmament question and to set the record straight on the origins of
the Paris Peace Conference demands for German disarmament. It
will, I hope, also contribute to the debate over the relationship
between internal and external factors in the formulation of foreign
policy and to an understanding of the problem of arms control.

My original intention had been to examine the Lloyd George
government's policy towards execution of the disarmament
provisions of the Treaty of Versailles. However, in doing research
for what was planned as a background chapter to that study I found
that though disarming Germany was a fundamental objective of
Britain's Peace Conference policy, postwar German disarmament
had not been a British war aim. Intrigued, I therefore turned my
attention to the unexplored area of how and why German
disarmament became such an important goal of British policy.

The resulting book examines the political, diplomatic and
strategic reasons why German disarmament was neither a British war
aim nor an armistice condition demanded by Britain. It also considers
the politics and diplomacy of the issue of general disarmament, the
government's approach to which was decisive in making German
disarmament a British objective. Beginning with the election
campaign of 1918, the study traces the process by which postwar
German disarmament became a goal of British policy and then
analyses Britain's Peace Conference diplomacy, which resulted in
the inclusion of Britain's disarmament demands in the disarmament
provisions of the Treaty of Versailles. A brief survey of Britain's
postwar policy towards enforcement of the treaty's disarmament
provisions discusses the consequences for the interwar period of

Britain's wartime and Peace Conference approach to the question of German disarmament.

Robert Bunselmeyer, Gaddis Smith and Robin Winks provided guidance and assistance during the preparation of the Yale University doctoral dissertation upon which this book is based. Grants from the Concilium on International and Area Studies and the International Relations Council at Yale and an Anne S. Richardson Fellowship from the Yale Graduate School helped make possible my research in the United Kingdom. I would also like to express my appreciation to Paul M. Kennedy for his interest and assistance and to Zara Steiner for her valuable suggestions. David R. Davis, Gertrude Dieken, Jonathan Dull, Herbert Ershkowitz, John E. Jessup and Wayne Maxson also provided valuable assistance. I wish to thank, too, the publishers and editors and all the others who aided my work. I alone, of course, am responsible for the book's contents.

For their assistance, I wish to express my appreciation to the staffs of the archives listed in the bibliography and of the Conservative Research Department and the Institute of Historical Research, University of London. For permission to use and to quote from private papers, I am grateful to Viscount Addison; the Rt Hon. Julian Amery; Lady Arthur; the Trustees of the First Beaverbrook Foundation; Mrs Mary Bennett; Mr Mark Bonham Carter; the British Library; the Trustees of the late Lord Bryce; the Master, Fellows and Scholars of Churchill College in the University of Cambridge; the Hon. Mrs Harriet A. M. Tyrrell Crawshay; Lord Croft; the Earl of Cromer; the Earl of Derby; Viscount Esher; Earl Haig; Baron Hardinge of Penshurst and the Hon. Julian Hardinge; Professor Agnes Headlam-Morley; the Clerk of the Records, House of Lords Record Office; the Trustees of the Imperial War Museum; Professor Ann K. S. Lambton; the Trustees of the Liddell Hart Centre for Military Archives, King's College, University of London; Liverpool City Library; the Marquess of Lothian; Mr Philip Mallet; the National Library of Wales; the Warden and Fellows of New College, Oxford; Mrs Mary Z. Pain; the Earl of Perth; Lord Robertson; Sir Anthony Rumbold; the Marquess of Salisbury; Mr L. P. Scott; Mr J. C. Smuts; Mrs Edith Stonequist; the University of Birmingham; Baroness Eirene Lloyd White; Yale University Library. Quotations from Crown copyright material in the Public

Record Office, India Office Library and Records and private collections appear by permission of the Controller of Her Majesty's Stationery Office. Every effort has been made to trace and to secure permission from the copyright-holders for all manuscript material under copyright quoted in this book. If I have inadvertently infringed upon such rights, I offer sincere apologies.

L. S. J.

Philadelphia, Pennsylvania
June 1983

Introduction

The most comprehensive examination of Britain's war aims in the First World War makes no mention of German military disarmament as a wartime British objective,[1] and as recently as 1981 a study of Britain's peace conference diplomacy attributed the disarmament provisions of the Treaty of Versailles to France.[2] While one historian of Britain's postwar defence policy has asserted that 'the first object of British defence policy in the aftermath of the Great War was to disarm Germany and to keep her disarmed',[3] studies of British policy in the 1920s point out Britain's willingness to make concessions to Germany regarding the fulfilment of the treaty's disarmament provisions.[4] Yet Britain's insistence at the Paris Conference on the necessity of disarming Germany has long been a matter of record.[5] Indeed, it was Great Britain which introduced the disarmament question at the Paris Peace Conference and took the lead there in pressing for German disarmament.

Why was German disarmament not a British war aim? How did it then become one of Britain's chief objectives at the Paris Peace Conference? Do the answers to these questions also suggest an explanation for Britain's early flexibility on the question of interpreting German compliance with the disarmament provisions of the Treaty of Versailles?

In seeking to answer these questions, this study of the politics and diplomacy of Britain's German disarmament policy examines British strategic thinking in its political context, exploring the interrelationship between domestic and imperial politics and foreign and defence policy. While arguing that the demands of public opinion and party politics played a pivotal role in making German disarmament an object of British policy, it also emphasises that strategic and geopolitical considerations were critical determinants of Britain's policy on the question of German disarmament.

It also suggests that there was another crucial influence on British policy-makers. This was the profound impact of the war itself. Neither Britain's war leaders nor its bureaucrats were men deciding policy aloof from the horrors of war. The overpowering presence of mourners' stationery in their private correspondence conveys some sense of the impact of the war on their lives. The sons of both of Britain's war premiers served in the war as did the sons of other ministers and officials. Prime Minister Henry Asquith's oldest son was killed in action. Conservative leader Andrew Bonar Law lost two sons. The oldest son of Arthur Henderson, first Labour member of the Cabinet, died on the Somme. Sir William Tyrrell and Lord Charles Hardinge of the Foreign Office each lost a son. The brother of Prime Minister David Lloyd George's secretary and mistress Frances Stevenson was killed in action as was the brother of Philip Kerr, his chief foreign policy adviser. When Lloyd George himself visited the front and hospitalised wounded, he was devastated by what he saw.[6] British policy-makers' experience of the war's devastation fostered a determination to prevent the recurrence of war, and it was from this perspective as well that they approached the issue of German disarmament.

Britain's changing position on postwar German disarmament reflected an ongoing debate about how best to guarantee postwar peace. At the heart of this debate were differing assumptions about the causes of war, about the nature of world politics and about Britain's appropriate strategic role. This debate was not confined to official circles but was carried on as well in the press and in political pamphlets, in Parliament and on the public platform. Through this debate, pressure groups and the moulders of public opinion affected government policy, and the government influenced public opinion. The interplay of ideas in this debate shaped the way in which British policy-makers perceived the political and strategic developments with which they had to deal and provided the framework within which they decided British policy on the question of German disarmament.

1

Destroying Prussian Militarism

The British declaration of war against Germany in August 1914 required a complete reorientation of Liberal attitudes towards Germany. After the Agadir crisis the Liberal government, despite repeated rebuffs, had worked for an improvement in Anglo-German relations. When attempts to reach a naval understanding with Germany proved unsuccessful, the Asquith government sought other areas of agreement. During the First Balkan War Britain and Germany worked together to avert a general war, prompting the Liberal *Nation* to exult, 'In the long tension of this crisis Berlin and London have learned to know each other, and the knowledge has brought only respect for each other's loyalty and good-will in purpose.'[1] While this appraisal was more wishful thinking than accurate assessment, the successful outcome of co-operation with Germany reinforced 'the liberal government's fixed idea of overcoming her hostility by kindness'.[2] Between 1912 and the summer of 1914 tensions between the two powers eased as a result of the Liberal government's interest in conciliating Germany.

By July 1914 Britain and Germany had reached agreements on outstanding colonial differences and relations with Germany appeared to be at a new high point. J. A. Spender, editor of the Asquithian Liberal *Westminster Gazette*, later recalled, 'I was more hopeful of British and German relations in the early months of 1914 than at any time since 1906'.[3] Spender believed that his perception was typical of journalists specialising in foreign affairs.[4] It was certainly the view held by Liberal journalists. The *Contemporary Review*, a journal edited by the Liberal historian G. P. Gooch, while not as euphoric as the more Radical *Nation*, also found encouragement in the direction of Anglo-German relations. In its review of foreign affairs the July issue reported that 'the Anglo-German estrangement . . . is happily losing its acuteness'.[5]

The Liberal government shared this optimism. In early June members of the Cabinet reacted with disbelief when President Wilson's emissary Colonel Edward M. House reported the war fever which he had found on his recent visit to Berlin.[6] Three days before the assassination of Archduke Ferdinand of Austria and his wife at Sarajevo Foreign Secretary Sir Edward Grey told Sir Francis Bertie, Britain's Ambassador to France, 'We are on good terms with Germany now and we desire to avoid a revival of friction with her'.[7] Speaking in the House of Commons only twelve days before Britain declared war on Germany, Chancellor of the Exchequer David Lloyd George, a leading member of the Cabinet, went even further. Despite the international situation he spoke optimistically of the improvement in Anglo-German relations:

> Our relations are very much better than they were a few years ago . . . those two great, I will not say rival nations, but two great Empires. The feeling is better altogether between them. They begin to realise they can co-operate for common ends, and that the points of co-operation are greater and more numerous and more important than the points of possible controversy.[8]

Friendship with Germany was a touchstone of the prewar Liberal approach to foreign policy. Apprehensive that it might be dragged into Continental quarrels by either France or Russia, the Liberal government wished to maintain good relations both with its Entente partners, on the one hand, and with Germany on the other. Objecting to the government's Entente policy and fearing the domestic consequences of Anglo-German rivalry, its Liberal critics preached friendship with Germany. They were particularly vociferous in their opposition to the accord with Russia, contrasting backward and autocratic Russia with civilised Germany, with which they felt that Britain shared a special relationship.

This image of Anglo-German relations was particularly strong within the Radical wing of the Liberal Party. Two leading Radicals, Noel Buxton and Arthur Ponsonby, in 1912 formed the Liberal Foreign Affairs Group to promote an improvement in Anglo-German relations. Over seventy members of the Liberal Party joined the group, which remained active until the outbreak of war. In January 1912 the Executive Committee of the National Liberal Federation, the chief political organisation of the Radicals, affirmed that group's commitment to an understanding with Germany, 'a country with which we have . . . many powerful ties of race, commerce, and historic association'.[9] Addressing the federation's 1912 Annual Conference, Sir John Brunner, the organisation's president, further enunciated this Liberal view of Anglo-German relations: 'Racially, intellectually, and morally we were much nearer Germany than France. It was only necessary to know Germany well in order to desire to draw nearer to her. The Germans were a strong and manly people like the English. He wanted these two strong, manly people to work together'.[10] This emphasis on common background and interests and on the desirability of co-operation was a view of Anglo-German relations which persisted in Liberal circles until the German violation of Belgian neutrality.

Even when it became clear that a general European war was imminent, leading Liberals cited Britain and Germany's community of interests and Germany's contributions to civilisation as arguments for British neutrality. The Radical journalist and author Norman Angell organised a Neutrality League, which issued a manifesto arguing that 'Germany . . . is . . . highly civilised, with a culture that has contributed enormously in the past to Western civilisation, racially allied to ourselves, and with moral ideals largely resembling our own'.[11] The 1 August issue of the *Daily News*, London's best-selling Liberal daily, carried a declaration in support of neutrality from its Radical editor A. G. Gardiner, who called German civilisation 'the most enlightened intellectual life of the modern world'.[12] Gardiner's leading article evoked a long supporting letter to the editor from the eminent Liberal historian G. M. Trevelyan opposing war against 'the kindred civilisation of Germany'.[13] Among well-known Liberals, particularly among intellectuals and journalists, then, the traditional Liberal view of Anglo-German relations prevailed until the very eve of British entry into the war.

This view appeared in Parliament as well as in the press. Liberal MPs who opposed British intervention, like their counterparts outside Parliament, stressed the congruence of British and German civilisation. Opposing Grey's statement in the House of Commons in favour of intervention, Joseph King, Liberal MP for North Somerset, called the war 'a war against German civilisation, and the German people who are our friends'.[14] The Radical Arnold Rowntree, MP for York and, like King, a member of the Liberal Foreign Affairs Group, reminded the government:

When we go to war against Germany we go to war against a people who, after all, hold largely the ideals which we hold . . . the German civilisation is in many ways near the British civilisation. We think of their literature, we think of what they have done for progressive religious thought, we think of what they have done for philosophy, and we say that these are not the men we want to fight.[15]

For most Liberals Germany's invasion of Belgium produced an almost overnight reversal of these attitudes. In the words of R. C. K. Ensor, himself a prewar Radical, 'For years past the liberals . . . had been making it an article of party faith that militarist Germany was not so black as it was painted. Now in a flash it seemed to them self-revealed as much blacker'.[16] The reaction of the protagonist of H. G. Wells's wartime novel *Mr. Britling Sees It Through* exemplifies this transformation: 'He hadn't realised . . . how angry and scornful he was at this final coming into action of the Teutonic militarism that had so long menaced his world. He had always said it would never really fight – and here it was fighting! He was furious with the indignation of an apologist betrayed'.[17]

Feeling thus betrayed, most of the Liberals who had been such outspoken proponents of Anglo-German friendship became ardent supporters of the war effort. The Liberal Foreign Affairs Group ceased to exist. The National Liberal Federation did not meet during the war; Brunner, its president, gave his wholehearted support to the British cause. The 5 August edition of the *Daily News*, after criticising the direction of British foreign policy over the past ten years, declared nevertheless, 'Being in, we must win'.[18] On 15 August the *Nation* published a leading article entitled 'Why Britain is right', and on 24 October its Radical editor, H. W. Massingham, issued a *mea culpa*: 'The Liberal miscalculation was in thinking that Germany was less in the hands of an explosive militarism, framed to burst on Europe at any convenient hour, than she proved to be.'[19] While some Liberals, including Ponsonby, King and Rowntree, did not join this chorus of support for the war, the preponderance of Liberal opinion threw its weight behind the government's prosecution of the war.

The Liberals who endorsed the war did not, however, totally repudiate their prewar views. Two weeks into the war C. P. Scott's perception of Germany was little different from prewar Liberal pronouncements. In a leading article in the *Manchester Guardian* the Radical proprietor and editor described the German people as 'to-day . . . our enemies but . . . not always to be our enemies, a great nation whose achievements in every sphere of human activity have made the world richer and whom the world can never spare'.[20] The distinguished Liberal elder statesman Lord Bryce, who in the years before the war had worked to improve Anglo-German relations and had, like so many other Liberals, come to support British participation in the war only after the German violation of Belgian neutrality, expressed a similar point of view. Writing in the *Daily Chronicle* at the beginning of October, Bryce, who had studied law at Heidelberg before German unification and had written a major work on the Holy Roman Empire, pointed out the close ties between Britain and Germany and reaffirmed his respect for the contributions of German intellectuals.[21]

The persistence of these earlier attitudes affected Liberals' approach to the war. Rationalising the sudden transformation of their position on British participation in war against Germany, Liberals contended that Britain was fighting not the German people but, rather, what they described as Germany's Prussian militarist governing class. Within days of the British declaration of war Liberal journals were proclaiming this distinction. On 8 August the *Nation* asserted, 'With the German people we have still, in spite of war, no individual quarrel'.[22] In that day's edition of the *Daily News* Gardiner agreed: 'Let us be quite clear in our minds as to the real enemy. We have no quarrel with the German people . . . No, it is not the people with whom we are at war. It is the tyranny of personal government armed with the mailed fist, the tyranny of a despotic rule.'[23] Even the erstwhile Liberal elder statesman Lord Cromer, who had been instrumental in bringing about the Anglo-French Entente and had consistently warned against the German danger, shared this point of view: 'There is a very bitter feeling, not so much against the German people as against the German Emperor and the militarist party in Germany.'[24]

Having made this distinction and believing that the war's 'one salient good will be the early and complete destruction of German militarism',[25] Liberals felt justified in giving all-out support to the British war effort. Indeed, Cromer, who retained his faith in Liberalism despite his defection from the Liberal Party, argued that his commitment to the war derived from his commitment to

Liberalism: 'One of the reasons I wish to do so [go on fighting] is *because* I am a Liberal, and believe that unless Kaiserism is suppressed, the cause of Liberal progress, not only in Germany, but also throughout the world, will receive a deadly blow.'[26]

Thus while they disavowed any interest in destroying Germany, Liberals insisted none the less that the war must continue until the Allies had destroyed German militarism. The first issue of the *Nation* published after British entry into the war declared, 'The struggle must now be carried on with the utmost energy, not indeed until Germany is crushed, but until a German aggression is defeated and German militarism broken.'[27] In the *Daily News* Gardiner outlined the same objective: 'Our war is with the Kaiser and Kaiserism; let us destroy them, but do not let us aim at destroying Germany.'[28] In February 1915 when Colonel House, in England on a peace mission, asked J. A. Spender for Liberals' views on peace terms, Spender replied that Liberals were 'specially resolute to pursue the war until the whole Prussian system & the order of ideas it represented could be brought to book and stamped out'.[29] Mr Britling popularised this Liberal concept of the war:

> Even now I cannot believe that a whole great people can be possessed by war madness. I think the war is the work of the German armaments party and of the Court party. They have forced this war on Germany . . . So long as they win, Germany will hold together, so long as their armies are not clearly defeated nor their navy destroyed. But once check them and stay them and beat them, then I believe that suddenly the spirit of Germany will change.[30]

In this way Liberals helped to turn the British war effort into a crusade against Prussian militarism and fostered the notion that complete victory would be necessary in order to achieve their objective.

The Liberal distinction between the German people and Prussian militarists was also part of government thinking. In attributing responsibility for the war to Germany, British leaders blamed the dominance of the Prussian military class for Germany's aggressive policy. This perception shaped their thinking about the purposes for which they were fighting, and the concept of the war as a crusade against Prussian militarism soon became official policy.

During the July crisis the prevalent view within the Cabinet was that there was a struggle in Berlin between a military war party and a civilian peace party. This had been the assessment of the Lord Chancellor, Viscount Haldane, since visiting Germany at the beginning of his tenure as War Secretary in 1906.[31] Grey had based his post-Agadir policy towards Germany on his belief in the existence of this conflict and his hope that a policy of conciliation would strengthen the peace party. The Foreign Secretary later wrote of Anglo-German co-operation during the First Balkan War: 'We got on very well with Germany at that time, because the Prussian military party did not think the time for war had come, and left the civil element alone.'[32] Throughout July 1914 he continued to base his actions on the hope that the civilian element would win the struggle and that Germany would act as a brake on Austria. The Austrian declaration of war on Serbia dashed these hopes.

Haldane's comment on 28 July that 'the German General Staff is in the saddle'[33] encapsuled the perception of other members of the Cabinet as well. Both Attorney-General Sir John Simon and Lloyd George told C. P. Scott on 3 August that the war party had gained control in Berlin.[34] On 4 August Grey told the American Ambassador Walter Hines Page: 'We must remember that there are two Germanys. There is the Germany of men like ourselves . . . Then there is the Germany of men of the war party. The war party has got the upper hand.'[35] When Horace Rumbold, chargé d'affaires in Berlin, who in the absence of the ambassador had conducted negotiations with the German government during the last days of the crisis, returned to London, he confirmed this analysis.[36] By the end of August even the bellicose First Lord of the Admiralty Winston Churchill, who had not shared his colleagues' hopes about maintaining peace, was telling an interviewer that the Prussian military autocracy had started the war.[37]

The belief that the war had come about only because the military party had gained control of decision-making in Germany was an illusion – an illusion fostered by the very civilian elements within the German government which the British leaders had thought to be working for peace – for there was no peace party in Berlin in July 1914. Their mistaken notion of the origins of the war led British ministers in August 1914 to conclude that in order to prevent a recurrence of war it would be necessary to discredit completely the German military party and so prevent its ever again directing

German policy. Only then would Europe – and Britain – be secure. How this was to be accomplished was neither clearly defined nor agreed upon, with the views even of individual ministers fluctuating with the fortunes of war and their own political fortunes. Nevertheless, despite military setbacks and changes in political leadership, from British entry into the war through the pre-Armistice discussions of October 1918 this belief – though sometimes held simultaneously with totally contradictory assumptions about the general causes of war – formed the basis of the British government's attitude towards the war. Grey's October 1914 description of his own position summarised this guiding principle of British policy: 'I can see nothing for it but to fight on till we can get a peace that will secure us against Prussian militarism. Once freed of that, Germany will have nothing to fear, because we shall have no more to fear from her.'[38]

In their references to Prussian militarism the statements of Britain's war leaders read much like the Liberal interpretation of the war which found expression in the columns of the *Nation* and the *Daily News*. Their public statements expressed their belief that the domination of the Prussian military class within Germany had caused the war and that the war must therefore bring about the end of that domination. In a letter addressed to a meeting of his constituents Grey asserted, 'It is against German militarism that we must fight . . . It is not the German people, but Prussian militarism which has driven Germany and Europe into this war.'[39] Asquith approached the war from a similar perspective. In a speech at Cardiff on 2 October 1914 he was careful to distinguish between the German people and those in control of German policy.[40] Lloyd George, a renegade Radical who had opposed British entry into the war until Germany invaded Belgium, justified the change in his position by making the same distinction. In one of his first speeches on the war he declared, 'We are not fighting the German people. The German people are under the heel of this [Prussian Junker] military caste.'[41]

On 9 November 1914 Asquith first included the destruction of Prussian militarism among Britain's publicly declared war aims. He told an audience at the Guildhall, 'We shall never sheathe the sword . . . until the military domination of Prussia is wholly and finally destroyed'.[42] In April 1916 in response to a speech by the German Chancellor which contended that the Allies wanted to destroy Germany the Prime Minister restated the British position:

Great Britain . . . entered the war not to strangle Germany, not to wipe her off the map of Europe, not to destroy or mutilate her national life . . .

As a result of the war we intend to establish the principle . . . that this settlement [of international problems] shall no longer be hampered and swayed over by the over-mastering dictation of a Government controlled by a military caste. That is what I mean by the destruction of the military domination of Prussia: nothing more, but nothing less.[43]

Thus over a year and a half into the war Asquith continued to maintain the distinction between Germany and the Prussian military caste, which he believed controlled the German government.

When Lloyd George became Prime Minister, he reaffirmed Asquith's declarations. In his first speech to the House of Commons as Prime Minister, Lloyd George attributed the war to 'the arrogant spirit of the Prussian military caste'. Rejecting the notion of destroying Germany, he asserted: 'The Allies entered this war to defend themselves against the aggression of the Prussian military domination, and having begun it, they must insist that it can only end with the most complete and effective guarantee against the possibility of that caste ever again disturbing the peace of Europe.'[44]

Asquith's and Lloyd George's language was characteristic of wartime public pronouncements. Lloyd George, in particular, used rhetoric designed to inflame or inspire his audiences. But it is a mistake completely to discount such statements as 'verbiage'.[45] They reflected a basic presupposition about the origins of the war and a genuine belief about the purpose for which Britain was fighting. Private communications and departmental memoranda echoed these public statements, and the underlying assumptions of these public pronouncements affected attitudes towards the question of disarming Germany after the war.

The private attitudes of public officials were identical with the views expressed on the public platform. Lloyd George, for example, wrote to his wife stating that he favoured 'beat[ing] the German Junker but no war on the German people'.[46] In his correspondence Grey, too, reiterated his public position, calling attention to the 'distinction we draw between Germany and the Prussian military caste'[47]: 'It is the Prussian Junkers alone, I believe, who have created all this, and the rest of the Germans are people more akin to ourselves than any other race.'[48] These sentiments were typical of the attitudes of the leading members of the Liberal government.

What was for Liberal journalists an ideological justification for British participation in the war became an underlying assumption of government policy. The first departmental attempts at defining Britain's war aims unquestioningly accepted the Liberal interpretation of the war. Comments by Admiral Sir Henry Jackson, who became First Sea Lord in May 1915, reveal that the Admiralty certainly regarded Asquith's public statements as declarations of the basis of British policy: 'These observations [the Admiralty's recommendations for peace terms] have been made on the assumption that the policy of Great Britain is that which was announced at the beginning of the war, viz., the breaking down of the military Government and domination of Prussia.'[49]

Within the Foreign Office, career officials – obviously not writing for public consumption – manifested the same attitude expressed in Asquith's and Lloyd George's speeches. In a memorandum drafted in August 1916 Sir William Tyrrell and Sir Ralph Paget attributed the war to Prussian aggression but disavowed any intention of crushing Germany: 'The Allies . . . are not out to crush Germany, but . . . to impair the hegemony of Prussia . . . The preparations for this war, the impulse to this war, the aggressive designs connected with this war, are all traceable to Prussian enterprise.'[50] Another memorandum submitted the following January to the Committee of Imperial Defence Sub-Committee on Territorial Changes by Tyrrell, Sir Louis Mallet and George Clerk, the Foreign Office representatives on the committee, employed the Liberal distinction between 'the naturally peaceful inclinations' of the German people and the aims of their Prussian militarist rulers. It, too, rejected the notion of destroying Germany: 'We are not out to destroy a race of 70,000,000 people in the centre of Europe.'[51] Paget had belonged to the pro-German minority within the prewar Foreign Office, and in the two years before the war Tyrrell had worked to achieve an Anglo-German understanding. Their adoption of the Liberal perspective on the war did not therefore call for a significant departure from their earlier views. However, Mallet, who chaired the CID sub-committee, was self-described as one of 'the 3 most prominent & outspoken anti-Germans in the [foreign and diplomatic] service'.[52] Just four months before, he had written a rabidly anti-German letter to his equally Germanophobe friend

Leopold Maxse, editor of the *National Review*, expressing his wish to destroy Germany.[53] His willingness to attach his name to a memorandum embodying quite the opposite views indicates the extent to which the Liberal interpretation had permeated official thinking. Indeed, Arthur J. Balfour, Conservative First Lord of the Admiralty in Asquith's Coalition government, acknowledged that the Liberal outlook had become the common view when he wrote in 1916 that 'most observers think' that 'the driving force behind German aggression be due . . . to Prussian organisation and Prussian traditions'.[54]

It is clear from their correspondence that, other than Mallet, Foreign Office civil servants were not simply grudgingly promulgating an official policy basis with which they disagreed. For example, Eric Drummond, who became Grey's private secretary in the spring of 1915, wrote privately of 'the difference between the German military clique & the German people'.[55] After becoming Minister to Denmark Paget affirmed his belief in the need 'to dictate terms to Germany' because 'otherwise we may consider the war as practically lost . . . negotiating & bargaining . . . would mean that the military party in Germany still possessed life & its one thought would be to prepare for a war of revenge'.[56] Tyrrell, who as Grey's private secretary had concurred in his chief's interpretation of the dichotomy within the German leadership, in 1918 retained his belief that 'when the extravagant hopes of German generals remain unfulfilled', there would be 'a change for the better' in German policy.[57]

The notion of a conflict between the civilian and military leadership in Germany and its companion concept, the distinction between the German people and their government did not, however, gain universal acceptance among those in positions of influence. Opposing these assumptions were the two extremes of, on the one hand, fanatical Germanophobes who painted with the same brush all Germans, including Britons of German origin and, at the opposite pole, equally fanatical pacifists who denied any German responsibility for the war. There were also government officials who rejected the prevailing interpretation. Foremost among these was Sir Eyre Crowe, the Foreign Office permanent official most knowledgeable about Germany. During the July crisis Crowe, author of the famous 1907 memorandum on Anglo-German relations, argued that 'the one restraining influence' on German action was fear of British entry into a war involving France and Belgium, not any efforts of the civilian elements within the German government, which he believed, rather, to have 'egged on the Austrians'.[58] At the Foreign Office the Permanent Under-Secretary, Sir Arthur Nicolson, agreed with Crowe, warning Grey in July 1914 that 'Berlin is playing with us'.[59] Not even all the Liberal press unequivocally accepted the Liberal distinction between the German people and the German government. On the same day on which the *Daily Chronicle* featured the Bryce article cited earlier it also ran a leading article questioning Bryce's – and other Liberals' – uncritical acceptance of the existence of this distinction: 'Some of us are perhaps rather incautious in the sharp line which we draw between the German Government and its people. The line in reality is not sharp.'[60]

Others went further. In a series of lectures delivered in the autumn of 1914 the noted historian of late-eighteenth- and nineteenth-century Europe J. Holland Rose, who attributed the war to Germany's dynamic growth and increased population's having led it to seek world power, accordingly took sharp issue with the prevailing view, declaring that 'our war with Germany is one of people against people. The fact must be faced. It has been asserted that the war was due to the Kaiser or to a few wicked persons at Berlin. That is incorrect.'

> We must therefore dismiss from our minds the thought that we are at war merely with a Government which has blinded its subjects. That is inconsistent with the facts of the situation. It is also not a struggle with a dominant military caste, which may be overthrown after a few defeats. We are at war with a practically united nation.[61]

Also disagreeing with the common view of the war, the *éminence grise* Lord Esher used language virtually identical to Rose's: 'We are not fighting the German Emperor or the German military caste. We are engaged in a life-or-death conflict with the German people of all sorts and classes.'[62]

Two leading imperialists, the Conservative backbenchers Leopold S. Amery and W. A. S. Hewins, worried that the government's emphasis on Prussian militarism would deflect Britain from what they conceived to be its true imperial interests. Fearing in the summer of 1917 that the Lloyd George government would agree to a negotiated peace, making impossible the economically punitive terms which he and his cohorts in the Unionist Business Committee desired, Hewins complained of 'the persistent error of our politicians that we have in Germany an enslaved people driven into war unwillingly by the Kaiser & the military caste'.[63] Amery shared Hewins's economic concerns and, like Rose, saw the war in terms of a German bid for world power.[64] In 1915 he wrote to his mentor, the imperialist doyen Lord Milner, that 'all this harping on Prussian militarism as something that must be rooted out . . . is wholly mischievous. It all tends to drag us into a false little England position.'[65] Furthermore, Amery disagreed with the contention that it was only the military party in Germany which sanctioned war as the best means of attaining Germany's objectives, that the war would discredit this position in the eyes of the German people and that a basic change in the German system would prevent future wars: 'The war may end by curing the German people of its belief in force as the sovereign remedy – it has done the converse so far – and if it does the German system of government may be upset or modified. But the dethronement of the Hohenzollerns . . . will not materially affect the general causes which lead to war.'[66]

These dissenting opinions did not represent the only challenge to the prevailing view. It was clear from the German press and from German propaganda pamphlets, to which both the government and newspaper correspondents had access through neutral countries, that there was widespread support in Germany for that government's war policy.

However, by the end of 1914 the idea of the war as a crusade against Prussian militarism had become a powerful motivating myth. The autumn issue of the imperialist quarterly the *Round Table* included an article entitled 'Germany and the Prussian spirit', which declared, 'The war between the British and German Empires is not in its essence a war of interests; it is a war of ideals'.[67] So pervasive was this belief that when Norman Angell revised his bestselling *The Great Illusion*, he devoted the new portions of the book to a discussion of this concept and entitled the edition, which appeared in December 1914, *Prussianism and its Destruction*.[68] With the exception of a few dissenters, virtually all shades of political opinion accepted the concept of the war as a struggle against Prussian militarism. Concluding a series of articles on suggested peace terms, Clifford Sharp, editor of the Fabian socialist *New Statesman*, asserted that 'the destruction of Prussian militarism . . . by general consent, is not merely an item, but the chief item, in the programme of the Allies. If Prussian militarism does not cease to exist as a factor in European politics the victory of the Allies will have been won in vain'.[69] Such a statement certainly appealed to popular anti-Germanism, fanned most effectively by the Northcliffe press, especially the *Daily Mail*. Extreme Germanophobes like Lord Northcliffe could accept the idea of destroying Prussian militarism and adapt it to their own purposes while rejecting the premise on which that notion was based. Most pacifists did not object to ending Prussianism. Rather, they defined the term more broadly than did the government or mainstream opinion and directed their attention to the necessity of ending militarism in Britain, too. The government, however, remained committed only to the destruction of German militarism.

This approach to the war, while grounded in genuine beliefs, also served useful propaganda purposes. The idea of the war as a crusade against Prussian militarism would, it was hoped, win American support for the British cause, rally public opinion at home as casualties mounted and spirits flagged and undermine the German people's support for their government's continued prosecution of the war.

At the outset the British recognised the importance of propaganda in their relations with the United States. When the Cabinet in August 1914 established an organisation to disseminate information abroad in order to influence public opinion in favour of the English case, one of its chief targets was the United States.[70] Influencing American opinion became even more important as the war continued.

From the summer of 1916 the British government was increasingly concerned about the policy implications of its dependence on American supplies and credit and, after American entry into the war in April 1917, American manpower. A series of Treasury memoranda drawn up in the summer and autumn of 1916 emphasised Britain's financial dependence on the United States and the possible consequences of that dependence. Chancellor of the Exchequer Reginald McKenna warned, 'If things go on as at present, I venture to say with certainty that by next June or earlier, the President of the American Republic will be in a position, if he wishes, to dictate his own terms to us'.[71] John Maynard Keynes,

McKenna's chief adviser at the Treasury, recommended 'that the policy of this country toward the U.S.A. should be so directed as . . . to conciliate and to please'.[72]

One way of attempting to conciliate the United States, while refusing Wilson's offers of mediation and tightening the blockade of Gemany to the detriment of American shipping, was to couch Britain's objectives in terms which would appeal to American public opinion and to Wilson's high-minded approach to the war. British representatives in the United States pointed out the importance of using Britain's pronouncements on the war to influence favourably American opinion. At the height of Anglo-American tension over the question of mediation Ambassador Sir Cecil Spring Rice counselled, 'We must proclaim our desire for a durable peace and show that we desire war for the sake of peace and not for the sake of war. From this point of view it is essential that we should avoid saying anything which would imply our desire to destroy the German people or irreparably break the power of Germany.'[73] Over a year later, with America already in the war but its resources not yet fully mobilised, Sir William Wiseman, head of British intelligence in the United States and after December 1916 the British government's chief liaison with House and Wilson, took a similar line: 'Any pronouncement they [the Allied governments] can make which will help the President to satisfy the American people that their efforts and sacrifices will reap the disinterested reward they hope for will be gratifying to him, and in its ultimate result serve to commit America yet more whole-heartedly to the task in hand.'[74]

From the beginning of American efforts at mediation House had stressed the need for ending 'militarism',[75] and Grey believed that the American's views about Prussian militarism coincided with his own: 'House left me in no doubt from the first that he held German militarism responsible for the war.'[76] Unwilling to make major substantive concessions to the United States, the British therefore had realistic grounds for hoping that the declarations about Prussian militarism, which they had already adopted as expressions of their conviction about the origins of the war, could play a role in maintaining good relations with the United States. Thus even when some British policy-makers were questioning the Allies' ability decisively to defeat Germany, there were diplomatic advantages to the continued promulgation of the destruction of Prussian militarism as Britain's chief aim.

There were also domestic political reasons for underscoring this objective. In the atmosphere of war-weariness and discontent which characterised 1917 it seemed to Lloyd George's advisers that only renewed emphasis on idealistic aims could justify to the British people the sacrifices they had already made and those still being demanded of them. In notes for Lloyd George's address to the inaugural meeting of the National War Aims Committee, organised in the summer of 1917 to counter the pacifist agitation which accompanied the discontent of that year, Philip Kerr, the member of Lloyd George's personal secretariat who handled foreign affairs, urged the Prime Minister to emphasise the necessity of destroying Prussian militarism in order to secure lasting peace:

> There is a growing body of people who are dissatisfied about the war aims of the Allies, who feel that they entered the war to down militarism and nothing else . . . The real way of dealing with the pacifist movement is to reaffirm our fundamental aims with which they really agree . . . and ask them whether there is any other way of attaining them save by vigorous prosecution of the war . . .
>   . . . The first condition of lasting peace, is that the domination of the Prussian military oligarchy over the German people and over their allies should be overthrown.[77]

Sir Maurice Hankey, the influential Secretary to the War Cabinet, also understood the propaganda benefits to be derived from promulgating lofty aims which pointed out the continued domination of Prussianism. At the end of 1917 Hankey encouraged Lloyd George to use his speech on the adjournment of the House of Commons 'to try & get the people back to the old idealistic spirit of the early days of the war' by making a speech on war aims, centring on the League of Nations and 'show[ing] how neither the Turkish nor Austrian nor even the German people stands in the way of this ideal, but only the spirit of the Prussian bureaucrat and militarist'.[78]

Emphasis on the Prussian spirit also played an important part in propaganda directed against Germany. As decisive military victory seemed less likely, British officials hoped through their public statements and later through organised propaganda to strengthen the moderates and weaken the militarists in Germany, thereby helping to accomplish their goal of destroying Prussian militarism. They utilised their belief that they were fighting an ideological war against Prussianism as the basis of their appeals to the German people.

In the autumn of 1917 Sir Eric Geddes, First Lord of the Admiralty since July and a Conservative, advised Lloyd George that using a forthcoming address as the occasion for telling the German people that Britain was fighting the Prussian spirit would have a significant impact in Germany: 'I am told that the catchword . . . for the Prussian spirit which we are supposed to be fighting against is the word "kulturkampf" . . . I am also informed that if in your speech you can say that this country is fighting everything that is embodied in that one word . . . it would have a very great significance to the German people.'[79] Heeding Geddes's advice, Lloyd George declared in his speech on 22 October, 'The real enemy is the war spirit fostered in Prussia'.[80] The Prime Minister also used his January 1918 address to the Trades Union Congress at least partly as a propaganda move against Germany.[81] In this major statement of Britain's war aims he once again disavowed any intention of destroying the German people, declaring that 'we are not fighting a war of aggression against the German people . . . The destruction or disruption of Germany or the German people has never been a war aim with us.'[82]

In May 1918 during the great German offensive Lloyd George instructed Crewe House, the headquarters of the recently established Department of Enemy Propaganda directed by Lord Northcliffe, to launch a direct propaganda campaign against Germany. With H. G. Wells in charge of the German Department from May until July it is understandable that the major policy statement adopted as the basis of Crewe House's propaganda campaign[83] had as one of its primary assumptions the Liberal distinction between the German people and their government. A memorandum drawn up by Wells with a preface written by Henry Wickham Steed, who worked at Crewe House while continuing as foreign editor of *The Times*, embodied the department's philosophy:

It should be pointed out that nothing stands between enemy people and a lasting peace except the predatory designs of their ruling dynasties and military and economic castes; that the design of the Allies is not to crush any people . . .

. . . Germany has therefore to choose between her own permanent ruin by adhering to her present system of government and policy, and the prospect of economic and political redemption by overthrowing her present militarists [*sic*] system.[84]

THE CHANGING OF GERMANY becomes a primary War Aim, the primary War Aim, for the Allies . . . The sharpest distinction has to be drawn, therefore, between Germany and its present government in all our propaganda and public utterances; and a constant appeal has to be made by the statesmen of the Alliance, and by a frank and open propaganda . . . from Germany Junker to Germany sober.[85]

Thus Crewe House took the concept of the war as a crusade against Prussian militarism to its logical conclusion. No longer would it be sufficient simply to discredit the German military party and thereby deprive it of its power but, in the propaganda agency's view, it would also be necessary for the German people to overthrow their government. As Hamilton Fyfe, who took over the German Department from Wells, later explained, 'What was emphasized and insisted upon was that guilt lay upon the Imperial Government and that if this Government were overturned the German People would not be held responsible for its misdeeds'.[86] In this way Crewe House in the closing months of the war gave new life to the idea of destroying Prussian militarism. By contributing to the belief that the overthrow of the German government would mean a complete break with the German past, it also laid the groundwork for a policy of appeasement of post-revolutionary Germany. The use of the idea of destroying Prussian militarism as a component of both domestic and foreign propaganda thus had implications far beyond its intended purposes.

Both a legitimately held justification of British participation in the war and a manipulated propaganda device, for Britain the idea of destroying Prussian militarism turned the war into an ideological battle. The overriding emphasis on the war as a crusade against Prussian militarism – with its origins in a misperception of the situation in Germany on the eve of war – had important consequences not only for wartime policy but also for policy towards post-Wilhelmian Germany and towards postwar security arrangements.

2
British War Aims and German Disarmament

It might be thought that British officials would have considered the disarming of Germany to be a logical means of assuring the destruction of Prussian militarism and that therefore German disarmament would have been a British war aim. Indeed, some outside government circles assumed that the government's insistence on destroying Prussian militarism meant that it hoped to disarm Germany after the war. When he attempted in the spring of 1916 to explain the British position to Colonel House, Ambassador Page, for example, interpreted the British emphasis on destroying German militarism as entailing the intention to disarm Germany: 'When the English say that the Germans must give up their militairism [sic], I doubt if the Germans yet know what they mean . . . It hasn't entered their heads that they've got to give up their armies and their military system.'[1] Labour MP J. Ramsay MacDonald also equated the destruction of Prussian militarism with the disarmament of Germany, declaring in a May 1916 attack on the government's objective of destroying militarism in Germany only, 'You cannot go to a people and say, "We are going to ask you to disarm yourselves; we are going to ask you to destroy your power of self-defence, and we are going to do nothing ourselves." '[2] Page and MacDonald, however, misinterpreted government policy. Most British policy-makers did not share the assumption that the destruction of Prussian militarism necessitated the disarming of Germany. For reasons which this and the next chapter will explore, the military disarmament of Germany was not a British war aim.

Before America's entry into the war in April 1917 a public call by a British official for German military disarmament would have opened the question of British naval disarmament. In the correspondence which he carried on with Grey on the subjects of American mediation and postwar measures for preserving peace Colonel House made it clear that he and President Wilson regarded the elimination of navalism as well as of militarism as essential to any mediated peace.[3] Navalism clearly referred to Britain just as militarism referred to Germany. Britain's use of its command of the seas to enforce its blockade of Germany had aroused anti-British feeling in the United States, leading to attacks on British navalism paralleling British outrage at German militarism. A June 1915 Cabinet paper examined this problem, warning that the issue of British navalism could be exploited as a propaganda weapon against Great Britain.[4]

British leaders were committed to maintaining Britain's naval supremacy, but they did not wish further to exacerbate Anglo-American tensions. The American emphasis on navalism and militarism as twin evils to be eradicated therefore raises the question of whether Wilson and House's stand influenced the British position on German disarmament. Was German disarmament one of what Amery referred to as Britain's 'real aims, conscious or subconscious',[5] a basic objective which, however, during the period of American neutrality British policy-makers found it disadvantageous to articulate? The American attitude towards navalism undoubtedly reinforced British opposition to American mediation, but there is no evidence to suggest that if Wilson and House had not linked the abolition of militarism to the abolition of navalism, British leaders would then have adopted German disarmament as a war aim.

Was German disarmament then one of what A. J. P. Taylor has described as assumptions which it was unnecessary to stipulate,[6] an objective that was so obvious and so generally accepted that there was no need to express it as a war aim? Examination of the formulation of war aims, of the context in which they were considered and of British officials' attitudes towards the future of German military power leads to the conclusion that just as the military disarmament of Germany was not a declared British war aim neither was it an underlying assumption of British policy. Few British officials advocated German disarmament other than destruction of the German navy.

All British officials regarded Britain's naval supremacy as essential to the country's existence. Since the 1890s the German navy had challenged that supremacy, posing a danger to the British Empire and the world trade upon which the British Isles depended. There was therefore understandable agreement not only that Britain must maintain its naval dominance but that the end of the war must also mark the end of German naval power. In March 1915 Churchill raised the question of German naval disarmament in the War Council. The First Lord posited the elimination of the German navy as one of the 'great objects of British policy', a means of assuring Britain's postwar security. Andrew Bonar Law, attending the meeting as leader of the Conservative Party, concurred: 'The first condition of peace was the elimination of the German fleet.'[7] The March 1915 War Council meeting reached no decision on German naval disarmament, and until the pre-Armistice discussions in the autumn of 1918 there was no further ministerial consideration of the question. Yet, the belief that Britain must insist upon the destruction of the Germany navy remained a tacit assumption of most British policy-makers.

There was no comparable common assumption about the destruction of the German army. As a naval empire, Britain traditionally had no interests on the Continent other than maintaining the balance of power there and ensuring that no Great Power controlled the Low Countries. Amery succinctly put the traditional British position when he stated, 'We are not a European power'.[8] Even after British entry into the war, ardent navalists doubted the wisdom of Britain's wholehearted commitment to a land war in Europe,[9] while imperialists like Amery were interested in protecting and expanding Britain's overseas empire and deprecated the idea of postwar interest in Continental affairs.[10]

While Amery represented an extreme imperialist point of view, most British policy-makers regarded Britain's involvement on the Continent as merely one more in a series of temporary interventions necessary to restore the European balance. They hoped after the war to return, as in the past, to a stance of detachment from European affairs. Consequently, the question of the German army was not a pressing concern for them. Their emphasis on colonial and economic objectives, together with their insistence on ending Germany's naval power, reflected their belief that punishing Germany economically and depriving it of its colonies as well as its navy would adequately weaken it in the only spheres in which it posed a direct threat to Britain's vital interests. This, of course, overlooked the fact that it was the power of the German army which gave Germany the potential for dominating the Continent and hence directly threatening Britain.

Very few officials expressed an interest in German military

disarmament. On the public platform the Germanophobe Australian Premier William Morris Hughes called for the crushing of Germany's military power and the destruction of the German 'military machine'.[11] But Hughes wanted this to be accomplished on the battlefield and, more concerned about German commercial rivalry,[12] he did not go beyond this rhetoric to push for postwar German disarmament in private policy sessions either when he attended Cabinet meetings in the spring of 1916 or when he sat as a member of the Imperial War Cabinet in 1918.

Lord Haldane, who at the invitation of the kaiser had observed the German military system during his 1906 visit to Berlin, was the only Cabinet member to recommend German disarmament to his colleagues. In a memorandum circulated in April 1915 Haldane, who at the time was, ironically, the target of a press campaign branding him as pro-German, argued the importance of ensuring German disarmament in order to prevent a repetition of German aggression: 'If Germany be left free to begin once more to build up her military system she may well, such is her energy and organising capacity, be able to build it up so that she will be more formidable than before.'[13] German disarmament was not, however, the major focus of Haldane's paper, which outlined an embryonic scheme for a league of nations, and the Lord Chancellor did not recommend unilateral German disarmament. Rather, he envisioned German disarmament as part of a general reduction of armaments.

A December 1916 memorandum by Sir Alfred Mond, one of Lloyd George's Liberal supporters and a minor non-Cabinet minister in the new regime, did broach the subject of unilateral German disarmament, mentioning the limitation of the German army as a point which would 'of course . . . require consideration'.[14] However, Mond pointed out that he had not included disarmament among his recommendations for possible peace terms because he considered the question of military forces to be an Allied rather than a British concern.

Some members of the Foreign Office staff and the Diplomatic Service disagreed; they believed that German disarmament was a matter of concern for Britain. In their August 1916 memorandum Tyrrell and Paget called for German disarmament as a step towards general disarmament. Presuming that Germany would not voluntarily submit to an arrangement for a general limitation of armaments, which they endorsed, the two Foreign Office officials contended that the Allies must achieve a decisive victory in order to impose disarmament on Germany:

> The danger we have to guard against is that if we succeeded in persuading the enemy to come to any kind of arrangement of the sort we must see to it that he is both able and willing to abide by his pledges. In view of the attitude which Germany has adopted in the past on this question we entertain but little hope that the Germans will be willing to approach the subject in any sincere and serious spirit unless they have no option.[15]

Like Haldane, then, Tyrrell and Paget envisaged German disarmament as merely part – though the necessary first stage – of a general limitation of armaments. For them, too, the disarmament of Germany was only a subsidiary recommendation. Their memorandum, which was the only official paper besides Haldane's to advocate German disarmament, concentrated primarily on territorial objectives.

Of Tyrrell and Paget's colleagues, Rumbold and Bertie each endorsed some form of unilateral German disarmament. Both hoped to destroy Germany's armaments factories, and Bertie also wanted 'disbandment of their military forces, and every possible difficulty placed in the way of a resuscitation of those forces'.[16] However, their views do not seem to have gone beyond private expressions of opinion.

Not only was there little official concern about the future of the German army, but there was surprisingly little press advocacy of German disarmament. Predictably, the Germanophobe *National Review* called for German military as well as naval disarmament. In November 1915 when it first outlined the terms which it wished to see exacted from Germany, it called for the surrender of the German navy but did not specifically deal with the question of the German army, stating only, 'Prussia to be permanently crushed and crippled by any means commending themselves to the Allies'.[17] In September 1916 an article by a contributor, which Maxse introduced with a statement that it was 'an attempt to prescribe a minimum and not a maximum', was more explicit. It advocated German land disarmament, particularly the reduction of war material.[18] The *National Review* did not, however, wage a campaign for postwar German disarmament and did not raise the issue again until after the Armistice.

The most detailed exposition of the need for disarming Germany after the war appeared not in the journals of the extreme right but in Clifford Sharp's autumn 1916 discussion of peace terms in the *New Statesman*. Sharp made German disarmament the cornerstone of his war aims programme, declaring that 'the paramount aim' of Britain must be 'to impose upon Germany a definite and drastic limitation of her military and naval establishments'. Like Tyrrell and Paget, he regarded German disarmament as the prerequisite for a more general reduction of armaments: 'The bald truth is that the problem of disarmament is the problem of disarming Germany.'[19]

None of these ideas received much attention during the war. The limited press support for German disarmament meant that there was no popular pressure on ministers to consider German disarmament as a British war aim. By the spring of 1915 when Haldane submitted his memorandum, the Lord Chancellor was no longer an influential member of the War Council. In addition, the government's attention was focused not on war aims but on the Dardanelles campaign and, shortly after, on attempting to salvage the failed Gallipoli expedition. An indication of how little impact Haldane's memorandum had is Lloyd George's later description of the Tyrrell–Paget memorandum, written sixteen months after Haldane's, as 'the first official document which contains a declaration in favour of . . . a reduction in armaments'.[20] The only minister formally to respond to the Haldane memorandum was War Secretary Kitchener, who did not address himself to the question of German disarmament.[21] Kitchener had earlier contended that imposition of an indemnity rather than specific disarmament measures would be the most effective way of dealing with German armaments: 'The question of armaments was entirely one of finance.'[22] Although both Haldane and Bertie had Asquith's ear, in the spring of 1915 Asquith was not ready to consider more specific peace objectives than those outlined in his Guildhall speech.[23] In addition to his other responsibilities, during the first two weeks of April he was temporarily in charge of the Foreign Office in Grey's absence, and his attention was devoted to the negotiations which resulted in Italy's joining the Allies. Moreover, he was soon preoccupied with reconstituting his government in order to ensure his own survival as Prime Minister. Less than two months after circulating his memorandum Haldane was out of the government and consequently no longer in a position to argue his views.

Even if he had agreed with Haldane, Asquith did not conceive of his role as Prime Minister as that of a policy advocate within the Cabinet or its committees. Lord Robert Cecil, who as Minister of Blockade was a member of his Coalition Cabinet, characterised him as 'apparently regarding it as no part of his duty to initiate solutions of any difficulty or to make suggestions for a new departure in policy',[24] and Balfour recalled that he 'would never give a lead of any kind in arriving at decisions'.[25] Even Grey in a defence of him commented that 'he was not disposed to go to meet the occasion and take it by the forelock'.[26]

Asquith's tendency to let matters drift coincided with Grey's unwillingness to sanction formal consideration of war aims. Preferring to avoid open debate, the Foreign Secretary had always been reluctant to discuss policy questions in the Cabinet. Devastated by the collapse of his efforts to preserve peace, he became convinced that during wartime there was little scope for diplomacy. Since the Allies had pledged to reach agreement on peace terms before demanding them from the enemy, Grey also feared that detailed consideration of war aims would exacerbate differences among the Allies.

Although Haldane was a close friend who occasionally deputised for Grey when the latter's health necessitated his absence from the Foreign Office and Grey himself hoped that arms reduction would result from the creation of a league of nations,[27] Haldane's paper apparently made little impression on him. He was away from his duties when the paper was circulated to the Cabinet and on his return plunged immediately into the negotiations with Italy which culminated in the Treaty of London of 26 April. With the strain which the paperwork involved in performing his duties as Foreign Secretary placed on his failing eyesight, it is possible that he did not even read Haldane's memorandum.

The views of the Foreign Office professionals who supported German disarmament fared little better with Grey than did Haldane's. Though Bertie was a career diplomat with close ties to the anti-German permanent officials at the Foreign Office, he had little influence on policy-making. From the beginning of 1915 until his appointment as minister in Berne in August 1916, Rumbold was head of the Prisoners Department at the Foreign Office and thus not involved in the central work of the Office. Even when requested by Asquith to submit the Foreign Office's views on possible peace terms, Grey did not instruct his staff to circulate the Tyrrell–Paget memorandum to the War Committee for almost another three weeks, over six weeks after its preparation.[28]

Grey expressed his own views on the question of disarming Germany in a May 1916 interview with Paul Miliukov, leader of the opposition in the Russian Duma. When Miliukov asked him what the British meant by 'crushing Prussian militarism' and whether Britain intended to disarm Germany, the Foreign Secretary replied that

> of course, if the Allies dictated peace in Berlin they could impose what conditions they liked, but Prussian militarism would cease to dominate Germany if the German people were convinced that the war had been a mistake. Prussian military policy being entirely devoid of all moral right, its only justification was success, and if it was not successful I believed it would cease to dominate Germany.[29]

Grey then went on to point out the difficulties involved in direct limitation of armaments. Thus he rejected the notion of imposing a direct limitation of armaments on Germany as both unnecessary and unworkable.

Paradoxically, Grey's view of the war as a struggle against Prussian militarism contributed to his lack of interest in disarming Germany after the war. Tyrrell and Paget considered ending the power of the Prussian army within the German state to be a means towards the end of German disarmament and Haldane, too, thought that disarmament must follow the 'dethronement' of 'military hierarchy in Germany'.[30] But for Grey the belief that Prussian militarism had been the sole cause of the war became a conviction that a decisive Allied victory would in itself destroy the Prussian army's political and social dominance in Germany, thus obviating the need for taking further steps to undermine its position. 'A changed spirit in Germany' would make possible 'enduring peace'[31] because 'a German democracy will not plot and plan wars, as Prussian militarism plotted wars'.[32]

Thus victory was essential: 'We believed . . . that defeat of the German armies was the only sure overthrow of Prussian militarism.'[33] Only if military victory proved impossible would it be necessary seriously to consider more limited objectives. Because he believed that military considerations should take precedence over diplomatic or political factors, as long as the generals expressed confidence in victory, Grey saw no reason to consider peace on other terms.[34] Therefore he not only discouraged war aims discussion by his Cabinet colleagues but also did not initiate departmental consideration of peace objectives.

Accordingly, during the first twenty-two months of the war the Foreign Office did not consider the conditions which it wished to demand for Germany. Nicolson believed that there was no point in discussing peace terms until the Allies were in a position to impose whatever terms they desired.[35] Although he recognised the problems inherent in attempting to impose terms which would secure a durable peace but not lead Germany to seek revenge,[36] the Permanent Under-Secretary did not encourage Foreign Office work aimed at resolving this dilemma. In early 1916 Drummond recommended creation of a committee to consider Britain's objectives regarding the reconstitution of Europe.[37] But when Hardinge, who had been serving as Viceroy of India, returned to the Foreign Office in June 1916, he found to his dismay 'that nothing had been done in the way of defining our desiderata when the time comes for peace negotiations'.[38] It was apparently under the impetus of Hardinge that Paget and Tyrrell prepared their memorandum and the committee chaired by Mallet began its work. Given Grey's attitude, however, in the summer of 1916 consideration of war aims probably would not have gone beyond the Foreign Office if it had not been for the intervention of Lord Esher.

In August Esher, unofficial liaison between British General Headquarters in France and the War Office, became convinced that the deadlock on the Somme would lead to peace negotiations.[39] Concerned that French preparation of peace terms would leave Britain at a disadvantage, he worked behind the scenes to secure British consideration of war aims. When Lloyd George, who had become War Secretary after Kitchener's death in June, came to Paris in early August, Esher discussed his concerns with him and recorded that Lloyd George 'admitted that no one in England had any idea of what our peace objectives should be, apart from vague generalities'.[40] From Paris, Esher then orchestrated a lobbying campaign aimed at producing ministerial consideration of peace objectives. He wrote to both General Sir William Robertson, the Chief of the Imperial General Staff, and Asquith urging definition of the principles on which Britain would insist in an armistice or peace.[41] Asquith responded by referring the matter to a War Office

committee, and the General Staff quickly produced a memorandum
on territorial objectives, which Robertson submitted to Lloyd
George with a covering letter taken almost verbatim from Esher's
letters to him.[42] When Lloyd George, who apparently believed it
best to keep objectives indefinite,[43] refused to circulate the paper to
his colleagues, Robertson took his case to Hankey, then serving as
Secretary to the War Committee. Hankey raised the question of
consideration of peace terms in a discussion with Asquith, Grey and
Edwin Montagu, Chancellor of the Duchy of Lancaster and
Financial Secretary to the Treasury and a close friend of Asquith.
When he found the Prime Minister and Foreign Secretary 'not very
encouraging',[44] the secretary, who was adept at manipulating
ministers, took it upon himself to get the issue discussed by the War
Committee. Balfour agreed to draw up a paper on peace terms,[45] and
Montagu, who in the earlier discussion had 'strongly supported'[46]
Hankey's position, submitted a memorandum on the need to
consider war aims.[47] In the face of this pressure Asquith on 30
August asked the members of the War Committee and the service
chiefs to consider the terms they would recommend if there should
be peace negotiations within the next few months.[48]

Asquith's request did not, however, produce the discussion which
Esher desired. Asquith himself devoted no attention to the issues
which he had asked his colleagues to consider, and most members of
the War Committee ignored the Prime Minister's call. In September
Grey finally circulated the Tyrrell–Paget memorandum but Balfour,
who in October produced the memorandum he had promised
Hankey, was the only member of the War Committee to prepare a
paper specifically in response to the possibility of imminent peace
discussions. Even those Liberals like McKenna who had increasing
misgivings about both the likelihood of the Allies' achieving decisive
victory and Britain's ability to conclude peace on its own terms free
from American influence if the war continued much longer did not
respond to Asquith's request.

Rather than submitting a paper to the War Committee, Lloyd
George, who had not been present at the 30 August meeting, chose a
public forum for the expression of his views. In the famous
'knock-out blow' interview with Roy Howard of the United Press,
he emphatically rejected the notion of peace negotiations: 'Peace
now or at any time before the final and complete elimination of this
menace [the Prussian war machine] is unthinkable.'[49] It is not clear

what Lloyd George's true position was – if he had one. In contrast to the bellicosity of this interview, just a month before he had privately expressed moderate views and had opposed public discussion of the European settlement because 'the war spirit' prevented sober consideration of aims.[50] There was a common thread in these contradictory statements, however, and that was his opposition to the consideration of peace terms.

Not only were Asquith, Grey and Lloyd George reluctant to define war aims, but important members of the Conservative wing of the Coalition vehemently opposed any consideration of the question of peace negotiations. Foremost among these was Lord Curzon. In May when the War Committee was considering one of Wilson's mediation offers, Curzon had written to Asquith to express his opposition to 'even the discussion of a premature and inconclusive peace'.[51] Curzon believed that the role of the Conservatives within the Coalition was to prevent the Liberals from concluding peace on any basis other than decisive military victory. In August he told Lord Bertie that 'he and his Unionist friends had made sacrifice of many of their views so as to remain in the Cabinet and there oppose an undesirable peace'.[52] Though Curzon knew the terms he wished to see imposed on Germany – and, despite his militance, these did not include disarmament – he interpreted any discussion of peace terms as a sign of weakness and wavering on the part of the government.[53] Strengthened by Lloyd George's public position and the support which it received in the House of Commons[54] and bolstered, too, by the agitation of the Unionist War Committee under the leadership of Sir Edward Carson, who after his resignation from the Coalition in October 1915 had become the focus of Conservative discontent with Asquith's conduct of the war, the militant Conservatives within the Coalition constituted a powerful bloc. Their opposition to consideration of a negotiated peace virtually assured that there would be no serious discussion of war aims by the Asquith Coalition as long as the issue of war aims was linked to the question of peace negotiations.

Besides Grey and Balfour, the only ones to submit detailed examinations of the question of peace terms were General Robertson, who immediately presented the paper which he and the General Staff had drawn up, and Admiral Jackson, who submitted the Admiralty's views in October. Of the four papers circulated to the War Committee, only the Tyrrell–Paget memorandum, which had been prepared earlier, proposed disarming Germany as a condition of peace. The two Foreign Office officials recognised, however, that decisive military victory would be necessary in order to impose disarmament on Germany.

Neither of the service chiefs recommended German disarmament. Since the General Staff had drafted its views in response to Esher's concerns about impending peace negotiations, it is understandable that it did not include German disarmament among its recommendations. As Paget and Tyrrell pointed out, it was unrealistic to expect Germany to accept such a proposal as part of a negotiated settlement. Moreover, deeply suspicious of the French, the CIGS, like Esher, wished to prevent Britain's being bested by France in any discussion of peace terms, and as Mond later commented, the question of disarmament seemed to be more an Allied than a British concern. While Robertson included 'tentative surrender of a certain portion of the enemy fleet' in the conditions upon which the General Staff believed an armistice might be granted and also recommended restriction of the German navy as a peace condition, he did not mention any conditions relating to the German army. Not only did the CIGS not recommend German disarmament as a condition of either an armistice or peace but, as will be more fully discussed in the next chapter, he advocated the maintenance of Germany as a strong military power.[55] In his memorandum the First Sea Lord, who naturally turned his attention to naval peace terms, based his recommendations upon a conclusive Allied victory rather than a stalemated end to the war. Assuming that such a victory would mean 'the destruction of Prussian militarism', which he accepted as Britain's chief aim, Admiral Jackson did not recommend destruction of the German fleet, and he expressed reservations about the 'practicability' of imposing naval disarmament on Germany.[56]

Although Asquith had asked for consideration of terms which Britain could put forward in peace negotiations, Balfour, like Jackson, based his recommendations on the assumption that Germany would 'either through defeat or exhaustion' have to accept the terms imposed by the Allies. Nevertheless, Balfour did not recommend German disarmament. He explicitly excluded from consideration the question of restriction of armaments, by which he seems to have meant a general limitation of armaments. Further, in a misreading of Prussian history – a misinterpretation which after Germany's defeat was to have an important effect on British policy towards the German army – he argued that Napoleon's attempt to destroy the Prussian army after Jena had led to the creation of the Prussian military system and hence militarist Germany: 'One of the few recorded attempts to crush militarism in a defeated State was Napoleon's attempt to destroy the Prussian army after Jena. No attempt was ever less successful. As everybody knows, Napoleon's policy compelled Prussia to contrive the military system which has created modern Germany.'[57] The implication was that a similar attempt after this war would be counterproductive, resulting in a resurgence of German militarism.

In his memorandum on peace objectives Balfour also outlined his belief that territory was the basis of military strength. He thought that if the Allies could apply the nationality principle in Europe, Germany's consequent loss of territory would have a significant impact on both the actual and the relative size of the German army: 'The resources of men and money on which the Central Powers could draw for purposes of aggressive warfare would be greatly diminished . . . and the men of military age thus withdrawn from the Central Armies would be added to the nations with which the Central Powers are now at war.'[58] However, Balfour made it clear that he did not expect a significant diminution of Germany's military power.

The War Committee did not discuss any of these memoranda, nor did it consider the question of war aims. French Premier and Foreign Minister Briand's well-publicised speech on 19 September rejecting a peace without victory removed the immediate reason which had motivated consideration of the war aims question. In late September Robertson complained to Esher that the War Committee would not read his memorandum and that no one was considering the problems which would confront Britain at a peace conference.[59] On 5 October when the War Committee discussed the question of negotiations at the end of the war, Admiral Jackson had not yet presented his memorandum. Since Balfour had just submitted his paper the day before, there can hardly have been time for serious examination of it by the other members of the War Committee before their discussion. This discussion did not include the subject of peace objectives.[60] When, in the absence of ministerial debate on war aims, Hankey prepared a paper summarising Asquith's statements on war aims and the territorial objectives on which the authors of the various memoranda agreed, he concluded that it would seem to follow from the opinions so far expressed that the minimum objects which we hope to achieve shall inflict on Germany such humiliation that she will never again repeat the experiment of forcing Europe into war. This would seem to be as far as the War Committee could go at present in defining the objects of the war.[61]

Thus despite Esher's efforts war aims remained undefined.

Although most members of the War Committee seemed determined, as Hankey wrote, to ensure a German defeat that would make impossible a repetition of German aggression, in the autumn of 1916 there were serious doubts about whether the Allies would be able to inflict such a defeat. As we have seen, McKenna and his officials at the Treasury expressed concern about increasing financial dependence on the United States. Walter Runciman, Liberal President of the Board of Trade, was alarmed at the prospect of a shipping breakdown leading to collapse in 1917 and Grey, too, worried about the shipping losses resulting from Germany's submarine campaign.[62] On 30 October Admiral Jellicoe, Commander-in-Chief of the Grand Fleet wrote to Asquith expressing his 'great anxiety at the possibility of our being forced to conclude peace on unsatisfactory terms owing to our losses in merchant ships by submarine attack'.[63]

It was in this atmosphere that Minister without Portfolio Lord Lansdowne, Conservative leader of the House of Lords, reopened the question of war aims and peace negotiations. On 13 November Lansdowne belatedly responded to Asquith's request for consideration of peace terms by circulating to the other members of the Cabinet a memorandum in which he called for an examination of the likelihood of the Allies' eventually being able to impose terms and asked whether it was worth continuing the war if they would not be able to obtain better terms later than were then possible.[64] Lansdowne did not, however, speak for even the more moderate of his Conservative colleagues. Cecil, for example, while acknowledging the gravity of the situation, rejected the idea of considering peace because any peace acceptable to Germany would leave Britain in a strategically weakened position.[65]

The Asquith Liberals, equally anxious about the military situation, nevertheless remained committed to decisive victory. They feared the consequences – political as well as strategic – of a negotiated peace more than the consequences of a continuation of the war. In the Nigerian debate on 8 November Carson and other Conservative malcontents in the House of Commons had challenged Bonar Law's leadership of their party and thus, indirectly, continued Conservative participation in a coalition which did not more vigorously prosecute the war. From mid-November Lloyd George, supported willy-nilly by Bonar Law, pressed for a major reorganisation of the civilian direction of the war in order to achieve the 'decisive finish'[66] he had advocated in September. In these circumstances it would have been political suicide for Asquith and his Liberal supporters to have considered a negotiated end to the war.

Despite the collapse of Allied hopes for a breakthrough on the Somme General Robertson responded to Lansdowne's memorandum by assuring the political leaders that decisive victory was still possible and warning against 'any peace which left the military domination of Prussia intact'.[67] Robertson thus reinforced the position of the majority of the Asquith Coalition, who had no inclination to give serious consideration to a negotiated settlement.

The determination to fight on did not, however, bring with it new interest in disarming Germany after the war. Among the political leadership, doubts about the Allies' ability to achieve a decisive military victory, and hence doubts about the likelihood of their being able to impose terms on Germany, persisted even after Lloyd George replaced Asquith as Prime Minister on 7 December. Although Lloyd George came to power as the man publicly committed to all-out prosecution of the war, privately he, too, was pessimistic about the military situation.[68] The worsening military situation exacerbated the politicians' doubts and by the spring of 1917 brought renewed interest in the possibility of peace negotiations. Unilateral German disarmament would obviously have no place in a negotiated settlement.

After his accession, Lloyd George's position on war aims and peace negotiations understandably changed with the changing military situation and his changing assessments of the prospects for a decisive Allied victory. At no time, however, until the pre-Armistice discussions of October 1918 was there even a hint on the part of the Prime Minister of interest in unilateral German disarmament. At the Imperial War Cabinet meetings in the spring of 1917 when he pressed for the inclusion of disarmament among Britain's war aims, his concern was for a general reduction of armaments, not unilateral German disarmament. Before he became Prime Minister, Lloyd George had, in fact, several times spoken of the necessity of Germany's remaining a strong power after the war. Moreover, at least publicly, he subscribed to Grey's view that the defeat of Germany would in itself so damage the prestige of the German army as to end its influence in German society. This was a recurrent theme of his war speeches. His speech of 3 February 1917 rejecting President Wilson's call for a 'peace without victory'[69] best exemplifies this attitude: 'If we destroy the prestige of the Prussian military idol, that cannot be set up again . . . If they lose confidence in their army, if that is broken, it cannot be restored . . . It is essential that this nation, with its great Allies, should destroy the delusion of the Prussian military power.'[70] According to this view, the war must be carried on to decisive victory because only victory would accomplish Britain's goal of destroying Prussian militarism, thereby making impossible a repetition of German aggression. If victory itself would achieve this end, then as long as victory seemed possible, there was no reason to call for German disarmament, particularly if one wanted a strong postwar Germany. Thus even when he was confident of victory, Lloyd George did not support unilateral German disarmament. In the late spring of 1917 as he became increasingly uncertain of the likelihood of a decisive Allied victory, he reportedly favoured 'a very moderate peace',[71] and in the summer of 1917 he began to think in terms of using Britain's conquests as bargaining chips in eventual peace negotiations. Realistic pursuit of this position also operated against support for German disarmament, an objective which could be achieved, if at all, only in the aftermath of victory.

The other members of the War Cabinet, which Lloyd George instituted as the small directing body of the war, showed no more interest than the Prime Minister in making German disarmament a British war aim. The most important members besides Lloyd George were men oriented towards the Empire rather than towards Europe. Lord Milner, one of the most influential members, was a leading imperialist who had spent a significant portion of his career in imperial posts. Although he had been born and educated partly in Germany, his imperial service and dedication to imperial unity more profoundly shaped his outlook on European affairs. Milner told General Sir Henry Wilson in 1917 that he hoped that after the war

Britain would be able to remain aloof from 'European complications'.[72] Like his protégé Amery, Milner did not endorse the prevalent belief in the necessity of destroying Prussian militarism. Early in the war he had written, 'I neither anticipate nor desire such a victory as will "crush German militarism for ever", whatever that may mean',[73] and in March 1917 he told an interviewer, 'If Germany comes out of the war with no gain of territory in Europe and her colonies lost, the people themselves will see that militarism is a failure'.[74]

As we have seen, Lord Curzon, the other former proconsul in the War Cabinet, did not agree with Milner's moderate approach to peace terms. Curzon espoused the extreme Germanophobe view of the war as a crusade against Prussian militarism, regarding Germany as 'not only an enemy to be beaten, but an evil spirit to be driven out'.[75] Nevertheless, despite his Germanophobia the Lord President of the Council and leader of the House of Lords had an outlook on Europe similar to Milner's. A former Viceroy of India, Curzon regarded Continental problems as subordinate to the necessity of maintaining the security of India and its communications.

Bonar Law, who as Conservative leader was second in power to Lloyd George, also had little interest or background in European affairs. An admirer of Joseph Chamberlain and a champion of imperial unity, he had not shown much interest in foreign policy before the war. Service as Colonial Secretary in Asquith's Coalition government had kept his attention focused on imperial problems. Although he was an extreme Germanophobe in some of his attitudes and opposed the idea of a negotiated peace,[76] he does not seem to have taken much interest in the war aims question. As Chancellor of the Exchequer, he was the only member of the War Cabinet with departmental responsibilities. In addition, he acted as Coalition spokesman in the House of Commons. Even if he had been more interested in the European settlement, his duties left him little time for pondering the broader questions of the war.

In addition to these Conservative leaders, General Jan Smuts, South Africa's Minister of Defence, who joined the War Cabinet in June 1917, was another influential member who represented the imperialist viewpoint. Unlike the other imperialists, Smuts, however, was not a Conservative. His views on war aims were an interesting blend of imperialist and Radical attitudes. Smuts believed that Britain was fighting primarily for the security of the empire and that European war aims were secondary to this objective. Accordingly, he wanted to assure the retention of the German colonies captured by the Dominions but, pessimistic about the military situation, he advocated limited war aims in Europe in the meetings of the Imperial War Cabinet in the spring of 1917.[77] Although Smuts became a leading proponent of arms limitation, he did not advocate unilateral German disarmament. Like Grey and Lloyd George, he believed that Germany's defeat would mean that 'German militarism will become bankrupt; that the German military leaders will be discredited in their own country'.[78] Hence a defeated Germany would no longer be a threat to world peace, and arms reduction in Germany would be merely part of a general reduction in armaments.

While some junior members of the Foreign Office agreed with the imperialists' priorities in war aims, neither Balfour, who served as Foreign Secretary in Lloyd George's administration, nor Cecil, who continued in the position of parliamentary under-secretary of state which he had held under Asquith, subscribed to the imperialist brand of Conservatism of their fellow Conservatives in the War Cabinet. Europe remained their central concern, prompting Amery to attempt to undermine the Foreign Office's 'purely European outlook'.[79] Within this European framework the Foreign Office, too, emphasised territorial objectives. Balfour, as we have seen, had not included German disarmament among the recommendations in his 1916 war aims memorandum and had, in fact, expressed doubts about the efficacy of destroying the German army. As Foreign Secretary, he gave no more support to Tyrrell and Paget's ideas on German disarmament than Grey had. Although he had drafted his 1916 memorandum in fulfilment of his promise to Hankey, Balfour himself saw no value in the specific definition of war aims until Britain was in a position to know whether it would be able to attain its desired objectives.[80] He deprecated the idea of adopting minimum aims because he feared the diplomatic consequences if such a step were to become known. Moreover, in contrast to Smuts, even as late as December 1917 he did not believe that the military situation necessitated or would ever be likely to necessitate such limitation.[81]

The Lloyd George Coalition confronted the question of war aims and peace negotiations almost immediately after assuming office when both the Germans and the Americans made overtures to the Allies. When the newly created War Cabinet considered Germany's 12 December 1916 offer of peace negotiations and President Wilson's 18 December request for a statement of war aims, its discussions, however, centred on how best to reject the German offer and answer the American note without alienating President Wilson, not on a serious consideration of Britain's war aims.[82] In suggesting terms for consideration at this time Alfred Mond mentioned, as we have seen, the limitation of the German army as a possible concern of Britain's allies. But at the Anglo-French conference which met in London at the end of December to prepare joint Allied replies to Germany and to President Wilson, the French did not put forward a demand for German disarmament. Hence, despite the uncompromising nature of the terms outlined in the Allied statement of war aims communicated to Wilson on 10 January 1917, there was no call for postwar German disarmament. Rather, the focus was on the European territorial settlement.[83]

In a follow-up note to the American government in which he elaborated on Britain's position, Balfour set forth arguments which further explain the lack of interest in German disarmament even among those members of the British government whose principal concern was Europe. According to the Foreign Secretary's note, the war was the result of 'great powers consumed with the lust of domination' existing within a community of nations 'ill prepared for defence' because it had no machinery for enforcing international law and its component states did not embody the principle of the self-determination of nations. While the attainment of the territorial objectives outlined in the Allied note would remove one of the causes of war, the only basis for a durable peace would be an Allied victory which by discrediting Germany's aims and methods among its own people and leading to the establishment of a system of international sanctions against aggressors would also remove the other causes of international unrest.[84] Thus, despite misgivings about the military situation, the British government in January 1917 still hoped for an imposed peace which would make impossible a recurrence of German aggression. In Balfour's view, a victory which produced their desired territorial rearrangements, the discrediting of Prussian militarism and the creation of a system of international sanctions would remove the causes which had led to war in 1914, thus accomplishing their objective. In this vision of the postwar world,

German disarmament would not be necessary for the maintenance of international stability.

When Lloyd George outlined his conception of Britain's war aims for the Imperial War Cabinet in March 1917, he advanced another belief which goes far to explain the lack of attention to the question of the future of the German army. This was the assumption, enunciated earlier by Grey, that a democracy would not wage aggressive war. Proclaiming that 'the democratisation of Europe' would be 'the only sure guarantee of peaceful progress', the Prime Minister argued that 'if Germany had had a democracy . . . we should not have had this trouble'.[85] British leaders who accepted this analysis hoped that a victory which destroyed the dominance of the military party in Germany would result in the institution of representative government there. Accordingly, they did not expect postwar Germany to pose a threat to peace.

Although discussion of peace terms was one of the announced purposes for the convening of the Imperial War Cabinet in the spring of 1917, Lloyd George apparently hoped to use empire consultation on war aims as a means for obtaining the wholehearted support of the Dominions for the campaign of 1918 rather than for eliciting genuine empire participation in the formulation of war aims. Having been warned by Kerr that the Dominion representatives would want to secure agreement on minimum terms,[86] he told the opening meeting of the Imperial Cabinet that the military situation did not warrant the delimiting of detailed minimum demands.[87]

However, the Dominion representatives, Smuts and Sir Joseph Ward of New Zealand, pressed for the definition of limited objectives and Lloyd George reluctantly agreed to the appointment of two committees to recommend terms that could be put forward in possible peace negotiations.[88] Chaired by Milner and composed predominantly of representatives of the Dominions, the committee appointed to examine non-territorial objectives considered the question of general disarmament and briefly discussed the issue of German submarines.[89] Not surprisingly, however, given the committee's composition and its charge to delineate terms for a negotiated peace, it did not consider the question of German military disarmament, nor did any member of the Imperial War Cabinet broach the question of unilateral German disarmament when the full Imperial Cabinet discussed the Milner Committee's report.[90] In a variation on the theme of the Prussian military party's responsibility for the war Lloyd George suggested that the existence of a professionalised army in Germany had been largely responsible for the war. However, he did not use this argument as grounds for demanding the abolition of the professional army in Germany only but rather as the basis for urging the universal abolition of professional armies.[91] Thus, in the first full-scale Cabinet debate on war aims unilateral German disarmament was not even a subject for consideration.

Not having expressed interest in German disarmament at this juncture of the war, the British government understandably did not consider it when officials in the winter of 1917–18 next addressed themselves to the question of defining war aims. By that time both the military-diplomatic and the domestic political situations had altered so drastically that the articulation of such a demand, even if British leaders had decided that it was desirable, would have been utterly unrealistic. Thus a variety of factors converged to account for the omission of German disarmament from Britain's war aims: the prewar history of Anglo-German relations, Britain's traditional attitude towards involvement on the Continent, the reluctance to define war aims, preoccupation with imperial concerns, the belief that a defeated Germany would no longer pose a threat to peace and, eventually, the realisation that the military situation might necessitate a negotiated peace. Moreover, as will be examined in the next chapter, many officials wished to maintain Germany as a strong military power after the war. Others, though dissenting from this aim, concluded that the curbing of German military power would be an impossible task which it would be fruitless to attempt.

3

The Future of German Military Power

While British policy-makers wished to destroy the Prussian army's dominance in Germany, they did not expect completely to destroy Germany's military power. Rather, British leaders fully anticipated that Germany would retain its Great Power status after the war. Australian Premier Hughes, urging the necessity of a decisive victory, might tell a cheering audience of Conservative businessmen that 'Germany's military power must be utterly crushed',[1] but Lord Cromer, who was in close touch with both official and influential outside opinion, more accurately reflected government policy. In a letter to *The Times* three weeks after Hughes's rabble-rousing speech Cromer succinctly stated the British position:

> So far as I know, no one in this country wishes to destroy the 'military power' of Prussia. The military strength of Prussia always has been, is now, and probably will continue to be very great. None in this country would object to its maintenance, provided that they could feel some definite assurance that it would be used for legitimate purposes and would cease to be an abiding menace to the rest of the world . . . we wish to destroy, not the military power of Prussia, but the militarist party dominant in that country.[2]

From the beginning of the war Britain's objective, as Harold Nelson has observed,[3] was the containment, not the elimination, of German power. In their January 1917 memorandum Clerk, Mallet and Tyrrell at the Foreign Office, believing that it would be impossible completely to destroy German power, were willing to sanction Germany's 'exploiting the position which she achieved for herself in 1870' as long as Germany confined its ambitions to Europe and did not challenge Britain's overseas empire.[4] In April 1917 when the

Curzon Committee recommended territorial war aims to the
Imperial War Cabinet, it based its recommendations upon the
assumption of a substantial weakening of Germany's strategic
resources and military strength, but not their destruction.[5]
Similarly, when General Smuts summarised the general war aims
defined by the Imperial War Cabinet, he included a European
settlement which would 'limit or destroy the military predominance', not the military power of, 'the Germanic powers'.[6]
Both Smuts and the Curzon Committee were, of course, outlining
terms for possible peace negotiations, and the January Foreign
Office memorandum also undoubtedly reflected the doubts awakened
by the deteriorating military situation of the winter of 1916–17.

Yet the expectation of Germany's continuation as a strong military
power predated doubts about the Allies' ability decisively to defeat
Germany. Little over a month into the war even the fiercely
anti-German Spring Rice argued that 'if Germany didn't exist she
would have to be invented'.[7] In March 1915 when most British
leaders still anticipated a decisive breakthrough, Lloyd George
acknowledged that he expected Germany to play a major role in the
postwar world. Recognising the permanence of German power, he
told the War Council, 'She [Germany] would always be a very
powerful nation'. None of his colleagues dissented from this view.[8]

Preoccupied with the prosecution of the war, British officials, in
fact, devoted little attention to the question of the future of German
military power. There was no systematic exploration of the problem.
Those who did consider the issue did not envisage a significant
long-term diminution of German military strength. Either they
believed that maintenance of the balance of power in Europe after
the war, and hence of postwar European stability, would necessitate
the preservation of a strong Germany, or they regarded a strong
postwar Germany, though undesirable, as an inevitable fact of
European power politics.

Maintenance of the balance of power in Europe was a basic
principle of British foreign and defence policy. As Amery noted in a
1917 memorandum on peace terms, historically Britain had always
based its intervention on the Continent on its desire to prevent any
one power's gaining military control there and then being able to
attain control of the seas, thereby threatening Britain's island
empire.[9] Grey had enunciated this principle when he told the
Committee of Imperial Defence in 1911 that a Europe united under

the domination of one power would leave Britain isolated and unable to maintain either its empire or its command of the seas: 'If control of the sea was lost, it would not only be the end of the British Empire as far as we are concerned, but all the Dominions would be separated from us, never to be rejoined; because the control of the seas, once having passed to a great European power, would never be allowed to return again.'[10]

The necessity of preserving the European balance had been the major underlying cause of British entry into the war. Writing in early August 1914, Asquith couched British interests in terms of maintenance of the balance of power and the deleterious consequences of an upset of that balance: 'It is against British interests that France should be wiped out as a Great Power.' 'We cannot allow Germany to use the Channel as a hostile base.'[11] When Grey presented the case for British intervention to the House of Commons on 3 August, he spoke in terms of Britain's interests as well as its obligations:

> If France . . . loses her position as a great Power, becomes subordinate to the will and power of one greater than herself . . . and if Belgium fell under the same dominating influence, and then Holland, and then Denmark, then would not Mr. Gladstone's words come true, that just opposite to us there would be a common interest against the unmeasured aggrandisement of any Power?[12]

Already economically outdistanced by Germany, its maritime and imperial position challenged by German naval expansion, Britain would find not only its position as a world power but its very independence threatened by German domination of the Continent. As Grey wrote to House in 1915, 'For us and for France defeat would mean our disappearance as Powers that counted in the world'.[13]

While Britain entered the war in order to prevent German domination of the Continent, British policy-makers did not want the war to result in either Russian or French predominance there. Although allied with France and Russia, British leaders did not lose sight of Britain's traditional rivalry with those two powers. Only seven months into the war, for example, Churchill was speaking of building a Mediterranean fleet against France and Russia after the war.[14] In his August 1916 memorandum Montagu pointed out 'that there is no community of aim [among the Allies] except detestation of Germany and a determination to avoid a repetition of her menace'.[15]

Concern about maintaining the balance of power after the war motivated some British officials to argue the necessity of preserving Germany as a strong military power. Montagu noted the attitude of some of his Cabinet colleagues: 'I have heard it said that, taking a long view, it would not be statesmanlike so to crush Germany as to leave no satisfactory balance in Europe.'[16] General Smuts's spring 1917 notes for a speech on war aims reveal the same assessment of Germany's role in Europe: 'I feel sure destruction of Germany not our aim . . . Germany cannot be crushed. Nor desirable. Into vacuum 7 worse *devils* may enter. Our policy traditionally based on *balance in Europe*.'[17] According to this view, a defeated and hence chastened Germany – no longer, it was hoped, controlled by militarists – would be a stabilising factor in postwar Europe. Such an outlook obviously militated against support for unilateral German disarmament.

Until the March Revolution in Russia those who advanced the idea of maintaining Germany in order to preserve the European balance contemplated a strong Germany primarily as a counter-balance to Russia. Although the centuries-old antagonism towards France remained an undercurrent throughout the war, particularly with regard to the disposition of the captured German colonies and territory of the defunct Turkish Empire, France was too weak in Europe to be considered a potential threat there. Britain's antagonism to Russia, which also predated its rivalry with Germany, had assumed increasing importance in the nineteenth century. For almost a century before the signature of the Anglo-Russian Entente in 1907 the imperial interests of the two powers in the Near East and Asia had clashed repeatedly, with Russian expansion posing a threat to India. In his seminal lecture to the Royal Geographic Society in 1904 in which he expounded his heartland theory of geopolitics, the noted political geographer Halford J. Mackinder had pointed out the danger to Britain of an expansionist Russia.[18] After the Japanese defeat of Russia in 1905 preoccupation with the growing challenge from Germany temporarily eclipsed concern about the Russian danger, and Mackinder himself, who had compared Germany's pivotal position in Europe with Russia's pivotal world position,[19] increasingly preached preparedness against Germany.[20] But the years of apparent improvement in Anglo-German relations following Agadir saw a marked growth of Russian power, prompting renewed concern about Russian ambitions. In June 1914, for example, when Grey told Bertie that Britain wished to avoid a revival of friction with Germany, he expressed anxiety about Russian policy in Persia.[21] Thus on the eve of the war there were two dynamic power centres in Europe, each of which posed a challenge to British interests. In August 1914 Germany was the immediate threat, but Russia remained a perceived potential danger.

In July and August 1914 the chief argument offered by those who opposed British participation in the war was that an Allied victory would strengthen Russia. Both Liberal activists who were ideological opponents of Russia and prominent academics who deplored Russian conduct in Persia protested against Britain's alignment with Russia. On 31 July a group of distinguished scholars issued a peace manifesto which contended that 'war upon her [Germany] in the interest of Servia and Russia will be a sin against civilisation'.[22] The manifesto of Angell's Neutrality League argued that a German defeat and Russian victory would produce such an increase in Russian territory and power as to upset the balance of power, giving Russia potential mastery of Europe.[23] In the *Daily News* when Gardiner urged British neutrality, he asserted that Germany's defeat would leave Russia all-powerful not only in Europe but also in Asia: 'If we crush Germany in the dust and make Russia the dictator of Europe and Asia it will be the greatest disaster that has ever befallen Western culture and civilisation.'[24] This point of view also found an adherent within the Cabinet. According to Lloyd George's confidant Lord Riddell, owner of the *News of the World*, one of the grounds on which the Chancellor of the Exchequer initially opposed British entry into the war was that intervention would strengthen Russia: 'L.G. strongly insisted on the danger of aggrandising Russia and on the future problems that would arise if Russia and France were successful.'[25]

During the early months of the war many who had supported Britain's action in August 1914 agreed that one outcome of the war might be an increase in Russian power. Balfour reportedly expressed concern about the danger to India of a Russian victory, while Cromer opposed a policy of crushing Germany because 'the only result would be an extreme predominance on the part of the Sclav [*sic*]'.[26] In contrast, Russophiles at the Foreign Office welcomed the prospect of a greatly strengthened Russia emerging from the war. Nicolson, a former ambassador to Russia who looked forward to a permanent Anglo-Russian alliance, believed that after the war Russia would be 'a great guarantee for general peace':[27]

> Though there is every likelihood that Russia will emerge from this war immensely stronger than she was before still she will not be a great menace like German militarism . . . It distresses me to hear . . . that in some years time we shall be fighting Russia in order to preserve the balance of power. You know as well as I do the baselessness of such an apprehension.[28]

Other officials, however, did not agree that such an apprehension was baseless. As Nicolson informed Sir George Buchanan, his almost equally pro-Russian successor at St Petersburg, there was 'among certain sections a kind of uneasy feeling that the downfall of Germany may result in the establishment of Russian predominance'.[29] Despite his Germanophobia Spring Rice, for example, believed that Russian hegemony in Europe would be as detrimental to British interests as German predominance there: 'If war continues either G[ermany] becomes supreme or R[ussia]. Both alternatives would be fatal to the equilibrium of Europe.'[30] Lloyd George, who even after deciding in favour of British intervention was not enthusiastic about the choice, retained a Liberal Russophobia, declaring in August 1914, 'I am dead against carrying on a war of conquest to crush Germany for the benefit of Russia'.[31]

Even while Britain was fighting to defeat Germany, many of the officials who feared postwar Russian predominance supported the idea of using Germany after the war to curb Russia's expansionist aims. As early as March 1915 Nicolson reported to Buchanan, 'There are many people – and even some in responsible positions – who think that before many years have elapsed we shall have to join with Germany for resisting the predominant power of Russia'.[32] Lloyd George was one of those who took this position. A few days after Nicolson's letter to Buchanan he suggested to the War Council that after defeating Germany Britain might want to take advantage of the fact of German power and use Germany to checkmate Russia: 'It might eventually even be desirable to have her [Germany] in a position to prevent Russia becoming too predominant.'[33] Continuing to hold this view of Germany's postwar role *vis-à-vis* Russia, in August 1916 he privately took an even stronger line: 'It is clear to me that Germany must be strong. We have to consider Russia . . . we shall want a strong Germany.'[34]

Through 1916 the idea of using a defeated Germany against Russia was apparently a fairly common view within the Cabinet. Commenting on the probable reaction to his own belief in the necessity of imposing harsh terms, including disarmament, on Germany, Lord Bertie, who shared the perception of Russia as a potential threat but opposed the idea of relying on Germany to meet the danger, wrote, 'I know that the argument against all this is that we may want to use Germany against Russian hegemony'.[35] In the autumn of 1916 when General Wilson, then Commander of the Fourth Army Corps in France, was on leave in London, he had an opportunity to talk with leading politicians. After sounding current opinion he complained in his diary about the Cabinet, 'They *will* talk . . . of not beating the Boch [*sic*] to the ground, as we shall want him against the Russians'.[36] Like Bertie, Wilson, an avid Germanophobe who had long feared the prospect of German hegemony in Europe, disagreed with the Cabinet's analysis of the appropriate strategical role for Germany in postwar Europe.

In contrast to General Wilson, officials at the War Office were the foremost advocates of the concept of a strong postwar Germany. The General Staff under the direction of Sir William Robertson, who served as CIGS from December 1915 until February 1918, looked forward to Germany's survival as a military power. In the war aims memorandum which he submitted in August 1916 Robertson outlined their belief in the need for a strong Germany in order to maintain the European balance. The military hierarchy in London was as sceptical of Britain's allies' postwar intentions as of Germany's: 'Our future relations with our Allies demand as close consideration as our relations with our enemies . . . It is well to remember that the present grouping of the Powers is not a permanency, and indeed it may continue but a very short time after the War is over.' Therefore Robertson and his subordinates put their faith in the balance of power and accordingly advocated leaving Germany strong on land as a counterweight to Britain's traditional foes Russia and France:

If the balance of power in Europe is to be maintained it follows that the existence of a strong Central European Power is essential, and that such a State must be Teutonic, as a Slav nation, the only other alternative, would always lean towards Russia, which would accordingly obtain a preponderant position and so destroy the very principle which we desire to uphold . . . It would be to the interests of the British Empire to leave Germany reasonably strong on land, but to weaken her at sea.[37]

Guided by this outlook, the General Staff during Robertson's tenure understandably expressed no interest in disarming Germany. As the Neutrality League's manifesto had pointed out, the disarmament of Germany would contribute to an increase in Russian power and the upset of the European balance.[38]

A General Staff memorandum prepared in early September for the Committee of Imperial Defence Sub-Committee on Territorial Changes again forcefully argued the necessity of a strong Germany, using much the same language as the earlier paper:

> If the maintenance of the balance of power in Europe is to be a fundamental principle of British diplomacy, it follows that a strong Teutonic State must be maintained in Central Europe . . .
> . . . the present grouping of the European Powers is no more likely to be permanent than previous ones have been, and it may well happen that in a few years' time Great Britain may be vitally interested in the existence of a strong and friendly Germany . . . any peace that may be concluded should be based upon such principles as tend to render it strong and reliable.[39]

The Director of Military Intelligence, General Macdonogh, whose views Robertson greatly respected,[40] opposed diminishing Germany's strength in the face of what he perceived to be increasing Russian power. In late September Robertson told Esher about a memorandum by Macdonogh which emphasised 'the danger of weakening Germany in view of the increasing power of Russia'.[41] In February 1917, according to Amery, Macdonogh and, to a lesser extent, General Maurice, the Director of Military Operations, both of whom had served on the War Office committee which had drafted the August 1916 memorandum, were 'entirely occupied . . . with the idea of leaving Germany strong after the war'.[42] While Amery undoubtedly exaggerated, the General Staff under Robertson's direction – because it believed in the principle of the balance of power as the proper basis of British strategy – did regard a strong Germany as essential to European stability after the war.

But, again because of its adherence to the principle of the balance of power, the military leadership did not want Germany to be too strong. In a December 1916 memorandum Robertson elaborated on its views on the desired strength of postwar Germany. Rejecting the notion of peace negotiations at a time when 'Prussia [was] absolutely predominant in all matters, military and political, in the Central European States', he emphasised 'that although we need to have a reasonably strong Germany, our position will become intolerable if she is left too strong'.[43] Although the General Staff believed that Germany must be allowed to retain some of its colonies 'if Germany is to be left as a strong European power',[44] Robertson specifically rejected the idea of acquiescing in German control of Central Europe because this 'would make the Central Empire the strongest S[t]ate in the history of the World, and tend to subjugate all other Western Kingdoms to that empire'.[45] Thus the governing concern for Robertson and the other members of the General Staff, just as for the civilian officials who supported the concept of a strong postwar Germany, was maintenance of the European balance of power, a traditional tenet of British foreign policy. Their perception of the relative strengths and postwar potential of the European Great Powers led them to conclude that a reasonably strong Germany would be necessary to the maintenance of that balance and therefore essential to the preservation of peace.

Not all those who considered the question of Germany's postwar potential thought that it was in Britain's interest to preserve German strength in order to maintain the postwar balance of power. Rather, many officials believed that Germany's industrial capacity and population base were so great that, regardless of the outcome of the war, Germany would remain the strongest power in Europe. In the late nineteenth and early twentieth centuries Germany had emerged as the greatest industrial power and most technologically advanced country in Europe. From 1905 the Mackinder school of strategic thinking had emphasised the connection between these developments, together with Germany's rapidly increasing population, and that nation's growing military strength and efficiency. Although Mackinder's views on the future importance of land power rather than sea power received only limited support at the time, when navalist thinking still predominated, their influence is evident in the thinking of those British officials who during the war believed that Germany's resources made inevitable its continuation as the strongest power in Europe.

Indeed, some feared that because of these resources Germany would emerge from the war even stronger than before. As early as November 1914 General Wilson, for example, worried that the breakup of Austria-Hungary resulting in an increase in Germany's population would be 'difficult' because even peace terms imposing the loss of important coal-producing regions would leave Germany potentially stronger after the war than before.[46] Haldane, who with Mackinder had been a member of the Coefficients, a group which in the early years of the century was convinced that Germany's efficient organisation and economic growth were pushing it inevitably into a confrontation with Britain, was also acutely aware of Germany's potential. As we have seen, in his April 1915 memorandum he pointed out the importance of Germany's 'energy and organising capacity' in determining its postwar military strength and position in Europe. He warned that unless the Allies took steps to prevent a recrudescence of German military power, German resources were so great that Germany might become even stronger after the war: 'The most crushing defeat will not prevent Germany from setting herself to work, with her population and national spirit and her great powers of scientific and industrial organisation, to accumulate wealth and diplomatic influence. The sequel may, if no counter step is taken, be a still greater military power than that which she now possesses.'[47] More optimistic than the other officials who feared Germany's potential military power, Haldane thought that the Allies could adopt measures to prevent an increase in German strength. He believed that Germany's defeat followed internally by the removal from power of the military hierarchy and externally by the organisation of a concert of the Great Powers, which would prevent the inordinate growth of armaments in Germany or any other nation and take action against potential disturbers of postwar stability, could be effective in curbing German power.

In contrast to Haldane, others who opposed the idea that there would be advantages for Britain in Germany's remaining a strong military power merely recognised the continuation of German power as an inescapable fact of European power politics and thought that Britain would simply have to deal with the consequences. They did not believe that even the most decisive Allied victory would result in a lasting diminution of German power, nor did they think that there were any peace terms which the Allies could impose which would permanently alter Germany's status as the strongest military power in Europe. Kitchener, for example, in his response to Haldane's memorandum argued that although the defeat of Germany would leave that nation temporarily impotent, in the long run a resurgence of German power directed against Britain was inevitable: 'Although this war may have an issue successful to our arms, Great Britain will inevitably have to face the consequence of German determination to take revenge upon us for having upset the calculations on which she commenced this war.'[48]

At the Foreign Office Eyre Crowe agreed with this aspect of Kitchener's analysis. Since at least 1907 Crowe had been convinced that Germany's expansionist tendencies would inevitably upset the balance of power; that because it was a military power, Germany would continue its attempts at establishing ascendancy in international politics; and that Britain and the other powers could do little to change the pattern of German conduct. As a student of modern European history, Crowe, whose mother and wife were German and who himself had been born and partly educated in Germany and maintained close contacts there, had before the war devoted his attention to Germany, against whose ambitions he had consistently warned. He knew little about Russia and did not grasp the new problems produced by Russia's re-emergence as a European power. Therefore, although for Crowe, too, the balance of power was an overriding concern, the principle of maintaining that balance led him to quite a different judgement about Germany's role in the postwar world from that formed by those who believed that balance of power considerations would necessitate a strong Germany as a counterweight to Russia.

In reviewing the probable postwar situation in a memorandum which he wrote in October 1916 against the concept of general disarmament Crowe asserted, 'The balance of power reappears as the fundamental problem'.[49] But, unlike the General Staff, he considered that Germany's potential was so great that despite defeat and the imposition of stringent peace terms it would retain the capacity for upsetting that balance. He pointed out the role of population in determining the size of armies, emphasising that the potential size of a nation's army was limited only by its manpower,[50] and he argued that 'the Central Powers . . . will not submit permanently to helpless inferiority'.[51] Crowe concluded therefore that, regardless of the outcome of the war, the Allies would not be able effectively to disarm Germany and that the re-emergence of Germany as a strong military power was inevitable.

It was Balfour who gave the most detailed exposition of the inevitability of German power. An authority on defence whose experience in dealing with Germany dated to 1878, when he had attended the Congress of Berlin as Salisbury's parliamentary private secretary, Balfour had no illusions about German power. In an article written in 1912 for publication in the German periodical *Nord und Sud* he had set forth his appraisal of Germany's potential: 'Without any fleet at all, Germany would remain the greatest Power in Europe.'[52] This remained Balfour's assessment of German strength. In his memorandum on peace objectives drafted in October 1916 he therefore challenged the General Staff's contention that Britain should be concerned about preserving German power.

As noted earlier, because a nation's territory determined its resources of men and money – Mackinder's dual concepts of manpower and money power – Balfour considered territory to be the basis of military power. Like other critics of the notion that it was in Britain's interest to preserve German power, he called attention to the potential for power furnished by the tremendous resources which Germany would possess regardless of the peace terms which the Allies might impose:

> I [do not] believe that anything which we and our Allies can accomplish will prevent the Germanic powers . . . from remaining wealthy, populous, and potentially formidable.
>
> . . . the Germanic states will be very well able to take care of themselves, whatever be the terms of peace to which they may have to submit.

Therefore he took issue with the General Staff's position that Britain should take steps to ensure the maintenance of a strong Germany in order to prevent either Russian expansion in Central Europe or the upset of the balance of power in Western Europe, which might leave France dominant there:

> I do not share the fears of those who think that the triumph of the Slav countries is likely to menace German predominance in

Central Europe . . .

   . . . Many of those who speculate about the future of Europe seem to fear that Germany will be so weakened by the War that the balance of power will be utterly upset, and Britain will be left face to face with some other Great Power striving in its turn for universal dominance. I doubt this.

Balfour shared Crowe's belief that it was a delusion to think that the Allies could effectively diminish Germany's military power:

It seems to me quite clear that, measured by population, Germany . . . will be more than a match for France alone, however much we give to France, and however much we take from the Central States. If, therefore, Europe after the war . . . is to be an armed camp, the peace of the world will depend, as heretofore, on defensive alliances formed by those who desire to retain their possessions against those who desire to increase them. In that event the *Entente* is likely to be maintained, Germany will still be the enemy, and an enemy strong enough to be dangerous . . . All I would for the moment insist on is that the greatest territorial losses which the Allies can or ought to inflict on the Central Powers will leave them powerful both for defence and offence.[53]

   In the closing months of the war, as Foreign Secretary, he reaffirmed this assessment, telling the Imperial War Cabinet in August 1918 that even if Britain attained all its European territorial objectives, 'Germany would still remain the biggest military power in Europe'.[54] Balfour thus remained convinced that the Allies could do little to end Germany's military power and thought that it was self-deceiving to hope otherwise. Rather, as he outlined in his January 1917 note to the American government, he hoped that the discrediting of Prussian militarism might change the way in which Germany exercised that power.[55] If not, then British participation in defensive alliances against Germany would be necessary.

   The collapse of Russia in 1917 mooted the question of maintaining a strong Germany as a counterpoise to Russia and, indeed, presented the prospect of a substantial increase in German power regardless of the outcome on the Western front. The developments in the East in 1917–18 brought home in a new way the interconnection, which

Grey had emphasised in 1911, of the European balance of power and empire defence. The breakdown of the Eastern front raised the spectre of German domination of Russia and awakened fears of a possible German advance across the Caucasus, through Persia and Afghanistan to India. German access to the Russian heartland could mean not only German ascendancy in Central Europe but eventual world dominion.

Some officials had already drawn attention to the danger to the empire of a possible German ascendancy in the East. After the 1916 House mission Montagu had commented on President Wilson's peace terms, which included German control of Anatolia, 'If Germany gets a footing in Asia Minor with an internationalised Dardanelles she can pursue the pressure in the East which has been her guiding principle and her best means of preparing an attack on the British Empire!'[56] On 22 March 1917, well before British leaders realised the impact of the March Revolution on Russian participation in the war, Balfour, seconded by Austen Chamberlain, the Secretary of State for India, warned the Imperial War Cabinet that Germany's ambitions included expansion eastwards to the Persian Gulf and eventually to India and the Far East and that success in achieving its objectives would alter the world balance of power, threatening the position not only of the empire as a whole but of its individual members as well.[57]

Amery was one of the first to recognise the strategical implications of developments in Russia: that the March Revolution meant 'the practical elimination of Russia' as a military factor in the war and possibly thereafter and that the Russian situation would require a rethinking of Britain's relationships with the other European Great Powers. Amery concluded from the changed situation that it was in British interests to strengthen France not only in Europe but also in West Africa and in Syria 'as a counterpoise to Central Europe'.[58] General Macdonogh, earlier the object of Amery's scorn because of his advocacy of a strong Germany and his lack of interest in retaining Britain's colonial acquisitions, agreed that Russia's collapse necessitated a reassessment of Britain's strategic options. After the failure of the Russian offensive in July 1917 the Director of Military Intelligence urged the necessity of destroying Germany's position in the Balkans and the Middle East, from which it could otherwise launch 'the next struggle against the British Empire and for the mastery of the world'.[59]

In September 1917 the British received reputed German peace overtures suggesting German willingness to enter negotiations on the basis of concessions to the Allies in the West and colonial concessions to Britain in exchange for Anglo-French acceptance of German annexation of Russian territory. While these proposals came to nothing, consideration of them revealed conflict between the Prime Minister and his colleagues about the future of German power. By removing the German threat from the Channel, restoring the prewar status quo in Western Europe and not only removing Germany's colonial challenge but also expanding Britain's overseas empire, the proposed terms would seem to have coincided with Britain's interests, if not with its proclaimed objective of destroying Prussian militarism. Yet Lloyd George was the only Cabinet member actively to advocate serious consideration of a compromise peace on this basis. The Prime Minister believed that if the proposals were rejected, Germany would still have access to Russia's vast resources, enabling the Germans to carry on the war indefinitely.[60] He was therefore willing to consider peace on the proposed terms, telling the War Cabinet, with apparent acquiescence, that if Germany annexed Courland and Lithuania, then 'two great Empires would emerge from the war, namely the British Empire and Germany'.[61]

Although these Baltic provinces were not on the route to India and German dominance there would not pose a direct threat to Britain's imperial interests, Germany's annexation of them would upset the postwar balance of power in Eastern Europe and eventually, as other ministers perceived, the equilibrium in the West which the proposed arrangement appeared to restore. Moreover, there was no assurance that Germany would be content with only these provinces. Therefore several of Lloyd George's colleagues protested that acquisition of Russian territory would leave Germany too strong, creating an unstable postwar situation. Milner who had never wanted to destroy Germany and believed, like Crowe and Balfour, that it could not be crushed,[62] nevertheless was not willing to sanction an increase in German power. Supported by Balfour and George Barnes, since August Labour's representative in the War Cabinet, he argued that the proposed arrangement would mean that Germany would emerge from the war even stronger than before, leading to another war in ten years' time.[63] For Curzon the issue was German ascendancy in Russia. He believed that German annexation of Russian territory would make Russia 'the vassal of Germany'.[64]

Churchill offered the most comprehensive objections to Lloyd George's position. Though not a member of the War Cabinet, the new Minister of Munitions took a great interest in matters of strategy. After Lloyd George discussed the question with him, he contended – in arguments reminiscent of Mackinder – that not only would acquiescing in German acquisition of Russian territory give Germany an 'enormous accession of military strength and population', but it would also risk the permanent alienation of Russia. Churchill believed that Russia would not always remain weak and that, as a result of such Anglo-French action, it would probably in future ally itself with Germany: 'Thus central & Eastern Europe w[oul]d stand against England, France & Italy, with America[,] in permanent antagonism.'[65]

Those ministers who opposed a negotiated peace giving Germany a free hand in Russia thus feared that such a peace would not be permanent; that if Germany emerged from the war stronger than before, it would soon again pose a threat to peace. While they did not expect Germany to cease being a strong European military power after the war, they clearly did not wish to contribute to an increase in German power. Unlike Lloyd George, whose attention focused on the military situation, they addressed themselves to the postwar geopolitical situation which the proposed arrangement would create. In their view, balance of power considerations as well as protection of the empire necessitated the checking of Germany's eastward expansion.

Lloyd George's position did, however, find adherents outside the Cabinet. For these officials as well as for the Prime Minister, a peace allowing German gains in Russia seemed a viable option *because* Germany was so strong. After the Bolshevik government opened separate peace discussions with the Central Powers, Hankey concluded that it would be advantageous for Britain and France to make a separate peace at Russia's expense, since Germany would take what it wanted from Russia in any case. He feared that if the war in the West were to continue after Germany made a separate peace with Russia, the outcome might be an increase in German power in both the West and the East: 'Anyhow, Germany will take what she can from Russia and would probably give up gladly what we want, whereas by prolonging the war we shall stiffen her back, and we may not be strong enough to take what we want by force. Thus Germany may be the gainer east and west.'[66]

Sir Douglas Haig, Commander-in-Chief in France, believed that since Germany's expansionist tendencies could not be checked, they should be diverted from areas of direct interest to the British Empire. He therefore thought that it was in Britain's interest to encourage German expansion into northern Russia, where German forces might encounter so many problems as significantly to diminish their danger to the empire: 'Encourage the latter [Germany] to exhaust herself in northern Russia . . . Germany must be allowed to expand somewhere. Guide her into Russia – and get her frost-bitten as much as possible *en route*.'[67] Thus, in marked contrast to Lloyd George's Cabinet colleagues, Haig and Hankey saw a peace granting Germany territory in Russia as a means of preventing Germany's becoming even stronger than it already was.

The terms of the Treaty of Brest-Litovsk, which Germany signed with Bolshevik Russia in March 1918, and German actions in the aftermath of the separate peace with Russia made it clear, however, that Germany's Eastern ambitions extended well beyond northern Russia. In addition to obtaining Poland, Lithuania and Courland and occupying Livonia and Estonia, the Germans gained *de facto* control of the Ukraine and with it access to the Black Sea and the Caucasus. A separate peace with Romania gave Germany economic dominance there. In a memorandum written in July 1918 after German troops had occupied the Crimea and advanced into the Caucasus, thereby accomplishing the first stage towards fulfilment of the British nightmare of a German advance on India, General Wilson, who had replaced Robertson as CIGS in February, expressed the essence of British fears about Germany's intentions. Not anticipating that the Germans were on the eve of a defeat which would undo their gains in the East, Wilson pointed out the strategical advantages which Germany possessed as a result of its expansion eastwards. He emphasised that Germany had gained access not only to additional reserves of raw materials and manpower but also to overland routes to Egypt and India, inaccessible to British sea power. Even if the Allies were victorious in the West, he thought therefore that the prospects for a durable postwar peace were bleak:

With this double increment of recuperative power [raw materials and manpower], Germany will be practically independent of maritime blockade and will be able completely to outstrip the rest of Europe in the reconstruction of their economic and military resources. Thus at no distant date Germany will be in a position again to threaten the peace of civilization and consummate the dominion of half the world.[68]

Under these conditions Germany would be a greater danger to Britain after the war than it had been before.

Only two weeks after Wilson had drafted this pessimistic memorandum, the British launched the offensive which gave the Allies the initiative in the war and led ultimately to Germany's October appeal for an armistice. But Germany's request for an armistice did not eradicate the anxieties of those who analysed the question of Germany's actual and potential power. Until a series of revolutionary uprisings in Germany in late October and early November changed the focus of their concern, they continued to worry about the consequences of Germany's present and future strength. The military leadership, in particular, believed that Germany, despite its wish for an armistice, was strong enough to remain a danger. Speculating on the probable course of postwar international relations, General Wake, a British military representative at the Supreme War Council, concluded on 26 October that for the foreseeable future Germany was 'likely to remain the strongest Power on the Continent'. While Churchill, as we have seen, anticipated an eventual Russian resurgence, Wake assumed that Germany would continue to have 'limitless opportunities of drawing supplies of all kinds from Russia'. He feared that if, in an attempt to weaken Germany, strong buffer states were established on Germany's eastern border, they would eventually become German satellites, thereby strengthening rather than weakening Germany.[69]

Three days after Wake expressed these views, however, the first revolt in Germany awakened new anxieties among British policy-makers. The concern even of many of those who earlier had deprecated talk of preserving Germany's military power shifted, as we shall see, from the consequences of continued German strength to a new emphasis on maintaining that strength so that Germany could serve as a barrier against the westward spread of Bolshevism.

For those officials who during the war seriously considered the issue of the future of German power there was never any expectation that Germany would cease to be a strong European military power after the war. Whether they simply accepted the reality of the permanence of German power or wished actively to exploit that power, they did not equate destroying Prussian militarism with destroying Germany's military power. Even early in the war when they were confident of the Allies' ability to achieve a decisive victory which would destroy Prussian militarism, most British policy-makers either did not wish or did not expect a significant weakening of Germany to be a consequence of such a victory. Some hoped that defeat would lead Germany to use its strength after the war in a fashion which would accord with British interests and believed, therefore, that a strong Germany would be a factor promoting postwar stability. With the exception of Haldane, those who believed that these expectations were unrealistic did not, however, envisage being able to diminish German military strength. Therefore, again with the exception of Haldane, the expectation of Germany's continued strength meant at least tacit opposition to German disarmament as a British war aim.

As decisive victory became increasingly uncertain and the Russian Revolution gave Germany new opportunities for increasing its power, British policy-makers certainly did not expect to be able to weaken Germany but rather became concerned about whether they would be able to prevent a further increase in German power. After Germany requested an armistice, General Wilson wished to include disarmament among the armistice terms and, as will be described in Chapter 5, for a brief period during the pre-Armistice discussions his views prevailed. But other considerations took precedence over this belated wish to see Germany disarmed, and when revolutionary outbreaks in Germany presented the possibility of the disappearance of Germany as a strong military power, the British response was to consider strengthening the German army as a means of preventing the spread of revolution.

4

The Question of General Disarmament

Although the British government showed no interest in unilateral German disarmament, general disarmament was the subject of serious consideration by both the Imperial War Cabinet committee appointed in April 1917 to recommend non-territorial peace aims and by two meetings of the Imperial War Cabinet itself. Moreover, in his January 1918 speech on war aims Lloyd George endorsed the concept of a general postwar reduction in armaments. Many both inside and outside official circles believed that when the war was over general arms reduction would be an important means of ensuring long-term peace. As will be discussed in Chapters 8 and 9, the government's approach to the question of general disarmament ultimately proved decisive in making German disarmament a goal of British policy. Therefore it is important to examine official wartime views and public statements on the question of a general limitation of armaments.

Opposition to armaments had been a tenet of prewar Liberalism, with Radicals arguing that armaments competition was one of the causes of war. From the beginning of the war many of the Liberal journalists and intellectuals who helped transform the war into a crusade against Prussian militarism found justification for their support of the British cause not only in their belief that an Allied victory would destroy Prussian militarism but also in their expectation that such a victory would make possible a general limitation of armaments. Writing in the *Nation* on 15 August 1914, H. G. Wells described the war as 'the opportunity of Liberalism':[1] 'Do Liberals realize that now is the time to plan the . . . collective disarmament of Europe . . . It is possible now to make an end to Kruppism. It may never be possible again.'[2] The same edition of the *Nation* carried a leading article which decried the idea of attempting to impose a unilateral limitation of armaments on the defeated enemy but called instead for universal arms limitation after the war.[3] In a series of lectures in which he outlined his reasons for supporting the war, H. A. L. Fisher, the distinguished Liberal historian of nineteenth-century France then serving as Vice-Chancellor of Sheffield University, argued that Britain must play a role in shaping the peace settlement in order to slow down 'the mad race of armaments',[4] as well as to free Europe from Prussian militarism.

These influential Liberal supporters of the British war effort thus hoped that Britain's participation in the war would advance the Liberal cause of arms limitation. In their view, the destruction of Prussian militarism, followed by a general limitation of armaments, would make the recurrence of war impossible. General disarmament would guarantee postwar security. From the first week of the war they used their positions to create a climate of opinion which fostered the belief that general disarmament would follow an Allied victory and that it would assure permanent peace.

During the early years of the war the idea of general disarmament received public support not only from these Liberal journalists and intellectuals but, even more insistently, from the Union of Democratic Control (UDC), formed in September 1914 by Radicals and Labourites who had opposed Britain's entry into the war. As one of the four cardinal points of its peace programme, the UDC called for Britain to 'propose as part of the Peace Settlement a plan for the drastic reduction of armaments'.[5] Throughout the war and during the peacemaking the UDC expounded its belief in the necessity of general disarmament as a means of assuring permanent peace. Through its propaganda it reached out to the rank and file of the Labour movement and, as we shall see, exerted pressure which led eventually to official declarations in support of general disarmament.

In their fervour these vocal advocates of general disarmament as the key to postwar peace ignored the problem of implementation. Although the *Nation*'s major objection to unilateral German disarmament was the belief that Germany would be able to evade any limitations imposed upon it,[6] the Radical journal's editor and contributors acknowledged no such problem in the enforcement of general disarmament. Indeed, the disarmament proposals put forward by one of these contributors, the economist J. A. Hobson,[7] an early member of the UDC, prompted Bryce, himself a supporter of reduction of armaments – but without the uncritical enthusiasm of its more ardent adherents – to prepare a memorandum outlining

the difficulties of determining the basis for arms limitation and of
ensuring compliance. Unlike Radicals such as Hobson and his fellow
UDC members, Bryce regarded the reduction of armaments as 'a
problem for solution',[8] not as an easy answer to the problem of war.

Some government officials – Conservative as well as Liberal – also
early expressed interest in the idea of general disarmament. Most
officials who endorsed the concept of arms limitation did not,
however, regard the limitation of armaments as in itself a guarantee of
peace. Rather, they believed that postwar stability achieved through
other means – a peace treaty favourable to British interests and, for
some, the creation of a league of nations – would make possible a
general reduction in armaments. Commenting in the spring of 1915
about the kind of peace he would like to see, Nicolson, for example,
wrote, 'We should all be liberated from this overburdening
competition in armaments'.[9] But his support for arms limitation took
the form of the vague wish that a stable peace might make possible a
reduction in armaments rather than the conviction of the committed
advocate of disarmament that arms limitation must be a cornerstone
of peace. In his memorandum on postwar relations among the Great
Powers Haldane, too, merely expressed the hope that a general
reduction of armaments would be a consequence of a league of
nations. As we have seen, he did not regard arms limitation alone as
the panacea for conflict among the European powers.

Although the official advocates of arms limitation did not share the
exalted hopes of the outside champions of general disarmament, most
of them gave no more attention to the problems of implementation
than did the non-official crusaders. In his memorandum Haldane, for
example, did not examine the difficulties intrinsic to the implementation of any plan for a general limitation of armaments. This omission
prompted Kitchener to point out that mutual reduction of armaments
was likely to be an area of contention between Britain and its allies:
'We and the Continental Powers look at these matters from different
angles, and . . . I greatly doubt whether they [the Allies] will not also
consider it necessary after the war to maintain armies as fully prepared
and numerous as before.'[10] Here the War Secretary correctly forecast
a basic divergence in the British and French approaches to the
problem of postwar security. In his response to Haldane's
memorandum Kitchener was one of the first officials to draw attention
to some of the problems involved in general disarmament.

Grey, though a supporter of the disarmament concept, also

recognised the difficulties of implementing any plan for a postwar reduction in armaments. Although he had been a prewar advocate of general disarmament and became a leader in the postwar disarmament movement, during his wartime tenure as Foreign Secretary he went no further than expressing his hope that a durable peace would make possible each nation's reduction of expenditure on armaments and that postwar stability, coupled with the creation of a league of nations, would therefore lead to arms reduction.[11] When Colonel House pressed him for a more definite commitment to arms limitation, he replied that he 'hesitated to advocate rules for directly limiting armaments not on the ground of principle but because of the practical difficulty in drawing up such rules'.[12]

When they advocated general disarmament in their August 1916 memorandum, Tyrrell and Paget, in contrast to their chief, did not acknowledge that there would be practical difficulties in drawing up such rules. Regarding the reduction of armaments as essential to the preservation of peace, the two Foreign Office clerks declared that general arbitration treaties leading to a reduction of standing armies and navies would be the best means of accomplishing this objective. Like Haldane, they failed to address themselves to the problems that might arise as the result of differences in the British and French concepts of security, to which Kitchener had earlier alluded. They, too, mistakenly believed that Britain's allies shared what they took for granted to be British interest in reducing armaments, asserting that 'this ideal is doubtless common ground amongst all the Allies'. As we shall see, however, the goal of arms reduction proved to be far from common ground between Britain and France. Although Tyrrell and Paget were more accurate in their assessment of Britain's probable postwar position on disarmament, they did not pursue the implications of this position. Correctly predicting that Britain would probably be the country most willing to reduce its army and navy, they nevertheless recommended a permanent alliance with Belgium and France, which would commit Britain to 'a probable increase of our military obligations'.[13] Their failure to deal with this inherent contradiction presaged a basic problem of Britain's postwar policy regarding both enforcement of the disarmament provisions of the Treaty of Versailles and the broader issue of preserving postwar security: how Britain could reduce its armed forces and at the same time honour its Continental commitments.

During Asquith's premiership Cecil was the most ardent official proponent of a definite plan for the limitation of armaments. In September 1916 he put forward specific proposals for a postwar agreement for the general limitation of armaments.[14] Deeply disturbed by the war's destructiveness, Cecil, an hereditary Conservative, not only believed that Britain's postwar interests would require peace but feared that another war would destroy the European order.[15] At the same time he seemed to have adopted the Radical outlook on the problem of militarism, warning that Prussian militarism was not the only form of militarism which threatened peace: 'Even if we succeed in destroying German militarism, that will not be enough. Militarism exists everywhere, even in this country. If the militarism of Germany is destroyed, what security have we that some other country may not take her place?'[16] Thus sharing the widespread doubts about the survival of the wartime alliance, he believed that general disarmament would be one of the best means of preventing another Great Power's domination of the Continent and that Britain's national interest therefore required the promotion of a plan for the postwar limitation of armaments. But, like most of the proponents of general disarmament, Cecil apparently did not think through the implications of his position.

Within the Foreign Office Cecil's draft memorandum evoked a speedy rebuttal from Eyre Crowe, who brought the full force of his considerable analytical abilities to bear in a telling critique of Cecil's advocacy of a general limitation of armaments. Crowe emphatically disagreed with the proposition that an agreement for a general limitation of armaments would coincide with British interests. Instead, he argued that 'nothing . . . but adequate force' would prevent the possibility of a postwar upset of the balance of power: 'It is all a question of real military preponderance.'[17] Thus, for Crowe, military strength was the only adequate guarantee of postwar security. Addressing himself to the technical aspects of disarmament, which its proponents largely ignored, he challenged the efficacy of any of the commonly suggested bases for limiting armaments: quantity, kinds, or expenditure. Profoundly suspicious of the Central Powers, he further contended that even with the adoption of all three bases, lack of good faith would make genuine disarmament impossible. In addition, differences in geography and national responsibilities would make the establishment of a universal standard of force impractical, and the powers could not, in his view, adopt a comparative standard because nations' needs changed with changing conditions. Lastly, Crowe held that an arms limitation agreement among a few countries only would be extremely dangerous.

When the Milner Committee met in April 1917 to formulate non-territorial peace aims, it considered Cecil's draft memorandum and Crowe's response, and both men were present to answer questions.[18] The Milner Committee's discussion of the Cecil and Crowe papers raised two points which had implications for postwar policy towards German disarmament. The first, the belief that it would be impossible to enforce a prohibition of Germany's building submarines, indicated a recognition of the general difficulties involved in enforcing disarmament. The other raised a more basic question about Britain's postwar defence policy. This was the prophetic but ultimately unheeded realisation that, in Britain, war hatred was so great there was a risk of abandoning military preparedness, the fear that a treaty which appeared to guarantee peace might, in fact, lead to 'supineness'.[19] Such weakness would, of course, mean that Britain would lack both the capability and the will for undertaking enforcement of German disarmament and might even be unable to protect its own interests and security.

The Milner Committee included three strong proponents of disarmament.[20] General Smuts supported the concept of arms limitation and was soon to become the most outspoken official advocate of postwar disarmament. Arthur Henderson, Labour member of the War Cabinet, was a member of the Union of Democratic Control and until he entered the Asquith Coalition had served on the UDC General Council. When he resigned from that post to join the government, he reaffirmed his commitment to the UDC's four cardinal points which, as we have seen, included a call for general disarmament. H. A. L. Fisher, who had become President of the Board of Education at Lloyd George's accession, had, at the beginning of the war, expressed his belief in the need 'to abate or terminate the evil race of armaments',[21] and after the war he became a staunch advocate of disarmament.

The committee members, however, found Crowe's arguments so persuasive that they did not include general disarmament among their war aims recommendations: 'They felt . . . that any too comprehensive or ambitious project to ensure world peace might prove not only impracticable, but harmful.'[22] The committee even doubted the practical value of the surrender of the German navy.[23]

Henderson explained to the Imperial War Cabinet that, although he strongly supported disarmament, he had chosen to take a more judicious approach rather than to endorse the Cecil recommendations. He believed that implementation of a league of nations must precede disarmament: 'The policy with regard to disarmament would have to depend on the nature of the international relations set up after the conclusion of peace.'[24] Cecil, too, found Crowe's criticisms so convincing that he temporarily abandoned his position of support for general disarmament.[25] Thus, in the spring of 1917 even these leading government advocates of general disarmament recognised the practical difficulties involved in achieving that goal and were not willing to base postwar British security on merely the hope that their objective might be attainable. They wanted other guarantees of postwar stability to underpin any plan for a general limitation of armaments.

When the Milner Committee presented its recommendations to the full Imperial War Cabinet on 26 April, Lloyd George criticised the report for its failure to deal with the question of disarmament.[26] As a Nonconformist Radical member of the prewar Liberal government, Lloyd George had been the leading advocate of reduction of expenditure on armaments, preferring that the money so allocated be spent on social reform. During the war, however, he seemed to have abandoned his Radical roots. As Minister of Munitions from May 1915 until July 1916, for example, in addition to revamping Britain's munitions industry and greatly increasing its productivity, he had pressed for the introduction of conscription. Nevertheless, with characteristic inconsistency, he retained a Radical's interest in arms reduction.

Moreover, both domestic and international developments pushed him in the direction of supporting postwar disarmament. By the spring of 1917 there was a marked change in the British public's attitude towards the war. Germany's submarine campaign was taking a catastrophic toll of British shipping, and there were shortages of food and coal with resultant increased prices. In mid-March Germany resumed its Zeppelin raids on England, causing widespread alarm. As the war, which the British people had originally expected to be over by Christmas 1914, dragged on with no end in sight, war-weariness and discontent set in. After the March Revolution in Russia these feelings were particularly strong within the Labour movement, the left wing of which had already endorsed a peace programme which included a call for reduction of armaments as a means of preventing the recurrence of war. Always keenly aware of the importance of public opinion, Lloyd George concluded from these developments that he British people wanted some assurance that war would not happen again. He realised, too, that there was an influential and growing body of opinion which believed that general disarmament would be the best means for ensuring the preservation of postwar peace. Therefore, when he introduced the disarmament issue at the Imperial War Cabinet meeting, the Prime Minister told his colleagues that he thought there would be great disappointment unless the end of the war brought efforts to secure a general limitation of armaments.[27]

In addition, on 6 April the United States had declared war on Germany and entered the war as an associated, rather than an allied, power. In an address to the United States Senate on 22 January 1917 President Wilson had called for a 'moderation of armaments': 'The question of armaments, whether on land or sea, is the most immediately and intensely practical question connected with the future fortunes of nations and of mankind.'[28] With this ringing endorsement by the American President, wartime opposition to armaments had achieved a new respectability. Lloyd George recognised that, with America now in the war but its troops not yet committed, Wilson was in an even stronger position to exert pressure for the attainment of his idealistic objectives. The new leverage of American manpower had been added to the old one of American financial assistance. The Allied need for American military co-operation and the prospect of American participation in eventual peace negotiations meant that the American President could directly influence the Allied policy-makers. Indirectly, he could serve as a rallying point for opposition forces in Britain which shared his outlook on peace terms and the structure of the postwar world. The need to appease American as well as British opinion thus reinforced the Prime Minister's residual Radical commitment to arms limitation.

The Imperial War Cabinet discussions initiated by Lloyd George were the first collective examination of the disarmament issue by British leaders.[29] These deliberations had implications for subsequent British policy on German as well as on general disarmament and for Britain's approach to the broader question of the maintenance of international stability after the war. The members of the Imperial War Cabinet discussed some of the difficulties which Crowe had outlined in his attack on Cecil's paper, including the standard of armaments to be allowed each nation, methods for prescribing limitation and the guaranteeing of good faith. In considering the question of compliance, Austen Chamberlain, a staunch Germanophobe who had been mistrustful of Germany's intentions since attending Treitschke's lectures at Berlin University in 1887, voiced what proved to be very realistic misgivings. Like Tyrrell and Paget, he anticipated that public opinion in Britain would insist on strict adherence to any arms limitation agreement. However, he also prophetically warned that public opinion in Germany would support tacit evasion.[30] Thus Chamberlain, like Crowe, grasped the dilemma which would confront Britain if the peace treaty included plans for general disarmament.

Because Lloyd George and other officials who supported disarmament believed that Germany's defeat would bring a significant change in both the structure of government and the foreign policy of that country, they did not view the question of German compliance with such suspicion. With this division within the British leadership over the likelihood of genuine German co-operation in plans for the preservation of peace, it was clear that there would be no agreement on the issue of general disarmament in the spring of 1917.

The Imperial War Cabinet's consideration of the questions of enforcement measures and the kind of armies which nations should be allowed also revealed attitudes which directly affected the position on German disarmament adopted by Britain at the Paris Peace Conference. In their memoranda Haldane and Balfour had both cited what they believed to be the precedent of the development of the Prussian army after Jena as a warning against imposing the types of restrictions which would lead to Germany's developing an even stronger army after the war. In the 1917 Imperial War Cabinet meetings Lloyd George took up this theme,[31] and during the peacemaking it remained a cornerstone of his approach to German as well as general disarmament. As we shall see, his assumption that the existence of a professional army in Germany had been largely responsible for the war, together with the belief that Napoleon's limitation of the size of the Prussian army had led to the creation of the Prussian military system, greatly influenced the subsequent British position on the method of recruitment, length of service and strength to be allowed the postwar German army.

In their discussions the members of the Imperial War Cabinet touched, in addition, upon the central technological issue involved in disarmament: how in an era of total war and rapid technological change to define what constituted armaments. The realisation that Germany's industrial organisation was an essential part of its military strength highlighted the difficulty of defining armaments and hence of effectively ensuring disarmament.[32] The question of the definition of armaments, like the other questions raised in these discussions, was a fundamental question which needed to be resolved in order to institute a workable plan for arms limitation, whether for general disarmament or for German disarmament. They were questions which, however, remained unresolved and again confronted British policy-makers during their preparations for the Peace Conference and during the peace negotiations themselves.

The Imperial War Cabinet discussions also pointed up the basic conflict between the wish for general disarmament and the insistence upon maintaining British naval supremacy, a conflict between the ideals of the proponents of general disarmament and British interests as perceived by all British policy-makers, including those who supported the concept of disarmament. The chief concern expressed in the Imperial War Cabinet's discussions of disarmament was that one consequence of a general disarmament agreement would be to threaten the supremacy of the British navy.[33] When Lloyd George recommended substituting non-professional for professional armies, it was Cecil who offered one of the strongest arguments against this suggestion: that the British navy was highly professionalised and any call for deprofessionalisation of the military might prompt a concomitant demand for deprofessionalisation of navies.[34] British leaders were not willing to sacrifice Britain's naval supremacy even in exchange for a reduction in the military strength of the Continental powers. Despite his personal support for arms limitation, Smuts pointed out that if the European powers reduced spending for land defence, they would then have more to spend on big navies.[35] This would, of course, pose a challenge to British naval superiority and hence possibly threaten the empire, a particular concern for Smuts as South Africa's Minister of Defence.

Since British leaders expected that even a negotiated peace would end Germany's naval power, their apprehensions demonstrated their continuing concern about the possibility of a postwar challenge from one or more of their co-belligerents. The Milner Committee in its general consideration of the idea of a league of nations had indeed specifically expressed this apprehension: 'Who will be our next enemy? We may soon be quarreling with our Allies.'[36] If even Germany's defeat would not guarantee the protection of British interests, then before committing themselves to arms limitation British policy-makers would have to decide whether the benefits of general disarmament outweighed its risks to British security, a security which they believed would continue to rest on Britain's naval predominance.

None of Lloyd George's colleagues was willing to give whole-hearted support to the idea of a general limitation of armaments as an essential component of peace arrangements. Besides Lloyd George, only Canadian Prime Minister Sir Robert Borden declared that he believed reduction of armaments might be a direct British objective.[37] Although Borden had apparently either not so expressed himself in the Milner Committee meetings or had been overruled, his position in the full Imperial Cabinet meeting was consistent with the approach to the war which he had taken from the beginning. The Canadian Premier, whose attitude to the war in many ways resembled that of President Wilson, had an idealistic notion of Canada's role and aims in the war. He believed that Canada was not pursuing selfish interests but was fighting for 'the future destiny of civilization and humanity' and 'to uphold public right, to promote the ends of what is known as international law'.[38] Arms limitation as a British war aim fit in with this view of Canada's objectives. Nevertheless, Borden gave Lloyd George only lukewarm backing. Even Smuts, soon to become a public champion of disarmament, did not endorse Lloyd George's position. The Imperial War Cabinet agreed only that arms limitation should be one of the topics included in a projected Anglo-American discussion of a league of nations.[39]

The Imperial War Cabinet discussions thus raised a great many questions about the disarmament issue but resolved none. Just as the early memoranda advocating general disarmament did not influence policy, so, too, the Imperial War Cabinet discussions of general disarmament resulted in no policy decisions. But the memoranda, the responses to them and the Cabinet discussions revealed attitudes which carried over into both the peacemaking process and the postwar period and shaped the development of British policy on German as well as general disarmament. They raised important policy questions which continued to plague British leaders dring the peacemaking and after. British officials' consideration of the pros and cons of disarmament also foreshadowed points of conflict with France, which later emerged as divergent British and French policies on both German and general disarmament. They revealed, too, basic contradictions in the British approach to the problem of postwar security, contradictions which were not resolved during the war, the peacemaking, or the interwar period.

Despite the Imperial War Cabinet's failure to endorse the idea of general disarmament, arms limitation soon received the public approval of two leading members of the government. First General Smuts and then Lloyd George publicly espoused the concept of postwar disarmament. While these public endorsements reflected the two men's own views, they resulted as much from developments on the changing domestic and international scene as from private convictions.

After the Imperial War Cabinet meetings Smuts remained in London to attend the War Cabinet, and in late June he became a member of that body. Although not so intended, Smuts's appointment to the War Cabinet proved important for the development of Britain's disarmament policy. Among Smuts's friends were active members of the UDC, and the South African minister whole-heartedly accepted the UDC's call for reduction of armaments.[40] As evidenced by the position which he took during the Imperial War Cabinet discussions, Smuts recognised the difficulties involved in designing a workable programme for arms limitation. Nevertheless, he remained committed to the concept. He took the disarmament issue to the public platform, giving support for disarmament the imprimatur of a respected government official. Behind the scenes, too, he worked to make disarmament part of British policy.

Smuts enjoyed an enormous prestige and popularity in Britain. In June William H. Buckler, special agent at the American embassy, reported that it had become 'the fashion to hail [him] as the "leading orator of the Empire"'.[41] In September C. P. Scott told Lloyd George that Smuts was 'perhaps the most popular man in the country'.[42] In great demand as a speaker and recipient of honours, Smuts used many of these occasions to outline his views on disarmament. He was sincere in his commitment to disarmament but, like Lloyd George, he also recognised the importance of bolstering public opinion in support of the war. In the paper which he had prepared for the Imperial War Cabinet in April he had written, 'This war will be settled largely by the imponderables – by the forces of public opinion all over the world'.[43] Despite his own willingness to consider a negotiated peace, when the Imperial War Cabinet did not pursue this possibility, he maintained a public commitment to victory. He undoubtedly realised that to a war-weary public – particularly to a working class increasingly exposed to the UDC's propaganda calling for a negotiated peace – the prospect of postwar disarmament offered an incentive for supporting continued prosecution of the war.

An address to the first mass meeting of the League of Nations Society in London on 14 May 1917 was the first major speech in which Smuts raised the issue of disarmament, linking it to a league of nations. Acknowledging that disarmament was the most difficult aspect of the question of a league of nations, he nevertheless insisted that arms limitation was essential for an effective league:

> It is no use trying to prevent war when nations are armed to the teeth. If Governments are allowed with impunity to prepare for war over a long process of years . . . then inevitably you reach a point when not even a League of Nations is sufficiently strong to withstand the deluge. And however difficult – and it is a most difficult subject when it is thoroughly gone into – it seems to me that this matter will also have to be dealt with . . . namely, the devising of plans which will lead to the abolition or diminution of armaments and to less recourse being had by States to warlike preparations in future.[44]

This was the first public statement by a British official advocating a postwar limitation of armaments. Although Smuts spoke as an individual, the authority of his position as an adviser to the War Cabinet gave added weight to his views. In this speech Smuts confined himself to a general endorsement of the concept of disarmament, but he soon became more explicit in his recommendations for postwar disarmament.

During the late spring and summer of 1917 working-class discontent and labour unrest increased, and the Labour movement and the UDC pressed for a restatement of Britain's war aims. Smuts's speech to the League of Nations Society had taken place during the 'May Strikes', widespread unofficial strikes led by the shop stewards' movement, a segment of labour increasingly opposed to the government's war policy and hence receptive to calls for a negotiated peace. Shortly after this speech, in correspondence with a friend with contacts in the Labour movement, Smuts expressed his concern about 'the grave dangers to this country in this war and thereafter' if the government did not respond to the workers' grievances.[45]

Since the March Revolution in Russia members of the British government had become increasingly worried about labour unrest. Milner wrote to Lloyd George expressing his apprehension that England might ' "follow Russia" into impotence and dissolution'.[46] In late May Frances Stevenson, Lloyd George's secretary and mistress, whose opinions generally reflected the Prime Minister's, recorded in her diary that industrial unrest was 'the most sinister thing at present',[47] and in his capacity as Minister of Munitions, the Radical Christopher Addison was disturbed by Scotland Yard's reports of the shop stewards' movement's activities.[48] Across the political spectrum, British leaders feared the revolutionary potential of the shop stewards' movement.

Labour support for the war was essential both to the success of the government's recruitment efforts and to the smooth functioning of industries necessary to the war effort. The root cause of the industrial unrest lay in the workers' opposition to military conscription and their determination to resist industrial conscription. In May the War Secretary, Lord Derby, warned Lloyd George that labour unrest was having a deleterious effect on the production of war supplies.[49] Partly to allay the growing discontent, the Lloyd George government had accelerated planning for postwar reconstruction. In early June when the Leeds Convention, convened by the Independent Labour Party and the British Socialist Party, expressed its support for the Russian Revolution and the Russian programme of a peace without annexations or indemnities and called for the establishment of workers' and soldiers' councils in Britain, the War Cabinet also decided 'to undertake an active campaign to counteract the pacifist movement'.[50]

The chief instrument for conducting this campaign was the National War Aims Committee, which sponsored local meetings at which prominent speakers stressed the necessity of victory and the importance of unity on the home front. By autumn the committee was reporting that organised labour was unwilling to co-operate in setting up local committees because it wanted a more specific statement of the government's objectives, and the Cabinet was expressing concern that the campaign was not having the desired effect.[51] In Paris, Bertie received a letter from London informing him that the labour situation dominated everything, and Buckler reported that a member of the War Cabinet had said that he was 'willing to be blackmailed by Labour for the duration of the war provided I can keep them in it'.[52] This was the atmosphere in which Smuts delivered his next major speech calling for disarmament.

Smuts's 24 October speech at Sheffield, a munitions manufacturing centre, testifies to the impact of the government's and his own concern about labour unrest. At a meeting organised by the National War Aims Committee and attended by over 6,000 Smuts said that Britain was fighting not only to defeat the enemy but also to create a new England after the war. He declared that a necessary precondition for the creation of this new England was that 'militarism must be swept from the face of the earth'. Smuts's proclamation of the destruction of militarism as the overriding war aim did not go beyond the vagueness of other officials' war speeches, but he then added a new and specific demand. For the first time he called for the abolition of standing armies: 'And when we talk about our war aims, to my mind there is one great dominating war aim – the end of militarism, the end of standing armies.'[53]

In the first pamphlet issued by the UDC, E. D. Morel, the group's secretary and guiding force had spoken of abolishing standing armies,[54] and in a peace message issued in August the Pope, too, had called for the substitution of arbitration for armies.[55] Perhaps in an attempt to undermine the effectiveness of the UDC's propaganda favouring a negotiated peace and to counter the international impact of the papal appeal, Smuts now declared the abolition of standing armies – always an unpopular institution in Britain – to be the country's chief objective. Although Smuts clearly stated that this was his personal view, he was now a member of the War Cabinet and no doubt many of his listeners believed that his remarks represented government policy. The War Cabinet, however, had articulated no such objective.

Returning to the theme of the construction of a new England, Smuts then specifically linked disarmament to postwar reconstruction: 'So long as the burden of militarism is resting on Europe . . . you will not be able to solve the economic and industrial and social questions which are ahead of us.'[56] Here he echoed the prewar

Radical solution to financing social reform and foreshadowed the government's postwar approach to implementing reconstruction: reduction of expenditure on armaments would provide the money needed for domestic reconstruction.

Despite the work of the National War Aims Committee labour unrest increased. To replace the devastating losses suffered in the Passchendaele campaign, the government had extended its combing-out policy to the mines, the only remaining large manpower source. The miners had organised resistance to the combing-out measures, and the over 200,000-member South Wales Miners' Federation was scheduled to take a strike vote on 1 and 2 November. In the hope of defusing the situation the War Cabinet sent Smuts to address the miners. At Tonypandy, the centre of the unrest, he addressed a meeting arranged by local representatives of the National War Aims Committee. In a long speech Smuts stressed the necessity of a victory which would destroy Prussianism. Again he emphasised that such a victory was a prerequisite for establishing 'the world on the new basis',[57] a basis which must include the end of standing armies and the reduction of armaments because armies and armaments drained nations' economic resources, hindering economic and social progress. Thus, in a message likely to appeal to a discontented but basically patriotic audience Smuts again linked victory, disarmament and postwar reconstruction. The applause which greeted his call for victory indicated that he had struck a responsive chord with his listeners. From Tonypandy Smuts travelled through the coal-fields making a series of speeches in which he declared that disarmament must follow peace.[58] His mission was successful; the miners rejected the strike policy.

The effects of Smuts's speeches went beyond the immediate aim of quelling labour unrest. These speeches strongly supporting the war while calling for postwar disarmament were well received by people of widely differing political opinions.[59] In addition to the newspaper coverage which the disarmament sections of the speeches received,[60] the government quickly recognised the speeches' propaganda value and reproduced them for distribution at home and abroad.[61] Thus Smuts's speeches had an impact well beyond their actual audiences. In his attempts to rally public opinion in support of the war Smuts, even more than the Liberal journalists and intellectuals or the Radical propagandists of the UDC, helped create expectations that peace would bring disarmament. These expectations, in turn, were to affect the formulation of disarmament policy.

Within days of Smuts's visit to Wales the Bolsheviks seized power in Russia and issued a decree calling on all the belligerents to enter peace negotiations. The Bolshevik Decree on Peace increased the pressures in Britain for a restatement of war aims which might lead to a negotiated settlement. The most significant of the calls for a restatement of aims came not from the left but from the Conservative elder statesman Lord Lansdowne. Reviewing the impact of the Bolshevik Revolution, the collapse of the Italian front in late October and the deteriorating economic situation in France, Lansdowne was understandably more pessimistic about the prospects for eventual Allied imposition of terms than he had been in 1916. He feared that prolongation of the war might lead not only to serious strikes which would cripple the British war effort but also to financial collapse.[62] When Balfour rejected Lansdowne's suggestion that the latter ask questions in the House of Lords designed to evoke an official clarification of Allied war aims, Lansdowne sent his appeal to the press.[63] The publication of the Lansdowne letter provoked a public debate in Britain, and Lansdowne's position received considerable support. At the same time the United States was also exerting pressure for a restatement of war aims.

Nevertheless, when Lloyd George responded publicly to Lansdowne's letter, he reiterated his commitment to decisive victory. In a speech at Gray's Inn on 14 December he proclaimed that 'there is no halfway house between victory and defeat': 'Victory is an essential condition for the security of a free world.'[64] As late as 27 December he replied evasively to a Labour request for a restatement of British war aims.[65]

Events, however, soon led the Prime Minister to reassess his position. Hoping that it might be possible to persuade Austria-Hungary to consider a separate peace, the War Cabinet had sent General Smuts to meet secretly in Switzerland with the former Austro-Hungarian Ambassador in London, Count Mensdorff. Although Mensdorff rejected a separate peace, Smuts reported that Austria-Hungary would attempt to influence Germany to accept moderate terms and that to facilitate this Mensdorff had urged a clear and definite restatement of British aims.[66] On 25 December the Central Powers, which since the beginning of the month had been negotiating with the Bolsheviks at Brest-Litovsk, announced what *The Times* correctly characterised as their 'feigned acquiescence'[67] in the Bolshevik programme of a peace without annexations or indemnities provided that within ten days the Allies accepted the same principles as the basis for peace negotiations. This action led Lloyd George to conclude that a restatement of war aims was necessary in order to counter the propaganda value of the enemy's announcement. Moreover, on 28 December, the same day on which, according to C. P. Scott, *The Times*'s report of the Central Powers' announcement convinced the Prime Minister of the necessity of restating Britain's war aims,[68] a joint conference of the Trades Union Congress and the Labour Party approved a memorandum on war aims embodying the principles long enunciated by the UDC. The favourable reception of the Labour memorandum by many outside the Labour movement strengthened Lloyd George's belief that he must answer the Brest-Litovsk programme.[69]

It is not clear whether Lloyd George regarded a restatement of war aims as anything more than a propaganda move. On 28 December when the War Cabinet first discussed the question of replying to the Central Powers and the Bolsheviks, he again spoke, as he had in September, in terms of acquiescing in a peace which allowed Germany to annex Russian territory.[70] Yet on 3 January he told his colleagues that 'the terms which we were bound to set out in the document were not such as Germany could accept . . . Hence, it was essential that this statement should be regarded rather as a war move than as a peace move.'[71] After delivering his war aims speech he wrote to his wife that he had never thought it would mean peace, and at the Supreme War Council a month later he reiterated the familiar theme that 'peace could never be made' until the military party in Germany was overthrown.[72]

Because of the deteriorating military situation, however, several of his colleagues who had opposed his earlier advocacy of a negotiated peace at Russia's expense now agreed with Hankey that 'if we can get anything like a decent peace, we ought to do so'[73] and hoped that a restatement of aims might lead to peace negotiations. Milner, though opposed to a peace which might leave Germany stronger than before, had long favoured pursuing the possibility of peace negotiations. At the War Cabinet on 28 December he took up Smuts and Ward's earlier proposal for the definition of minimum objectives which might lead to peace negotiations.[74] That evening he met with Smuts and Curzon to discuss peace terms,[75] and a few days later Curzon, formerly so opposed to a negotiated peace, expressed his view of the planned war aims statement as 'a genuine and sincere attempt to secure a reasonable peace', albeit one which he did not expect to succeed.[76] Pessimistic about the chances for an improvement in the military situation, even the formerly bellicose Carson, a member of the War Cabinet since July, now strongly favoured 'a serious effort to secure a satisfactory peace'.[77]

Thus the desire on the part of some members of the War Cabinet for a negotiated end to the war coincided with the need for a propaganda statement on war aims, and on 31 December the War Cabinet authorised Smuts, Cecil and Lloyd George to prepare draft statements. Because of the continuing manpower crisis the War Cabinet also agreed that it would be best if Lloyd George could make the planned statement on war aims to a Trades Union Congress meeting which was discussing manpower.[78] Thus the statement was to serve as 'a counter-offensive'[79] to the statements not only of both the Bolsheviks and the Central Powers but also of British dissidents.

While the proposals of the Bolsheviks and the Central Powers dealt only with terms on which the war might be ended, the British decided that their reply should make some reference as well to means for preventing future wars. Lloyd George decided that one of the points to be made in his speech was the failure of the Bolsheviks and the Central Powers to include in their proposals any reference to the League of Nations or disarmament.[80] Therefore, in addition to reviewing Britain's specific territorial and economic objectives, each of the draft statements also considered the problem of postwar security. Their different approaches to the essential conditions for the maintenance of postwar peace affected the attitudes of the authors of the draft statements to the question of peace negotiations and hence their conceptions of the proposed statement.

The draft prepared by Smuts was based on the most optimistic assessment of the Central Powers' motives and intentions. Asserting that Germany's acceptance of Britain's territorial objectives would be sufficient to indicate its abandonment of militarism, his draft declared that in order to assure postwar security not only was it necessary for Germany to renounce militarism but all nations must abandon offensive war as an instrument of policy. Smuts believed that there were grounds for agreement between the Allies and the Central Powers about the character of the postwar world, and he hoped that the projected statement might become the basis of peace negotiations.

As might be expected, Smuts made general disarmament the

cornerstone of his recommended approach to the problem of maintaining postwar peace. In his suggestions for the Prime Minister's speech he went further than he had in any of his own speeches advocating disarmament, endorsing not only the limitation of armaments but turning his earlier appeal for an end to standing armies into a call for the abolition of conscription: 'We consider it essential that the peace treaty shall include general provisions which shall bind the Governments concerned to the abolition of Military conscription and the limitation of armaments and the means and scale of future warfare.'[81]

The abolition of conscription was a new element in a statement prepared by a British official. For Smuts it was to become the key to the whole question of disarmament. Throughout his stay in England he was in frequent and close contact with Quaker friends with whom he held long philosophical discussions and whose views he took very seriously. These friends and their activities on behalf of conscientious objectors undoubtedly influenced his thinking on conscription.[82] Moreover, the Prime Minister was to deliver his address to a Labour meeting on manpower, and the Labour memorandum on war aims began its call for disarmament with a demand for the end of conscription. Once again, then, Smuts's own beliefs corresponded with a politically advantageous approach to the question of war aims. Believing that disarmament provided the solution to the maintenance of postwar security, he proposed that the war aims statement include a definite and specific declaration that general disarmament was an essential British objective.

Lloyd George delegated the preparation of his draft to Philip Kerr, who had already submitted for his consideration a draft 'counter-statement'[83] to the proposals of the Bolsheviks and the Central Powers. For Kerr the conversion of Germany to democracy was a prerequisite for lasting peace and security, and he did not believe that it was possible to enter into serious peace negotiations with the current German government. In the memorandum which he had prepared before the War Cabinet had agreed to a public restatement of war aims Kerr, using against the Central Powers language which seemed to be lifted directly from the UDC and Labour, had presented his version of the appropriate British position regarding peace:

The Allies do not believe that there can be any security for lasting peace so long as the governments of the peoples of Central

Europe, controlling as they do the immense resources in armies and materials of war disclosed in this war, are not directly amenable to popular control. The Allies . . . believe that the competition of armaments, and secret diplomacy, with their inevitable outcome – war – spring directly out of the system of entrusting the supreme power in the state to autocratic and therefore irresponsible hands . . . the Allies do not believe it possible to bring into operation those measures for the reduction of armaments . . . or for the constitution of a League of all nations to formulate and defend international law and freedom by land and sea, which are necessary to the real peace of the world, until the people of Central Europe have fallen into line with the rest of civilised mankind, and have taken the practical control of their polity into their own hands.[84]

Thus Kerr's first draft statement differed significantly from the one prepared by Smuts, who, though he hoped that Germany would become democratic, did not make this a precondition for peace.

As the quotation above indicates, Kerr also differed from Smuts on the question of disarmament. While he supported moderation in the growth of armaments, he was nevertheless a proponent of military preparedness. Therefore when he prepared another draft based on the Smuts draft, he changed Smuts's strong endorsement of disarmament as an essential British aim into merely an expression of willingness to 'enter into arrangements with all nations for the abolition of military conscription [and] the limitation of armaments' provided that these nations accepted the principles of 'the great association of free peoples' which had united to fight against the tyranny of the Central Powers. For Kerr it was not arms limitation but this association of free nations which could 'become in itself the strongest guarantee that such a conflict as this shall never occur again'.[85] In his view only the creation of such a system of collective security, based on democratic principles, would make it possible safely to proceed with general arms reduction.

Like Kerr, Cecil believed that only 'a definite German defeat or a German revolution' would guarantee future security and he, too, opposed entering peace negotiations. When he wrote to Balfour giving his views on the appropriate British response to the Central Powers, he rejected both the League of Nations and disarmament as the foundation of postwar security. Expressing his agreement with an article which had appeared in Germany saying that disarmament was safe for that country because it would always be able to rearm more quickly than its neighbours, he went so far as to comment, 'Disarmament is, I believe, a fraud'.[86] Nevertheless, in his draft Cecil condemned the growth of armaments and the institution of conscription: 'The crushing weight of modern armaments, the increasing evil of compulsory military service, the vast waste of wealth and effort involved in warlike preparation, these are blots on our civilisation.'[87] While he did not believe that the League of Nations could be anything more than 'a buttress to security',[88] he thought that there must be such a league before there could be any workable plan for arms limitation, and his draft called for both the creation of a league and the limitation of armaments: 'We must seek by the creation of some international organisation to limit the burden of armaments and diminish the probability of war.'[89] Cecil was sufficiently independent and principled that these differences between his privately expressed views and his draft of a statement intended for public presentation were not simply the result of his carrying out the War Cabinet's charge despite his own convictions. The differences reflected as well his own ambivalence on the question of disarmament and his belief in the importance of Anglo-American co-operation. Before preparing his draft Cecil had several discussions on war aims with Wiseman, who had accompanied House to Europe for an inter-Allied conference, and Wiseman again communicated Wilson's views on war aims and the preservation of peace.[90] While Cecil had not yet recovered from Crowe's criticisms and remained sceptical of specific plans for the implementation of disarmament, he retained his philosophical commitment to the idea of arms limitation. Hence in his draft he espoused the concepts of the league and general disarmament as worthy goals for the future but did not call for their specific inclusion in the peace treaty.

For the section of his war aims speech which dealt with the maintenance of postwar peace Lloyd George chose the Cecil formulation, and on 4 January the War Cabinet approved the statement.[91] On 5 January the Prime Minister delivered this major address on war aims to the Trades Union Congress meeting on manpower. After reviewing Britain's war aims, he concluded by pointing out that the Central Powers' proposal had omitted the question of the maintenance of postwar security, and he used Cecil's language to state Britain's position.[92] While not committing himself to the inclusion of disarmament in the peace treaty, as Smuts had advocated, the Prime Minister in an official statement of Britain's war aims had expressed his approval of the concept of arms limitation. Though Lloyd George's endorsement of disarmament was much vaguer than Smuts's, his address, of course, had an even greater impact on public opinion than the South African's earlier speeches advocating disarmament.

Despite Smuts's and Lloyd George's public pronouncements, however, the British government had no policy on general disarmament. As we have seen, it had not even considered the question of German disarmament. In its deliberations before approving Lloyd George's war aims statement, the War Cabinet had not discussed the question of disarmament or other measures for the maintenance of postwar peace. After the Imperial War Cabinet meetings in the spring of 1917 the government did not consider the disarmament question again until Germany sued for an armistice. Nevertheless, Smuts's and Lloyd George's speeches were important for the development of Britain's disarmament policy. They created a climate of expectations which manifested itself during the election campaign of 1918 and affected the formulation of policy on German as well as general disarmament. Whether intentionally or not, the speeches also led – or pushed – the Cabinet in a direction in which both Smuts and Lloyd George, although with different levels of commitment and at different paces, wished to go.

With its explicit endorsement of general disarmament as an Allied objective, President Wilson's Fourteen Points address, delivered three days after Lloyd George's speech, had an even more profound impact on public expectations regarding postwar disarmament.[93] Eventually, too, Wilson's declaration of disarmament as an Allied aim had an important effect on Allied diplomacy, when the Americans insisted that the other Allies accept the Fourteen Points as the basis on which they would negotiate peace with Germany. Immediately, however, the Germans rejected both Lloyd George's and Wilson's proposals. Bolshevik Russia's acceptance of Germany's peace terms on 3 March, followed on 21 March by the launching of the German Western offensive, ended talk of war aims and peace negotiations. It was not until Germany sued for an armistice that disarmament again became a subject of both internal British and inter-Allied consideration.

5

Armistice:
The Disarmament Debate

Germany's overture for an armistice in October 1918 made the question of German disarmament an immediate issue for British policy-makers. When the Allied military advisers recommended disarming the surrendering German forces, the political leaders had to decide whether to demand disarmament as a condition of armistice. For the first time British officials debated the question of German disarmament. General Wilson insisted upon the necessity of disarming the German army before it evacuated Allied territory, but General Haig, summoned to London to give his advice on armistice terms, disagreed. The policy-makers themselves had no fixed position, their views changing with their changing perceptions of the military and international situations. As a result, between the German overture and the signature of the Armistice the British position on disarming the German army underwent several changes. British leaders were concerned not only about conditions in Germany and the German army but also about their own and their allies' continued military strength, about Britain's position in the postwar world and about the threat of the westward spread of Bolshevism.

An overriding consideration for Britain's political leaders as they deliberated armistice terms was the possibility that a demand for disarmament of the withdrawing German forces would lead Germany to reconsider its desire for an armistice, thereby prolonging the war. This was Lloyd George and Bonar Law's conclusion when the Allies first discussed possible armistice conditions at the beginning of October after French intelligence intercepted Germany's note to President Wilson requesting an armistice leading to peace on the basis of his Fourteen Points and subsequent pronouncements.

Not knowing how Wilson would respond to the German

approach, the Allied ministers discussed possible armistice terms and asked their military and naval representatives to submit recommendations as well. The ministers did not include disarmament of the surrendering German forces among the principles upon which they believed armistice conditions should be based.[1] The military and naval representatives contended, however, 'that the first essential of an armistice is the disarmament of the enemy under the control of the Allies'. They therefore advised that in order to maintain Allied military ascendancy during the period of the armistice, the armistice conditions should include the surrender of all German armaments in invaded territory and of key fortresses occupied by the Germans as well as the internment of Germany's surface ships, naval air force and a large number of submarines.[2]

These recommendations corresponded with the views of Britain's chief military adviser, the militantly Germanophobe Henry Wilson, who believed that 'we must make immediate disarmament a condition. Then keep Boch [*sic*] troops under Boch command & discipline . . . & march & train [them] over the Rhine, leaving all arms, munitions, depots, factories, etc., etc., intact.'[3] On 7 October British military intelligence had reported that, although Germany realised that it was on the verge of military defeat, it was 'playing for time' in order to withdraw its forces in a fashion which would 'baulk the Allies of complete victory'.[4] The CIGS concluded that in order to prevent renewed fighting by the Germans after the signature of an armistice, disarmament before withdrawal must be an armistice condition: 'I don't see what guarantee we shall get worth having unless we disarm the brutes.'[5]

The other members of the British contingent in Paris did not share Wilson's enthusiasm for including disarmament among the armistice terms. When he discussed his views with Lloyd George and Bonar Law, the two ministers found his recommendations 'too severe'.[6] Hankey, too, found the military and naval representatives' draft terms 'much too extreme' because 'they involved complete disarmament, and many most humiliating conditions'.[7] Lloyd George, Bonar Law and Hankey, in contrast to Wilson, feared that a disarmament demand would strengthen Germany's will to continue fighting and thus lose the opportunity for armistice. In the Supreme War Council, against the advice of the CIGS, Lloyd George and Bonar Law therefore opposed the military advisers' proposals.

The British ministers were not alone in their opposition to these proposals. In presenting their recommendations to the Allied ministers, the military representatives emphasised their belief that unless the Allies disarmed the German army before it withdrew from occupied territory, Germany would be able to shorten its line of defence and reconstitute its forces and thus be in a better position to resume fighting.[8] A separate memorandum submitted by Marshal Foch, Commander-in-Chief of the Allied armies in France, disagreed with this analysis. Arguing instead that occupation of the left bank of the Rhine and the bridgeheads on the right bank would provide the best guarantee of Allied military dominance, Foch contended that disarmament of the withdrawing German forces was not necessary to assure Allied military superiority during the period of the armistice. The only disarmament measure which he called for was the German army's abandonment without destruction of its military installations and of all materiel which a speedily retreating army would be unable to remove.[9] In the Supreme War Council discussions the British view that the Allies were not in a position to impose terms as severe as those proposed by either the military representatives or Foch prevailed, and neither set of proposals won approval.[10]

While Lloyd George and Bonar Law regarded both the military representatives' and Foch's proposals as demanding too much and hence risking the possibility of unnecessarily prolonging the war, Lloyd George was equally concerned that President Wilson should not commit the Allies to an armistice on insufficient terms. As we have seen, throughout the war most British officials had contended that a decisive Allied victory would destroy Prussian militarism. They were not convinced, however, that Germany's request for an armistice signified such a victory. Amery, for example, agreed with the early military intelligence conclusion that Germany's purpose in requesting an armistice was 'to make it easier for the German Army to fall back to a new line and for the German people to hold out through the winter'.[11] Moreover, members of the government doubted the genuineness of the announced democratisation of Germany, which had accompanied its request for an armistice. While the *Daily News* interpreted events in Germany as meaning 'that the military despotism of Prussia is overthrown',[12] some officials were less sanguine. On 8 October Arthur Murray of the Political Intelligence Department (PID) at the Foreign Office expressed concern that some segments of British opinion believed that the appointment of the apparently moderate Prince Max of Baden as German Chancellor meant that there had been a complete change in the character and intentions of the German government. He emphatically disagreed: 'This, of course , is not only not the case, but it is just exactly what the German Government wish us to believe.'[13] Lloyd George feared that an armistice on President Wilson's terms, rather than testifying to the destruction of Prussian militarism, might 'give militarism a fresh lease of life'.[14]

These were some of the considerations which motivated Lloyd George when, after reporting on the Paris conference to the Imperial War Cabinet on 11 October,[15] he convened a conference of his closest advisers at the press magnate Lord Riddell's home in Danny on 13 October to discuss the question of an armistice.[16] This meeting considered whether to agree to an armistice at all and, if so, whether to demand the inclusion of disarmament among the armistice conditions. At the Supreme War Council meetings the fact that Germany had sued for peace on the basis of the Fourteen Points, which called for reduction of armaments, had not deterred Lloyd George and Bonar Law from opposing the military representatives' disarmament proposals as too harsh. Nevertheless, at the 13 October meeting the Prime Minister contended that President Wilson's reply to Germany meant that 'we were practically bound to demand disarmament as a condition of armistice'.[17] He took the lead not just in arguing the necessity of disarmament but in opposing an armistice on any basis other than unconditional surrender.

General Wilson took advantage of this opportunity to argue forcefully for the necessity of disarming the German forces during the period of the armistice. Reiterating his position that '"pile your arms" should be the main condition of the armistice', the CIGS urged the immediate disarmament of the surrendering German army: 'The present opportunity of disarming Germany now should be taken. Otherwise the Germans would put up a great fight on their own frontier, and he wished to put this out of their power.'[18]

On the issue of exacting conditions sufficiently humiliating to prevent a recurrence of German aggression, Wilson did not think it necessary for the Allies to push on into Germany and demand unconditional surrender. Rather, supported by the Chief of the Naval Staff, Admiral Sir Rosslyn Wemyss, who proposed, too, the disarmament of the German fleet, he advised that Germany's surrender of arms would achieve Britain's objective of crushing

Prussian militarism: 'From a military point of view, he could imagine no greater degradation than for the [German] Armies to lay down their arms in foreign territory.'[19] Wilson believed that disarming Germany's surrendering forces would not only give the Allies an immediate tactical advantage but would also, by publicly disgracing the German military, be a means of promoting Britain's long-term strategic interest in peace on the Continent. Thus even the anti-German CIGS apparently subscribed to the view that discrediting Germany's military leadership would assure its permanent removal from power. He argued that disarmament of the retreating German army was essential both to demonstrate and to seal decisive victory. Although Wilson was thinking only of the immediate surrender of arms by the forces engaged in combat, this was the first time since the Haldane and the Tyrrell–Paget memoranda that an official had linked Germany's disarmament with the destruction of Prussian militarism.

Much to General Wilson's delight, the conference endorsed his views, thereby reversing the position which Lloyd George and Bonar Law had taken in Paris.[20] Churchill vigorously supported the recommendation for disarmament, pointing out that even if the German troops surrendered their arms, Germany would still be able to mount a formidable defence and that, if not disarmed, it would be able rapidly to recover from its current setbacks. He urged that armistice terms 'should be entirely disabling, and that Germany should be asked to put the worst construction on her ultimate fate'. Bonar Law reversed his earlier position – albeit as part of an argument against demanding unconditional surrender – and tacitly accepted disarmament as an armistice condition. In opposing Lloyd George's suggestion that the war continue until the Allies invaded Germany, the Chancellor of the Exchequer agreed with General Wilson that the retreating forces' surrender of arms would constitute decisive victory and hence the end of Prussian militarism: 'If the troops had to leave their guns and rifles behind, the defeat would be as complete as anyone could wish.'[21] While Balfour still regarded the surrender of arms as less important than the surrender of territory, he did not oppose disarmament. Only Lord Milner, who, however, subsequently made clear his support for the idea of disarming the surrendering German army,[22] maintained 'that German militarism was already overthrown'.[23]

While Lloyd George and Bonar Law were the only members of the

War Cabinet present at the 13 October conference at Danny, Hankey reported that after he circulated a note of the meeting to the other members, 'there was not the smallest disposition to cavil at the decisions taken at Danny which, by general assent, were agreed to be right ones'.[24] Before receiving this note Curzon had, in fact, submitted a memorandum on armistice terms in which he, too, endorsed disarmament as a condition of armistice.[25] Thus whether, like Milner, they believed that Germany's request for an armistice signalled the collapse of Prussian militarism or, like most other ministers, they thought that the armistice conditions must be such as would secure this collapse, British leaders seemed to agree that the German army's surrender of arms was necessary to indicate its decisive defeat. Significantly, however, the Danny conference, while endorsing the concept of disarming the German army, rejected the idea of fighting on for unconditional surrender. This decision indicated that if British leaders believed that Germany would refuse an armistice which required disarmament, thereby necessitating an Allied advance on Germany, they would be likely to reconsider their position. Indeed, the triumph of the CIGS's views proved short-lived. On the very day of the meeting which had approved the demand for disarmament, Lloyd George, who had played the decisive role in securing that endorsement, expressed reservations about the decision: 'I think it might have been wiser to have prescribed for Foch's terms . . . They are not so humiliating, and I think the Germans would be more likely to accept them.'[26] Subsequent developments strengthened this belief.

News from the United States contributed to a modification of the British position. Shortly after the conference Lloyd George received a telegram from Sir Eric Geddes, who was in America as head of the British Naval Mission. Geddes informed him, after a meeting with the President, that Wilson's attitude seemed to be 'hardening towards caution', that the President recognised the need to continue fighting and that, although Wilson feared that the military and naval experts might recommend unnecessarily humiliating terms, he apparently believed that the disintegration of Austria necessitated 'greater stringency in dealing with GERMANY, in order that she should no longer be a dominant military power surrounded by smaller impotent states'.[27] On 15 October the British learned the contents of President Wilson's second note to Germany,[28] which stipulated that the armistice terms would be determined by the

Allied military advisers and must guarantee Allied military supremacy. This information undoubtedly lessened Lloyd George's fears that the President would agree to an armistice which would mean a 'sham or humbugging peace'.[29] Moreover, Geddes had also informed the Prime Minister that Wilson recognised the necessity of consulting with the Allies and was therefore sending House to Europe as his representative.[30] This news somewhat mollified British resentment of Wilson's handling of the negotiations with Germany. Thus the atmosphere when Generals Wilson and Haig reported on the military situation was different from that at the Danny conference.[31] After hearing their military advisers' reports on the situation at the front, the political leaders once again became apprehensive about the possibility that Germany might refuse an armistice which included a demand for disarmament and about the possible consequences of such a refusal.

General Wilson contributed to the undermining of his own position. While he continued to insist upon the German army's 'lay[ing] down their arms',[32] the picture which he painted of the military situation offered no encouragement for believing that this was a realistic demand. Although the General Staff had concluded that the British army's continuing advance constituted 'a grave threat' to the entire enemy line in the north, making defence of that line for any length of time impracticable and thus giving the German army in that sector little chance of reorganising and resting its forces,[33] Wilson had a low opinion of the capability of the French and American forces which were fighting in other sectors. He told the War Cabinet on 16 October that there was nothing in the German army's military situation on the Western front to warrant surrender,[34] that the British army, though tired, was 'willing & able to fight' but the French army was 'very tired & neither willing nor able to fight' and the American army 'unfit to fight'. This assessment led him to conclude that although 'the Boches are in a bad way', the Allied armies 'are not in a position to take full advantage of their weakness'.[35]

Rather than leading to a moderation of his demands, Wilson's belief that 'the Boch [*sic*] Army is *not* beaten yet'[36] strengthened his conviction that it must be disarmed as part of the armistice. On 19 October at a meeting of the X Committee, the small group which had assumed responsibility for the conduct of the war after the launching of the German offensive in May, he 'kept on repeating' that Britain would not resume fighting once there was an armistice and that therefore unless the Allies disarmed the German army and occupied Germany up to the Rhine, they 'would *never* be able to enforce terms which would give us a durable peace'.[37] However, Wilson's inability to marshal evidence either that the condition of the German army made it likely that Germany would accept disarmament as an armistice condition or that the Allied forces could speedily impose disarmament seriously damaged his case.

In addition, Wilson did not receive support from the commander in the field. When Lloyd George summoned Haig from the front to give his evaluation of the situation, Wilson unsuccessfully attempted to convince the Commander-in-Chief that 'we ought to insist on the disarmament of the Boches'.[38] Haig, however, was not a Germanophobe, and he worried about the consequences of demanding 'stiff terms'.[39] Moreover, like most of his fellow officers, he distrusted Wilson. The CIGS's arguments did not win him over.

Haig concurred in Wilson's appraisal of the Allied armies' fighting ability and of the German army's capacity for resistance, but this analysis led him to quite a different conclusion from Wilson's. He thought that the Allied armistice terms should not include disarmament, a condition which he considered tantamount to unconditional surrender. Throughout the war – and, indeed, as late as 10 October – Haig had taken a singularly optimistic view of Allied prospects.[40] However, his Chief of Staff, General Lawrence, upon whose paper Haig based his presentation in London, was pessimistic,[41] and German resistance to the British attack of 17 October had convinced Haig 'that the enemy was not ready for unconditional surrender'.[42] He believed that insistence upon humiliating terms would restore the morale of the German army, which would resist the imposition of such conditions. He reported that if forced to fight on its own territory, the German army would fight fiercely and the war would continue for at least another year. In these circumstances, he argued, the British army would bear the brunt of Allied fighting, but Britain would gain nothing in return. Moreover, Haig pointed out that he lacked reinforcements and that therefore the morale of his troops was bound to decline. In addition, he expressed doubts about the willingness of British soldiers to continue fighting in order to impose disarmament if Germany were willing to accept an armistice on other terms. Since he believed that the Allies had already achieved a victory sufficient to safeguard British interests, the

Commander-in-Chief preferred terms which he believed Germany would accept immediately and recommended letting the German soldiers withdraw without surrendering their weapons.[43] Fearing that harsh armistice conditions would 'produce a desire for revenge in years to come',[44] Haig, in contrast to Wilson, believed that moderate terms would best serve Britain's long-term interests.

Haig and Wilson had little information about conditions in the German army when they made their presentations. However, the figures available on the comparative strengths of the Allied and German armies were more encouraging than the two generals' interpretations of the situation. An 8 October memorandum fairly accurately reported the strength of the German army on the Western front and correctly pointed out its dwindling reserves and declining morale. Although the report contained an arithmetical error, which led it to underestimate Allied superiority, even with this mistake and the apparent incorrect equating of the strength of a German division to that of an Allied division, it indicated that there were over 750,000 more Allied than German forces engaged on the Western front.[45] A War Office summary of battle conditions from 11–17 October, a period which included the attack which had affected Haig's judgement of the situation, minimised the strength of the enemy's resistance and also called attention to the critical state of German reserves.[46]

In their reports to the political leaders, though Wilson and Haig emphasised the exhaustion of the Allied troops and expressed concern about their continuing morale, they did not give even equal weight to the exhaustion of the German forces or the effect on their morale both of knowledge of their government's armistice request and of being continually forced to retreat. On the German side, Crown Prince Rupprecht of Bavaria, Army Group Commander on the Western front, wrote on 18 October that the German troops were surrendering 'in hordes', that there were no more prepared lines of defence and none could be dug.[47] Contrary to the British belief that the Germans would be able to retreat, regroup and resume fighting in the spring when the active campaign season began again, he informed the Chancellor that he did not think there was any possibility of holding out through December.[48]

Just as Haig and Wilson overestimated Germany's capacity to resist, they underestimated their allies' fighting ability and determination and the Allied advantages in weaponry and strategic position. In contrast to Haig's and Wilson's misgivings about the French army, its censors reported, after examining the troops' mail, that French soldiers, though tired, strongly favoured continuing the war to decisive victory.[49] General Spears, who as Chief of the British Military Mission in France served as liaison officer between the British and French General Staffs, also discounted reports of French soldiers' unwillingness to continue fighting.[50] Even though the American troops were not fully combat ready, their sheer numbers – over 2 million at the time of the Armistice – were bound to have an effect, and the American advance in early November proved to be a decisive factor in the German surrender. In addition, Wilson's and Haig's assessments ignored Allied superiority in munitions and tanks. Moreover, they focused only on the Western front and did not take into account the effects of the military collapse of Germany's allies.

Nevertheless, Wilson's and Haig's reports were the information on which the ministers had to base their decision about armistice terms. The generals' analyses of the military situation raised serious questions about the likelihood of Germany's accepting disarmament unless forced to do so by a continuation of the war. Partly at the insistence of the government,[51] the right-wing press was clamouring for harsh terms,[52] and even the *Daily News* declared that if Foch should insist upon the Germans surrendering their weapons, 'the whole of the Allied peoples would be ready to stand by that demand'.[53] However, the *Daily News* also cautioned that demands for vengeance might 'reinstate the militarists and unite people and Kaiser in a war of desperate defence'.[54] Politicians, too, worried about the consequences of demanding harsh terms. Mond agreed with the *Daily News* that insistence upon unconditional surrender or upon terms which were its equivalent might lead to a reaction which would restore 'the Junker Military Party' to power. He warned Lloyd George that the consequences of this might be civil war, leading to 'the creation of a second Russia'. In an argument based on belief in the Prussian military party's responsibility for the war and on the assumption that democracies do not wage aggressive war, he contended that if Germany continued on the road to democracy, 'that surely would be the greatest step towards the peace of the world which could probably be taken'.[55] By 24 October Lloyd George, too, was describing demands for unconditional surrender as 'folly'.[56]

On 21 October the British knew that Germany had accepted the conditions of President Wilson's second note, and on 23 October the President sent them his correspondence with Germany with the recommendation that the Allied military representatives begin preparation of armistice terms. With Germany willing to sign an armistice under these conditions, Foch and Haig opposed to General Wilson's and the Allied military representatives' disarmament proposals and the CIGS and the Commander-in-Chief agreeing that continued fighting would be necessary in order to exact surrender of arms, the War Cabinet had to decide whether disarming Germany was a sufficiently vital objective to justify continuing the fighting.

While some ministers spoke of fighting on to secure the surrender of the German fleet, none was willing to prolong the war in order to disarm the German army. This was, of course, consistent with Britain's traditional stance and with wartime attitudes towards the future of German naval and military power respectively. After Haig's presentation Bonar Law returned to the position which he had taken during the Supreme War Council meetings in Paris. He considered even Haig's recommendations to be harsher than the military situation warranted,[57] and he opposed continuing the war in order to impose military – as opposed to naval – disarmament.[58] On 25 October Balfour seemed to assume that the decision of the 13 October conference still held,[59] but, as we have seen, he had never been a proponent of military disarmament. In the meeting at which the Cabinet reached its decision about armistice terms, although the former First Lord advocated surrender of the German fleet, he expressed no willingness to continue the war in order to secure the German army's surrender of arms.[60] Even the Germanophobe Chamberlain did not include surrender of arms among his desired armistice conditions.[61]

On 26 October the members of the War Cabinet debated whether to agree to an armistice or to demand terms which they believed Germany was unlikely to accept, thereby necessitating a prolongation of the war. At this meeting Curzon, too, backed off from his endorsement of disarmament. He at first implied continued support for disarmament as an armistice condition, saying that 'he attached vital importance to the imposition of conditions which would render Germany impotent to renew the War. On this point we must have secure guarantees.'[62] Yet he would not commit himself on the question and did not object to an immediate armistice although it seemed likely that a speedy armistice would preclude the imposition of disarmament.[63] Geddes, attending the War Cabinet in his capacity as First Lord, maintained that 'he would insist on the surrender of so much of Germany's naval and military power as to reduce her to a second-class Power'.[64] But he specifically disavowed interest in continuing the war. Smuts had submitted a memorandum in which he argued that Germany was not sufficiently defeated to accept disarmament, a condition which, he maintained, 'only an utterly defeated enemy could be compelled to concede'.[65] Having already renounced any interest in a crushing military victory,[66] he emphatically rejected the idea of continuing the war.[67]

Although Lloyd George again raised the question of fighting on to achieve unconditional surrender,[68] he was acutely aware of Britain's continuing manpower problems. He knew that the British Expeditionary Force could not maintain its current level of military strength, much less provide the additional forces necessary for continuing the war as long as the military advisers indicated would be necessary if disarmament were a condition of armistice. Moreover, when he had visited the front a year before, he had been told that the army would not continue fighting simply to achieve a military triumph,[69] and Haig's observations confirmed this assessment.

Accordingly, the War Cabinet decided that it did not wish to continue the war. Rather than endorsing specific terms, it adopted as guidelines for Lloyd George and Balfour in their negotiations with France and the United States the vague formulations that 'the British Government desires a good peace if that is now attainable' and that 'the naval conditions of the armistice should represent the admission of German defeat by sea in the same degree as the military conditions recognise the corresponding admission of German defeat by land'.[70] Even when the Deputy CIGS, General Harington, informed the War Cabinet that conditions in the German army had deteriorated so badly that if the war continued Germany would probably have to accept whatever terms the Allies wished to impose,[71] Britain's political leaders expressed no interest in continuing the war in order to disarm the surrendering German army.[72]

During these discussions British leaders had another preoccupation besides a possible German refusal of harsh terms. They were also quite concerned about the impact of a prolongation of the fighting on Britain's position in the postwar world. In 1917 Lloyd

George had told the king of his determination that British arms be chiefly responsible for the attainment of victory. He wanted Britain to be in a strong position in relation to its allies at the end of the war so that it could play the chief role at the peace conference: 'It was his duty to ensure that whenever the climax is reached England is at the zenith of her military strength and in a position more than to hold her own among the Nations of the World.'[73] This was, of course, an objective of all British policy-makers. In October 1918 there was considerable uneasiness that if the war continued as long as Haig and Wilson believed would be necessary to impose disarmament, Britain would, in the process, lose its dominant position in world affairs. Milner, for example, had told H. A. L. Fisher in August that 'we should run great risks by prolonging [the] war beyond this year and that the British Empire will never be so strong again'.[74]

In evaluating Britain's strategic position as they debated whether to agree to an armistice or to continue the war, British leaders therefore considered Britain's status in relation to its allies as well as the Allied military position *vis-à-vis* Germany. As they had indicated periodically throughout the war, they were not optimistic about maintaining the wartime alliance into the postwar period, and they were suspicious of their allies' postwar intentions. Smuts epitomised this outlook when he wrote, 'We have to bear in mind that our opponents at the peace table will not only be our enemies . . . history teaches us that our friends of to-day may not be our friends of to-morrow'.[75] British policy-makers feared that if the war continued, the United States, newly emerging as a world power, would soon rival and even surpass Britain's power. In addition, they were concerned about coming out of the war in a weak diplomatic position in relation to France and feared that the exhaustion of the British army by continued fighting would leave Britain in a poor bargaining position at the peace conference. With Germany baulked of conquest of the Continent, the German colonies captured and Britain in possession of much of the territory of the collapsed Turkish Empire, Amery's perception of the British position in October 1918 seemed to many British leaders to be correct: 'As far as the British Empire is concerned we have practically got all that is required for our security, and any difficulty that may arise about its retention will come from our Allies and not from the enemy.'[76] Therefore they wished to end the war while Britain still played the leading military role and would as a result be in the best position for attaining its colonial and economic objectives at the peace conference and for maintaining its primacy in the postwar world.

As we have seen, British leaders had for some time been concerned about the extent and implications of American influence on Britain's war and peace aims policy. As early as 1916 McKenna had expressed fears that the United States might be able to 'dictate to us' 'the time and terms of peace'.[77] In March 1918 Wiseman had used almost identical language to describe the 'unpleasant truth' of the Allied relationship with the United States: 'They are in a position almost to dictate the war policy of the Allies.'[78] As Paul Cambon, the French ambassador in London, noted, the prospect of America's assuming the role of Europe's patron after the war caused considerable uneasiness in Britain.[79]

Wilson's handling of the negotiations with Germany exacerbated these concerns. When Addison wrote on 23 October that 'there is no greater autocrat in the world at the present moment than President Wilson',[80] he vividly expressed British resentment at the President's actions. The American attitude towards British sea power caused particular anxiety. Not only did Wilson insist upon basing peace upon the Fourteen Points, which called for freedom of the seas but, during his stay in Washington, Geddes received the impression that 'President Wilson wished to create a sea power other than ours'. The First Lord became convinced that it was 'the aim and purpose of the President to reduce comparatively the preponderance in sea-power of the British Empire'.[81] This would, of course, strike at the basis not only of British predominance but also of British security.

The longer the war continued the more dependent Britain would become on the United States for money and manpower and hence the less freedom of action Britain would have in the peace negotiations and in the postwar world. During the Flanders offensive a year before, Lloyd George, increasingly disturbed by Haig's conduct of a war of attrition, had confided to Hankey his apprehension that if the depletion of British manpower continued, the United States would play the decisive role in the achievement of victory and Britain might therefore become a second-rate power:

A continuance of Sir Douglas Haig's attacks might conceivably result in bringing Germany to terms in 1919. But in that case it would be the United States of America who would deal the blow and not we ourselves . . . He was particularly anxious to avoid a situation at the end of the War in which our Army would no longer be a first-class one. He wished . . . that this country would be the greatest military power in the world.[82]

At a meeting of the Imperial War Cabinet in August 1918 the Prime Minister had again expressed the view that if victory meant the exhaustion of the British army, then 'the substance [of victory] would have passed to America'.[83]

Although Lloyd George was sceptical of Haig's judgement, it is likely that the Commander-in-Chief's assessment that the brunt of continued fighting would fall on the British forces reawakened the Prime Minister's earlier misgivings about the deleterious effects of achieving an Allied victory at the expense of the British army. The opinion of the formerly so optimistic Haig that continuing the war in order to disarm the German forces might indeed exhaust the British army undoubtedly affected Lloyd George's thinking on armistice terms. Despite his talk of unconditional surrender he appears to have been as disturbed about the possibility that continuing the war would weaken Britain's position, leaving it open to postwar challenge from the United States, as about the possibility of a resurgent Germany.

Other Cabinet members and advisers were equally apprehensive about the growth of American power at the expense of Britain. Addison recorded his concern that as a result of the exhaustion of the Allied armies and the increasing numbers of American troops arriving in Europe 'we might be in danger next year if things went on until then and if Wilson were in a position to dictate a Peace to France and ourselves'.[84] Lord Reading, who had become ambassador to the United States in January, agreed that if the war continued the United States would pose a threat to Britain's position: 'Every month that the War continued increased the power of the United States . . . by continuing the War it might become more difficult for us to hold our own.'[85] One reason why even the anti-German Chamberlain favoured a speedy armistice was his belief that Britain had reached the zenith of its contribution to the Allied war effort. He, too, worried that if the war continued, Britain's military role would inevitably decline while that of the United States would increase. This, he feared, would result in a diminution of Britain's power to determine armistice and peace conditions and a corresponding growth in America's power to impose its will:

If we fight on, Germany is ruined, but at what a cost to ourselves! Our armies must dwindle; the French are no longer fighting; a year hence we shall have lost how many thousands more men? & American power will be dominant. Today we are top dog. Our fleets, our armies have brought Germany to her knees and today (more than at any later time) the peace may be our peace.[86]

Smuts was the member of the War Cabinet most disturbed by the prospect of a decline in Britain's world power. He feared the rising power of not only the United States but also Japan. In August 1918 he had first voiced his apprehension that fighting on to achieve complete military victory might result in Britain's becoming a second-rate power.[87] On 24 October when he circulated a memorandum to the War Cabinet urging an early peace, Smuts focused on the United States as Britain's chief competitor for world power:

If peace comes now, it will be a British peace . . . now at the supreme crisis of the war we are at the height of our power . . . If unwisely we let slip this opportunity, the war may drag on for another year – till no doubt Germany is utterly broken and finished, but also (and this is my point) till we have lost the first position; and the peace which will then be imposed on an utterly exhausted Europe will be an American peace. In another year of war the United States will have taken our place as the first military, diplomatic and financial power of the world.[88]

Smuts's assessment of the relative strengths of the Great Powers led him to conclude that if the Allies continued the war in order to crush Germany, they would also destroy Europe as a power centre: 'If we were to beat Germany to nothingness, then we must beat Europe to nothingness, too.'[89] He warned that the United States would fill the power vacuum thereby created, with unpredictable consequences for Britain: 'A new centre of gravity will have been given to the great system of western civilisation, with results for the world and the British Empire which no man can foresee.'[90] Thus Smuts worried that continuing the war until unconditional surrender or the imposition of terms amounting to its equivalent would lead not only to America's replacing Britain as the leading world power but also to a collapse of the world order. Underlying Smuts's and other British leaders' anxieties about America's growing power, then, was the critical question of Britain's survival as a world power.

British misgivings about French intentions were of a different order. France was a rival, not a threat to Britain's status as a world power. Britain's economic relationship with its Entente partner was the reverse of that with the United States. During the war France had become increasingly dependent upon Britain for money, merchant ships and supplies. Thus Britain was the economically weaker France's creditor. More importantly, as a land power which before the war had not attempted to outbuild the British fleet and seemed unlikely after the war to have the resources for expanding its navy, France posed no challenge to Britain's naval supremacy. When Balfour complained during the final pre-Armistice negotiations about Foch's opposition to the Admiralty's recommendations for the naval conditions of armistice, he nevertheless made it clear that he had no fear of France's naval power: 'As for the other Allied Powers [besides the United States] . . . they simply do not count . . . without British assistance they would be powerless [at sea].'[91] Hence, unlike the United States, France did not threaten Britain's dominant position in world affairs. But, as a result of Germany's loss of its colonies, the Bolshevik regime's renunciation of tsarist Russia's imperialist ambitions and the wartime consolidation of both Britain's and France's positions in the Middle East, France remained Britain's chief imperial rival.

Although the two powers had temporarily subordinated their differences to the common war effort, British leaders never lost sight of this traditional rivalry, and they expected it to be an important factor in postwar diplomacy. As we have seen, the impetus for Asquith's request for war aims recommendations had been fear of losing out to France at the peace table. When the 1917 Milner Committee report had emphasised that Britain and France would be competitors for shares of any economic compensation from Germany,[92] it also had pointed to the likelihood of the resumption of an antagonistic relationship with France in the peace negotiations. In the autumn of 1917 Lloyd George had expressed his concern about conflict with France not only at the peace conference but after. He had told King George V that continuing the war into 1919 would not only promote the growth of the United States as a world power but also give France the opportunity to recruit fresh forces, which would then be available at the end of the war for possible use against British interests.[93]

With victory in sight, it became clear that there would be many areas in which British interests would clash with those of France, and mistrust of French intentions became more pronounced. French Premier Clemenceau's later remark to Lloyd George that 'within an hour after the Armistice I had the impression that you had become once again the enemies of France'[94] was inaccurate only in that the resumption of British antagonism towards France did not await the signature of the Armistice. The British were suspicious of French territorial designs against Germany, manifested in Foch's demand for occupation of the Rhine. They disagreed with the French over the disposition of the territories of the defunct Ottoman Empire, where concessions to France might interfere with Britain's strategic interest in protection of the route to India. This rivalry in the Middle East caused particular concern to Curzon, whose focus remained the empire, especially India. He distrusted French ambitions in the area and regarded France as 'quite likely' to be Britain's 'real rival in 20 years' time'.[95] Lloyd George, too, complained of French aims in the Middle East that 'the French are rather greedy; they want everything'.[96]

Thus there were many potential areas of conflict. British leaders therefore had no desire to continue the war if continued fighting would, as Haig believed,[97] further French, but not British, interests and might indeed, by weakening Britain's military and diplomatic position, risk the attainment of British objectives. Entering the final Allied armistice discussions, the British representatives, then, had the support of their colleagues for pursuing moderate military terms which did not include disarmament of the German army.[98]

The terms presented for their consideration in Paris, however, called for partial disarmament of the German army. These were the terms formulated by Foch on Clemenceau's instructions after the receipt of President Wilson's 23 October letter. In his proposals Foch elaborated on his 8 October recommendation by specifying the kinds and amounts of weaponry he wished Germany to surrender. While he thus recommended partial disarmament of the surrendering enemy forces, the cornerstone of his proposals remained occupation of the Rhine.[99] According to Hankey, Lloyd George 'made a good representation of Haig's appeal for moderation'[100] when the Allied prime ministers and Colonel House considered the military terms of armistice on 1 November. However, Foch insisted that his terms were necessary to prevent a renewal of hostilities. Although Foch was unable to guarantee immediate German acceptance of his proposed terms, Lloyd George accepted his argument and, along with the other prime ministers and House, agreed to the Foch proposals,[101] which the Supreme War Council then approved.[102] Thus, contrary to the War Cabinet's instructions, Lloyd George and his colleagues at Versailles endorsed military conditions which might necessitate a prolongation of the war. By the time the Germans received these terms, however, they were in no condition to refuse them. The military terms which Germany accepted on 11 November therefore included the surrender of large quantities of war material.[103]

In addition to considering the military and naval terms of armistice, the prime ministers and House also debated the question of accepting the Fourteen Points as the basis for peace. As we have seen, the spring 1917 session of the Imperial War Cabinet had refused to endorse the idea of general disarmament, and the Imperial Cabinet's members had pointed out the difficulties of implementing arms reduction. Moreover, the War Cabinet had not discussed the concept before Lloyd George endorsed it in his Trades Union Congress address, nor did it debate the issue in October during its discussion of armistice terms. Nevertheless, the British went to Paris prepared to accept Point Four of the Fourteen Points, which called for reduction of armaments.[104]

As Reading noted, they expected implementation of Point Four to depend upon 'the formation of a League of Nations which would become an efficient instrument for securing International Peace'.[105] Thus their interpretation of this Wilsonian principle conformed with Lloyd George's call in his 1918 war aims speech for the creation of an international organisation which would make possible the limitation of armaments. The construction of Point Four as 'conditional upon [an] effective League' – an interpretation which House confirmed to Reading[106] – meant that its implementation would be sufficiently far in the future to pose no immediate challenge to British naval supremacy. In addition, the elaboration of Point Four in the intercepted copy which the British obtained of a commentary on the Fourteen Points prepared for House's use as a talking paper in his negotiations with the Allies showed that the Americans were primarily interested in securing acceptance of the principle of arms limitation, not in working out specific plans for its implementation:

IV. Adequate guarantees given and taken that armaments will be reduced to the lowest point consistent with domestic safety.

'Domestic safety' clearly implies not only internal policing, but the protection of territory against invasion. The accumulation of armaments above this level would be a violation of the proposal. What further guarantees should be given and taken, or what are to be the standards of judgment have never been determined. It will be enough to adopt the general principle and then institute some means to prepare detailed projects for its execution.[107]

This definition of domestic safety gave the British wide latitude for asserting the necessity of a large navy to protect their empire. Hence Point Four, though clearly intended to encompass naval as well as military disarmament, seemed sufficiently vague to permit Britain full freedom of action in future attempts to implement it.

It was instead Point Two, calling for freedom of the seas, which became the focus of British concerns about an American challenge to British naval superiority. Disagreement over acceptance of Point Two produced heated exchanges between Lloyd George and House and led to a crisis in Anglo-American relations, resolved only when House agreed to reserve the question of the freedom of the seas for discussion at the peace conference. With House's acceptance of this reservation having safeguarded Britain's strategic position and his acceptance of another reservation relating to reparations having ensured Britain's right to claim compensation from Germany, Lloyd George agreed to accept the Fourteen Points as the basis of peace, and the other Allied ministers also indicated their acceptance. Thus, in addition to the military and naval terms of armistice which Foch and Wemyss presented to the Germans, President Wilson communicated to the German government the pre-Armistice agreement by which the Allies agreed to conclude peace on the basis of the Fourteen Points. On the question of disarmament, however, the Fourteen Points were so vague that their acceptance did not necessarily indicate an intention to demand further disarmament as part of the treaty with Germany.

In fact, while these discussions were under way, events were taking place in Germany which led British leaders to question whether the military terms of armistice to which they had agreed might not reduce German armaments to a point below that consistent with the maintenance of Germany's domestic safety and indeed the safety of all Western Europe. In late October and early November there was a series of revolutionary outbreaks in Germany, culminating in the abdication of the emperor and the proclamation of the German republic on 9 November and the formation the next day of a revolutionary government. Already concerned about the possibility of the spread of Bolshevism to Germany, British leaders were profoundly affected by these events.

Since British officials were unaware of the circumstances which had prompted the German request for an armistice and their military advisers reported that there was nothing in the military situation to warrant the request, they attributed Germany's action to internal conditions. In early October Addison recorded that the government was receiving 'rumours of the very bad state in Germany and signs of a breakup there',[108] while Lloyd George told Geddes, 'Our information as to conditions in Germany shows considerable demoralisation and panic'.[109]

Since similar conditions had preceded the revolutions in Russia, British leaders feared that Germany, too, might succumb to Bolshevism. In an interview published in the *Evening Standard* on 17 October Milner expressed his concern that the Allies' armistice demands might lead to '*Bolshevism and chaos*'[110] in Germany. Information which he received when he went to Paris for the meetings of the Supreme War Council reinforced this apprehension. A memorandum prepared by one of the officers attached to the Supreme War Council concluded that 'Bolshevism may be too unsympathetic to the national genius of Germany ever to find a home there; but its brother is knocking at the door'.[111] From Paris, too, Lord Derby, who had become ambassador to France in April, reported that the French government expected a Bolshevik revolution in Germany and that Foreign Minister Pichon feared the consequences for France.[112]

The situation in Germany and the belief that Bolshevism was contagious reawakened British leaders' fears of class war. As we have seen, the labour unrest of 1917 had aroused their concern about the possibility of a revolution in Britain. Since the Bolshevik Revolution they had tended to identify any form of social upheaval with

Bolshevism. When Haig returned to London in October 1918, Wilson told him of their continuing 'fear of the Trades Unions, of strikes'.[113] On the government's instructions, therefore, while the Political Intelligence Department of the Foreign Office reported on conditions in Germany, the Home Office regularly circulated to the War Cabinet intelligence reports on the activities of allegedly revolutionary organisations in the United Kingdom.[114]

Thus British leaders feared a Bolshevik revolution in Germany not just because of its expected consequences there but because it might threaten the whole European order and pose a danger even to Britain. In his 24 October memorandum Smuts cited the danger of 'the grim spectre of Bolshevist anarchy . . . stalking to the front' as an argument for the immediate conclusion of peace: 'There is no doubt that under the pressure of this vast world war a fundamental change is coming over the spirit of Europe. Its tremendous and far-reaching pressure is felt even more on the home fronts than on the battle fronts.'[115] While Smuts urged peace as a means of stemming the revolutionary tide and preserving European stability, for others the prospect of peace did not lessen the fear of revolution. As the war came to an end, Chamberlain, for example, worried about the growth of a revolutionary atmosphere in Britain: 'I am anxious about the future which seems to me full of difficulty & danger – strikes, discontent & much revolutionary feeling in the air when the strain & patriotic self-repression of the last four years are removed.'[116] The revolutionary uprisings in Germany in late October and early November understandably heightened the British government's concern about the threat of Bolshevism not only in Germany but also in the rest of Europe and Britain.

Exacerbating the War Cabinet's fear of revolution, these events led to consideration of the possibility of strengthening the German army in order to prevent the westward spread of Bolshevism. Even before the first uprising in the German fleet on the night of 29–30 October, Milner and General Wilson had opposed demobilising the German army because 'Germany may have to be the bulwark against Russian Bolshevickism [*sic*]'.[117] After the outbreaks in Germany British ministers increasingly believed that Germany must serve as a barrier against the expansion of Bolshevism and must consequently be left an army strong enough both to put down internal unrest and to defend its borders against the contagion of Bolshevism. General Bliss, the American military representative on the Supreme War

Council, reported on the eve of the Armistice that 'there was running through the minds of all the high political men the fear of revolution and Bolshevism in Germany and their belief that the only barrier against the spread of it would be to leave the German army sufficiently armed to put down such revolution'.[118] Their fear of Bolshevism transformed British leaders' attitude towards the German army. By early November, with the armistice terms agreed upon, concern about the German army's imminent collapse had replaced their earlier anxiety about the possibility of armed German resistance to harsh armistice terms.

Between the first German revolt on 29 October and the signature of the Armistice on 11 November the War Cabinet devoted significant portions of several meetings to consideration of the German situation and its implications for British policy.[119] What emerges from the records of these meetings and from intragovernmental and private communications during this period is a conviction that Germany would now be unable to resume fighting, a marked concern about the demoralisation of the German army and the possibility that its deterioration might open the way to the triumph of Bolshevism in Germany, and a genuine fear of the prospect of revolution in Britain.

The War Cabinet discussion of 10 November best reveals the extent of British concern at the prospect of a Bolshevik revolution in Germany and the effect of this anxiety on attitudes towards the role of the German army. The Allies had presented the armistice terms to the Germans on 8 November and were awaiting their response. Lloyd George opened the discussion by stating his fear that 'events were taking a similar course in Germany to that which had taken place in Russia'.[120] Fearing that there would be no German government to authorise signing an armistice, the War Cabinet discussed what the Allied response should be in that event.

The Prime Minister's conjecture that Foch would probably want to continue fighting in order to destroy the German army and capture its war material provoked vehement protests from his colleagues. Milner, who thought that the prospect in Germany was 'very black',[121] argued that 'the German Army was no longer a danger to us', while General Wilson, who had earlier so adamantly recommended disarmament, predicted the army's imminent disintegration in the face of the disorders in Germany. The strongest response came from Churchill, who had become obsessively anti-Bolshevik. For the aristocratic former Tory the threat of Bolshevism in Germany produced a complete reversal of attitude about the German army. On 13 October he had been a leading advocate of disarmament; now he argued equally forcefully for strengthening the German army as a means of countering Bolshevism: 'It was important that we should not attempt to destroy the only police force available for maintaining order in Germany. We might have to build up the Germany [*sic*] Army, as it was important to get Germany on her legs again for fear of the spread of Bolshevism.'[122]

The British government preferred the idea of strengthening the German army to that of using Allied forces to restore order in Germany. British leaders were reluctant to send British troops into areas where they would be exposed to revolutionary ideas, which they might then import into Britain. General Wilson, who was 'certain that Bolshevism will sweep over Germany',[123] cautioned against the involvement of British forces in putting down revolutionary outbreaks there, and Lloyd George warned that British working-class soldiers might be the means for transmitting Bolshevism from Germany to Britain: 'Marching men into Germany was marching them into a cholera area. The Germans did that in Russia and caught the virus, i.e. of Bolshevism.'[124] The British certainly did not wish France to take unilateral action in Germany and thus gain a foothold there. Therefore if the disorders continued and they wished order to be restored and maintained, the only alternative seemed to be to strengthen the German army. Thus, even before the war was officially over, British officials' fear of Bolshevism led them seriously to consider bolstering their enemy's armed forces.

General Wilson expressed the prevalent outlook when he wrote on 10 November, 'Our real danger now is not the Boch [*sic*] but Bolshevism'.[125] After the uprisings in Germany only a minority still feared a militarist reaction there. Chamberlain thought that there was 'always the possibility of a military reaction',[126] while Cecil forwarded to the British representatives at the Supreme War Council information from a recent returnee from Berlin that harsh terms were more likely to revive a military national spirit than to promote Bolshevism.[127] By the time of the Armistice, however, for most British leaders the containment of Bolshevism, not the destruction of Prussian militarism, had become the focus of their concerns about Germany.

6
The Aftermath of Victory

With the German signature of the Armistice having removed the fear that Germany might refuse to accept the Allied armistice terms, and leftist agitation in Germany threatening to topple the new republican regime there, the British government initially adopted a charitable attitude towards Germany. In the euphoria of victory British leaders believed that a new Germany had emerged from the war. When the *Daily News* proclaimed, 'The old Germany is gone for ever',[1] it expressed the sentiments of most government leaders as well. They shared the view of Bryce, who had written a few days before the kaiser's abdication that William II's removal would mean the collapse of Prussian militarism: 'If the Hohenzollern dynasty disappears, the keystone will be taken out of the arch upon which the German militarist system rests, and Germany will have her own troubles to come, and be no wise disposed to resume militarism or aggression.'[2] Concerned that these 'troubles to come' might have repercussions which would affect the victors, too, and convinced, as a military intelligence survey of the London press put it, of 'the fact that the drastic armistice terms render further German aggression impossible for many years to come',[3] the government in the immediate aftermath of victory assumed a conciliatory posture towards Germany.

While popular Germanophobia had increased as the war went on, reaching its height during the last months of fighting, the war had not completely eradicated the admiration for the German people and the feeling, which had characterised a significant segment of prewar thinking, that there was a special affinity between Britain and Germany. Despite widespread popular antipathy towards Germany and all things German, official ambivalence continued to manifest itself in the distinction drawn between the German people and their Prussian leaders. Like many of his colleagues, Lloyd George hoped that a revolution in Germany ending the war would lead to the resumption of good relations between Britain and Germany: 'The

Germans w[oul]d in that case become our friends.'[4] Accordingly, in one of his last major speeches before the German request for an armistice, while arguing the necessity of victory, he had again sounded the theme of the distinction between the German people and their rulers. He had welcomed the prospect of Germany, purged of its militarist rulers, entering the projected League of Nations: 'If, after the war, Germany repudiates and condemns her perfidy, or, rather, the perfidy of her rulers, then a Germany freed from military domination will be welcome into the great League of Nations.'[5] To most British leaders, Germany in early November seemed indeed to have been 'freed from military domination', and this perception profoundly affected their attitude towards the new German government and towards Germany's place in the European system.

The belief in Germany's transformation overshadowed the doubts which had been raised by the German sinking of the mailboat *Leinster* just a few days after the overture for an armistice. This German action had caused even the usually reserved Balfour publicly to question the validity of the distinction between the German people and their rulers:

> I wish I could think that these atrocious crimes were the crimes of a small dominant military caste. I agree that the direction of policy . . . may be in the hands of a small caste, but it is incredible that crimes like these . . . should go on being repeated month after month of four years of embittered warfare if it [*sic*] did not commend itself to the population which commits them.[6]

The certainty of victory, however, coupled with fears of Germany's imminent collapse, had brought a temporary softening of the attitude of British leaders.

Within official circles, for a time this attitude of restraint tempered the strong wave of anti-Germanism which swept Britain at the end of the war. The government's attitude prompted Maxse to complain in the *National Review* that the Cabinet was out of step with public opinion: 'It is incontestable that the Man in the Street to-day has an incomparably keener grasp of the German danger and infinitely sounder views upon it than the Man in the Cabinet, who perpetually strikes false notes from living in the pre-war atmosphere when the Anglo-German legend . . . dominated our public life, equally infecting Parliament and the Press.'[7] As Maxse correctly asserted, the government's conciliatory attitude had its roots in the prewar assumptions about Germany described earlier. It derived, too, from British leaders' beliefs about the origins of the war and their repeated wartime assertions that Germany's military defeat would mean the end of Prussian militarism. Fear of Bolshevism and concern about Britain's economic future also fostered an initially conciliatory attitude towards Germany.

While Hughes, like Arthur Murray, had dismissed the government of Prince Max of Baden as 'a sham', describing its members as 'puppets whose strings were pulled by the Kaiser and Hindenburg',[8] for many other officials Germany's military collapse had signalled the end of militarism there. Not only had Milner told his colleagues at the Danny conference that Prussian militarism was overthrown, but in his *Evening Standard* interview he had asserted that it was 'a serious mistake . . . to imagine that the German people are in love with militarism', that an armistice which guaranteed Allied military supremacy would bring about 'the utter collapse of Prussian militarism'.[9] After the Armistice Amery, too, declared that 'Kaiserism has been discredited by the defeat of its armies'.[10] Milner and Amery, it is true, had early rejected the idea of the war as a crusade against Prussian militarism, and Milner had long advocated a moderate peace. Yet, in the aftermath of the German Revolution, others who had wholeheartedly subscribed to the view of the war as a struggle against Prussian militarism and had strongly argued the necessity of complete military victory shared this perception of the situation in Germany.

Members of the Political Intelligence Department at the Foreign Office – those, in fact, most knowledgeable about Germany – agreed with Milner's and Amery's assessment. Throughout the war these men had insisted upon the necessity of a decisive military victory. With victory achieved, they were now convinced that there had been a genuine change in Germany. The PID's specialist on Germany, the historian Alfred Zimmern, who, in contrast to Hughes and Murray, believed that the appointment of Prince Max as Chancellor had marked 'a definite and decisive change in the Government of Germany',[11] applauded Milner's interview as 'both wise and courageous'.[12] He later wrote of the PID's perception of the situation at the time of the Armistice that 'Prussian militarism lay in very truth in the dust'.[13]

Sir James Headlam-Morley, assistant-director of the PID and, like Zimmern, an expert on Germany, agreed. In the introduction to a collection of his articles published in 1917 he had argued that Germany's military defeat, which he considered essential, would achieve the destruction of militarism, 'the ultimate object of the war'.[14] On the basis of his knowledge of Germany and of German history, Headlam-Morley, who had studied with the German military historian Hans Delbrück, had attended Treitschke's lectures and had written a biography of Bismarck, had therefore contended that 'with a Germany defeated no artificial securities will be wanted, for there will be a stronger security in the consciousness of defeat'.[15] Thus a defeated Germany would be a new Germany, promoting European security and therefore deserving of generous treatment by the Allies. Convinced that the events in Germany in early November had vindicated his wartime analysis but that the Allies had not taken advantage of the conditions created by the German Revolution to assure that Germany's new direction marked a permanent departure from the past, he later wrote, 'The revolution in Germany was, as far as I can make out, as thorough, complete and sincere as any revolution of which there is any record'.[16]

In the first weeks after the Armistice, however, British officials had little information from Germany on which to judge the genuineness of the German commitment to democracy or to base their assessments of conditions there. The situation in Germany remained, as Chamberlain had described it a few days before the Armistice, 'very obscure'.[17] As Rumbold reported from his post in neutral Berne, a centre for intelligence activity, 'The state of things is so extraordinary and history is being made at such a pace that it is impossible to take it in'.[18] The difficulty, which he noted, of determining and reporting 'the exact conditions in Germany'[19] was, of course, even greater in London.

In addition to reports from British diplomats in neutral countries, the PID relied initially on the intelligence sources it had developed during the war, on press surveys and on information obtained from newspaper correspondents and returning prisoners of war. PID agents did not enter Germany until mid-December. Between an 11 November survey of Germany's new political leadership[20] and a report from the *Daily Chronicle*'s Geneva correspondent circulated in late November[21] the PID provided the War Cabinet with no written reports on conditions in Germany. Balfour was obviously not satisfied with the information he was receiving at the Foreign Office. Although the first PID agents to go into Germany submitted a report on 21 December,[22] on 30 December Drummond wrote to General Thwaites, who had replaced Macdonogh as Director of Military Intelligence, about the need for reliable information from Berlin.[23]

During this period the War Office was an even less productive source of information for the political leadership. At the War Office information on Germany received from the British representatives on the Armistice Commission supplemented that provided by the various sections of military intelligence, which continued to operate as they had during the war. Through General Spears, General Wilson also received French intelligence reports on conditions in Germany.[24] In addition, on 11 November the War Cabinet approved the CIGS's request to send a military attaché to Berlin, 'as it was very necessary indeed that we should have somebody on the spot to furnish us with inside information of what was happening in Germany'.[25] Nevertheless, during the rest of 1918 the War Office submitted no formal reports to the Cabinet on conditions in Germany or the German army.

The lack of reliable detailed information about the situation in Germany heightened British leaders' uncertainty about Germany's future, reinforcing their fears of a Bolshevik revolution there and hence encouraging a generous attitude towards the defeated enemy. In his *Evening Standard* interview Milner had warned that Germany's susceptibility to Bolshevism would depend upon its treatment by the Allies. The War Secretary believed 'that in order to save themselves [the] Allies must first of all save Germany from anarchy'.[26] Milner, like most of his colleagues, regarded a stable Germany as essential to the preservation of the European order. Zimmern agreed: 'It is in our interest as much as theirs that they [the Central Empires] should not be carried over the abyss. There will be a moment at the end of the war . . . when we shall have to do a quick change, as on the battlefield, between fighting Germany and picking up her wounded.' Failure to make this transition, he believed, would be 'a source of real danger to Europe'.[27] Smuts, fearful of a total European collapse and the triumph of Bolshevism in its wake, shared these sentiments. On the night before the signing of the Armistice he told Lloyd George, 'It is for us now to be large and generous'[28] to the defeated enemy. From the Armistice until late November, when members of the government became caught up in the anti-Germanism of the election campaign, this attitude prevailed over that of Hughes, who believed that the Armistice terms were not sufficiently harsh.[29]

On 11 November the War Cabinet received word from Admiral Wemyss, who represented Britain at the presentation of the armistice terms to the Germans, that, according to the information available to the German Armistice Mission, 'conditions in Germany are far worse than were thought'.[30] Although Wemyss questioned the German representatives' motives in emphasising the danger of Bolshevism[31] and permanent Foreign Office officials apparently believed that 'Germany is not drifting to Bolshevism',[32] Wemyss's report increased the anxieties of those for whom fear of Bolshevism overrode any suspicions of German intentions. While barely a month before, Lloyd George and Churchill had strongly argued the necessity of crushing Germany, the changed situation led them not only to reconsider their position on the status of the German army but also to adopt a magnanimous attitude towards the recent enemy. In a retrospective account of an Armistice night meeting with Lloyd George, Churchill described his own mood as 'divided between anxiety for the future and desire to help the fallen foe' and recalled that both he and the Prime Minister worried that Germany would succumb to Bolshevism. It was in this atmosphere that, according to Churchill, 'the conversation ran on the great qualities of the German people, on the tremendous fight they had made against three-quarters of the world'.[33] Thus fear of Bolshevism continued to temper British leaders' attitude towards Germany.

They feared not just the direct consequences of a Bolshevik revolution in Germany but, as we have seen, its possible impact in Britain. Esher warned that 'the toppling over of Thrones is very catching. As bad as influenza.'[34] Milner called attention to 'the revolutionary tendency, greater or less, in all countries',[35] and Churchill expressed concern that the coming of peace would leave Britain with 2 million discontented men.[36] The Home Office continued to compile its fortnightly reports on allegedly revolutionary organisations in the United Kingdom, with its first post-Armistice report charging that 'since the tremendous events of a week ago, the Pacifists have been busy tearing off their disguise, and re-appearing in their proper garb as revolutionaries'.[37] Basil Thomson, who as head of the Criminal Investigation Department and the Special Branch at New Scotland Yard was responsible for political intelligence in Britain, recorded in his memoirs that much of his work in the months after the Armistice dealt with 'the Red propaganda from Moscow which had fascinated the Labour extremists in England . . . Certainly at that time there was cause for alarm.'[38] The War Cabinet was so alarmed that on 14 November it decided to launch a counter-propaganda campaign to inform the British public 'what Bolshevism meant in practice'.[39] This, however, was only a supplementary measure. British leaders believed that preventing a Bolshevik revolution in Germany would be one of the best means of averting revolutionary outbreaks at home.

At the same time they hoped to receive economic compensation from Germany, and most hoped that after the return of peace Britain would resume its formerly profitable trade with Germany. The attainment of these objectives would require a stable German society. Haig's conviction that 'it is our interest . . . to have Germany a prosperous, not an impoverished country'[40] reflected the prevalent belief that Germany's economic well-being was vital to Britain's future. While the desire for reparations and indemnity soon led to demands for a retributive peace, initially it, too, focused attention on the advisability of promoting German stability. In this way, economic considerations joined with anti-Bolshevism to produce a charitable attitude towards Germany. Milner's 17 October interview clearly linked the economic and anti-Bolshevik issues: '*As reparation has to be obtained, we do not wish to see Bolshevism and chaos rampant there.*'[41] Churchill's description of his Armistice night conversation with Lloyd George also juxtaposed fear of revolution and concern about economic recovery, stressing the necessity of German recovery to European and hence British recovery. His list of the topics which he and Lloyd George discussed concluded with 'the impossibility of rebuilding Europe except with their [the German people's] aid'.[42]

Thus the British government's momentary expansiveness, epitomised by the War Cabinet's decision on 11 November immediately to consider steps to begin provisioning the enemy,[43] had as its object the preservation of a stable government in Germany. British leaders believed this necessary in order to prevent the triumph of Bolshevism in Germany and its possible spread from there to Britain. In addition, they hoped to ensure that Britain would receive its share of economic compensation from Germany and that

Germany would be available as a future trading partner. In contrast to the *National Review*, much of the Liberal press agreed with this approach to the treatment of Germany. In the *Daily News* Gardiner proclaimed that the Allies 'must act at once and generously [in providing food and supplies to Germany] if they are to prevent a universal drift into Bolshevism and anarchy . . . The restoration of order and prosperity to more than half Europe is, on the lowest and most selfish ground, a necessity for ourselves.'[44] Both the *Star* and the *Westminster Gazette* also regarded a merciful policy towards Germany as the best means of avoiding anarchy and Bolshevism.[45] Thus in the immediate aftermath of victory both the government and a significant segment of the press agreed that adopting a beneficent attitude towards Germany would further Britain's long-term interests.

When Lloyd George recommended to his colleagues that they should provide food to the defeated enemy, he raised another issue: preventing future German aggression. Bolstering the new German government would, he believed, prevent Germany's eventually seeking revenge for its defeat: 'It behoved us now . . . to do nothing which might arouse and harbour a spirit of revenge later.'[46] Yet, except for this almost offhand comment, British leaders in the first weeks after the signature of the Armistice seemed unconcerned about a possible resurgence of German power.

The Cabinet was more interested in returning Britain's armed forces to a peacetime basis than in taking additional steps to disarm Germany. Anxious to begin the work of postwar reconstruction, ministers were particularly concerned about the shortage of coal. Even before the Allies had reached final agreement on armistice terms, Sir Albert Stanley, President of the Board of Trade, had written to Lloyd George requesting the release of miners from the army because of 'the extreme gravity of the coal situation'.[47] Within hours of the signature of the Armistice the War Cabinet agreed to begin implementing plans for partial demobilisation, with miners and the key men needed by industry to be released first.[48] On 12 November the Minister of National Service, Sir Auckland Geddes, ended recruiting, much to the consternation of General Wilson.[49]

Throughout early November the CIGS recorded in his diary his anxieties about the army's future and his inability to get the War Cabinet to consider the question of the postwar army.[50] Apparently forgotten was Lloyd George's earlier determination that Britain 'be

the greatest military power in the world'.[51] On 13 November
Milner, who at the end of October had requested special legislation
to retain men in service at the end of the war,[52] wrote to Lloyd
George: 'I hope it may be possible to get the Cabinet or yourself to
give one clear half hour's attention without delay to the question of
the future of the Army . . . unless some provision is made for
recruiting or keeping men, you run the risk of finding yourself
without any Army at all in six months!'[53] Both Milner and Wilson
favoured the retention of conscription as the only means of providing
sufficient forces to meet Britain's postwar responsibilities.[54] By
mid-November, however, the campaign for the election of a new
Parliament was under way and, as we shall see in the next chapter,
the idea of continuing conscription was extremely unpopular among
the electorate.

Moreover, while the War Office was pressing for a decision on the
postwar army, the public was demanding demobilisation. On 11
November Esher had warned Hankey that 'unless you put
"demobilization" on a sound basis before you become absorbed in
the [Peace] Conference you will have two general elections in lieu of
one'.[55] The *Daily Mail* took the lead in the campaign for speedy
demobilisation. On 29 November a leading article asked, 'Cannot
the machinery of demobilisation be speeded up?'[56] and on 3
December Northcliffe instructed the staff to deal with demobilisation every day.[57] Stanley continued to push for the release of miners
from military service and, according to General Wilson, Lloyd
George, too, was concerned that miners were not being released
quickly enough.[58] On 10 December Lloyd George wrote to Balfour
that the problems connected with demobilisation 'might easily
become menacing if not attended to'.[59] In these circumstances the
Prime Minister was reluctant to make a decision on the army until
after the election.[60] When two days before the election the Imperial
War Cabinet considered a memorandum by General Wilson on
Britain's postwar military commitments,[61] Lloyd George agreed to
the War Office's recommendations for maintaining forces in Europe,
the Middle East and Russia only on condition that their maintenance
should not be permanent. The Imperial Cabinet then approved the
gradual demobilisation of the army down to a level which, at the
completion of demobilisation, would leave those British forces
charged with responsibilities other than home and empire defence at
roughly one-third their current strength.[62]

While General Wilson anticipated many minor wars in the next year,[63] most of those in responsible positions did not believe that there would be another war between major powers for the foreseeable future. When Milner had urged on Lloyd George the necessity of reaching a decision on the postwar army, he had referred not to the need for defence against a potential aggressor but to 'the disturbed state of Europe and the revolutionary tendency, greater or less, in all countries'.[64] Although they feared revolution, most British leaders did not believe that this threat alone warranted Britain's continuing after the signature of peace the level of military preparedness it had attained during the war. After the German request for an armistice Kerr had written that once hostilities ceased, 'nobody will dream of starting a new war if they can possibly help it for at least a generation'.[65] Both the Chief of the Air Staff and the Air Minister concurred in this assessment. Like Milner and General Wilson, General Sykes foresaw 'a period of deep-seated disturbance throughout the world'. However, he thought it 'improbable that for some years there will be a great war between first-class powers'.[66] Lord Weir was even more optimistic. On 12 December he informed the War Cabinet 'that the military situation foreshadows a probability of a real and enduring peace, not merely a suspended state of war'.[67] Thus, well before the adoption of the ten-year rule, British leaders were being advised that there was no prospect of a major war for many years to come. To those outside the War Office, it therefore seemed reasonable for Britain, a victorious naval power beset by serious domestic problems, drastically to reduce its military forces.

British leaders' assumptions about the origins of the war and the consequences of Germany's defeat help explain their acceptance of the premise that there would be no early war between major powers. They believed that Germany had been the chief aggressor in 1914 and in the aftermath of its defeat did not expect another major power to pursue similar policies. Moreover, in the immediate aftermath of victory, they believed that Germany's defeat and the collapse of the German Empire, followed by the imposition of severe Armistice terms, meant an end to Germany's aggressive policies as well. Thus they no longer regarded the German army as a threat to European stability. Rather, as we have seen, they hoped that it might be used to promote Germany's internal stability and to act as a bulwark against the westward spread of Bolshevism.

The reports which British ministers received assured them that the German army was no longer capable of offensive action. During the pre-Armistice discussions Foch had told the Allied leaders that it would be impossible for Germany to rearm during the peace negotiations, and in mid-November he informed a British general that in their retirement from many sectors the German troops were 'leaving *all* their guns behind'.[68] A 14 November analysis by Amery, the member of the Cabinet Office responsible for editing regular summaries of events in Western Europe, concluded that the German army, though still a factor internally, was no longer 'a force to be reckoned with in external, affairs',[69] and in a memorandum approved by Crowe and Hardinge of the regular Foreign Office staff Headlam-Morley asserted that the German army 'need no longer be taken into consideration as a fighting force'.[70] In December, after meeting with the German delegates to renew the Armistice, Wemyss reported to Lloyd George that the German army was 'simply melting away'.[71] Thus, from a variety of sources British leaders received assurances that the German army had ceased to be a danger.

Although in response to Foch's request the forces which the Imperial War Cabinet agreed to retain after the signing of peace included provision for reserves on the Western front and a possible army of occupation in Germany, in considering whether to provide these forces the members of the Imperial Cabinet expressed no concern about possible future danger from Germany. Their private discussion on 12 December contrasted sharply with the public position taken by the Coalition late in the election campaign. In a major speech just the day before, Lloyd George – for reasons which, as the next chapter will examine, had nothing to do with fear of a resurgence of German power – had attacked the German army as a threat to world peace.[72] His position within the Cabinet, however, provides a significant contrast to his platform performance. In discussion with his colleagues he questioned the need for reserves on the Western front, referring to German claims that their surrender of machine guns left them without sufficient weapons for dealing with internal disorders.[73] Despite his platform rhetoric, Lloyd George, like other British leaders, seemed convinced that the German army posed no immediate danger. In addition, most of these officials hoped, as we have seen, that Germany's internal transformation would mean the permanent abandonment of policies which might lead to war. Consequently, despite the Coalition's campaign position, between the Armistice and the general election members of the British government privately expressed no interest in further disarming Germany.

7
The Election Campaign

The heat of the election campaign, which began in mid-November, soon led Coalition leaders to abandon – at least publicly – their attitude of restraint towards Germany. Faced with a fiercely anti-German electorate, members of the government, along with other Coalition candidates, adopted a rhetoric which matched that of the most extreme Germanophobes. By 26 November Churchill was telling his constituents, 'Practically the whole German nation was guilty of the crime of aggressive war conducted by brutal and bestial means . . . They were all in it, and they must all suffer for it.'[1] Churchill's speech marked a significant departure from both the repeatedly declared wartime position that there was a distinction between the German people and their Prussian militarist government and his own Armistice night attitude. Austen Chamberlain's address at Birmingham two days later also contrasted sharply with government officials' statements during the war and with their conciliatory early post-Armistice attitude: 'I say until we are satisfied – and we cannot be satisfied until we have proved it – that in the German people there is a changed heart and changed mind, no single scapegoat [the kaiser] can bear their sins. They have made their bed and they must lie upon it.'[2] Like Churchill's remarks, Chamberlain's speech indicated an abandonment of the distinction between the German people and their former rulers and of the position that vengeance was not in British interests. Regardless of their private beliefs, most Coalition candidates followed Churchill's and Chamberlain's lead and publicly adopted an anti-German stance. No longer proclaiming the collapse of Prussian militarism, in response to the demands of the voters in their constituencies they instead promised revenge on the German people.

Yet, despite the virulent anti-Germanism which characterised the campaign, German disarmament was not among the electorate's anti-German demands. A week before the election *The Times* reported that 'every question, foreign and domestic, in which the public is taking interest is being brought out into the light'.[3] Unilateral German disarmament was not among these. Rather, demands for a retributive peace and candidates' responses to these pressures concentrated on reparations and indemnity, the punishment of those Germans considered responsible for the war, especially the kaiser, and the expulsion of German aliens from Britain.[4]

Only the most vehement anti-Germans called for disarming Germany beyond the terms of the Armistice without the concomitant disarmament of other nations, and even they did not turn this demand into a significant campaign issue. In its 'Fundamental Points of Policy', issued shortly before the Armistice, the Germanophobe right-wing National Party had listed German disarmament as one of its primary demands for the peace terms.[5] However, in later enunciations of the party's peace policy neither General Henry Page Croft, leader of the party, nor Sir Richard Cooper, one of its founders, mentioned disarmament.[6] While the ultra-Conservative *Morning Post* criticised the Armistice for not requiring demobilisation of the German army, its solution to the problem of maintaining Allied dominance was continued military preparedness, not further German disarmament.[7] Although the *Morning Post* advocated the annihilation of German naval power, it did not include a call for German military disarmament in any of the leading articles outlining its desired peace terms.[8] When renewal of the Armistice with Germany was under discussion, the *Daily Mail*, too, criticised the omission of demobilisation from the original Armistice conditions and urged that demobilisation be a condition for extending the Armistice. Anxious to speed British demobilisation, the *Daily Mail* based its support for demobilisation of the German army primarily on the assumption that German demobilisation would make possible demobilisation of the Allied armies and thus bring social and economic benefits to the Allies.[9] Despite the shrillness of its anti-German campaign, the *Daily Mail*, like the *Morning Post*, did not during the election campaign demand the inclusion of German disarmament in the peace treaty.[10] In the *National Review* Maxse did advocate further disarming Germany, criticising the Armistice not only for not including demobilisation but also for omitting complete disarmament or even the surrender of small arms.[11] However, even Maxse did not turn his disarmament demand into an election issue. Instead, asserting that the only means of preventing

Germany's waging war for the foreseeable future and thereby guaranteeing British security would be to impose a peace which 'crippled [Germany] financially as well as in arms', he used the pages of the *National Review* to argue that the 'acid test' for candidates was their position on indemnity.[12]

Maxse's analysis of the interrelationship between the economic terms of peace and Germany's potential for reasserting its military power reflected the right's emphasis on the correlation between economic strength and national power. His line of reasoning was similar to one of the arguments advanced by the Imperial War Cabinet committee charged at the end of November with determining Germany's capacity to pay the Allies' war costs. In its reports this committee, chaired by the anti-German Hughes, contended that payment of a large indemnity would deprive Germany of the resources necessary for financing aggressive war.[13] This belief that the imposition on Germany of severely punitive economic terms would provide military as well as economic security helps account for the extreme Germanophobes' lack of interest in German disarmament as an election issue. For them the crucial concern was making Germany pay the cost of the war. This, they believed, would assure Germany's military as well as its economic paralysis.

Moreover, in the obverse of the Hughes Committee's argument, Crewe House's peace proposals, which had appeared in the Northcliffe press bearing the proprietor's by-line, had asserted that 'to insist on the disarmament of another country may be to present that country with a huge annual income that can be used in commercial rivalry'.[14] The most intensely anti-German publicists and politicians were, like Maxse and Hughes, also ardent protectionists. Such an argument was likely to have reinforced their preoccupation with the economic rather than the military terms of peace.

While not demanded by the electorate, Germany's disarmament became a declared campaign goal of the Coalition as a result of two other issues raised during the campaign. The first, the reduction of armaments, was an endorsed objective of Labour, independent Liberals and the Coalition. The second, the abolition of conscription, was the only domestic concern to capture the electorate's interest. The government's approach to these two questions led to its adoption of German disarmament as one of its avowed peace conference aims. In this way the election campaign played a major role in transforming German disarmament into a goal of British policy.

The belief that war had now become unthinkable joined with philosophical opposition to armaments and economic realities to create a climate in which, with the exception of a minority on the right, both public and politicians agreed that Britain should reduce its armaments expenditures. This outlook, which dominated British foreign and defence policy in the late 1920s and 1930s, began to take hold in the immediate post-Armistice period. Its initial consequences, however, were quite different from its long-term results. The desire to reduce spending on arms led in late 1918 and early 1919 to a demand for German disarmament as a prerequisite for a general limitation of armaments which would, in turn, make possible a substantial reduction in Britain's expenditures on armaments.

Though reduction of armaments was not a central campaign issue, concern with limiting armaments was evident in party platforms, campaign speeches and editorials and articles in leading journals. Publications as disparate in their politics as the Conservative *Observer* and the Radical *Nation* supported an end to competitive armaments.[15] Only extreme nationalists demanded a continued high level of military expenditure, basing their demand on Britain's lack of military preparedness in 1914.[16] The Coalition, the Labour Party and Asquith Liberals all endorsed a reduction of Britain's armaments expenditures and also envisioned some form of general limitation of armaments as part of the forthcoming settlement.

A deep revulsion against war characterised postwar Britain. In its first post-Armistice issue the *Nation* accurately described the impact of the war on popular opinion: 'Never till now have they [the mass of men] seen it [war] panoplied in its complete armor of destruction.'[17] With the fighting finally over, the prevalent feeling was that such a bloodletting must never happen again. Even before the Armistice A. G. Gardiner had proclaimed that 'the abolition of the institution of war is the capital necessity'.[18] In its memorandum on war aims, Labour had declared the prevention of war to be its overriding objective: 'Of all the war aims, none is so important as that there shall be henceforth on earth no more war.'[19]

Such sentiments were not the monopoly of the left. As Kerr told Lloyd George, 'What they [the British people] are concerned about is to know that you personally are determined to do all you possible [*sic*] can . . . to make another war such as the last impossible'.[20] Recognising the pervasiveness of antiwar sentiment, especially among the newly enfranchised women voters, a sample Unionist election handbill addressed to women took up Labour's cry, proclaiming, 'There must be no more war.'[21] The Coalition's first election manifesto defined the government's 'first task' to be 'to conclude a just and lasting peace and so to establish the foundations of a new Europe, that occasion for further wars may be for ever averted',[22] and Bonar Law, who had lost two sons in the war, declared that it would be Britain's 'chief aim' at the peace conference 'to try . . . to make it as certain as we can that a calamity like this will never happen in the world again'.[23]

While the punishment of Germany, the territorial rearrangement of Europe, continued military preparedness and the establishment of a league of nations were among the different solutions offered for achieving 'a just and lasting peace', to many, general disarmament offered the best hope for attaining this objective. On the left, the No Conscription Fellowship argued that 'complete Disarmament' was 'the only practical remedy for war'.[24] The Labour Party and the Radical *Nation* also epitomised this outlook. As we have seen, the wartime movement for a general limitation of armaments had popularised the prewar Radical concept that armaments competition was one of the causes of war. Beginning with its first pamphlet, the UDC, in particular, had expounded this view: 'The policy of gigantic armaments . . . leads, and can only lead, to an intolerable situation from which war comes to be regarded by diplomacy as the only escape.'[25] Having adopted the UDC's analysis in its 1917 war aims statement, the Labour Party brought this viewpoint into the campaign. On 30 November a Labour meeting voiced unanimous support for the 'total disarmament' of all nations.[26] The *Nation* took the UDC's analysis a step further: 'For let it be clearly and uncompromisingly said, the cause of war is armaments.'[27] Accordingly, as it had throughout the war, the *Nation* opposed unilaterally disarming Germany, which it believed the Armistice had done, and insisted that universal disarmament must now follow: 'Disarmament for one must mean disarmament for all.' It argued that the Armistice had left Germany powerless to resume fighting and that, as a result, Britain had entered a new era in which armaments were no longer necessary: 'The last great British war has been fought and won . . . If therefore we unarm, it is because the long day's work is done.'[28]

Although only the left advocated immediate total – and, if necessary, unilateral – disarmament, opposition to armaments was, as we have seen, also part of Liberal ideology. Prewar Liberalism had opposed both the use of force and the expenditure of funds on armaments rather than social reform. Before the war Lloyd George had been the leading proponent of this viewpoint. While most Liberal politicians had abandoned their traditional position in wholehearted support of the Allied war effort, at the end of the war they reasserted the principle of opposition to armaments. In November 1918 when H. A. L. Fisher, deputed to draft the Coalition's election manifesto, asked Montagu, since July 1917 a member of the Lloyd George government, for his views on policy, the latter's only recommendation regarding postwar foreign and defence policy was that 'something ought to be said about the reduction of armaments and the League of Nations'.[29] The 10 November draft prepared by Fisher, himself an early advocate of arms limitation, emphasised both concepts.[30] In addition to the Coalition Liberals, Asquith's supporters also advocated the limitation of armaments. Early in the campaign, for example, Herbert Samuel, a leading Asquithian, expressed his support for general disarmament, which he expected to result from creation of a league of nations.[31]

Lloyd George acknowledged the importance of this aspect of Liberal political philosophy when he addressed a group of over 200 Liberals whom he had invited to a meeting at Downing Street on 12 November in the hopes of winning their continued support for the Coalition. There, in what those attending described as 'a magnificent Liberal speech',[32] he announced his intention to hold an election and readily won their endorsement.

The programme on which Lloyd George and Bonar Law as leader of the Conservatives had agreed on 2 November to wage the Coalition's campaign made no reference to the peace treaty, to the Wilsonian peace programme on which the Allies were then negotiating with Colonel House, or to any aspect of postwar foreign and defence policy.[33] When Lloyd George met with a small group of Coalition Liberals on 6 November to discuss his postwar policy, there was no discussion of these subjects.[34] However, in the summer of 1918 when the Prime Minister had first begun making preparations for an election, Coalition Liberal chief whip Frederick Guest had advised him that in order to secure Liberal support for the continuation of the Coalition 'the only safe programme is a guiding principle which ensures improved conditions, both for the world and for this country as a result of the war' and 'that adoption and explanation of the Wilsonian policy of a League of Free Nations . . . will attract to the Government the vast majority of the electors'.[35] Lloyd George obviously had Guest's advice in mind when he addressed the 12 November meeting. Moreover, between the 6 November discussion and this meeting he had received Fisher's manifesto endorsing the same concepts which Guest had earlier recommended.

Telling his Liberal audience that the two great questions facing the country were the peace terms and reconstruction, the Prime Minister proclaimed that it was 'the business of the Liberal Party primarily to insist' that the postwar world should see 'the reign of peace'. Going well beyond his Trades Union Congress address, he expressed his commitment to the creation of a viable league of nations and wholeheartedly endorsed a general reduction in armaments. Indeed, his support of the inclusion of general disarmament in the peace settlement echoed the Radical analysis of armaments as a cause of war:

> We must have a guaranteed reduction of armaments. You cannot allow great countries to have armies of three or four millions, and some of the best brains of these communities devoting their minds to thinking out how those great armies can be hurled against other countries, and what the consequences will be, without ultimately producing the very thing which in their own brain they have been working out through the years. It is an inevitable consequence of it . . . We must not permit that risk to take place again (Hear, Hear).

He went on to promise that 'the moment you come from the Peace Congress, armies will be purely police in arms'.[36] Thus Lloyd George expressed his support for two of the principles embodied in the Fourteen Points, implying that the Wilsonian peace programme was also that of the Coalition.

While the analysis of armaments competition as a cause of war coincided with his prewar beliefs and as early as 1917 he had expressed interest in general disarmament as a peace aim, part of his intention in declaring general disarmament to be 'the first essential'[37] was, as we shall see later in this chapter, to appease the Coalition Liberal opponents of conscription who were pressing him for a commitment to the abolition of conscription in Britain. By declaring that inclusion of general disarmament in the peace arrangements must precede the end of conscription in Britain, for which he also expressed his support, he correctly calculated that he would win their support as well as that of those Coalition Liberals for whom his announced commitment to the League of Nations, general disarmament and postwar reconstruction was sufficient to ensure their willingness to continue the Coalition.

A general limitation of armaments would, of course, include a reduction of Britain's armaments. The Coalition election manifesto published on 22 November indeed suggested, as the Imperial War Cabinet decision of 12 December confirmed, a willingness to begin reducing Britain's armaments and armed forces even before the establishment of a viable league: 'The brilliant and conclusive triumph of the Allied Armies will, we hope, render it possible to reduce the burden of our armaments and to release, by successive and progressive stages, the Labour and Capital of the Empire for the arts of peace.' Another section of the manifesto spoke of the government's intention to implement 'the inevitable reductions in our military and naval establishments'. While declaring that the eventual size of Britain's armed forces would be contingent upon empire and League of Nations needs, the manifesto clearly stated the Coalition's intention to begin reductions 'meanwhile'[38] before these requirements were known.

Supporting such a reduction was a consistent position for the Liberal minority within the Coalition partnership to take. A reduction in armaments in order to free funds for domestic concerns echoed Lloyd George's prewar sentiments and reflected his interest in postwar reconstruction. Both Fisher, who had prepared the manifesto, and Addison, Minister of Reconstruction since July 1917, had, like Lloyd George, come from the Radical wing of the Liberal Party and were committed to social reform. On a more pragmatic level, they would need funding for the long postponed programmes of their respective departments. Fisher had made the availability of funds for his department a condition of his acceptance of the position of President of the Board of Education.[39] Addison's diaries for October and November 1918 reveal his concern with plans for postwar reconstruction.[40] Discussing the relationship between 'the creation of conditions affording, or even seeming to afford, security from war' and reconstruction, he took the position in an October

1918 memorandum that 'diminishing expenditure on armaments would by so much make possible expenditure of a more fruitful kind.'[41]

To suggest, even tentatively, the diversion of national resources from defence to social needs was, however, an important departure from the traditional position of the dominant Conservative Party. In contrast to the Liberals, the prewar Conservatives had supported increased armaments. A guide for Unionist speakers issued in 1914 asserted that the claims of national defence were 'paramount': 'The Unionist Party . . . has always treated the needs of the Army and Navy as of primary importance.' While the social imperialist wing of the Conservative Party was also committed to social reform, it believed in a strong defence and had never advocated arms reduction as a means of financing social reform. The 1914 campaign guide specifically and emphatically rejected the notion that 'to maintain adequate armaments necessitates the sacrifice of Social Reform and that we have to choose between the two'.[42] Understandably, then, despite the language of the Coalition manifesto many Conservative candidates, in contrast to the party's leadership, agreed with Eric Geddes's outlook on the postwar world: 'There were those who thought and hoped that after this war the world might become so Utopian that wars could not occur, and armaments would become unnecessary . . . He was not one of those who believed in that Utopian state.'[43] Significantly, however, Conservative leader Bonar Law had not taken much interest in the problems of defence before the war or in naval and military affairs during it.

The key to the Conservative Party's postwar position on armaments expenditures lay in the election manifesto's words 'to release . . . the Labour and Capital of the Empire for the arts of peace' and in the manifesto's declaration that the government intended to carry through its planned reductions in Britain's armed forces 'to the best advantage of Industry and Trade' and to 'endeavour to reduce the war debt in such a manner as may inflict the least injury to Industry and credit'.[44] Conservatives as well as Liberals had practical reasons for seeking to reduce expenditures on armaments. Leading members of both parties were concerned about the postwar economic situation. The tremendous cost of the war had transformed Britain from a creditor to a debtor nation. In December 1918 the war debt was over £600 million, not taking into account continuing expenses such as soldiers' pay and pensions. The war adversely affected Britain's world trade position. British gold reserves fell substantially, the merchant marine suffered great losses, and in 1918 Britain had an unfavourable international balance of payments. Inflation was also a problem, the pound by 1919 buying only one-third what it had purchased in 1914. The diversion of labour and capital to the work of war had resulted in an acute housing shortage, a scarcity of many essentials, such as clothing and furniture, and problems in the railway and coal industries. As businessmen, leading Conservatives were perhaps more uneasy about this situation than their Liberal counterparts.

While the Liberal Party had been the traditional home for industrialists and Lloyd George had recruited many Liberal businessmen to his administration, these men, with a few exceptions, did not occupy key decision-making positions in either the government or the party hierarchy. In contrast, Conservative businessmen held central positions in both their party and the Coalition. Since the late nineteenth century business, rather than landed, interests had increasingly dominated the Conservative Party. Bonar Law, a Glasgow iron merchant who had entered the House of Commons in 1900 and had replaced Balfour as leader of the party in 1911, symbolised this transformation. The war had accelerated the entry of businessmen into important positions in the Conservative Party. In 1916, for example, Sir George Younger, owner of a Scottish brewing firm, became Chairman of the Party Organisation, replacing Arthur Steel-Maitland, a product of Rugby and Balliol.

The business orientation of these influential Conservatives made them especially interested in reducing the war debt and re-establishing Britain's trading and financial position. Responsible for Britain's finances as Chancellor of the Exchequer, Bonar Law in particular was concerned about Britain's economic problems. In addition, Conservative philosophy stressed 'faith in a balanced budget, a stable currency, and a reduction of the public debt'.[45] These concerns, together with the Coalition's reluctance either to abandon its programme of reconstruction or to increase taxes and Bonar Law's own doubts about the likelihood or the wisdom of obtaining a large indemnity from Germany, explain the willingness of the Conservatives to consider reducing expenditures on armaments.

Financing the war debt by reducing public spending was not feasible in the post-Armistice political atmosphere. As Addison later recalled, the war had produced 'a definite public demand' for 'a progressive domestic policy'.[46] Fear of revolution was a powerful motivating force for satisfying this demand. Explaining his rationale for continuing the Coalition, Bonar Law wrote to Balfour that the traditional Conservative Party had no future and the alternative to a Coalition government led by Lloyd George would be a Lib–Lab combination which, when faced with a Conservative opposition, would 'be driven to act in a much more extreme way' on the domestic problems facing the country. Bonar Law believed that if the Coalition continued, 'there would at least be a chance that the reforms which undoubtedly will be necessary should be made in a way as little revolutionary as possible'.[47] Lloyd George referred to this fear of revolution in his address to the 16 November meeting opening the Coalition's campaign. In his speech to the same audience Bonar Law, while in one breath disclaiming fear of 'the revolutionary spirit', in the next expressed the essence of the Conservative approach to reform – reform from above in order to prevent revolution from below: 'The danger of a revolution will come only if the social and economic conditions become intolerable. It is our business to do what we can to prevent that.'[48] Hence even Conservatives who did not belong to the social imperial wing of the party joined with Coalition Liberals in endorsing a programme of domestic reconstruction.

Paying for the war had necessitated the postponement of long-promised social reforms, while the concentration of resources on the war effort had exacerbated pre-existing problems. Promises of postwar reconstruction dated from early in the war, and in its election programme the Coalition pledged itself to domestic reforms. Its first election manifesto outlined a programme of social betterment, while the day after the manifesto's publication Lloyd George emphasised the necessity of reconstruction, telling a campaign audience that Britain must become 'a fit country for heroes to live in'.[49] Even when later in the campaign anti-German peace issues overtook the government's initial emphasis on domestic concerns, the Coalition remained committed to reconstruction. Implementing social reforms would mean an increase, rather than a reduction, in public spending. Therefore the government would have to seek other means of financing the war debt.

The Coalition rejected another alternative, a further increase in taxation. The Labour Party proposed both a higher income tax and a capital levy to eliminate the war debt.[50] However, as Chancellor of the Exchequer, Lloyd George had earlier maintained that even a 75 per cent tax on the income of the rich would not pay for the war,[51] and in 1917 when Bonar Law had indicated that he might favour a capital levy after the war, the Conservative Party had vehemently opposed his position.[52] Thus these two means of increasing revenues were ruled out.

As we have seen, an indemnity from Germany was the popular solution among the electorate to the problem of paying for the cost of the war, and agitation by the proponents of indemnity made it one of the chief issues of the campaign. Under the exigencies of the campaign many Coalition candidates adopted the demand for a German indemnity as the central part of their platforms, and the official election manifestos issued by the Coalition in December stressed the importance of making Germany pay. Yet, informed opinion within the government doubted Germany's ability to do this. Bonar Law opposed an indemnity, maintaining that reparation alone would cost far more than Germany could pay. Despite Lloyd George's public declarations late in the campaign in support of indemnity the Prime Minister, too, remained sceptical of Germany's ability to pay the whole cost of the war. Even Sir Eric Geddes, famous for his call for getting from Germany 'everything you can squeeze out of a lemon and a bit more',[53] doubted whether Germany could make major payments without harming British trade and employment.[54] Thus, relying on an indemnity from Germany did not seem to be a realistic means of solving Britain's economic problems.

Reducing armaments offered another alternative for cutting expenditures and thereby financing the war debt. In his repeated attempts to win British support for his scheme for a temporary postwar prohibition of the manufacture of munitions, one of the arguments which Colonel House had used was that 'the money it would save to each nation every year would be sufficient to pay the interest on the great war debts that they are now piling up'.[55] In 1915 Francis W. Hirst, a Radical, then editor of the *Economist*, had advocated arms limitation as the preferred method of eliminating the war debt itself.[56] During the campaign the *Daily News* framed the economic aspect of the arms reduction issue starkly as a choice between armaments and bankruptcy, on the one hand, and disarmament and social reform on the other.[57]

While the government certainly did not contemplate unilateral

British disarmament, its first election manifesto articulated a willingness to reduce British armaments as a means of dealing with Britain's postwar fiscal problems. An early and rather vague campaign document, the manifesto did not commit the Coalition, but it did not stand alone. As we have seen, behind-the-scenes decisions also pointed in the direction of an early reduction in the size of Britain's armed forces, and on 9 December demobilisation began. Moreover, on 23 November Bonar Law in his capacity as Chancellor of the Exchequer informed Geddes, the First Lord, of the necessity of reducing naval expenditure.[58]

In addition, public expectations, kindled not only by campaign pledges but also by Smuts's 1917 speeches, Lloyd George's Trades Union Congress address and the Wilsonian peace progamme, acted as a continuing pressure on the government to demonstrate its commitment to peace by reducing armaments and turning its attention to domestic problems. Officials' reactions to this pressure and to the even more insistent pressure for the abolition of conscription were, as we shall see, important factors in the adoption of German disarmament as a specific goal of British policy.

Introduced as a war measure in 1916 despite considerable opposition, conscription was alien to Britain's liberal tradition. Popular antipathy to a large standing army in peacetime dated to the seventeenth century. As *The Times* pointed out in 1919, 'Continental Powers have never quite understood what a clean break we made with our traditions when we raised armies of millions by compulsion'.[59] In 1918 there was considerable apprehension that the Coalition government intended to continue compulsory service after the war. During the election campaign opponents of conscription played upon this fear, orchestrating a public outcry against the retention of compulsion and exerting pressure on the Coalition to address itself to the conscription issue.

As a prime mover in securing the adoption of conscription, Lloyd George had violated Liberal principles and alienated orthodox Liberals. In 1918, before the Armistice, he privately showed no inclination to abolish conscription after the war. In discussions with Haig during the final pre-Armistice negotiations in France, the Prime Minister envisaged the retention of at least some of the conscript forces then serving.[60] When on 24 September he offered Asquith the Lord Chancellorship and eight places for his supporters in the postwar government if the Liberal leader would pledge his electoral support, one of the conditions of the arrangement was that Asquith should agree to the extension of conscription to Ireland.[61] At the 6 November meeting with his Liberal supporters, the Prime Minister said nothing about conscription.[62]

Some prominent Coalition Liberals, however, soon made clear their opposition to the continuation of compulsory service and their conviction that a commitment to the abolition of conscription should be part of the Coalition's platform. On 8 November Guest met with a small group of Liberal newspaper proprietors to discuss co-ordination of their newspapers' handling of the campaign. At this meeting Lord Rothermere, owner of the *Daily Mirror*, insisted that the abolition of conscription must be part of the Coalition's programme.[63] Fisher, too, believed that the Coalition should promise to end compulsory service and just before Lloyd George addressed the Downing Street meeting spoke with the Prime Minister about the issue.[64]

Fisher's concern apparently had an impact on Lloyd George. While the Prime Minister's notes for his speech did not mention conscription,[65] he did briefly refer to the issue in his remarks. Asserting that a guaranteed reduction of armaments was 'the one guarantee that you can get rid of conscription here', he explained that with a general reduction in armaments to the level at which all armies would perform only police functions there would be no need for conscription.[66] Thus Lloyd George made the abolition of conscription in Britain contingent upon the implementation of a general limitation of armaments. With this typically vague and hedging pronouncement he professed his support for the traditional Liberal position on both conscription and arms limitation. As Amery commented afterwards, he 'dodged' the conscription issue 'very cleverly'.[67] Although he declared that, as soon as the peace conference was over, the only function of armies would be to maintain civil order and conscription would therefore be un-necessary, he made no specific commitment to its abolition and offered no timetable for ending compulsory service.

Lloyd George had gauged his audience correctly. Most Coalition Liberals had not been strongly anti-conscriptionist. Several of those present belonged, like Lloyd George, to the conscriptionist wing of the party.[68] Others attending had, like most Liberals, eventually consented to conscription as a wartime necessity despite their philosophical opposition. Even Fisher was satisfied with Lloyd George's statement. Although he had refused to commit himself in advance to proposing the resolution of support for the Prime Minister's intention to fight the election in partnership with the Conservatives, after hearing Lloyd George's speech he moved the resolution of endorsement and later pronounced the address 'a thoroughly satisfactory speech from the Liberal p[oin]t of view'.[69]

Lloyd George's brief reference to the elimination of conscription at some undefined future time did not, however, satisfy most anti-conscriptionists. Furthermore, neither the Coalition's election programme contained in Lloyd George's letter to Bonar Law nor its first manifesto, though prepared by Fisher, mentioned conscription. Opponents of conscription therefore launched an attack on the Coalition for its failure to promise an immediate end to compulsory service.

The No Conscription Fellowship, in particular, directed its energies towards making the abolition of conscription a campaign issue. The 14 November issue of its organ the *Tribunal* promoted a letter-writing campaign aimed at having those MPs who had voted against the introduction of conscription make its abolition a prominent part of their election addresses. The same edition featured an editorial urging readers also to enlist other voters to write to candidates, to ask questions at campaign appearances and to organise deputations to visit candidates to discuss the conscription issue.[70] Two weeks later the fellowship issued a series of questions on conscription and disarmament for voters to ask candidates in their constituencies.[71]

Churchill was an early target for the anti-conscriptionists' tactics. On 26 November after a speech in which he, like other Coalition candidates, had not mentioned conscription, a questioner asked him, 'Will there be conscription after the war?' In his reply Churchill set forth what eventually became the Coalition's official position on conscription – that at the peace conference the Coalition intended to demand the universal abolition of conscription but that the British government's policy on postwar conscription would depend upon what other countries did: 'No one will try harder than the British Government to prevent conscription being continued after the war. We shall go to the Peace Conference to demand that all nations shall give it up, but what we do must depend on what other nations do.'[72] Churchill's statement angered rather than mollified opponents of conscription, who wanted a definite commitment to its abolition. Despite Coalition attempts to defuse the conscription issue, the anti-conscriptionists did not let up. Until the last day of the campaign, hecklers continued to interrupt Coalition speakers with taunts and questions about conscription.

Asquith Liberals also joined the attack. The first sally from this quarter came from McKenna, an avowed enemy of Lloyd George. In a speech on 25 November he denounced the Coalition's election programme for its failure to mention conscription.[73] Runciman soon joined him in criticising the Coalition for failing to state clearly its position on the retention of conscription.[74] Other Asquith Liberals also took up the issue. Ellis Davies, whom Lloyd George described as his 'most bitter critic',[75] repeatedly accused the Coalition of planning to continue conscription.[76] Sir John Simon, who had resigned from Asquith's Cabinet at the end of 1915 over the conscription issue, was another vocal critic of the government's policy. Simon vehemently opposed the position adopted by the Coalition later in the campaign that ending conscription in Britain depended upon its abolition elsewhere: 'Conscription has got to go. It has got to go now. It has got to go for ever. It has got to go, whatever other countries do.'[77] Although Asquith had not referred to the conscription issue when he announced his election programme,[78] as the question attracted more attention in the campaign, he, too, called for an end to conscription: 'With the return of the troops . . . naturally must come to an end compulsory military service. Conscription was carried on the distinct understanding that it was for the duration of the war, and that understanding had got to be observed.'[79]

The Labour Party played an important role in making conscription an election issue. While some Labourites chose to remain with the Coalition, the Labour Party withdrew its support from the government and for the first time contested an election on its own as a truly national political party. On 27 November the Labour Party issued its election manifesto, which included a call for 'the complete abolition of conscription'.[80] The Parliamentary Committee of the Trades Union Congress challenged the Coalition with the statement that 'unless conscription is abandoned, there can be no sincerity in the promise regarding the League of Nations, and whole or partial disarmament',[81] and the Independent Labour Party took up the No Conscription Fellowship's campaign, polling candidates on their views on conscription.[82]

While the Labour Party hoped to see 'such concerted action as may be possible for the universal abolition of compulsory military service in all countries',[83] it wanted Britain to abolish conscription regardless of what other countries did. Labour believed that the abolition of conscription, rather than following from the creation of a league of nations, must be one of the bases of such a league.[84] The left maintained that the terms of peace being advocated by Coalition candidates, particularly the demands for a large indemnity, would require an army of occupation in Germany and would therefore mean the continuation of conscription. The publication of the Labour manifesto and the emphasis on the conscription issue by Labour candidates, speakers and journals intensified the anti-conscriptionist pressures on the Coalition. And, as we shall see below, J. H. Thomas's contention that he had proof that the government intended to retain compulsory service led directly to Lloyd George's major campaign statement on conscription.

As the campaign progressed, reports from Coalition Liberal candidates revealed the increasing importance of the conscription issue and thus the effectiveness of the anti-conscriptionist agitation. From Gloucestershire came word of 'a dread of conscription', while in the last reports from one section of Yorkshire the 'abolition of compulsory military service everywhere' headed the list of issues in which the voters were showing the most interest.[85] Two days before the election Mond wrote to Lloyd George that Labour's assertion that the Coalition intended to continue conscription had given him 'considerable trouble' in his Welsh constituency.[86] Looking back on the campaign, Montagu observed that the accusations of the *Daily News*, which rivalled the *Tribunal* in the intensity of its campaign against conscription,[87] had been 'the most potent weapon' against him.[88] A post-election survey of voter attitudes confirmed the reports of individual candidates, noting that 'the possibility of the survival of Conscription aroused the deepest hostility' among the Liberal electorate.[89] In its report on election issues, *Gleanings and Memoranda*, the publication of the National Unionist Association, also gave high priority to conscription.[90]

By the last week of the campaign it was clear that the protests against conscription were having an impact on voter sentiment and in turn upon the Coalition. On 9 December *The Times* reported, 'Some unrest has been produced among Carnarvonshire electors by Mr. Davies's repeated statements that conscription is to be continued'. To counter the effects of the anti-conscription campaign in the Prime Minister's own district, posters proclaiming 'Vote for the Prime Minister and No Conscription' appeared in Lloyd George's neighbouring constituency of Carnarvon Borough.[91] The *Manchester Guardian*'s political correspondent wrote on 12 December that, according to reports from London, 'the conscription issue is becoming the most important in the election', and the weekly *Nation* entitled its election issue 'Conscription or Peace?'[92]

The Cabinet, as we have seen, having yet made no decision about the future of the British army, Lloyd George attempted to turn the electorate's attention from the issue of conscription in Britain to that of the existence of large conscript armies on the Continent, particularly in Germany. Kerr had been urging him to deal with the conscription issue by pledging that if the Coalition were returned to power, working for 'the universal abolition of conscript armies in time of peace' would be for its representatives at the peace conference an objective second only to securing the trial and punishment of those responsible for the war.[93] He had stressed the importance of pointing out that 'to be effective . . . the policy must be universal throughout the world'.[94] This was the position adopted when, in response to the questions and accusations about the Coalition's position, Lloyd George's headquarters issued a statement 'that it is the definite intention of the Coalition Government at the Peace Conference to propose the abolition of compulsory military service throughout Europe'.[95]

Elaborating on this statement in a speech at the Queen's Hall on 9 December, the Prime Minister introduced the issue of German disarmament into the campaign. His notes for this section of his speech revealed no particular concern about the German army and, indeed, indicated a desire to temper public expectations regarding both the imposition of harsh terms on Germany and the likelihood that the various measures being advocated for the preservation of peace could in fact prevent war:

> Don't want terms that will keep hundreds of thousands
> of our boys in Germany to hold down a hostile popula-
> tion.
> Disarmament.
> Put an end to conscript armies.
> In same category as League of Nations.

> Don't say it will prevent war,
> it will make it difficult.[96]

In his speech, however, he singled out the German army for special attention and implied that getting rid of Europe's large conscript armies would ensure peace:

> You must see when you come to settle the terms of peace that these gigantic Armies which have been the means of provoking war, and tempting rule[r]s to war, shall not be permitted in the future (Cheers). There is no doubt at all that that immense Army with its great equipment and its clatter tempted the rulers of Germany to make war . . . If there is going to be peace on earth we must not have those great conscript armies in Europe in future (Cheers).[97]

While this approach drew warm support from a not entirely friendly audience, staunch opponents of conscription were not satisfied with 'the guarded allusion to Conscription'.[98] Moreover, another development soon undermined Lloyd George's attempt to deflect attention from the issue of conscription in Britain. In a well-publicised speech at Manchester on 10 December Labourite J. H. Thomas accused the Coalition of definitely planning to continue conscription after the war and documented his charge by reading a letter from one British general to another outlining plans for the postwar retention of conscription.[99] Thomas's charges produced a public outcry and an avalanche of telegrams to Downing Street.[100] At the same time Coalitionists were advising Lloyd George of the urgency of his making a statement on conscription. Guest wrote that he was 'sure a statement on *Conscription* is necessary – this being used against Gov[ernmen]t candidates both by Asquithians and Labour'.[101] Another of Lloyd George's followers was even more emphatic: '*You should flatly eny that you or your colleagues mean to perpetuate Conscription.*'[102]

The Prime Minister therefore issued an official reply to Thomas's charges, stating that the government intended to end conscription at home as well as in other countries, but that the abolition of conscription in Britain would depend upon the outcome of the peace conference: 'The policy of the Government is to abolish conscript armies in this and every other country, and they hope to be able to accomplish this at the Peace Conference.'[103] At the same time Lloyd

George announced his intention of dealing with the conscription issue in his speech at Bristol on 11 December.[104]

On the defensive about the conscription issue, Lloyd George thus chose his last major campaign speech as the occasion for an important statement on conscription. The cheers which greeted the Prime Minister's announcement that he would begin his speech with the conscription question revealed the depth of public feeling about the issue. The reporting of the Bristol speech further indicated the importance which the conscription issue had attained and the acceptance of its linkage to the question of disarmament. Although Lloyd George also made major statements on reparations and indemnity, the headline in *The Times* read, 'Prime Minister on Conscription', while the *Morning Post* headed its report, 'Disarmament All Round'.[105]

Denying – probably honestly – knowledge of the plans set forth in the letter which Thomas had read the previous day, Lloyd George said that the government did not intend to maintain 'a *great* conscript Army *in this country*'.[106] These qualifications were typical Lloyd George devices. While the government hoped to rely on a volunteer army for empire and home defence, the War Office was urging the retention of conscript forces both for the army required to supervise fulfilment of the Armistice conditions and for the troops which would be necessary if, as seemed likely, the treaty with Germany were to require an army of occupation.

Less duplicitously, the Prime Minister, like Churchill earlier in the campaign, told his audience that the future of conscription in Britain would depend upon the peace terms. He criticised the anti-conscriptionists, particularly Labour candidates, for their refusal to concede this connection: 'Whether you will require conscription in the future in any shape or form depends not upon the opinion which I express here on this platform, or which any other political leader expresses upon any other platform. It will depend entirely upon the terms of peace (cheers).'[107]

Then, as in his Queen's Hall speech, he shifted the issue to the danger of conscript armies on the Continent. He devoted the rest of his remarks on conscription to the necessity of abolishing these armies as part of the peace settlement before ending conscription in Britain: 'The real guarantee against conscription in this country, and in every other country, is to put an end by the terms of the Peace Conference to these great conscript Armies. If you forbid Germany to raise an Army of five millions . . . what need will there be for other countries to raise these big Armies?' Blaming the war and Britain's subsequent adoption of conscription on the existence of the German army, he skilfully played upon the crowd's anti-German feelings to turn their concern with ending conscription at home into support for his new demand for German disarmament: 'The swagger, the clatter, the trampling over peoples, the boastings, the threatenings, the interferings with neighbours, the bullying and arrogance [of Germany], with these five millions behind them – this was a menace to the peace of the world, and unless the Peace Conference puts an end to it you might as well not open its doors.'[108] No longer, then, were Germany's defeat, the apparent collapse of Prussian militarism and the change in Germany's government sufficient to prevent a repetition of German aggression. Now he also demanded the end of Germany's conscript army.

In this way Lloyd George responded to demands generated by the left with a statement designed to win the support of the majority of the electorate without alienating his Conservative colleagues. His appeal to anti-Germanism would not only win votes for the Coalition but undoubtedly would also enhance his position with the more militant of the Coalition Conservatives, whereas an unequivocal pledge to end conscription in Britain might have produced strains within the Coalition partnership, since many Coalition Conservative candidates had made ' "National Service" a main plank in their platform'.[109] Moreover, in the light of the pressures being exerted by the War Office for the at least temporary extension of conscription to meet Britain's postwar responsibilities, Lloyd George certainly knew that a definite pledge to end conscription in Britain would return to haunt him after the election. Hence he made the abolition of conscription in Britain contingent upon its abolition in Germany and the rest of Europe.

The Prime Minister's Bristol speech by no means appeased diehard anti-conscriptionists nor ended the conscription controversy. While Mond related that in his constituency the Bristol speech had 'dispel[led] the last lingering doubts' about the government's position,[110] the *Daily News* reported that soldiers had heckled Lloyd George's remarks.[111] In a box on the front page of the 12 December edition that journal proclaimed, 'A vote for the Coalition is a vote for Conscription', and a long leading article denouncing the Prime Minister's position declared that conscription was 'the issue of the election'. In the *Manchester Guardian* Scott also expressed dissatisfaction with Lloyd George's statement on conscription.[112] The No Conscription Fellowship, of course, continued its campaign, and many cries of 'What about conscription?' interrupted Lloyd George's last campaign speech.[113] After the election the *Tribunal* urged its readers to 'SEE THAT THE PRESSURE IS MAINTAINED',[114] and agitation against conscription continued well into 1919.

Rather than promising a definite end to conscription in Britain, as the opponents of compulsory service were demanding, Lloyd George had led the British public to believe that the peace conference would demand an end to Germany's conscript army and that this, in turn, would make possible the return to a voluntary system at home. Thus, to the extent that any public pronouncement could, the Bristol speech and Lloyd George's subsequent reaffirmation of his Bristol statement[115] pledged the Coalition to seek the end of Germany's large conscript army as part of the peace settlement.

This campaign pledge, together with the government's desire to reduce expenditures and Lloyd George and Bonar Law's consequent interest in securing an agreement for the general limitation of armaments, meant that with the Coalition's victory at the polls German disarmament was well on its way to becoming an important part of Britain's peace policy. This substantial shift in position came about not as a result of anti-German pressures or – notwithstanding Lloyd George's platform rhetoric – of fears of a resurgent Germany but as the consequence of the government's concern about Britain's fiscal problems and of Lloyd George's handling of the conscription question, a domestic issue which was causing the Coalition great embarrassment in the campaign. As we shall see in Chapter 9, concern about the consequences of the continuing domestic opposition to conscription was an important determinant of Britain's peace conference position on the future of the German army and therefore of its approach to the whole question of German disarmament. From the election campaign of 1918 through the Paris Peace Conference – and after – domestic concerns played a central role in the development and implementation of Britain's policy towards the disarmament of Germany.

8
The Decision to Disarm Germany

To much of the British public it must have seemed in mid-December 1918 that the government had a policy on both general and German disarmament. In his Trades Union Congress address the Prime Minister had endorsed the concept of general arms limitation, and Britain had accepted the modified Fourteen Points as the basis for peace negotiations with Germany. The Coalition's first election manifesto had spoken of reducing Britain's armaments, and during the campaign Lloyd George had not only expressed his commitment to a general limitation of armaments but had specifically introduced the issue of German disarmament. Despite these public statements, however, the Cabinet, as we have seen, had reached no policy decisions on the questions of either general or German disarmament.

Consciousness of the depth of popular feeling against war and of the Coalition's campaign pledges on arms reduction and the abolition of conscription played an important role as British officials, with the experience of the campaign fresh in their minds, joined with their empire colleagues to determine Britain's peace conference policy. Significantly, however, in their consideration of the disarmament question there was no evidence of the extreme Germanophobia in which most Coalition candidates had been caught up during the campaign. Rather, just as when at the height of the campaign they had discussed the future of the British army, they seemed generally unconcerned about the question of German power. In deciding Britain's peace conference position on both general and German disarmament and on the broader question of the maintenance of postwar stability, British leaders had, of course, to take into account the public expectations created by their wartime and campaign utterances. They also had to reconcile divergent viewpoints within the government and among British Empire representatives as well as the conflicting pressures being brought to bear by their American and French allies. These concerns, rather than the question of Germany's future role in Europe, provided the framework for their consideration of the disarmament question.

The United States and France had radically different conceptions of what the peace settlement should accomplish. President Wilson envisaged the creation of a new world order based on the League of Nations. As Wiseman had reported, 'The one fundamental problem . . . which is the key-note to the whole American attitude is the League of Nations'.[1] Moreover, Wilson hoped that the newly democratic Germany would eventually become an equal partner in this new system of collective security. In contrast, the French wished to perpetuate the preponderance of Allied power achieved by the Armistice. Their overriding concern was long-term security against a revival of German power. This they hoped to assure not only by a punitive peace but also by a continued Anglo-American commitment to Europe.

The British had misgivings about basing their postwar policy on either of these strategies. The choice of either as the sole basis for maintaining postwar stability would be a departure from traditional policy, while its complete rejection would present problems for Britain's future relations with the proponent of the discarded option. In deciding Britain's disarmament policy Lloyd George attempted to reconcile these opposing strategies so that Britain could pursue its interests as he perceived them without alienating either ally.

Acceptance of the Wilsonian peace programme would mean the abandonment of Britain's traditional imperial naval strategy and its longstanding interest in maintaining the European balance of power. R. E. Prothero, the President of the Board of Agriculture, summarised Britain's predicament as it attempted to decide how to respond to Wilson's programme. A postwar strategy based on Wilson's conception of the League of Nations would mean the sacrifice of Britain's naval supremacy and of British autonomy in determining the use of its sea power: 'British sea-power is to be translated into League of Nations sea-power, and the control of the League of Nations will not lie in the hands of Great Britain.' This would strike at the foundation of Britain's position as a world power and potentially its survival as an independent nation: 'The retention of sea-power is, to us, a matter of life and death; and . . . we cannot put our hands to any treaty which, at this moment of complete victory, will lead to our ultimate extinction.' But, as Prothero also pointed out, the dilemma which Britain faced in dealing with Wilson was its continued economic dependence on the United States: 'The immediate economic stability of this country largely depends on the co-operation of the United States.'[2] Hoping that Wilson might agree to an adjustment of Britain's war loans, British leaders could not afford to disregard his wishes on the larger question of the preservation of postwar peace.

The question of supporting the French approach to peace was an even more complicated one. As Borden observed, France's peace plans 'would keep the German people under the allied nations as taskmasters for half a century'.[3] Acquiescence in the French peace strategy would thus entail a long-term involvement on the Continent. This would be a significant departure from the traditional British policy of intervening in Europe only long enough to restore the balance of power there. In addition, at a time when the British people were demanding speedy demobilisation and an end to conscription and the government hoped to reduce armaments expenditures, such a policy would present domestic difficulties. Moreover, as we have seen, in the revolutionary atmosphere of post-Armistice Europe most British policy-makers did not believe that a drastic weakening of a democratic Germany would accord with Britain's interests. However, Germany had come sufficiently close to domination of the Continent to confirm that Britain's security was indeed bound up with that of Western Europe, particularly France. Therefore British leaders could not ignore with impunity the demands of French security.

Despite the geographic reality that French security was essential to British security, most British policy-makers who addressed themselves to the question of how Britain should align itself at the peace conference denounced France's aims and advocated co-operation with the United States. The fact that the war had ended with Britain still apparently at the height of its power and that Lloyd George, in the pre-Armistice negotiations over the Fourteen Points, had secured Allied acceptance of Britain's reservation regarding the freedom of the seas had somewhat allayed British leaders' earlier anxieties about the growing power of the United States and about American intentions regarding British sea power. In contrast, French actions in the aftermath of the Armistice had exacerbated British misgivings about France's intentions, and these misgivings outweighed concern that American power might be used against British interests.

Concern about France's intentions reflected both the traditional British interest in maintaining the balance of power on the Continent and the re-emergence of Britain's historic rivalry with France. As we have seen, once victory had been assured, residual British fears of French predominance in Europe had reappeared. The outcome of the war had ended Germany's threat to the European balance, and the Armistice terms had considerably diminished German power. In addition, since the Bolshevik Revolution Russia had ceased to be a factor in the European balance. British leaders recognised that, at least temporarily, France was the dominant power on the Continent, a power with worldwide interests, which in many places clashed with British interests.

The British government certainly did not view France as either a direct military threat or a danger to European security. During the war British leaders had repeatedly expressed misgivings about France's ability to hold its own militarily.[4] In October 1918, as we have seen, Generals Haig and Wilson had given a negative assessment of the French army's capability, and other analyses were equally sceptical about France's military strength.[5] Although British leaders did not perceive France as a threat to British or European security, they did regard French ambitions as a real challenge to British interests. France was Britain's chief competitor for economic compensation from Germany and for the territorial spoils of war. Moreover, French designs on the Rhineland would, as previously noted, involve Britain in a long-term military commitment on the Continent. Therefore British policy-makers approached the question of Britain's postwar relationship with France with more apprehension than they viewed the prospect of a continuing association with the United States. They regarded French policy as a factor which would create instability in Europe and the rest of the world, while they thought that the United States would be more likely to use its power in a way which would promote postwar stability.

At the end of November the French ambassador, Cambon, presented Balfour with a plan for concerting Anglo-French peace conference policy so that France and Britain would be united in opposing President Wilson's peace plans. Balfour's reaction to this proposal was that 'from the point of view of immediate diplomacy, Cambon's policy is little short of insanity': 'Their [the French's] deliberate effort to exclude the Americans from any effective share in the world settlement is, in my judgment, neither in our interest nor in that of the French themselves.' Rather, Balfour advocated close co-operation with the United States. The specifics of France's peace objectives also disturbed the Foreign Secretary. As others had done during the pre-Armistice discussions, he complained about France's greed: 'Diplomacy apart, the French seem to me so greedy that even if America & Italy did not exist we might find some difficulty in swallowing their terms whole.'[6]

French demands during the Allied conference which met in London from 1 December to 3 December increased British suspicions of France's peace policy. A peace conference procedural outline which the French had submitted for the consideration of the other Allies listed as military and naval conditions to be discussed at the Paris conference 'military guarantees on land and sea, number of troops, dismantling of fortifications, reduction of armaments, territorial occupation'.[7] At the London conference, however, when the Allies discussed peace issues, there was no discussion of disarmament except in the context of the extent to which Germany had fulfilled the Armistice conditions.[8] Instead, when Foch and his Chief of Staff, General Weygand, met with Lloyd George, Bonar Law, Hankey and General Wilson, Foch made it clear that France's central proposal for the military peace terms would be detachment of the left bank of the Rhine. Both Lloyd George and Bonar Law opposed this proposal on the ground that it would create another Alsace-Lorraine. General Wilson, though sympathetic to the security needs of 'the poor French', also thought Foch's proposal too extreme.[9] Although he expected the British army to provide its share of troops for an army of occupation, Britain's military overextension troubled him. Believing that in a period of limited military resources Britain's primary object should be protection of the empire, the CIGS deprecated the idea of allowing troops from areas along the route to India 'to be dragged into European complications'.[10] Therefore, despite his longstanding anti-Germanism and his prewar advocacy of an alignment with France, he opposed peace terms which would require an extensive military commitment on the Continent for enforcement.

Others whose orientation was towards the empire rather than towards Europe feared not only France's aims on the Rhine but, like Balfour, its overall peace objectives. Borden's reaction to France's proposed peace terms was similar to Balfour's: 'Nearly everything that is to be exacted [from Germany] is for France.'[11] Unenthusiastic about his British Empire colleagues' colonial ambitions, he clearly would not accede to France's terms. Borden's objections to French policy went beyond an antipathy to using victory for territorial aggrandisement. Uncertain whether he would be able to provide Canadian troops for an army of occupation, he opposed a Continental commitment on practical as well as idealistic grounds. On 30 December he told the other members of the Imperial War Cabinet that the British Empire 'should keep clear, as far as possible, of European complications and alliances'.[12] Understandably, Borden preferred to co-operate with Canada's neighbour, the United States, and with President Wilson with whose outlook on world affairs he largely agreed.[13]

As we have seen, Curzon's preoccupation with the empire also made him mistrustful of the French, but his attitude towards the question of whether Britain should align itself at the peace conference with the United States or with France reflected the ambivalence of the British position. Curzon, whose speciality was Asia and who had little interest in European problems, was profoundly suspicious of the French. On 2 December, in an Eastern Committee discussion of postwar territorial arrangements, he again expressed his fears about French competition. Although he hoped that the wartime relationship with France would last, he had grave doubts about the likelihood of maintaining amicable relations: 'I am seriously afraid that the great Power from whom we may have most to fear in the future is France, and I shudder at the possibility of putting France in such a position. She is powerful in almost all parts of the world, even around India.'[14] Nevertheless, on 30 December when Lloyd George reported to the Imperial War Cabinet that President Wilson would not support the British position on indemnity, Curzon said that 'it might be necessary, on some issues at any rate, for Mr. Lloyd George to work at the Conference in alliance with M. Clemenceau'.[15]

General Smuts displayed no such flexibility in his attitude towards the course which the British Empire should follow at the Paris Peace Conference. At the Eastern Committee meeting he went even further than Curzon, ruling out the possibility of a resurgent Germany at any time in the near future and warning against France's territorial ambitions: 'With Germany practically wiped off for a generation we must deal with France. France is a great military Power. We know the character of French policy in the past, and what it may be in the coming generation again. France may be our great problem.'[16] Smuts elaborated on these ideas in a paper recommending the concerting of peace conference policy with the United States against France. Although he had earlier expressed great concern about the growing power of the United States, the achievement of victory while Britain was apparently still in a dominant position had ameliorated his anxiety about America's growing power. After the Armistice his jealousy of France's colonial acquisitions in Africa and the Middle East led him to advocate Anglo-American co-operation against France in the peace negotiations. He hoped that such co-operation would lead to American aid in freeing Britain from its obligation to support France's territorial claims.

Smuts presented his desire to undo the wartime Allied territorial arrangements to the advantage of the British Empire in the broader terms of Britain's probable postwar position *vis-à-vis* the other Great Powers. In a retreat from his earlier concern about Japan's emerging power and a discounting of Germany's continuing capacity to make its power felt on the world scene, Smuts asserted that the outcome of the war had left only three first-class world powers: the British Empire, France and the United States. Operating on the assumption that Britain must choose to work at the peace conference either with France or with America, he advocated co-operation with the United States because he did not trust France:

> France was a bad neighbour to us in the past . . . I am afraid her arrogant diplomacy may be revived by the great change which has come over her fortunes. She has always been very ambitious, is militant and imperialist by temperament, and her politics have generally a nasty trail of finance and concession-hunting over them. I fear we shall find her a difficult if not an intolerable neighbour. She will do her best to remain mistress of the Continent. Incidentally she will keep Germany in a state of humiliating subjection which must create a hopeless atmosphere for future peace and co-operation.[17]

Smuts's arguments embodied the essence of British anxieties about postwar France: concern about French imperial and economic rivalry, fear of the consequences of French domination of Europe, and the expectation that France would thwart efforts either to reintegrate Germany into the European system or to include it in a new international order. Since Smuts perceived France as a greater threat than the United States to British interests, he recommended collaboration with America in the peace negotiations as a means of attempting to moderate French demands and thus lessening the challenge from France. Moreover, Smuts was sincerely committed to the League of Nations, and an Anglo-American strategy would be the only means of securing its adoption at the peace conference. Here again, as in his 1917 war aims speeches, he approached an issue in a way which allowed him to reconcile his perception of Britain's interests with his ideals.

An Anglo-American strategy, as expounded by Smuts, thus offered a meeting ground for those like Amery who thought chiefly in terms of Britain's imperial interests and an adherent of the league like Cecil. While cautioning that the United States should not be allowed to interfere in British interests, Amery, too, believed that 'to place Anglo-American relations on a permanent footing of mutual understanding and co-operation is the most important external object that the British Empire can aim at as the outcome of the war'.[18] Cecil, who had been appointed head of the Foreign Office's League of Nations section, argued that the best guarantee of a stable peace would be 'a good understanding with the United States', which he believed could only be obtained by British support for the League of Nations.[19] Cecil rejected the notion that 'the world domination of the Entente or any other group of powers' could provide the basis for permanent peace.[20]

These considerations about Anglo-American and Anglo-French relations, together with the public expectations manifested in and created by the election campaign, formed the background to the Imperial War Cabinet's discussion of the disarmament question on the eve of the Paris Peace Conference. The Imperial Cabinet had reconvened in late November to reconsider Britain's war aims in light of the Allied victory. On 18 December it decided the main peace issues which Lloyd George and Balfour should discuss with President Wilson during the American President's forthcoming visit to London in preparation for the Paris Peace Conference. While the main emphasis was on territorial terms, Lloyd George included disarmament among the 'other large and vital problems on which attention should be concentrated immediately' in order to formulate guidelines for these conversations.[21] The Prime Minister here referred to general disarmament under the auspices of the League of Nations, but the resulting Imperial War Cabinet discussion on 24 December produced a stat ment of Britain's disarmament policy in which German disarmament emerged as the key to a general limitation of armaments.

This formulation of a German disarmament policy took place in the context of consideration of several memoranda on the League of Nations. These included the report of the Phillimore Committee, appointed in early 1919 to study the question of the league, two Foreign Office memoranda, an Admiralty memorandum and a memorandum by General Smuts. Only the Smuts memorandum advocated general disarmament. The Foreign Office and Admiralty memoranda explicitly rejected the concept, while the Phillimore Committee report did not deal with the disarmament question.

The Admiralty memorandum understandably dealt only with the question of the limitation of naval armaments. It argued that the existence of a strong navy was essential to the survival of the British Empire and that therefore the British navy performed a purely defensive function. Accordingly, Britain should not participate in any arms limitation agreement which would not allow it to retain a margin of naval superiority.[22] The Admiralty's position was consonant with that taken by British leaders throughout the war, but its adoption would jeopardise the chances for reaching agreement on a general limitation of armaments. All nations could argue that their own armies and navies served only a defensive function while those of their potential adversaries were intended for aggressive purposes. In particular, France regarded its army in the same light in which the British viewed their navy, and the French would resent British efforts to limit the French army while insisting upon the maintenance of Britain's naval supremacy.

The Foreign Office memoranda, prepared by two members of the Political Intelligence Department who were also members of the Round Table movement, also flatly opposed including disarmament in the plans for the league. Both Alfred Zimmern and Eustace Percy shared the Round Table movement's opposition to charging the league with specific responsibilities which it might be unable to fulfil. In an article which appeared in the December 1918 issue of the *Round Table* Zimmern set forth the movement's approach to the provisions of the treaty and of the covenant which would constitute the league:

It is better to avoid provisions which, however desirable in the abstract, cannot be worked out in such form as to be subject to scrutiny and control. The history of diplomacy is full of pious provisions of this kind, and experience has invariably shown that they are not only useless, but actually harmful; for they tie the hands of law-abiding and trustworthy powers whilst leaving the untrustworthy free to pursue their purposes in secret. The best instances of such provisions in the past . . . have been the attempts to secure the limitation of armaments and the mitigation of the rules of war.[23]

Zimmern, who had given much thought to the disarmament question, believed that there was no practicable scale or form of control on which to base general disarmament. As Kitchener had contended, he, too, believed that finance was the key to disarmament. Discussing the disarmament question with Jones, Zimmern had commented that instead of being incorporated into the provisions of the League of Nations, arms limitation should be left to the taxpayers in each nation.[24] In addition, the problem of defining armaments troubled him. When Jones had suggested restricting the manufacture of armaments to state-owned workshops, [25] Zimmern had replied that '"armaments" is too wide a term'.[26] Accordingly, in his memorandum Zimmern rejected both 'any definite arrangement for the limitation of armaments according to an agreed scale, since the term armament defies accurate analysis' and 'provisions designed to limit the weapons or methods by which war can be carried on' because unscrupulous powers would not uphold such provisions.[27] These arguments echoed some of the concerns about the problem of implementing general disarmament which had been expressed in Crowe's 1916 memorandum and in the 1917 Imperial War Cabinet discussions. They also presaged the difficulties which were to prove to be at the heart of the problem of enforcement of the eventual treaty provisions.

Zimmern's colleague, Percy, was more succinct in his rejection of the disarmament concept, simply stating that 'disarmament should form no part of the treaty creating the League'. He dismissed the idea of attempting to implement Point Four of the Fourteen Points, describing President Wilson's wording of his call for disarmament as 'only safe because it is meaningless'.[28]

The Phillimore Committee, a Foreign Office committee composed both of Foreign Office civil servants and distinguished outsiders,[29] apparently did not consider the disarmament question to be worth its consideration. Its chairman, Lord Phillimore, a former Lord Justice of Appeal and an authority on international law, had been the only one at a 1917 League of Nations Society lawyers' conference on the league to dissent from the view that disarmament was essential to a viable league.[30] In addition, as we have seen, Crowe, one of the Foreign Office members, was a firm opponent of a general limitation of armaments. Although Tyrrell, another Foreign Office member, had been an early advocate of arms limitation, there is some indication that in his new position as head of the PID he had modified his views. The Foreign Office memoranda opposing any scheme for general disarmament were the work of his subordinates in the PID. Since these papers embodied policy recommendations, Foreign Office procedures required that they be channelled through Tyrrell before being distributed outside the department.

Although the Phillimore Committee held fourteen meetings between January and July 1918, it never discussed the disarmament question.[31] The only mention of arms limitation occurred when a visiting American judge reported on the Phillimore Committee's French counterpart, the Bourgeois Committee. However, no member of the Phillimore Committee even commented when the American reported that the Bourgeois Committee thought that the principle of arms limitation would have to be accepted.[32] Accordingly, the Phillimore Committee's report made no reference to disarmament.[33]

Of the papers under consideration by the Imperial War Cabinet the Smuts memorandum presented the most detailed analysis of the disarmament question. In it Smuts elaborated on his earlier support for general disarmament. He raised the disarmament issue first in the section of his memorandum devoted to the territorial settlement. Here he proposed both that the league prohibit mandatory states from establishing military forces beyond those needed for internal policing and that to gain admission to the league the new states resulting from the breakup of the old European empires should agree to raise only those military forces and accumulate only those armaments which the league would deem reasonable. The adoption of such a policy would, he hoped, lead to general disarmament: 'The result will be that militarism will be scotched *ab initio* in the case of all new States . . . In such case it will also be much easier for the older States and Powers to adopt a policy of disarmament and reduction of military forces.' In these conditions, he argued, 'perhaps even Germany' would then have to follow suit.[34] Unlike Tyrrell, Paget and other officials who during the war had regarded German disarmament as a prerequisite for a general limitation of armaments, Smuts, then, hoped for German disarmament to result from, rather than to precede, general disarmament. Unconcerned, as we have seen, about German power – either actual or potential – Smuts did not advocate separate treatment of Germany in the implementation of disarmament.

Having recommended that one of the functions of the league should be to formulate for the approval of its members an arrangement for the limitation of armaments, Smuts in the section of his memorandum entitled, 'The League of Nations and World Peace' turned his attention directly to 'the most important and vital issue before the civilised world': the prevention of war. In this portion of his paper he more fully explored the disarmament question, reviewing the three most common proposals for general disarmament and some of the problems involved in their implementation. He surveyed and endorsed, in turn, the concepts of the abolition of conscription, the limitation of armaments and the nationalisation of munitions production. Of greatest importance for the Imperial War Cabinet discussion and for subsequent British policy were his views on the abolition of conscription and the limitation of armaments.

Smuts endorsed the abolition of conscription in much stronger terms than he had used in his draft for Lloyd George's Trades Union Congress address. Urging that the peace conference should abolish conscription, he argued that the abolition of conscription was 'by far the most important' of the three disarmament proposals, that it was essential to the maintenance of peace. His analysis of the relationship between conscription and militarism coincided not only with the prewar Liberal identification of conscription with militarism but also with the view of the role of conscript armies on the Continent enunciated in Lloyd George's late campaign speeches:

> I would go so far as to say that while the Great Powers are allowed to raise conscript armies without hindrance or limit, it would be vain to expect the lasting preservation of world peace. If the instrument is ready for use the occasion will arrive and the men will arise to use it. I look upon conscription as the taproot of

militarism; unless that is cut, all our labours will eventually be in vain.

This analysis, reinforcing as it did Lloyd George's campaign position, was influential in the development of Britain's position on German disarmament. As we shall see in the next chapter, Smuts's perception of conscription as 'the taproot of militarism' prevailed over the Foreign Office's later attempt to discredit it.

Smuts offered additional reasons for supporting the universal abolition of conscription. After the outlawing of conscription he hoped that the league would limit the size of volunteer or militia forces. Still concerned about the threat of Bolshevism, he maintained that ending compulsory service would, by freeing capital and labour for the improvement of social conditions throughout Europe, stem the revolutionary tide. This was, of course, the same argument which motivated many British leaders' interest in reducing Britain's armaments expenditures. Lastly, perhaps having in mind the role of the conscription issue in the British election campaign, Smuts argued that, of the three disarmament proposals, the abolition of conscription would receive the greatest public support in all countries.

Although he admitted that there would be difficulties in deciding what system would replace conscription and whether – and, if so, how – the league would limit the size of volunteer armies, Smuts failed to deal with the problem of enforcement. He recognised that good faith would be necessary for successful implementation, but, unlike Zimmern, Crowe, or some of his colleagues in the Imperial War Cabinet, Smuts assumed good faith on the part of all powers: 'I see nothing inherently insoluble in the problems presented, so long as States are *bona fide* willing to make the new system workable.'

Smuts was less optimistic about resolving the problems involved in implementing a general limitation of armaments. He pointed out the difficulty of defining armaments and of establishing a system of comparative values for different types of weapons:

The weapons of war are no longer limited in range and use as in former wars. It is practically impossible, after our experience of this war, to say what things could be excluded from the list of armaments in the broad sense. The war was fought throughout and ultimately won, not only by the usual military weapons in the narrower sense, but by the whole economic, industrial, and financial systems of the belligerent Powers. Food, shipping, metals and raw materials, credit, transport, industries and factories of all kinds played just as important a part as guns, rifles, aeroplanes, tanks, explosives and gas, warships and submarines.

Even if . . . the list of armaments selected for limitation is confined to direct instruments of war . . . then the second question arises, how one instrument is to be valued against another. How is an aeroplane valued as against a tank, a Zeppelin against a submarine, a machine gun against a field gun or a Stokes gun or a can of poison gas? Unless a whole system of comparative values is settled, the armaments of one State may exceed in striking power those fixed for another State of equal military standing. And new inventions may at any moment upset the applecart with all its precious tables of values.

Here then was a comprehensive statement from a proponent of arms limitation of the complexity of the technological problems of disarmament and an acknowledgement of some of the obstacles to the achievement of arms limitation, obstacles which Zimmern and other critics of disarmament found insurmountable.

Smuts offered no direct solution to 'these perplexities'. Rather, he proposed bypassing them through a narrower interpretation of arms limitation. Significantly, his proposal for a workable solution to the problem of arms limitation was contingent upon the abolition of conscription. Smuts suggested that, if conscription were abolished, the league should then determine a scale of direct armaments and equipment to be allowed the volunteer or militia forces of each state: 'Such a provision seems almost a necessary corollary to the abolition of conscription and the limitation of volunteer or militia forces to definite numbers.'

This approach to the twin issues of the abolition of conscription and the reduction of armaments reversed that outlined by Lloyd George in his 12 November speech to Coalition Liberals, when the Prime Minister had anticipated instead that the universal abolition of conscription would follow a general reduction of armaments. By mid-December, however, the mounting pressures for an end to conscription at home had apparently convinced Lloyd George of the political wisdom of calling first for an end to compulsory service throughout Europe. Smuts's views therefore found a receptive audience in the Prime Minister, who opened the Imperial War

Cabinet's consideration of the various memoranda on the League of Nations by referring to the Smuts paper as 'one of the ablest State Papers he had read'.[35]

In the subsequent discussion the idea of including general disarmament within the purview of the League of Nations elicited both strong support and stiff opposition. The chief opponent was Prime Minister Hughes, a vocal advocate of national military preparedness as the best means of preserving peace. Taking his cue from the Percy paper, the recalcitrant Australian Premier contended that 'there was no question of disarmament' in President Wilson's proposal for a league of nations. Since he represented one of the empire's farthest outposts, a continent vulnerable to the increasing power of the Japanese navy, Hughes naturally was most concerned about the question of naval disarmament, which Smuts had ignored. Expressing his 'complete agreement' with the Admiralty memorandum, he asserted that 'nothing should be done to impair our right to maintain and to control exclusively such navy as was essential to our safety'.[36] Churchill supported Hughes's position. Believing that reduction of armaments would occur 'gradually and naturally'[37] if the peace settlement removed most of the causes of war, Churchill was not willing to entrust Britain's security to an untested league in the interim: 'A League of Nations could be no substitute for national defences.'[38]

Reading, the ambassador to the United States, also opposed the idea of including disarmament among the league's responsibilities. Rather than approaching the issue from the point of view of exclusively British interests, however, he focused on how linking the league's establishment to agreement on arms limitation might affect the viability of the league. On this basis he offered cogent criticism of Smuts's disarmament proposals. Reading thought that Smuts expected too much from the League of Nations at its inception and that attempting to resolve the difficulties involved in general disarmament might well prevent the establishment of the league. Since he put a high value on Anglo-American co-operation, he thought that Britain should not support a proposal, insistence on which might jeopardise the achievement of Wilson's chief goal, the creation of the League of Nations.

Reading also raised the question which had remained unresolved since it was first put forward in the 1917 Imperial War Cabinet meetings and which continued to go unanswered throughout the interwar period, that of guaranteeing good faith. Addressing himself to the crucial interrelated questions of confidence in the league and enforcement of its authority regarding disarmament, issues ignored by Smuts and the other advocates of general disarmament, Reading went to the heart of what became major problems of the post-Versailles period. In the ambassador's view, if the Allies adopted Smuts's proposals and limited all armies, then the question would arise as to what guarantee there was that Germany would not evade its obligations and secretly build up a larger army than that authorised it. Thus, in the context of setting forth his opposition to the linking of general disarmament to the creation of the league, Reading introduced the issue of German disarmament into the discussion. His framing of the question presaged the Paris Peace Conference controversies with France over the best means of achieving French security. Reading's analysis also pointed out the crux of the dilemma which Britain would face once further German disarmament became part of its policy and was, in turn, incorporated into the peace treaty. This was the question of how Britain could ensure German disarmament while reducing its own armed forces. Again, as in 1917, the Imperial War Cabinet did not deal with these basic questions. Reading was the only one to voice concern about the question of German compliance and to imply thereby that the German army of the future might pose a danger to European security.

On the question of the relationship between disarmament and the league, Bonar Law, in this discussion the strongest advocate of Smuts's disarmament recommendations, took a position diametrically opposed to Reading's. Also concerned about the future of the League of Nations, the Conservative leader, in contrast to Reading, believed that general disarmament should be an integral task of the league: 'Unless something definite was accomplished in regard to disarmament any discussion on the League of Nations would be in the main academic.' Answering the critics of naval disarmament, while at the same time proffering a means of satisfying France's security needs without acquiescing in Foch's plans for the Rhine, he endorsed Smuts's proposal for a system of relative armaments: 'The question of safety was a relative one. If our Navy were reduced but retained the relative supremacy which it possessed at the present moment we should lose nothing. The same applied to France and her army.'[39] From Bonar Law's point of view as Chancellor of the

Exchequer Britain would, in fact, gain something from acceptance of this proposal. The adoption of a scheme of relative armaments would allow a reduction in expenditures for the British army and navy, while agreeing to France's proposals would not only make this reduction impossible but would probably necessitate increased funding. Supporting general disarmament thus was consonant with Bonar Law's concern about Britain's financial future as well as with his views on the best means of maintaining postwar stability.

Borden, who as early as the 1917 Imperial War Cabinet meetings had considered a general reduction of armaments to be a possible British objective, now invoked public opinion as a reason for supporting disarmament: 'It was the very strong view of the common people that something should be done to reduce armaments.'[40] He elaborated on this assessment with a statement which revealed the extent to which the Radical interpretation of the armaments question, a minority viewpoint in 1914, had by 1918 permeated public opinion. According to the Canadian Premier, the public believed that profit-making in the manufacture of armaments led to war.[41] Therefore, 'if we did not take steps to reduce armaments the Peace Conference would be a sham'.[42] As political head of his country, Borden was, of course, particularly sensitive to the pressures of public opinion. His interpretation of public expectations reinforced his support for President Wilson's Fourteen Points and his own idealistic conception of the purposes for which Canada had fought the war.

Cecil continued to waver on the disarmament question. He remained committed to the ideal of arms limitation but still doubted the feasibility of general disarmament under current conditions. As late as 12 November, in an address at Birmingham University in which he outlined his plan for a league of nations, Cecil had called attention to the fact that his proposal said nothing about disarmament. He had assured his audience that he still considered disarmament to be the key to the maintenance of peace: 'It is, indeed, most true that without disarmament there can be no complete security against future war.' But he had told his listeners, 'After giving considerable thought to the subject, I have not yet come upon any plan for this purpose which seems safe and practicable'. Instead, he had expressed the hope that 'nations will gradually disarm as and when the necessity for national armament disappears'.[43] In the covering synopsis of an advance copy of this speech which he had circulated to the War Cabinet in October Cecil had reiterated, 'Compulsory national disarmament is not proposed'. Rather, the prospects for general disarmament would depend upon 'the growth of international goodwill'.[44] Hence before the election his position on the reduction of armaments had been that arms limitation was a goal which might be achieved in the future but that general disarmament would only be possible when the causes of war disappeared.

Cecil's experience during the campaign, however, apparently convinced him of the importance of taking some step towards achieving the goal of disarmament. He remained convinced that another war would destroy not only the European system but civilisation as well.[45] The Bolshevik Revolution and its aftermath had added a new dimension to his Conservative concern about the preservation of Western civilisation. He had played an active role in the government's anti-Bolshevik press campaign,[46] and during the election campaign he had expressed fears that growing class antagonism in Britain might lead eventually to Bolshevism there.[47] As a Coalition candidate, he had had to field questions from opponents of conscription,[48] and he had formed the impression that the working class believed that the rich did not oppose war. On the basis of this exposure to popular feeling during the election campaign, Cecil told the Imperial War Cabinet that he feared class conflict in Britain if the government did not demonstrate its commitment to ending war. Accordingly, he endorsed Borden's position on armaments reduction and also advocated 'some provision' against the private manufacture of armaments and against conscription. However, he voiced misgivings about agreeing to a definite plan for disarmament, 'as this involved the question of the Freedom of the Seas, and this question was partial disarmament of the naval Powers'.[49] Hence, despite his idealism and his desire to work closely with the United States, Cecil, too, was unwilling to sacrifice Britain's naval supremacy and therefore would endorse only imprecise disarmament proposals.

The Imperial War Cabinet's inability to agree about general disarmament led to the adoption of additional German disarmament as a goal of British policy. This was Lloyd George's solution to the domestic, imperial and foreign policy problems which confronted him in dealing with the disarmament question. As we have seen, Lloyd George had early expressed interest in general disarmament.

Like Bonar Law, the Prime Minister believed that disarmament would be essential to the success of the league: 'Disarmament would be regarded as the real test of whether the League of Nations was a farce, or whether business was meant.' In addition, for Lloyd George, as for Borden, public opinion – as always – played an important role in determining his position. He thought that in order to meet public expectations the league must make some provision for disarmament: 'If the League of Nations did not include some provision for disarmament it would be regarded as a sham. Without some check on armaments there would be the greatest disappointment among the people.'[50] However, it was clear that there was no agreement among the members of the Imperial Cabinet on including general disarmament within the purview of the league.

Therefore Lloyd George proposed that the league first limit the size of the defeated powers' armies to a definite minimum necessary for police purposes only and prohibit conscription in these countries. This proposal, of course, coincided with his campaign call for an end to Germany's large conscript army. He apparently hoped that this approach would reconcile the conflicting viewpoints within the Imperial Cabinet as well as satisfy public opinion. Proposing first the disarmament of Germany and the other defeated powers would have the advantage of satisfying anti-Germans and, by initiating the disarmament process and thereby demonstrating Britain's commitment to disarmament, the proponents of arms limitation as well. Moreover, the end of conscription in Germany and its allies would, he believed, make possible the universal abolition of conscription and hence the fulfilment of his campaign pledge: 'If the League of Nations began by the abolition of conscription in the enemy countries, all the other countries would follow.'[51] According to this scenario, then Britain, too, would be able to abolish conscription.

Disarming Germany and the other defeated powers under the auspices of the league also seemed to offer a means of conciliating both France and the United States. Lloyd George thought that the adoption of his suggestion would allay French anxieties about a revival of German power and that once the league imposed restrictions on the German army, France would then abandon its own tradition of conscription: 'If this were done the French people would never stand sending their children into a conscript army for defence against a shadow.'[52] Lloyd George must have hoped, too, that if the United States and Britain insisted upon disarming Germany, France would then abandon its demand for the detachment of the Rhine and a long-term British military commitment to the Continent. Moreover, Lloyd George hoped to use British support for the league as leverage in obtaining American support at Paris for Britain's aims.[53] By expressing Britain's commitment to both the league and the concept of general disarmament, a proposal that the league disarm the defeated enemy as the first step towards general disarmament would provide a way to placate President Wilson without sacrificing British interests.

Although Lloyd George's proposal was the first direct call for German disarmament in either a wartime or post-Armistice Cabinet meeting, it prompted no discussion. Perhaps he simply articulated what the other Cabinet members had tacitly assumed since the election. A hard-liner like Hughes undoubtedly welcomed this specific statement of the intention further to disarm Germany[54] – albeit under the auspices of the league – while those who supported general disarmament must have recognised that France would never be party to any scheme for a general limitation of armaments unless the Allies first disarmed Germany. There being no objections to Lloyd George's suggested approach to the disarmament question, it became the basis of Britain's position, first, in the discussion with President Wilson and then, with modifications resulting from that discussion, at the Paris Peace Conference. In this way Lloyd George transformed his campaign statements on the abolition of conscription in Germany and his own interest in postwar disarmament into a formal declaration of Britain's disarmament policy. In so doing he seemed to have achieved a masterful resolution of the complex disarmament question.

However, although Lloyd George's solution provided a way out of the impasse within the Imperial War Cabinet, it overlooked several important factors. Enforcing German disarmament would involve the same problems – none of which had been resolved – as the enforcement of general disarmament. Indeed, it would present even greater difficulties. Although Germany had accepted the Fourteen Points as the basis of peace, this acceptance had been the result of military and political exigencies, not of commitment to the Wilsonian principles. Therefore German disarmament would have to be imposed, whereas proposals for general disarmament envisaged at least some measure of mutual agreement. As Cecil pointed out in a commentary on Smuts's proposals written in opposition to the idea of proceeding with definite plans for disarmament, 'the permanent disarmament of a great nation against its will means permanent occupation and difficulties so great as to make it almost impossible'.[55] Among these difficulties, which Cecil also outlined, were the existence in the defeated powers of large numbers of trained soldiers, of quantities of armaments and of industrial resources readily adaptable to war purposes. In addition, the league's enforcement of German disarmament would require the commitment of Allied forces to the league, and few British leaders were willing to use scarce British troops for that purpose.

Moreover, in assuming that France would willingly accept his proposal as the answer to its security needs, Lloyd George misjudged both the depth of the French preoccupation with the problem of security against Germany and the integral role of the conscript army in modern French history. As Cecil recognised, France would oppose the abolition of conscription.[56] In addition, with the British preoccupied with security against Bolshevism and disturbed by the unstable conditions in Germany while the French worried about security against a German revival, even if they agreed to limit Germany's army, they were bound to differ in their interpretations of the number of troops necessary for police purposes and, indeed, in their definitions of police functions. Such disagreement might delay the imposition of German disarmament. That delay, together with French opposition to the abolition of conscription, would mean therefore an indefinite postponement of the abolition of conscription in Britain and hence the disappointment of hopes raised in the election campaign. Thus Lloyd George's solution entailed more problems than it resolved.

Yet Lloyd George's approach, with one major modification, became the basis of the planned Anglo-American peace conference strategy on the disarmament question. When Lloyd George reported his and Balfour's 27 December meeting with President Wilson to the Imperial War Cabinet,[57] he informed his colleagues that the President had originally wanted the peace conference to reach a definite decision on universal disarmament before the actual establishment of the League of Nations rather than entrusting disarmament to the league and first disarming the defeated enemy as the British proposed. Wilson had, however, conceded that the problems of relative disarmament were too complicated to be settled by the conference, and they had reached a compromise by which they had agreed 'that the Conference should not separate before a definite provisional limitation of armaments had been imposed on Germany and her allies, a limitation which would enable them to maintain order in the troubled conditions of their territories but no more'.[58] However, they had decided that Germany could later petition the league for a revision of this provisional limitation. Hence they did not envisage Germany's permanent disarmament to the level which the peace conference would prescribe. Lloyd George also apparently presented his case for the prohibition of conscription in Germany, and they seem to have agreed on this as well.[59] Insisting upon further German disarmament would, then, be part of the Anglo-American strategy at the Paris Peace Conference.

It is significant that the enunciation of German disarmament as a goal of British policy emerged from discussion of the responsibilities of the League of Nations rather than from debate over the peace terms to be demanded from Germany. Despite Lloyd George's late campaign rhetoric, British policy-makers' discussion of the disarmament question showed a distinct lack of concern about the potential for a revival of German military power. Admittedly, the reports they were receiving from Germany indicated that both the society and the army were disintegrating, and they feared the westward spread of Bolshevism. During the war they had not seriously contemplated the destruction of German military power, and most British leaders believed that they had accomplished their goal of destroying Prussian militarism. Germany's loss of its colonies and its navy had removed its direct threat to the British Empire. Its territorial losses confined it to Europe, while France remained a colonial power. Yet Germany had almost succeeded in gaining control of the Continent, and Russia no longer existed as an effective counterbalance to German power. Few other ministers thought, as Hughes did, that they would be able to impose economic terms which would deprive Germany of the foundations of its military strength. Even with the imposition of the economic terms which they contemplated and the loss of Alsace-Lorraine, in terms of its population and its industrial base, Germany would remain, as Balfour had pointed out as late as August,[60] the strongest power in Europe. The unstable situation in Germany meant that there was no assurance that Germany's conversion to democracy would be lasting or that, if it were, Germany would therefore, as Balfour hoped and other policy-makers apparently believed, use its power in accordance with British interests.

Yet, in reaching their decision to disarm Germany British leaders ignored the reality of German power. Notwithstanding the experience of the war, they overestimated France's potential. The peace conference strategy which Lloyd George devised with President Wilson seemed designed as much to curb French as German power: 'They felt, that if the German army was limited France would have to follow suit, and that she could hardly maintain an immense army under those conditions.'[61] The fact that the British decision to disarm Germany did not derive from a concern about German power had important consequences for the way in which British policy-makers approached both the question of German disarmament at the Paris Peace Conference and the enforcement of that disarmament once it was embodied in the Treaty of Versailles. They had reached their decision in the context of consideration of the problem of general disarmament against a background of public expectations of disarmament and an end to conscription. The desire to implement general disarmament and the need to appease British public opinion remained essential elements of the framework within which they viewed the issue of German disarmament. Moreover, Lloyd George had framed their decision in terms of an Anglo-American effort to check the growth of French power while at the same time assuring French security. At the Paris Peace Conference and in the post-Versailles period the attempt to reconcile Francophobia and the recognition of France's security needs into a coherent position continued as an important motif not only of Britain's policy towards German disarmament but of its whole German policy.

9

Peace Conference Policy:
Drafting the Military Clauses of the Treaty

Having, so most of them believed, achieved their objective of destroying Prussian militarism, British policy-makers wanted to prepare a peace settlement which would not only ensure against its revival but also prevent the recurrence of a major war. The desire for a return to normal peace conditions was so great, however, that neither the British public nor the British government wished to continue Britain's military commitment to Europe. Therefore at the Paris Peace Conference British leaders worked to achieve a settlement which would promote European stability but require minimal British participation in Continental affairs. As far as the new conditions created by America's decisive contribution to the war and its central role in the peacemaking process made it possible, they hoped to restore the European balance of power. To accomplish their objectives, most of them believed that it would be necessary eventually to reintegrate Germany into the European system, to preserve the wartime relationship with France while curbing French ambitions and preventing French domination of the Continent, to contain Bolshevism while preventing a Russo-German combination and to assure continued American participation in the maintenance of European security. Therefore while they wished in the peace treaty to achieve their specific colonial, naval and economic aims and to deprive Germany of the means of achieving Continental ascendency, they did not wish unduly to weaken Germany as a land power. Rather, they expected republican Germany, limited territorially to Europe, to play a role in the maintenance of postwar stability.

Pursuit of these diplomatic objectives not only coincided with Britain's traditional foreign policy interests but also would make possible the achievement of the Coalition's domestic aims of speedy demobilisation, the abolition of conscription, reduction of armaments expenditures and concentration on reconstruction. It was also consonant with the new imperial situation created by Britain's expanded overseas responsibilities and the Dominions' unwillingness to commit themselves to participate in upholding a European settlement. At the Paris Peace Conference British policy during the preparation of the military clauses of the treaty with Germany reflected the interplay of these complex external and internal factors.

The information which the Cabinet received on the eve of the peace conference confirmed earlier reports that Germany no longer posed a threat to the Allies. Foch, for example, reported the 'notable diminution of the military power of the enemy' resulting from its surrender of most of the war material required by the Armistice and the partial demobilisation of its army.[1] At the beginning of January War Secretary Milner told Lloyd George, 'I don't believe . . . that, whatever the state of their [Germany's] Army, it has much fight left in it'.[2] Reports which the Director of Military Intelligence circulated to the War Cabinet agreed with Milner's assessment. These accounts by men recently returned from Germany were unanimous in their opinion that Germany would not resume fighting.[3] Nevertheless, at the Paris Peace Conference Lloyd George vigorously pursued the strategy on disarmament which he had outlined in December and indeed went beyond it to demand that Germany be further disarmed as a condition of again renewing the Armistice.

Domestic concerns continued to play a key role in the development of the British position on German disarmament. There was considerable discontent among British soldiers as well as the general public over both the rate and the method of the demobilisation scheme implemented on 9 December. Furthermore, contrary to popular expectations, demobilisation did not mean discharge. In addition, there was widespread misunderstanding of the fact that the government did not intend to order general demobilisation until after the signature of the peace treaty. The government's failure adequately to deal with the demobilisation problem fuelled growing discontent in the army.

In early January there was a series of mutinies and demonstrations by thousands of soldiers protesting against the government's demobilisation policy. Soldiers who had been home on leave refused to re-embark for France, while at two army camps in England the men formed soldiers' councils patterned on the revolutionary workers' and soldiers' councils which had been formed in Russia. These developments exacerbated the already prevalent fears of Bolshevism. Esher wrote to Lloyd George of 'the *danger* of "unsympathetic demobilization"', which he believed could lead to Bolshevism,[4] and General Wilson worried that agitators would exploit the situation in the army.[5] On 8 January when a deputation of over a thousand soldiers marched on the Prime Minister's residence, the CIGS told the War Cabinet that 'the soldiers' delegation bore a dangerous resemblance to a Soviet'.[6]

The demobilisation discontent confronted the government not only with a potentially dangerous situation within the army and at home but also with the problem of satisfying the public's equally insistent demands for rapid demobilisation and a punitive peace. While speeding up the demobilisation process might allay the discontent, Milner believed that the consequent rapid reduction in the size of the army would make difficult the attainment of Britain's diplomatic objectives. During the December Imperial War Cabinet sessions the War Secretary had warned his colleagues that even the gradual reduction of the size of the army upon which they had agreed would run 'a grave risk of throwing away the fruits of the victory'.[7] At a meeting with members of the press during the January demonstrations he asserted that fulfilment of the public's demand for a harsh peace would require a disciplined army: 'If we were to appear at the peace conference with an army out of hand and generally speaking with a sense of dissatisfaction and discontent throughout the country, our position would be enormously weakened and the enemy would be correspondingly strengthened and encouraged.'[8]

Faced with what Esher correctly described as the 'incompatible requirements' of 'reserve power to enforce the decisions of the [Peace] Conference and the *necessity* of reducing the Army',[9] the government did not, however, directly attack the problems created by the existing demobilisation scheme until Churchill replaced Milner at the War Office. On 17 January, just days after assuming office, the new War Secretary – much to the consternation of Lloyd George, who was in Paris for the peace talks – presented to his colleagues in London a proposal for a new demobilisation plan, which provided for the retention until the end of April 1920 of over

1 million conscript forces to serve in armies of occupation.[10] Lloyd George refused to allow the Cabinet formally to consider the War Office proposal.[11] He resented Churchill's having initiated discussion of a policy matter without consulting him and believed that the numbers requested by the War Office were unnecessary. Moreover, he feared the political consequences of introducing a bill for the continuation of conscription and thought that there might be further trouble in the army if the government announced that it intended to retain so many conscripts.[12] Other politicians also worried about the consequences of continuing conscription. When members of the Cabinet met informally with War Office officials on 22 January to discuss the proposed plan, Bonar Law expressed concern about the impact on the House of Commons of asking for the continuation of conscription.[13] Austen Chamberlain, now Chancellor of the Exchequer, objected to the size of the proposed force on fiscal as well as political grounds.[14] Nevertheless, disturbed by the situation in the army and unable to offer an alternative proposal, those at the meeting gave their 'unwilling assent'[15] to the War Office plan, and Churchill, Haig and Wilson went to Paris to attempt to win Lloyd George's approval for its formal presentation to the War Cabinet.

When he met with the War Office representatives, Lloyd George, who believed that German disarmament would make it unnecessary to keep a British army on the Rhine after the signature of peace,[16] initially wanted to discuss how to disarm Germany rather than to consider the War Office proposal for a conscript army of occupation.[17] However, the Prime Minister eventually agreed in principle to the retention of conscription although he insisted upon a reduction in the number of divisions to be retained.[18] Despite the opposition of Bonar Law, who feared that 'a formidable opposition would be roused in the country' if 'the Government's first act in Parliament were to pass a Conscription Bill',[19] the Cabinet approved the new demobilisation plan.[20]

The publication on 29 January of the new demobilisation plan providing for discharge on the basis of first in, first out did not end the unrest in the army. On 8 February about 250 troops on leave marched to Whitehall to protest against their return to duty. This so-called Horse Guards Revolution coincided with widespread industrial unrest throughout Britain. Military officials were so alarmed that the War Office distributed questionnaires to all commanding officers to determine whether their troops could be relied upon to maintain domestic order.

Not only did the demobilisation plan's publication not end the unrest in the army, but Churchill's announcement of the need for an interim army – by which he clearly meant a conscript army – to serve while a permanent volunteer army was being created[21] brought the political reaction Bonar Law had predicted. The government's announced policy gave added impetus to the observance of 'No-Conscription Sunday', sponsored by the National Council for Civil Liberties on 2 March. In the House of Commons debates on the bill extending conscription, Labour and independent Liberal MPs – and even a few Coalition Liberals – attacked the government for betraying its election promises.[22] In the March and April by-elections at West Leyton, Central Hull and Central Aberdeen-shire the conscription issue played an important role in the defeat of Coalition candidates by their independent Liberal opponents.[23]

So widespread was the charge that the military service bill violated Lloyd George's campaign pledges that Coalition headquarters provided Coalition MPs with notes for a rebuttal: 'It does not break the Prime Minister's election pledge against conscription. On the contrary it is expressly designed to enable us to carry out the Terms of Peace, one of the objects of which will be to destroy conscription everywhere once and for all.'[24] Thus, once again when faced with opposition to the continuation of conscription at home, Lloyd George linked its abolition in Britain to the peace settlement's assuring its universal abolition.

While the anti-conscription sentiment was not sufficient to prevent passage of the Naval, Military and Air Service Bill, which came into force in mid-April when approved by the House of Lords, the military unrest and opposition to the continuation of con-scription had a significant impact on the position on German disarmament taken by the British policy-makers in Paris, who were considering the fate of the German army while these events were taking place in Britain. The pressures for speedy demobilisation, an end to conscription and a reduction in the size of the British army led the British delegation at the Paris Peace Conference to press for further disarming Germany even before the Allies drafted the peace treaty.

It was the British delegation which introduced the question of German disarmament early in the peace conference's deliberations.

Believing that the speedy disarmament of Germany would make possible Britain's return to a small volunteer army, British policy-makers insisted on the urgency of demanding additional German disarmament. Before his departure for Paris, Balfour had spoken to his niece of the importance of an early return to normal conditions,[25] an important element of which, he believed, would be the return of British troops from Europe.[26] When, despite the pre-conference Anglo-American agreement on disarming Germany as part of the peace settlement, German disarmament was not among the questions proposed for immediate peace conference consideration, the Foreign Secretary on 21 January – at the height of Lloyd George's controversy with Churchill – proposed the appointment of a committee to consider the disarmament question, particularly the disarmament of Germany. In presenting his proposal Balfour not only paid deference to American sensibilities by emphasising the relationship between disarmament and a visible league of nations, but he also introduced the concept which the British hoped would lead the French to abandon their designs on the Rhine, that of the relationship between disarmament and strategic frontier:

He would like to suggest a fourth [committee], namely disarmament, which was so closely related to strategic frontier. He pointed out that if the League of Nations is to be practical, the delegates must make up their minds as soon as possible regarding the question of disarmament. It was most important in this connection, to come to some agreement as to what arms Germany was to be allowed to have. It is evident that a League of Nations would be a sham if there is no disarmament.[27]

The Council of Ten having taken no action on Balfour's proposal, Lloyd George – undoubtedly hoping thereby to undermine Churchill's plan – on 23 January formally submitted a resolution calling for the appointment of a commission to consider the disarmament question: 'to advise on an immediate and drastic reduction in the armed forces of the enemy' and 'to prepare a plan in connection with the League of Nations for a permanent reduction in the burden of military, naval and aerial forces and armaments'.[28] In informing Churchill of his opposition to the retention of a large conscript army, Lloyd George had emphasised the interconnection between German disarmament and the size of the British army: 'If the German Army is to be demobilized, it is absurd to retain so big an Army.' Just as during the election campaign and the Imperial War Cabinet discussions, he had insisted that German disarmament was the prerequisite for British disarmament: 'German demobilization must be the first step.'[29] Accordingly, at the peace conference he followed the approach to which he had secured President Wilson's agreement in December, recommending immediate action on the question of German disarmament but postponement of consideration of general disarmament.[30] Since the French did not want to reduce their armed forces and the Italians had expressed no interest in general disarmament, it is not surprising that they offered no objections to the separation of the issue of German disarmament from that of general disarmament. Rather than creating a disarmament commission, the members of the Council of Ten considered the question of German disarmament themselves, continuing for these discussions to use the title Supreme War Council and appointing committees of experts to advise them on various aspects of the problem. They left to the League of Nations Commission the definition of arms limitation as a universal goal. In this way Lloyd George's general approach to the handling of the disarmament issue became the framework for the peace conference's consideration of the question.

In its specifics, however, Lloyd George's proposal went beyond his agreement with President Wilson and the plan he had presented to the Imperial War Cabinet. Reluctant, as we have seen, to accept Churchill's proposal for the continuation of conscription, Lloyd George urged not just that German disarmament be included in the peace treaty but that further German disarmament be made a condition of again renewing the Armistice, which was due to expire in mid-February. He argued that the immediate reduction of the German army was essential so that Britain would not have to continue conscription: 'Unless the enemy's forces were immediately reduced, the British Government might be forced to maintain compulsory service. He did not know what might be the political result of such a decision.'[31]

Moreover, in addition to demanding a reduction in the size of the German army to the minimum necessary for maintaining internal order, he called also for the limitation of German armaments. Lloyd George's peace conference position on German armaments reflected his belief, strengthened by his experience as Minister of Munitions, in the crucial role played by materiel in determining the outcome of the war. In his wartime speeches he had stressed that the war was a war of equipment, that in the long run supplies were more important than men.[32] While these speeches had been designed to encourage increased munitions production, at the peace conference he expressed the same belief: 'If the Germans maintained armaments and munitions sufficient for an army of two or three million men, their demobilization would be nugatory.'[33] This argument presaged a major theme of his government's post-Versailles policy towards enforcing German disarmament: that Germany's continued possession of war material – rather than the size of its army – was the key to its potential military revival.

At the peace conference, however, he placed equal emphasis on limiting Germany's army and on curbing its armaments. German disarmament was Lloyd George's alternative to the maintenance of a British army large enough to provide the occupation forces requested by Foch: 'Marshal Foch had forwarded a demand for British troops which it would be extremely difficult for the country to honour. It was for this reason that he had suggested as an alternative to increasing the Allied forces the reduction of the enemy's troops.'[34] So convinced was he that immediate German disarmament would provide the solution to the demobilisation difficulties at home that, as we have seen, he initially refused to discuss the War Office's proposal with Churchill and Generals Wilson and Haig.

Lloyd George's demand for speedy German disarmament also reflected Britain's continuing concern about French power and about the implications for Britain's postwar policy of France's European aims. Lloyd George and other British leaders continued to overestimate France's military potential. In early January, House commented on British apprehensions 'over France's growing imperialistic [*sic*] tendencies [*sic*]': 'Every day now there is an indication that she [France] intends to assert herself as the dominant Continental Power . . . I see many evidences that the English are concerned and do not like the prospect.'[35] While French attitudes justified this concern, France's resources did not. General Spears correctly pointed out the discrepancy between French ambitions and French strength:

To-day, perhaps the first time for fifty years, the French are taking themselves seriously as a first-class power.

With a cheerful disregard to the small and shrinking population

and to the economic weakness of FRANCE, many Frenchmen
are giving free rein to violently imperialistic ideas . . .

It must, however, be clearly realised that there is very little
material force behind this aggresiveness [*sic*].[36]

Nevertheless, France's ambitions troubled Lloyd George. Early in
the peace negotiations he denounced French intentions regarding
the Rhine: 'They are on their hind legs . . . Their nightmare is over.
Now they are very imperial in spirit, and I should think they want to
maintain a big army.'[37] Such a policy would, of course, not only
thwart his plans for general disarmament but also threaten the
European balance of power. Although he understood that the quest
for security was a strong motivation for French behaviour,[38] Lloyd
George was disturbed by the size of the French army and especially
by French desires to impose on Germany terms the enforcement of
which would require the maintenance of a large British army. He
believed that disarming Germany would satisfy France's security
needs and therefore end French designs on the Rhine and France's
desire for a continuing British military commitment to the Continent
after the signature of peace. As we have seen, he also expected
German disarmament to lead to a reduction in the size of the French
army.

Lloyd George's desire to impose further German disarmament in
order to make possible a reduction in the size of the Allied
occupation forces brought him into conflict with Foch. Their
disagreement revealed a basic difference in the British and French
concepts of what was necessary to preserve the security of Western
Europe. While Lloyd George believed that the disarmament of
Germany would adequately guarantee France's security, Foch
insisted that only Allied control of the Rhine, which would, of
course, necessitate the retention of large armies of occupation, could
safeguard France. These conflicting viewpoints represented
different approaches to the problem of maintaining postwar
European stability. Lloyd George believed that weakening Germany
without, however, permitting an inordinate increase in French
power would maintain the European balance and hence guarantee
peace. And, as we have seen, he anticipated that the disarmament of
Germany would lead to general disarmament, which would further
ensure the preservation of peace, allowing Britain to concentrate on
domestic problems. In contrast, Foch, doubting the possibility of

effectively disarming Germany, thought it more important to maintain a preponderance of Allied military power in Europe.

On 24 January when Foch and the Allied military advisers attended the Supreme War Council, these two points of view clashed head-on. Foch argued that even if the Allies included additional disarmament demands in the Armistice renewal, in order to have any hope of enforcing these demands – a prospect about which he was pessimistic – they must still retain the occupation forces which he requested. In response Lloyd George sounded a theme which, after the conclusion of peace, became an increasingly important element in the divergence of British and French attitudes towards execution of the disarmament provisions of the treaty: 'Marshal Foch's argument really meant that Germany could never be trusted, and, therefore, that the armies of occupation could never be materially reduced.'[39] Lloyd George contended that, instead of maintaining large armies of occupation, the Allies could better control the situation in Germany through the leverage of food and raw materials and the seizure of arms and that, contrary to Foch's assertion, Germany could be immediately and effectively disarmed. To resolve the impasse, the Supreme War Council appointed a committee, chaired by Louis Loucheur, France's Minister of Armament during the last year of the war, to report both on the strength of the Allied armies which should be maintained in Western Europe during the duration of the Armistice and on demobilisation of the German army, and the guarantees which would be necessary to ensure the surrender of German arms and munitions factories.

The Loucheur Committee's report, which endorsed in principle Lloyd George's proposals, produced even more disagreement than those proposals had, evoking the opposition not only of Foch but also – for quite different reasons – of President Wilson. The Loucheur Committee reported that Germany could be sufficiently disarmed to warrant continued Allied demobilisation before the conclusion of peace if the Allies established an adequate system of control. It recommended a reduction in the size of the German army, the surrender of additional war material, restriction of the manufacture of certain enumerated weapons through the destruction of designated weapons-producing machinery and supervision of factories by an inter-Allied control committee, and military occupation of the Ruhr basin, location of Germany's largest armaments manufacturer and the heart of its mining district.[40]

Despite this last proposal, Foch rejected the idea that there could be effective control of disarmament and insisted on the necessity of maintaining the Allied armies at their current strength.[41]

However, the most important opposition to imposing additional German disarmament as a condition of Armistice renewal came from President Wilson, who opposed the imposition of additional Armistice conditions as 'not sportsmanlike'.[42] Although the Loucheur Committee's technical subcommittee, which had been charged with the task of determining how to prevent Germany's replacing surrendered materiel, had rejected the notion of controlling the manufacture of all armaments as both impracticable and unnecessary and had recommended instead restricting only those weapons which its members regarded as essential for the resumption of hostilities,[43] Wilson criticised its proposals as 'a panic programme.'[44] When the Supreme Council appointed another committee to modify the Loucheur Committee's proposals, he objected to its recommendations as well.[45]

The President still supported the idea of disarming Germany. It was, in fact, he who introduced the concept of German disarmament as punishment, telling the Supreme Council on 12 February that 'the world had a moral right to disarm Germany, and to subject her to a generation of thoughtfulness'.[46] However, Wilson preferred imposing disarmament as part of an early peace rather than as a revision of the Armistice terms.[47] As a result of his objections to the various proposals for demanding disarmament as a condition of Armistice renewal and of Clemenceau's refusal to negotiate the matter with the Germans,[48] one week before the expiration of the Armistice the Supreme Council could agree only to demand that Germany report the quantities of weapons still in its possession.[49]

While the President formally registered his protests against adding to the Armistice conditions, House worked behind the scenes to secure British co-operation in pressing for the immediate drafting of peace terms. Lloyd George had returned to London on 8 February and, according to House, on 9 February Balfour, who headed the British delegation in the Prime Minister's absence, agreed to join with the Americans in working for early agreement on preliminary peace terms.[50]

Other members of the British delegation also reached the conclusion that it was preferable to draw up preliminary peace terms rather than to change the Armistice. Foch's behaviour at the 11

February meeting of the military members of the Joint Military and Economic Committee, which the Supreme Council had appointed to recommend methods for assuring German compliance with the naval and financial conditions of the Armistice, convinced Cecil, Thwaites and Haig that it was in Britain's interest to conclude a preliminary peace. At this meeting Foch reversed his position and, apparently disregarding the wishes of the other members of the subcommittee, submitted a recommendation for the imposition of harsh military conditions at the Armistice renewal.[51] Cecil angrily refused to accept this recommendation and instead supported Thwaites's proposal for the immediate presentation of military and naval peace terms,[52] a recommendation which coincided with the American position. The subcommittee eventually endorsed the Anglo-American position, and the Joint Military and Economic Committee in turn adopted it, agreeing to recommend to the Supreme Council the appointment of a commission to draw up military and naval peace terms.[53] Haig then enlisted Hankey to work behind the scenes to obtain Balfour's and Milner's support for the committee's proposal.[54]

Although Lloyd George still preferred to impose disarmament as a condition of Armistice renewal,[55] the Supreme Council considered the question of a preliminary peace before his views were communicated to Paris. Balfour shared the Prime Minister's concern about the need for speeding up the demobilisation process but, won over by House and Hankey, he now believed that the imposition of preliminary military terms was the best way to accomplish this.[56] Accordingly, on 12 February he endorsed the Joint Military and Economic Committee's recommendation, arguing that Germany must accept final military and naval terms 'in order to enable Europe to demobilise and so to resume its life on a peace footing and re-establish its industries'.[57] On Balfour's initiative, the Supreme Council agreed to renew the Armistice indefinitely and to appoint a committee chaired by Foch to draw up military, naval and air conditions for a preliminary peace.[58] In this way the Supreme Council accepted Lloyd George's view of the importance of prompt attention to the problem of disarming Germany while it rejected his call for making German disarmament a condition of Armistice renewal.

Although Foch now favoured disarming Germany, it soon became clear that there were basic differences in the British and French approaches to accomplishing this objective. These differences derived from the different French and Anglo-American conceptions of the role which German disarmament would play in the preservation of peace. The French continued to believe that German disarmament would not provide an adequate guarantee of their security. Rather, they regarded disarmament as just one – and not the primary – means of weakening Germany. Control of the Rhineland remained the central element of their strategy for permanently diminishing German power. The British and the Americans also wanted to prevent a resurgence of German power, but they did not view the maintenance of postwar peace solely – or even principally – in terms of curbing German power. Even the Francophile Henry Wilson 'want[ed] a Germany sufficiently strong to be no temptation to the French'.[59] Moreover, Lloyd George and President Wilson placed German disarmament in a larger context. As we have seen, they expected German disarmament to be, in the words of Kerr, only 'the first great step in the de-militarisation of the world'.[60]

When the military advisers formulated their recommendations for the military peace terms, these different strategic conceptions, together with domestic political considerations, played a more important role than technical concerns. At the end of December the Imperial War Cabinet had instructed the CIGS to prepare recommendations on both the strength to which the enemy forces should be limited, 'taking into consideration the need for maintaining internal order', and the way in which these forces should be recruited, and Lloyd George had made clear his opposition to the retention of conscription.[61] In January when the Prime Minister had directed Haig to negotiate with Foch the number of British divisions to be retained in the occupation army, he had set forth as the basis of these negotiations the assumption that Germany would be thoroughly disarmed, its military organisation broken up and its munitions works destroyed.[62] Although General Wilson thought that it would be technically impossible to limit either the number of trained men in Germany or the amount of armaments there and was convinced that a nation's potential manpower was the principal determinant of its military strength,[63] he put aside these reservations about the technical difficulties involved in implementing disarmament, and both he and Haig submitted recommendations which clearly coincided with Lloyd George's disarmament policy.

Wilson and Haig based their recommendations upon the idea of destroying 'the system of the "Nation in Arms"'.[64] To accomplish this objective, they advocated the abolition of conscription, the requirement of long-term service in order to prevent the creation of a reserve, limitation of Germany's forces to those necessary to maintain internal order and defend the eastern border against Bolshevik Russia, limitation of Germany's armaments to what they regarded as defensive weaponry and demilitarisation of the Rhineland.[65] Although the proposal for the retention of sufficient forces to protect against an incursion by Russia went beyond the specific directives which they had received, this recommendation corresponded with the political leadership's strategic objective of containing Bolshevism. For this purpose, the military advisers proposed the retention of fifteen divisions[66] – sufficient, they believed, to repel a Russian attack but not enough to enable Germany to exploit the situation in Russia, gain control of the border states and eventually 'obtain a preponderating influence in Russia',[67] a continuing British concern.

For the military advisers, too, strategic and political considerations took precedence over technical ones. In opposing the concept of the nation in arms, the British military advisers were striking not only at what the British believed to be one of the foundations of German militarism but also at the basis of the French military system. Having already blocked inclusion in the league covenant of any reference to the possible abolition of conscription, the French were apparently quite correctly concerned that prohibiting conscription in Germany might set a precedent which the British and the Americans would then attempt to apply to them. Although they offered technical reasons for preferring to allow Germany a short-service conscript army,[68] it seems unlikely that they truly believed that a volunteer army would provide a greater source of national strength. As Paul Birdsall has astutely observed of the French position on German conscription, 'It is hard to take seriously the technical arguments of an expert who declines to turn them to his own advantage'.[69] Rather, the desire to maintain their own large conscript army was undoubtedly a more important motivation.

Several days' debate among the military representatives followed the presentation of the various proposals to the whole committee. Haig, though willing to concede the issues of conscription and length of service since 'the problem concerned France most of all',[70] contended that Foch's scheme did not permit the Germans sufficient forces to oppose Bolshevik Russia; Wilson argued that Lloyd George had promised during the election campaign to abolish conscription; the Americans criticised both the British and the French proposals as humiliating; while, except on the question of the number of troops, Foch held his ground.[71] So that the committee could complete its work and submit proposals to the Supreme Council, the CIGS finally agreed to the submission of Foch's draft, modified to allow the Germans to retain – for the sole purpose of maintaining internal order – an army of 200,000 organised in fifteen divisions.[72] Wilson's willingness to sanction proposals with which he fundamentally disagreed reflected the increasing British concern about the situation in Germany as well as at home and the consequent desire to hasten the conclusion of peace in order to restore both Continental and domestic stability.

Although most British officials – with the exception of some members of the PID[73] – undoubtedly agreed with Lloyd George and Kerr's assessment that German actions since the Armistice indicated that Germany was still 'unrepentant',[74] they nevertheless remained more concerned about the possibility of anarchy leading to the triumph of Bolshevism there than about an early resurgence of German power. According to military evaluations, Germany continued to pose no military threat. Before the February Armistice renewal the Quartermaster-General in London received a report from his representative at the peace conference that even though 'the Boche' was 'getting in a very truculent and defiant mood', he was 'in no condition to fight',[75] and an 18 February report on the condition of the German army described it as 'no longer fit to take the field'.[76]

British officers who had gone into Germany in January and February to evaluate conditions there also reported that Germany posed no military danger.[77] They expressed no concern about the German government's reliance on the Free Corps, the irregular military formations which had put down the January Spartacist outbreak in Berlin and several subsequent uprisings, or the potential for undermining the new republic and perpetuating the tradition of militarism which these forces represented. Indeed, one officer, whose report both Headlam-Morley and General Wilson commended to Lloyd George,[78] concluded after almost a month in Germany that 'any renewal of militarism at the present time, or, indeed, for many years to come, is entirely out of the question'. Ignoring the role of the Free Corps, he reported that the German government lacked the forces for crushing Bolshevism.[79] What these officers feared was not a revival of militarism but a collapse into anarchy leading to Bolshevism, which they believed would not be contained in Germany. One, for example, warned of the danger of Germany's succumbing to Bolshevism, which would then spread westwards: 'I believe that Germany at the present moment is on the brink of a volcano which may burst forth at any moment. It would be folly to suppose that the ensuing disaster would be confined to Germany.'[80] Notwithstanding that much of these officers' information had been derived from official German sources, the War Office officials who processed their reports accepted them as accurate assessments of the German situation.[81]

Events in Germany beginning in late February seemed to British officials monitoring the situation there to bring closer the complete collapse of order. The 21 February assassination of the Bavarian prime minister was followed quickly by further political violence in Munich, the adjournment of Parliament and the calling of a general strike. In Berlin, street violence and armed Communist uprisings followed the proclamation of a general strike on 3 March. Three days after the onset of civil disorder in Bavaria the head of the War Office's division of military intelligence responsible for intelligence on Germany concluded from the first returned officers' reports and other recent information that although 'from a military point of view, the present German Army is no danger to the Allies, and can only become so by a complete change in the spirit of the nation', 'the infectious nature of Bolshevism' meant that the instability in Germany constituted a serious threat to the Allies.[82]

Some officials in London were sufficiently concerned about the situation in Germany to sanction an increase in the power of the German army. The Deputy Director of Military Intelligence was so alarmed at the prospect of Bolshevism in Germany that in a reaction reminiscent of that of the political leadership in November he told Thwaites, 'I personally would run any risk of Germany recovering its military position rather than see it go Bolshevist'.[83]

The reaction of George Saunders of the PID provides an even more striking example of the extent to which fear of anarchy in Germany affected attitudes towards the role of the German army. As Berlin correspondent of *The Times* during the years of heightened Anglo-German rivalry, Saunders had played a major role in arousing British suspicions of Germany. Unlike many of his colleagues in the PID, he did not believe that Germany's defeat meant the permanent crushing of Prussian dominance in Germany.[84] Yet, despite his revulsion against Prussianism,[85] he regarded a 'great Central European Teutonic State or close alliance of States' as essential to European stability.[86] Since Bolshevism threatened internal order in Germany and therefore European order, he did not believe that the Allies should further weaken the already disintegrating German army: 'In order to suppress it [Bolshevism] the Government must be allowed by the Allies to reestablish some sort of military order and discipline. This it is very difficult for Germany to do, while at the same time conforming to the demands of the Allies with regard to the Army.'[87] Thus, even at the time when the peace conference on Britain's initiative was considering how to disarm Germany, the idea that German military power might be a force for preserving European stability had not completely disappeared. By the end of March, this idea had gained greater currency not just in London but also among the British policy-makers in Paris.

In February and early March, however, most British officials did not go this far, although they were deeply disturbed by the situation in Germany. On his return to Paris from London, General Wilson found his own 'grave fears of anarchy in Germany' confirmed by other military members of the delegation as well as by Milner.[88] The events in Munich and Berlin contributed to the British delegation's concern and uncertainty about conditions in Germany and strengthened pressures not only for providing food relief, as those returning from Germany urged,[89] but also for speeding the presentation of peace terms before Germany sank into 'a sea of anarchy'.[90] On 4 March Headlam-Morley reported from Paris:

The parole now is to speed up and to get the Preliminaries of Peace settled with Germany . . . The reports from Germany during the last few days have been very bad, and it looks as if the second revolution, which has been so often foretold, is on the point of breaking out. If it does, the consequences, not only in Germany but throughout Central Europe, will be very serious.[91]

Hankey worried that if the peace conference did not quickly reach agreement on terms, there might be no German government to which to present them: 'All the evidence we get shows that there really is an appalling state of affairs in Germany. The question is: can we get through the preliminaries of peace in sufficient time, and in such form, as to save Germany?'[92]

At the same time, the continuing demobilisation discontent and growing industrial unrest at home were also propelling British leaders to seek the speedy conclusion of peace, while Dominion prime ministers had begun to express their impatience with what they regarded as the conference's dilatoriness in addressing itself to the work of drafting the treaty with Germany. In urging his colleagues in the British Empire Delegation to support the hastening of the peace conference's work, Balfour on 20 February cited 'the growing impatience' of Allied public opinion.[93] The *Daily Mail* continued its campaign for the speedy conclusion of peace, with a 24 February leading article calling attention to the deleterious economic consequences for Britain of delay, and on 27 February Jones wrote to Hankey that 'the Conclusion of Peace is really becoming urgent from a Trade and Labour standpoint'.[94] Borden, too, added his voice to those protesting at the delay in demobilisation, communicating to Lloyd George the impatience of the Canadian troops because the failure to conclude peace with Germany was preventing their return home.[95] While Borden expressed his views privately to Lloyd George and other members of the delegation,[96] Hughes typically chose a public forum to voice his discontent. Towards the end of February he left Paris to deliver a series of speeches to the Australian Corps in Belgium in which he criticised the slow work of the peace conference.[97]

Foch, too, wanted to hasten settlement of those terms in which France was directly interested. On 18 February, with Clemenceau's approval, he proposed that the preliminary peace terms include not only the disarmament of Germany but also the definition of its frontiers and the imposition of an indemnity.[98] Foch's proposal led Balfour and House, acting as head of the American delegation in President Wilson's absence, again to discuss the question of accelerating the work of the peace conference,[99] and on 20 February the Foreign Secretary, as we have seen, submitted the question to his colleagues in the British Empire Delegation. The Dominion leaders were divided in their approach to the question of the desirable scope of a preliminary peace. Borden predictably endorsed Balfour's proposal for speeding completion of preliminary economic and territorial as well as military, naval and air terms, while Sir Joseph

Cook of Australia and Sir Joseph Ward of New Zealand preferred to proceed with the immediate settlement of military and naval peace terms. The Australasian ministers, who favoured a more punitive peace than Borden, believed that Germany's early disarmament would reduce the likelihood of resistance to other peace terms. The Cabinet members who were present also disagreed. Milner supported Balfour, but Barnes preferred to impose the military and naval terms first. As the ranking defence official present, Admiral Wemyss told the ministers that early settlement of the military and naval terms would simplify the work of Britain's defence services. The meeting eventually agreed to reject the idea of postponing the presentation of the military and naval terms until the territorial and economic terms were formulated but to recommend that the Supreme Council begin consideration of these terms as well.[100] After obtaining Lloyd George's approval, Balfour submitted this proposal to the Supreme Council, which on 24 February agreed to proceed with consideration of other preliminary peace terms, leaving open the question of presenting first the military, naval and air terms.[101]

The separate presentation of the military terms was, in fact, a dead issue. Both the French and the Americans wanted to present the peace treaty to the Germans as a whole.[102] Moreover, the main impetus for speedy German disarmament had come from Lloyd George, and he no longer seems to have been particularly interested in immediately disarming Germany. On 26 February Kerr wrote to the Prime Minister stating that he, Balfour and Hankey agreed that unless Lloyd George was 'anxious to push through the disarmament of Germany independently of the other preliminaries of peace', there was no need for him to rush his return to Paris.[103] While speedy disarmament of Germany might have made possible the announcement of a reduction in the number of conscript forces the government intended to retain, thus damping some of the political heat generated by its plan to extend conscription, Lloyd George did not return to the peace conference to press for Germany's immediate disarmament. Instead, he remained in London to address two sessions of the National Industrial Conference, which the government had convened as a means of allaying labour discontent. In addition, General Wilson did not agree to the presentation of Foch's draft military terms until 28 February, and the Supreme Council did not begin to discuss them until 3 March,[104] by which time the work of the commissions formulating the other treaty provisions was well under way. Hankey wrote to Lloyd George on 1 March: 'All the questions . . . are more or less connected. We are coming to a stage when they will have to be considered, more or less, as a whole.'[105]

The military conditions submitted by Foch aroused considerable uneasiness among British policy-makers, already disturbed by French proposals for the Rhine and by what they perceived as Germany's internal disintegration and its susceptibility to Bolshevism. Their reactions underscore the differences between the British and French approaches to postwar security. Both nations expected the treaty to provide security against Germany, but influential members of the British delegation believed that any postwar security arrangement which did not also provide security *for* Germany would be undermined from its inception. Kerr foresaw that if the treaty did not allow Germany sufficient forces for defending its borders, circumstances would force the Allies to make concessions in this area, thereby setting a precedent for further revisions: 'Necessity will force us to allow Germany to increase her forces and once we begin this process we shall never be able to stop it.'[106] Balfour argued that if German armaments were to be 'mercilessly cut down to the amount necessary to maintain internal order', then Germany must be given some guarantee against external aggression.[107] According to Haig, the Foreign Secretary continued to recognise 'the dangers of a strong Germany'.[108] He apparently objected to Foch's proposals because he believed that the drastic disarmament of Germany without a concomitant guarantee of German security would lead to evasion and the resurgence of militarism[109] as he believed that Napoleon's restrictions had led to the rise of Prussian militarism.

The British, as we have seen, also believed that a stable Germany was essential to European security. Even Hughes was willing to concede Germany the forces necessary for preserving internal order.[110] Most British officials wanted to strengthen the new government in Germany, and they feared that French policies might instead undermine its position. The PID had reported in December that significant segments of French opinion preferred, at least temporarily, an anarchic to an orderly Germany either because they hoped that instability would lead to Germany's disintegration and hence encourage the separation of the Rhineland or because they feared France's being outstripped by a stable democratic Germany.[111] The French position during the Armistice renewal discussions had awakened the same concerns. Haig worried that France's object was 'revenge; to grind Germany to powder',[112] that the French wanted 'the destruction of the German people with his machinery so that there will be no competitor against French trade'.[113] Even Derby, who sympathised with the French point of view,[114] reported that Clemenceau was 'a revengeful old man' who wished 'to absolutely crush Germany so that quite apart from any Military position she shall be unable to do anything commercially for 100 years'.[115]

British policy-makers also wanted stringent peace terms but for different reasons than the French. They wanted severe economic terms in order to assure that Britain would receive its share of economic compensation from Germany. Moreover, the anti-German sentiment manifested in the election campaign was now expressed in the House of Commons by a group of Conservative MPs whose demands for a harsh peace focused on the economic terms, and Lloyd George 'did not want to let the Conservatives "throw him" on a question of such popular concern'.[116] In addition, Lloyd George believed that a punitive peace, by demonstrating that militarism did not pay, would act as a deterrent to the revival of militarism in Germany and to the resort to aggression by other powers as well.

But, unlike the French, the British no longer perceived Germany as a direct threat to their security. During the pre-Armistice negotiations the Supreme Council had agreed that the interned German fleet would not be returned, and early in the peace conference it had ordered the destruction or surrender of those German submarines not already delivered under the terms of the Armistice. It had also agreed in January that the captured German colonies would not be returned. Although the Supreme Council had not yet agreed upon the terms of Germany's aerial disarmament, few civilian leaders fully realised the potential of air power. Ignoring the lessons of 1914, British policy-makers therefore did not consider the safety of the British Empire to be at stake in the negotiation of the remaining peace terms, whereas from the French point of view the survival of France depended upon the territorial and military terms still to be arranged.

Most British policy-makers feared the consequences for Germany – and hence for Europe – of what they regarded as France's unnecessarily humiliating demands. They thought that Foch's military proposals, which General Wilson characterised as 'full of pinpricks'[117] and Bonar Law decried as 'a mass of pinpricks, involving every calculated humiliation',[118] were part of a French pattern of vengeance, which would thwart their own hopes for stabilising the situation in Germany. When Kerr reported Foch's proposals to Lloyd George, he urged that on his return to Paris the Prime Minister should 'insist on a sane policy towards Germany': 'I am all for imposing stiff terms on Germany, but they must be terms which give the German people some hope and some independence. If the French have their way they will give them neither.'[119]

In addition to being concerned about the immediate consequences of presenting humiliating military terms, the British government viewed the long-term strategic implications of such terms very differently from the French. Britain's defence policy was predicated on the maintenance of the balance of power in Europe and hence in the view of most policy-makers required a counterbalance to France, now the strongest power on the Continent. The Coalition expected the eventual reintegration of Germany into the European system both to fulfil this function and to prevent its allying itself with Bolshevik Russia, thus not only drastically altering the European balance but again posing a potential danger to British holdings in the East. The French, in contrast, believed that perpetuating the relationship of victor to vanquished was their only safeguard against renewed German aggression.

Despite their insistence on stringent military terms, the French had made clear their continuing lack of faith in German disarmament as an adequate guarantee of their security.[120] Lloyd George believed – quite correctly – that Foch's Rhineland proposal meant that, regardless of the treaty's military provisions, he did not expect effective German disarmament: 'Marshal Foch was not going on the assumption of a Germany disarmed, but on that of two or three millions of German soldiers under arms.'[121] Although the problems raised in the 1917 and 1918 Imperial War Cabinet discussions and in the various memoranda which had considered the disarmament question had still not been resolved, Lloyd George was convinced that the Allies could effectually disarm Germany. For the Prime Minister, the destruction of Germany's weapons-producing machinery provided the key to its immediate disarmament. He doubted the long-term efficacy of Allied inspection and control,[122] but he believed that the efficiency of British intelligence would prevent extensive clandestine rearmament.[123]

In addition to this technical control, Lloyd George apparently believed that there would be economic, strategic and popular constraints on German rearmament. Echoing the Hughes Committee's reports, he told the War Cabinet on 4 March that 'the imposition of a huge indemnity which would prevent the Germans spending money on an army' would provide the 'best safeguard' against Germany's rebuilding its army.[124] Thus while Ward had argued that disarming Germany would help to obtain an indemnity,[125] Lloyd George contended that exaction of an indemnity would ensure German disarmament. Since he told House two days later that he knew that Germany could not pay the indemnity which Britain was demanding,[126] there is a question as to how seriously he took his own argument. He may simply have been trying to convince those of his colleagues who seemed inclined to accede to French wishes regarding the Rhine that German disarmament would, as he believed, sufficiently guarantee France's security.

One of the assumptions upon which Lloyd George based his assurances that German disarmament could be enforced was American participation in upholding the European settlement. Despite the Republican victory in the American congressional election on the eve of the peace conference, widely interpreted in Europe as a repudiation of President Wilson, Lloyd George was confident that if Germany openly declared its intention to rearm, the United States would be prepared to enforce the disarmament provisions of the treaty: 'There was no doubt that the United States would be prepared to take up arms again in order to ensure the disarmament of any offending Power, though she would not go to war for indemnities or territorial acquisition.'[127]

However, for long-term German disarmament he placed his greatest reliance not on these strategic, economic and technical constraints but on the overriding constraint of public opinion. Explaining the basis of Lloyd George's policy for preserving peace, Kerr paraphrased its chief assumption: 'If only we can destroy armaments and interrupt conscription for five or six years . . . the people of Europe themselves who are now all democracies could be trusted to see that the armaments process was never started again . . . the public opinion of Europe being the only real security of disarmament.'[128] Retaining his Liberal beliefs about the responsibility for the outbreak of war in 1914 and the general causes of war, Lloyd George put his trust in the German people and the new

German democracy to ensure Germany's disarmament. According to this Liberal view, as democracies do not wage aggressive war, they do not need vast armaments and armies; since the German people, who had been led into war by a militaristic government, were now in control of their government, they would not sanction rearmament. Hence Germany – because it was a democracy – could be relied upon to comply with the disarmament provisions of the treaty. This trust in Germany's good faith – like the 1914 distinction between the German people and their Prussian rulers from which it derived – though based on Liberal assumptions, soon gained wider currency. It was to be an important element of post-Versailles British attitudes and policy towards Germany and to bring the British government into conflict with France over strategies for executing the disarmament provisions of the treaty just as it brought the two powers into conflict at the peace conference over the content of those provisions.

While the French viewed German disarmament as merely another means of weakening Germany, British policy, as enunciated by Lloyd George since the election campaign, regarded German disarmament as the first step towards general disarmament. Lloyd George wanted not just to ensure against a revival of Prussian militarism but to destroy militarism throughout Europe, including France. As Kerr explained the Prime Minister's policy to House, 'The real security for the future was to break the habit of militarism in Europe'.[129] This goal, of course, conflicted with France's aims of maintaining its own military preparedness through a large conscript army and of maintaining a preponderance of Allied military power in Europe after the signature of peace. These different conceptions of the function of German disarmament underlay the Anglo-French struggle at the peace conference over the question of the retention of conscription in Germany.

For Lloyd George, the prohibition of conscription in Germany was essential from the point of view both of political expediency and of political conviction. In the election campaign he had pledged to end conscription in Germany in order to make possible its abolition in Britain, and he was being accused of violating his campaign pledges. His peace conference notes on conscription indicate his concern with the domestic political consequences of the conference's decision on the issue: 'Promise [sic] there w[oul]d be no conscription after war. Suppression of conscription in Germany.'[130] Moreover, he was committed to the destruction of militarism, and he agreed with Smuts's identification of conscription as 'the taproot of militarism'. Hence, in order to prevent the revival of militarism in Germany, the Allies must prohibit conscription there.

In early January Headlam-Morley had drafted a memorandum to rebut Lloyd George's and Smuts's belief in the link between conscription and militarism. Disagreeing fundamentally with Smuts's December memorandum, Headlam-Morley maintained not only that conscription was not the cause of militarism but that it indeed made war less likely. Since under a conscript system the middle class, which had the greatest political power, would have to fight, its reluctance to do so would, he believed, lessen the likelihood of war. Drawing upon his knowledge of German history, he turned his attention specifically to the Prussian military system, which Lloyd George was fond of citing as justification for his position. Headlam-Morley pointed out that Prussian militarism had resulted from the special position of the officer corps in Germany, not from the policy of compulsory service. Contrary to the views of Britain's military advisers, he contended, moreover, that a long-term service army might well promote the growth of militarism.[131] Tyrrell and Cecil had considered this paper important enough to circulate to the Cabinet before the Peace Conference, and Cecil in circulating it had noted that 'its conclusions . . . seem to me to justify great caution in dealing with the Disarmament question'.[132] But in view of the diminished influence of the Foreign Office, the lack of support for Headlam-Morley's position among the more influential members of the delegation and the strong political and ideological motivations for ending conscription, it is not surprising that the paper did not alter the Prime Minister's position.

Whether or not they agreed that conscription was the source of militarism, Lloyd George's closest advisers joined him in opposing its retention in Germany.[133] Balfour, who had been away from the Foreign Office when the Headlam-Morley paper was drafted and circulated, did not agree with the paper's premise. Rather, he subscribed to Lloyd George's view that Britain and America were 'out to destroy Militarism' and therefore 'must necessarily look at the question [of conscription] with somewhat different eyes' from France and Italy. He attacked Foch's proposal not only from this perspective of 'high international policy' but also from the standpoint of 'Military expediency', arguing that by allowing the annual training of 200,000 men it would not accomplish its military objective but would over time provide Germany with millions of trained men. Acknowledging that fulfilment of the proposals for destruction and limitation of armaments would leave insufficient equipment for an army of this size, he asked somewhat sarcastically whether Foch intended to rely for Germany's disarmament mainly on the limitation of armaments, a notion which Foch had clearly rejected: 'Is he prepared, in other words, to admit that his scheme does not prevent the training of a large number of men, but only the supply of these trained men with materials of war?' While not actually rejecting Foch's proposals, Balfour called for their careful civilian review.[134]

General Wilson also made clear his opposition to Foch's proposal for a conscript army and lobbied for its rejection.[135] According to Wilson, the voluntary principle had wide support among the British delegation, with Hankey, Kerr, Cecil and Milner also opposing allowing conscription in Germany.[136] Therefore when Lloyd George on his return to Paris opposed Foch's proposal in the Supreme Council, he had the support of the most important members of the British delegation.

Accordingly, Lloyd George informed the Supreme Council on 6 March that Britain could not accept Foch's proposals 'without large modifications'.[137] Although General Wilson recorded in his diary that Lloyd George made clear his opposition to conscription, the minutes of the meeting indicate rather that, as House commented, the Prime Minister skilfully couched his objections in terms not of his opposition to conscription but of his concern for French security.[138] Employing Balfour's argument about the trained manpower potential which Foch's proposal would provide, he protested against the annual recruitment of men:

> Why should the Allies present Germany a scheme which would enable her to raise four or five million men in the next twenty years? . . . under the proposed scheme, Germany would have an Army of three to four million trained men led not by donkeys, but by officers who had had considerable war experience. Surely that could not be called disarmament. He himself would be very sorry to leave France after the signing of peace with that threat facing her across the Rhine.[139]

When Foch, using an argument similar to Headlam-Morley's, insisted that cadres, not soldiers, were the key to the reconstitution of a large well-trained army and that Lloyd George's proposal for long-term service would provide these cadres, the Prime Minister countered that the officers who had served in the war would be available for training recruits and that therefore 'the annual renewal of the whole army as suggested [by Foch] merely meant in the course of years the creation of an enormous army'.[140] Thus, in his determination to end conscription he did not recognise that long-term service was more likely to lead, as Headlam-Morley had pointed out, to the development of a professional army, to the existence of which Lloyd George himself attributed the war.

Lloyd George's tactics were successful. The Supreme Council having agreed to his submitting an alternative proposal for discussion,[141] he worked behind the scenes to ensure its acceptance. On 7 March in an unofficial meeting with Clemenceau and House in which they discussed the whole range of issues before the peace conference, Lloyd George, having enlisted House's support in advance, won the French Premier's acceptance of the principle of a long-term service volunteer army. The three agreed that the treaty would restrict Germany to a twelve-year service volunteer army of a maximum strength of 200,000.[142] With Clemenceau now supporting the requirement of a volunteer army, Supreme Council approval that afternoon followed as a matter of course despite the opposition of the French military advisers.[143]

Thus Lloyd George had fulfilled his campaign pledge and achieved what he regarded as the essential component of his overall policy objective regarding conscription and the destruction of militarism. The prohibition of conscription in Germany was a sufficiently severe peace condition to satisfy Conservative opinion in Britain while, since it held the promise of the complete abolition of compulsory military service, it pleased Radicals as well. Both the *Daily Mail* and the *Daily News* greeted the abolition of conscription in Germany as the most significant accomplishment of the peace conference thus far.[144] Lloyd George himself believed, like the *Daily News*, that the end of conscription in Germany would mean its abolition throughout Europe. Clemenceau's acquiescence in the application of the voluntary principle to Germany apparently reinforced the Prime Minister's belief that once Germany was deprived of a large conscript army, France would abandon conscription. He told Stevenson after the meeting, 'What I proposed practically amounts to the abolition of conscription in Europe'.[145]

Having won his point on the method of recruitment of the German army, Lloyd George made a concession to Foch on the question of its size. When the military advisers met to adapt their recommendations to the guidelines adopted by the Supreme Council, they agreed – over the objections of the French – to limit the size of the German army to 140,000.[146] Foch, however, pressed for its reduction to 100,000. In another private meeting with Clemenceau and House the Prime Minister – against the advice of the CIGS – agreed to the French proposal,[147] and the Supreme Council approved it that afternoon despite Balfour's protest against so greatly weakening Germany.[148]

Except for the question of the duration of supervision, which was a point of contention between the French and the Americans, the other major military conditions were ratified without controversy.[149] On 10 March when the Supreme Council approved the reduction of the German army to 100,000, it also agreed that Germany would not be permitted heavy armaments and that other armaments would be drastically limited and their manufacture severely restricted, that German fortifications in the west would be dismantled and no new fortifications constructed and that Germany would be forbidden to maintain a general staff.[150] While the Supreme Council also agreed to establish an inter-Allied commission to supervise execution of these provisions, it did not resolve the issue of the duration of the commission's control until 17 March when it decided that supervision would last, in Balfour's words, 'during an indefinite, not an eternal period'.[151]

The reduction in the size of the army meant that the military conditions which the Supreme Council endorsed were – with the exception of the duration of control – more stringent than Foch's original proposals. General Wilson thought them 'much too drastic',[152] and Headlam-Morley warned other members of the Foreign Office that if similar restrictions were not applied to the rest of Europe, 'the inevitable result will be that Germany . . . will use her whole force to overthrow the settlement'.[153] As we have seen, Balfour, Kerr and Bonar Law had also expressed serious misgivings about the severity of Foch's proposals.

Moreover, in accepting the reduction of the army to 100,000, Lloyd George had put aside his own repeatedly reiterated concern that a drastic limitation of the size of the German army would promote evasion and hence foster the resurgence of militarism. Thus he had violated the precept which he had insisted should be a guideline in disarming Germany and had agreed to the type of restriction which he believed had led to the development of Prussian militarism. Although there is not sufficient evidence to reach a definite conclusion about why he not only disregarded the views of his closest advisers but also abandoned his own position, there is a clue in a decision taken at the 10 March meeting at which he agreed to the 100,000-man army. At this meeting Lloyd George, Clemenceau and House also agreed to appoint a committee to discuss the French proposals for the Rhine,[154] and it seems likely that Lloyd George hoped, by strengthening the disarmament provisions, to win concessions from the French in these negotiations. The imposition of severe military conditions (which, as we have seen, he not only anticipated the League of Nations would eventually revise but expected would lead to general disarmament) would have a less destabilising impact on Germany than its dismemberment through detachment of the Rhineland. Moreover, the prospect of Germany's disarmament might be used as leverage to lessen France's territorial demands.

If Lloyd George expected his acquiescence in the reduction of the German army to lead France to abandon its insistence on a strategic frontier,[155] he again misjudged the extent of French concern about security against a revival of German power. The military conditions approved by the Supreme Council would deprive Germany of the means for waging war and for making preparations for war. Special provision had been made to ensure against a German invasion of France and Belgium. The failure to specify the duration of control, though intended by the British and Americans to prevent permanent control, would nevertheless give France a basis for asserting the right to continued control. Yet the French remained unconvinced that German disarmament would guarantee their security. In the aftermath of the failure of the committee discussing the Rhine to reach agreement, when Lloyd George and President Wilson offered an Anglo-American guarantee of French security if France would abandon its demand for separation and occupation of the Rhineland, Clemenceau demanded other physical guarantees in exchange because 'the limitation of the military forces of Germany will not be a sufficient guarantee against this danger [a recurrence of German aggression]'.[156] Thus the achievement of Lloyd George's objective regarding German disarmament had not produced one of its intended results. The incorporation of stringent disarmament

10

Peace Conference Policy:
The Politics and Strategy of Moderation

For Lloyd George, especially, Clemenceau's insistence that German disarmament and an Anglo-American guarantee were not adequate safeguards of France's security meant that the peace conference had reached a crisis. Inability to reach agreement on guarantees of French security meant a further postponement of the conclusion of peace and the British still regarded the treaty's speedy completion as a matter of urgency, both because of their continuing fears of Bolshevism in Germany and the rest of Europe and because of the need to deal with domestic problems. The situation in Germany still appeared threatening. Although by 16 March the Free Corps had succeeded in crushing the Berlin uprising, the Political Intelligence Department reported that 'it is impossible at present to say whether the danger of Spartacism in Berlin and throughout Germany has been finally arrested'.[1] At home there was increasing labour unrest. Lloyd George feared 'a Soviet Republic' in Britain if the government did not gain the upper hand in a threatened miners' strike,[2] but the pressures of the peace negotiations prevented his return home to deal with the situation.

Although he had been successful on the conscription issue, the rest of his peace conference strategy seemed on the verge of collapse. In Lloyd George's view the failure to reach agreement on French security jeopardised the continued existence of the alliance,[3] already troubled by disagreements in other areas. The British had not yet attained their objectives regarding reparations and were meeting resistance from the French as well as the Americans. As in the pre-Armistice negotiations, there was a conflict with the United States over the question of sea power. The British and the Americans disagreed over the disposition of the German fleet, and the United States was threatening to outbuild the British navy. In addition, the conference had been unable to decide how to deal with the problem of Russia.

Moreover, there was growing concern among leading members of the British delegation about the cumulative severity of the peace terms being drafted by the various commissions. In addition to the military, naval and air terms upon which agreement had just been reached and the decision early in the conference not to return the German colonies, the British anticipated the imposition of a heavy indemnity. Territorially, Germany would lose Alsace-Lorraine. In the east it seemed likely that parts of Prussia would be included in Poland; while in the west the French were demanding control not only of the Rhineland but also of the Saar, and the Belgians were claiming the districts of Eupen and Malmédy.

Those British policy-makers who expressed concern about the severity of the peace conditions were apprehensive about the consequences for British interests of an inordinate temporary weakening or a permanent alienation of Germany. On 21 March Wiseman reported to Reading that 'general opinion seems to be tending towards fairly moderate treatment of Germany, in order not to crush her morale, the idea that a reasonably strong German State is a healthy thing for Europe'.[4]

Balfour was one of those who was concerned about the consequences of imposing drastic terms on Germany. Fearing a repetition of what he believed had happened after Napoleon's defeat of Prussia, the Foreign Secretary, as we have seen, thought that the military terms were too severe. In opposing the reduction of the German army to 100,000, he reiterated the argument he had used against Foch's proposals for reduction of German armaments, asserting that if the Allies demanded such a reduction in the German army without also devising a plan for general disarmament, then they must give Germany some other guarantee against invasion:

> The army of Germany was to be reduced to a police force, and that a small one. In that case Germany must be secured against invasion . . . If the Germans were told that they were to have only 100,000 armed men, while France, Poland or Bohemia could have as many as they wished, they would say that the Allied Powers were leaving them at the mercy even of their small neighbours . . . some such guarantee [against invasion]

would have to be found if the Conference made Germany powerless for attack and weak for defence.[5]

Otherwise, he implied, the Allies would be inviting non-compliance.

Balfour believed that French policy was misguided. Although French assumptions about an inevitable revival of German power closely paralleled the views which he had expressed in his 1916 memorandum, the Foreign Secretary, commenting on Clemenceau's demand for physical guarantees, argued that the changes in European power politics resulting from the war wouuld lead a resurgent Germany to direct its ambitions eastwards rather than against France: 'If there is a renewal of German world politics, it is towards the East rather than towards the West that her ambitions will probably be directed.' He therefore thought that any effort to preserve European stability which focused only on Germany's western borders would be doomed to failure: 'No attempt to guard against the dangers of the future can be deemed other than narrow and incomplete which concentrates its whole attention upon bridge-heads and strategic frontiers, upon the Rhine and the Treaty of 1814, and draws all its inspiration from Generals and Statesmen absorbed in the Military memories of 1870 and 1914.' Rather, the only solution to the problem of the re-emergence of a Germany determined 'again to pursue a policy of world domination' would be 'a change in the international system of the world'.[6]

Like Balfour, General Wilson rejected the notion of the Rhine as the Allied powers' strategic frontier[7] and focused on the likelihood of Germany's turning its attention eastwards. Unlike Balfour, however, he was concerned that such a development would eventually have a devastating impact on the West. Alarmed by 'the crushing terms, in every sphere, we are proposing to put on the Boches', he feared that Germany would reject them[8] and then, if the Allies did not take preventive steps, ally itself with Russia and Japan, with the result that 'we would see East and West over-run by Bolshevism in one form or another'.[9] Scoffing at the idea of the creation of a new international system, he rejected reliance on the League of Nations and a continued alignment with the United States to counter this development and advocated instead a return to the prewar system of alliances. So completely had anti-Bolshevism superseded his longstanding Germanophobia that he endorsed an alliance with France and Germany against Russia and Japan as a strategy for

preserving Western Europe and the British Empire from
Bolshevism.[10]

After hearing Wilson propound his views, Hankey drafted a
memorandum for Lloyd George in which he asked the Prime
Minister to hear the CIGS's case firsthand and also expressed his
own reservations about the way the treaty was developing and the
implications of the projected peace terms for the maintenance of
European stability. He reminded Lloyd George that Kerr had
frequently pointed out that 'while every exaction on Germany can be
justified on its merits, the accumulation of these will put Germany in
an utterly impossible position',[11] and his memorandum reflected this
outlook.

Like General Wilson, Hankey feared Bolshevism as a fundamental
threat to European civilisation; he contended, therefore, that the
peace terms must promote the creation of a barrier against its
westward spread. Pointing out that in the new situation which the
war had created in Central and Eastern Europe only Germany was
potentially strong enough to serve as this barrier, he maintained that
the treaty, as it was developing, would instead foster the disintegrating tendencies in an 'exhausted, depleted, crippled and reduced'
Germany, thus opening the way to Bolshevism. Not only did
Hankey, like Balfour, assert that the 'humiliating naval, military and
air terms' already adopted would 'deprive Germany of the physical
force required to resist external attack', which, he believed, was
'more likely to come from Bolshevism than any other quarter', but
he also declared that the psychological impact of the other terms
being prepared would make the German people susceptible to
Bolshevik propaganda, Bolshevism's 'other and perhaps more
dangerous weapon'. He argued that though the terms being
contemplated were justified as punishment, strategic considerations
should take precedence over the desire to impose a vindictive peace
and the Allies should not pursue a policy which would promote the
alignment of a Bolshevik Germany with Bolshevik Russia:

> Our first object is not to secure the humiliation of Germany, but
> the peace of the world. What prospect is there of peace if the
> teaming [*sic*] millions of Russia and Siberia are to be organised
> by German brains under the banner of Bolshevism? Look at a
> map of the world. Germany may either become the barrier
> against the westward penetration of Bolshevism, which may

then burn itself out, but it is equally well situated to become the head and the brain. Are we not at the parting of the ways? May not the future of civilisation depend upon which path Germany is forced or allowed to take?[12]

Like General Wilson, Hankey advocated an eventual anti-Bolshevik alignment with Germany. He thought that through the peace terms 'the ground should be so prepared that an eventual cooperation with Germany against Bolshevism should be capable of realisation'. He recommended as guidelines for a policy which would accomplish this objective: (1) impressing the German people with 'the enormity of their crimes', (2) providing them with the physical force for resisting Bolshevism and (3) bolstering their self-respect so that they would be resistant to Bolshevism. To reconcile these principles in application, he made several specific recommendations, including the imposition of drastic penalties of limited duration, such as a temporary occupation of the Rhineland, and stockpiling the weapons to be surrendered by Germany so that they could be gradually returned 'if it becomes necessary to use Germany as a physical barrier against Bolshevism'. In addition, like Balfour, he advocated guaranteeing Germany's frontiers, but only on condition that Germany aid the Allies against Bolshevism.[13] Probably drawing upon Kerr's earlier proposal that rather than presenting the disarmament demands 'as a new humiliation on Germany', the Allies should present them to the German people 'as part of the peace programme of the world',[14] he recommended 'a preamble to the naval, military, and air terms of Peace indicating that the disarmament of Germany was part of the disarmament of the world', and, like Kerr, he advised generally avoiding 'the appearance of vindictiveness' in the treaty.[15] Thus Hankey recommended a policy of moderate conciliation in order to win Germany over to the anti-Bolshevik camp.

After receiving Hankey's memorandum Lloyd George decided to meet with a small group of advisers to review Britain's peace conference strategy and its postwar strategic options. For this task he chose not experts on Germany or Europe but a committed navalist and three men whose primary concern was the empire, and on 22 March he withdrew to Fontainebleau with Hankey, Kerr, Wilson and Montagu to consider the situation.[16] According to Stevenson, Lloyd George went to Fontainebleau 'determined to force decisions on the vital points during the coming week'.[17] The result was his famous Fontainebleau Memorandum. The memorandum was a manifestation not only of Lloyd George's desire to break the impasse in the negotiations but also of his belief that public opinion in Britain, impatient for a return to peace conditions and unwilling to tolerate a settlement which would require the commitment of British forces to Europe, was becoming more moderate.[18]

While Lloyd George regarded Germany in defeat as 'just a bleeding torso of the Germany that was',[19] in the Fontainebleau Memorandum he acknowledged its potential power for overturning the European settlement:

> France itself has demonstrated that those who say you can make Germany so feeble that she will never be able to hit back are utterly wrong . . . You may strip Germany of her colonies, reduce her armaments to a mere police force and her navy to that of a fifth-rate power; all the same in the end if she feels that she has been unjustly treated in the peace of 1919 she will find means of exacting retribution from her conquerors.[20]

Rather than addressing itself to the question of that potential power, however, the Fontainebleau Memorandum assumed that the adoption of a conciliatory posture towards Germany would prevent the use of renascent German power against Allied interests. Reminiscent of the prewar Liberal stance towards Germany, this attitude also foreshadowed British policy towards Germany for the next twenty years.

Drawing heavily upon Hankey's memorandum, the Fontaine-bleau Memorandum appealed for a peace which, though punitive, would contain 'no provocations for future wars', a peace which would be capable of fulfilment and hence likely to be accepted. Such a settlement was necessary, Lloyd George argued, to save Germany and Europe from Bolshevism and to ensure a lasting peace: 'The greatest danger that I see in the present situation is that Germany may throw in her lot with Bolshevism and place her resources, her brains, her vast organising power at the disposal of the revolutionary fanatics whose dream it is to conquer the world for Bolshevism by force of arms.'[21]

Lloyd George's appeal, though couched in the language of impartiality, did not, as Clemenceau pointed out in his reply,[22] sacrifice any of Britain's vital interests. Indeed, while intended to provide the basis for a lasting peace, it was also designed to achieve specifically British aims: to assure British naval supremacy and to avoid a Continental commitment. Applying Wilsonian principles against both France and the United States in order to achieve these British aims, it employed the tactics which the Prime Minister had enunciated in December of enlisting the support of the United States to curb French aims and of using British support for the League of Nations as leverage against the United States.

In so doing, it reiterated Lloyd George's position that general disarmament was the prerequisite for permanent security. A paper entitled 'British Empire Interests', which Hankey and Kerr had drafted at Fontainebleau, listed German naval disarmament and an agreement with the United States on naval shipbuilding, together with 'limitation of armaments of all nations consequential upon military terms of peace imposed upon Germany', as Britain's top requirements,[23] and the memorandum embodied these priorities. Although a marginal note, apparently by Kerr, on an early draft of peace terms had called for a modification in the number of troops allowed Germany,[24] the final memorandum endorsed the military, naval and air terms already adopted by the Supreme War Council. On the issue of conscription, the memorandum and all of its drafts called specifically for the abolition of compulsory service only in Germany and the small states, but, according to General Wilson, the intention was to 'force the other great Powers to follow suit'.[25]

Of more immediate importance for the diplomacy of the peace conference was the memorandum's call for general arms limitation. Not only did Lloyd George adopt Hankey's recommendation that a preamble to the disarmament section of the treaty should state that German disarmament was the first step towards general disarmament, but he made approval of the league covenant contingent upon prior Allied agreement on arms limitation: 'The first condition of success for the League of Nations is . . . a firm understanding between the British Empire and the United States of America and France and Italy that there will be no competitive building up of fleets or armies between them. Unless this is arrived at before the Covenant is signed the League of Nations will be a sham and a mockery.' Thus, while declaring that the League of Nations was an 'essential element' of the peace settlement, he threatened to withhold Britain's signature from the covenant if the United States did not abandon its programme of naval expansion.[26]

As for France, the main target of the memorandum, Lloyd George invoked the principle of self-determination against French demands for the Rhine. While offering a just peace and universal arms limitation as the ultimate guarantees of French security, for the short term he renewed the offer of an Anglo-American guarantee and endorsed the demilitarisation of the Rhineland.[27]

The Fontainebleau Memorandum was primarily a tactical device intended to win American and French co-operation in rapidly reaching a settlement which would preserve European peace and stability and maintain the alliance without sacrificing British interests. Certainly Lloyd George wanted to contain Bolshevism: he was concerned about conditions in Germany, about the labour situation at home, about the coup which had brought a Bolshevik regime to power in Hungary while he was at Fontainebleau. Yet when he drafted the memorandum, he was aware that Lenin had expressed willingness to make peace on terms acceptable to the Allies, and he did not withdraw the memorandum or alter the basis of his argument after receiving firsthand confirmation of this from the American who had undertaken a mission to Russia to determine the terms on which the Bolsheviks would be willing to make peace. Above all, the kind of peace which Lloyd George proposed in the Fontainebleau Memorandum would not require a British military commitment to Europe. It would not increase France's power on the Continent as realisation of the French programme would do. Moreover, it would ensure continued American participation in European affairs, while the constitution of the League of Nations only after agreement on arms limitation would preserve Britain's naval hegemony. General Wilson believed that achievement of the Fontainebleau programme would mean that 'even if Paris & League crashed England would come well out of it'.[28]

Lloyd George was only partially successful in achieving his objectives. On the issue of British naval supremacy, his strategy was ultimately successful, although he had to adopt a slightly different tactic from that outlined at Fontainebleau. Although he continued to threaten to withhold Britain's signature from the covenant until he had reached an agreement with the United States on naval building,[29] President Wilson had secured confirmation of the covenant as an integral part of the treaty the day before Lloyd George circulated the Fontainebleau Memorandum. In early April, however, in exchange for British support for an amendment to the covenant protecting the Monroe Doctrine, House assured Cecil that the United States did not intend to engage in naval competition with Britain, and the President agreed to consider suspending the naval building programme then before Congress. In May when Wilson withdrew Administration support from the programme, British naval hegemony was, at least temporarily, assured.

The inclusion of a preamble to the military, naval and air clauses of the treaty declaring that German disarmament was a preliminary to general disarmament coincided with Point Four of President Wilson's Fourteen Points, and the Americans worked with the British to secure its adoption, the President introducing the British draft for Council of Three approval.[30] Fatefully, therefore, the treaty – on Britain's initiative – defined the purpose of German disarmament not as the curbing of German power but as 'render[ing] possible the initiation of a general limitation of the armaments of all nations'.[31] Thus it embodied Lloyd George's approach to the whole disarmament question.

On the question of the Rhineland, however, Lloyd George's diplomacy suffered a major defeat. The Fontainebleau Memorandum did not break the deadlock in the negotiations for an arrangement to guarantee France's security; final agreement was not reached until the end of April. Moreover, the provisions regarding the Rhineland which the French finally accepted in exchange for an Anglo-American guarantee of their security went further than Lloyd George would have liked. Until mid-April he and President Wilson maintained a united front against the French demands regarding both the Rhineland and continued control of disarmament. They rejected all demands for a Rhineland occupation and, in response to the demand for league control of disarmament after withdrawal of the control commission, agreed only to include in the military clauses of the treaty a provision for league inspection, thus rejecting the idea of permanent control in Germany.[32] But when Lloyd George returned to London to confront a group of Conservative MPs, outraged at news of the contents of the Fontainebleau Memorandum, Wilson and Clemenceau reached an agreement to which Lloyd George on his return only reluctantly consented. It provided for a fifteen-year occupation of a permanently demilitarised Rhineland and the bridgeheads of the Rhine. The occupation was to serve as a guarantee of the execution of the treaty and was to be subject to extension if, at the end of the prescribed period, the Allies considered the existing guarantees against German aggression inadequate or to early termination if the Germans fully complied with the treaty before that time.[33] Thus the treaty would require the long-term commitment of British forces to Europe. While this military commitment would be mainly symbolic, Lloyd George having promised only to provide 'a battalion with the flag',[34] it, nevertheless, marked a significant departure from Britain's traditional role in Europe.

The Rhineland arrangement did not bode well for the future of Anglo-French relations. Rather, it seemed likely to perpetuate and indeed to exacerbate tensions between Britain and France. Given the different British and French approaches to the question of security and the differing political pressures on the leaders of the two countries, conflict over interpretation both of German compliance and of adequate guarantees of security semed inevitable, particularly if, as Lloyd George presciently told the British Empire Delegation was likely,[35] the United States refused to ratify the guarantee and it then lapsed, leaving – in French eyes – only the occupation as a sure guarantee of France's security.

Moreover, the commitment to the Continent came at a time when the British people were eager for an early withdrawal from Europe and the CIGS, complaining that he lacked sufficient forces for empire defence, was contemplating transferring troops from the Rhine to imperial posts and was recommending extension of conscription to meet imperial responsibilities.[36] Hence, in its broadest implications, the Rhineland arrangement was a setback for Lloyd George's domestic policies as well. But once Wilson and Clemenceau had reached a compromise, there was little the Prime Minister could do but accept it unless he wished further to postpone the conclusion of peace. The Rhineland arrangement meant the resolution of the last major issue of the German settlement and hence a return to peace conditions if the Germans signed the treaty. Lloyd George could hope that, as Wiseman had concluded after an April visit to Britain, 'people want peace and normal conditions, are not interested in details of the peace settlement'.[37]

The Dominion leaders were, however, quite interested in the details of the peace settlement, and their reluctance to commit themselves to the guarantee to France led to the adoption of a procedure whereby each Dominion was to have the option of ratifying or rejecting the treaty of guarantee. Hence the Rhineland arrangement marked a watershed in Britain's relations with its Dominions and a setback for those, like Kerr, who had hoped that the experience of the common war effort would promote greater imperial unity. No longer could London count on the Dominions automatically to follow its diplomatic lead.

It was indeed from a Dominion representative that the greatest opposition to the completed treaty came. At the beginning of May, Smuts, who had not been at the centre of decision-making during the peace conference, launched a campaign for the 'drastic revision'[38] of the draft treaty. Bombarding Lloyd George – and, to a lesser extent, President Wilson – with letters and memoranda and lobbying the British and American delegations, he attacked the treaty as incapable of fulfilment and likely to lead either to another war or to revolution.[39] In late March when Smuts had written to Lloyd George to express his displeasure with the way the treaty was developing, his ideas had coincided with those which Lloyd George had just expressed in the Fontainebleau Memorandum, and he had found the Prime Minister receptive to his views.[40] By May, however, Lloyd George's attitude had changed. Incensed by the chief German delegate's defiant reception of the peace terms,[41] the volatile Prime Minister was speaking of 'smashing the Junkers' and was urging the occupation of Berlin and the reinstitution of the blockade in order to force the Germans to sign the treaty.[42]

However, Lloyd George soon found that many of his colleagues preferred Smuts's approach to his own. Of the ranking British officials, initially only Barnes joined Smuts in calling for the treaty's revision,[43] but before the end of May it was clear that others shared their viewpoint and believed that concessions should be made in order to assure acceptance of the treaty. While Barnes communicated the likelihood of Labour dissatisfaction with the draft treaty,[44] Cecil reported that dissatisfaction in Britain extended well beyond Labour circles.[45] Expressing the misgivings which he had felt since March,[46] he also warned that British acquiescence in an unrevised treaty would destroy Britain's 'moral leadership of the nations' and that an eventual American reaction against the treaty would undermine the growing Anglo-American *rapprochement* for which not only he but Lloyd George, too, had worked.[47]

After Lloyd George had authorised Foch to make arrangements with Churchill for the British army to march on Berlin if the Germans refused to sign the treaty,[48] the War Secretary wrote to the

Prime Minister stating that while Britain could contribute to a Rhineland occupation, it lacked the military resources to occupy and hold 'the heart of Germany'. He argued that an early peace was therefore in Britain's interest, and he recommended that in response to any counter-proposals which the Germans offered, the Allies should 'split the outstanding difference' in order to 'reach a settlement with the present German Government, and to reach it as speedily as possible':

> The British Empire is in a very fine position at the present moment, and we now require a peace which will fix and recognise that position. Let us beware lest in following too far Latin ambitions and hatreds we do not create a new situation in which our advantages will largely have disappeared. Settle now while we have the power, or lose perhaps for ever the power of settlement on the basis of a military victory.

Such an argument, of course, suggested that Britain would not be able to enforce the peace terms if Germany failed to comply with a treaty revised in its favour. But, anticipating German compliance, Churchill asserted that 'everything shows that the present German government is sincerely desirous of making a beaten peace and preserving an orderly community which will carry out its agreement'.[49]

Soon after, Jones informed one of Lloyd George's secretaries that Fisher and other Liberal ministers were 'deeply apprehensive about some aspects of the Peace Settlement and at the growing signs of criticism in this country'.[50] Fisher himself wrote to Lloyd George in support of Churchill's views, adding political arguments to the War Secretary's military rationale for revising the treaty. Assuring the Prime Minister of 'the undivided support of the Liberal member[s] of your Government in any efforts which you may make to bring the representatives of the Allied Powers to acquiesce in such concessions as may be necessary in order to obtain peace at the earliest possible moment', he warned of 'a violent revulsion of feeling against the Government in this Country if there were to be a renewal of the war'.[51]

When Lloyd George met with the British Empire Delegation and with Cabinet members he had summoned from London to discuss the counter-proposals which the Germans submitted on 29 May, he found a unanimous desire to revise the draft treaty.[52] This desire for treaty revision was based not on sympathy for Germany but on assessments of Britain's interests. While Smuts denounced the draft treaty for betraying the principles for which Britain had fought the war, at the root of his demand for revision was fear of the long-term consequences for the British Empire of imposing a treaty which he believed could not be fulfilled: 'Many of the terms were impossible to carry out. They would produce political and economic chaos in Europe for a generation and in the long run it would be the British Empire which would have to pay the penalty.' As we have seen, Cecil, too, believed that abandonment of the principles which had motivated the Allied cause would – by undermining Britain's moral prestige and rupturing its relationship with the United States – damage long-term British interests. Like Smuts, Chamberlain believed that the proposed peace was unworkable, and he worried that it would 'involve the Allies in liabilities which the Allies could not meet or in risks which they need not incur'.[53]

Others were, like Churchill and Fisher, more concerned about the short-term military and political consequences of Germany's refusing to sign the treaty, and it was on this basis that they supported treaty revision. Ward epitomised the position of those who had not altered their attitude towards Germany but who concluded that Britain's limited military resources and the British public's unwillingness to renew the war necessitated concessions in order to assure acceptance of the treaty. Describing himself as 'one who, if it were possible, would not concede an inch to an enemy responsible for the war', the New Zealand leader none the less urged that 'the opportunity should not be lost, by avoiding reasonable concessions, of ensuring that the *present* German Government should sign the peace terms'.[54]

In advocating revision, however, British leaders were no more willing in June than Lloyd George had been in March to make concessions in areas which they regarded as vital to British interests. Hence, even Hughes could go along with the consensus reached at these meetings: that Lloyd George would press for specified concessions and, if necessary, communicate Britain's unwillingness to march on Berlin or participate in the reimposition of the blockade if these revisions were not made and Germany therefore refused to sign the treaty.[55]

Predictably, the provisions for the Rhineland occupation,

generally regarded as contrary to British interests, aroused considerable opposition. Since British officials agreed with the German contention that Germany was not capable of waging aggressive war,[56] they thought that French security did not require both the guarantee and the occupation. Moreover, they disliked the fact that Germany's responsibility for the cost of the occupation army would constitute a drain on the funds available for reparation payments, and they feared that the French forces would provoke incidents which would require British intervention. They therefore decided that the Prime Minister should press for a reduction in both the size of the occupation force and the duration of the occupation.[57] Lloyd George had already attempted to reopen the whole question of the occupation, but Clemenceau had agreed only to the appointment of a commission to rewrite its regulating convention.[58] Raising the question again when he presented his colleagues' views to the Council of Three, Lloyd George again met the French Premier's adamant opposition.[59] The issue was finally resolved to Lloyd George's satisfaction when Clemenceau, though continuing to refuse to alter the treaty provisions, consented to an inter-Allied agreement that the number of troops would be reduced when Germany disarmed.[60] Thus the size of the occupation force would be directly linked to German compliance with the military clauses of the treaty. France thereby acknowledged that Germany's disarmament would provide it with sufficient security to warrant altering an arrangement which it considered essential to its defence. To this extent, the French had implicitly accepted the British concept of the link between disarmament and security. Yet the agreement ignored the likelihood of contention over the question of German compliance and hence over reduction of the occupation force. Inherent in it, as in the Rhineland arrangement itself, was the potential for continuing Anglo-French conflict.

Although the military clauses were not among the provisions which Lloyd George's colleagues charged him with seeking to modify, the German comments on disarmament impressed the British. In their counter-proposals the Germans agreed to accept the disarmament provisions of the treaty on condition that Germany be admitted to the League of Nations, the other signatory powers reduce their armaments and abolish conscription within two years and Germany be allowed a transition period before fulfilling the military terms. They demanded that during this transition period

Germany should have the right to maintain the forces necessary for preserving internal order and to determine the organisation of its army and armament, and they rejected any special supervision of German disarmament.[61]

Despite the intransigent tone of the German note, Chamberlain thought 'that it was written by men who wanted to sign a Treaty which it would be possible for them to keep', and he not only agreed with the Germans that, under the terms of the draft treaty, they would be unable to preserve internal order but he also believed that they would be unable to defend their borders.[62] Although Balfour thought that 'if the Germans were to be given an army to-morrow . . . they would immediately begin a war of revenge',[63] he nevertheless considered the German disarmament proposals 'in a sense reasonable unless Germany were given guarantees of safety'.[64] General Wilson termed the German attitude towards the military terms generally 'satisfactory' and considered the demand for retention of a larger number of troops during a transition period 'fully justified',[65] while Cecil considered the conditional acceptance of the principle of a 100,000-man volunteer army 'of immense importance'. Moreover, Cecil thought that the German proposals coincided with Britain's goals regarding general disarmament and hence should be seriously considered: 'It would be a great mistake to lose this opportunity of finally destroying German militarism by consent, and indeed it is to our interest that the German conditions should be fulfilled.'[66]

Proposals put forward by British officials in response to the German counter-proposals became the basis of modifications of treaty provisions relating both to general and to German disarmament. The British League of Nations section drafted a proposed reply to the counter-proposals on the league suggesting that the Allies inform Germany that it would be admitted to the league when it had demonstrated that it had a stable government which intended to observe its international obligations and to disarm. The proposed reply recommended, too, that the Allies reiterate their own commitment to disarmament, announcing their intention immediately to open negotiations at which the question of conscription would be considered, but pointing out that implementation of any scheme for general disarmament would depend upon Germany's fulfilment of the treaty's disarmament terms.[67] However, Clemenceau objected to the mention of conscription; so this was omitted from the draft which was submitted to and – with minor modifications – accepted by the Council of Four.[68] Thus the attempt to obtain a general commitment to the abolition of conscription was again blocked by the French. Elaborating on the covenant's provision for reduction of armaments, the reply to the German comments on the league did, however, promise that the Allies would work for the adoption of a programme for general disarmament, contingent upon German compliance with the disarmament terms of the treaty.[69]

Although the Germans had also presented their demands relating to their own disarmament under the heading of the League of Nations, in their reply the Allies treated these proposals separately, reaffirming their right as victors to determine the conditions of Germany's disarmament. They did, however, make minor modifications in the military clauses. The committee appointed to draft this section of the Allied reply accepted the German contention that Germany needed a transition period before reducing its army to treaty level. The committee did not, however, go as far in recommending modifications as its British member would have liked. While General Wilson thought that Germany should be allowed six months in which to reduce its army to 300,000 and a year to reach its permanent level, which – despite Germany's acceptance of eventual reduction to 100,000 – he wished to increase to 200,000, the full committee recommended reduction to 300,000 within three months, with subsequent reductions to be determined by a conference of Allied military experts and the permanent level of 100,000 stipulated in the draft treaty to be reached by 31 March 1920 at the latest. The committee recommended corresponding adjustments in the rate of reduction of small arms, but it did not go along with the CIGS's proposal for an extension of the period for fulfilling all the disarmament conditions, recommending extension only of the deadline for the destruction of specific fortifications. Emphatically reasserting the right of control, neither Wilson nor the committee as a whole was willing to make concessions to the other German demands.[70] When the committee submitted its recommendations, Clemenceau, who had initially rejected the notion of a transition period,[71] objected to the 300,000-man transition army, and its size was accordingly reduced to 200,000.[72] Thus while granting Germany an extension of the deadline for reducing its army, the Allies made no substantial modifications in the terms of its disarmament.

In their reply they did, however, modify both the premise and the implied commitment of the preamble to the disarmament section of the treaty. In his memorandum General Wilson had ignored the German call for general disarmament, and the military committee's draft reply specifically refused to make any commitment to arms reduction, stating that only when Germany had renounced 'military methods in the application of her politics', could the Allies consider limiting their armaments.[73] According to Lloyd George, however, in informal conversations he, Clemenceau and President Wilson agreed to include a statement on general disarmament in the Allied reply,[74] and on 12 June Lloyd George introduced, and the Council of Five accepted, two paragraphs drafted by Kerr which reaffirmed the Allied commitment to general disarmament.[75]

Yet, in proposing these paragraphs Lloyd George did not mention general disarmament but spoke rather of the necessity of strengthening the military committee's draft, 'as it was a matter of great importance before coming to the concessions to indicate the great trouble that had been caused in the world by the development of the German military machine'.[76] And the paragraphs themselves, while pledging the Allies to their own disarmament even more forcefully than the preamble or their reply on the League of Nations, also introduced concepts condemnatory of German policy, which were absent from the disarmament section of the treaty. The paragraphs adopted by the Council of Five denounced German militarism for its responsibility for the war and, unlike the preamble, asserted that the purpose of Germany's disarmament was not just to make possible general disarmament but also to prevent a recurrence of German aggression:

I. The Allied and Associated Powers wish to make it clear that their proposals in regard to German armaments were not made solely with the object of making it impossible for Germany to resume her policy of military aggression. It is also the first step towards that geneal reduction and limitation of armaments which they seek to bring about as one of the most fruitful preventives of war, and which it will be one of the first duties of the League of Nations to promote.

II. They must point out, however, that the colossal growth in armaments of the last few decades was forced upon the nations of Europe by Germany. As Germany increased her power, her neighbours had to follow suit unless they were to become impotent to resist German dictation or the German sword. It is therefore right, as it is necessary, that the process of limitation of armaments should begin with the nation which has been responsible for their expansion. It is not until the aggressor has led the way that the attacked can safely afford to follow suit.[77]

Thus, with the substitution of Kerr's paragraphs, the introduction to the official Allied reply to the German counter-proposals on the military clauses of the treaty read like a summation of British Liberal assumptions: Prussian militarism's policy of aggression had caused the war; Prussian militarism, by fostering the growth of armaments, had created an unstable international atmosphere; competition in armaments leads to war; arms limitation can prevent war.

Missing, however, was the wartime distinction between the German people and their Prussian militarist government. Rather, the covering letter to the Allied reply, also drafted by Kerr, while holding out the prospect of 'early reconciliation and appeasement', asserted not just that a punitive peace was necessary to deter future aggression by Germany or any other power and that the new German government must demonstrate its commitment to pursuing a peaceful policy before the Allies would be convinced that the change in Germany was genuine, but that the German people shared responsibility for the conduct of their government: 'Throughout the war, as before the war, the German people . . . supported the war' and did not overthrow their government 'until . . . all hope of profiting by a war of conquest had vanished.' Therefore they could not 'now pretend, having changed their rulers after the war was lost' that they should not be held accountable for the actions of their government.[78] There was little to distinguish this assertion from Coalition candidates' pronouncements late in the election campaign. Not only had the speech of the German Foreign Minister, Brockdorff-Rantzau, on receipt of the draft treaty outraged the Allied leaders, but in their counter-proposals the Germans had focused on the question of responsibility for the war. Therefore the Allies felt compelled to justify the basis of the peace terms.

The Allied reply – largely through British influence – thus combined condemnation and conciliation. As a result of the pressures exerted on the Prime Minister by his colleagues and of Lloyd George's subsequent efforts within the Council of Four, it made a major concession on the question of Germany's eastern frontiers, and it promised that Germany would be readmitted into the community of nations when it had shown its determination to comply with the treaty. But, with Kerr's formulation of the Allied case, the reply also pronounced Germany responsible for the war and 'for the savage and inhuman manner in which it was conducted',[79] a judgement which neither the German government nor the German people were willing to accept.

The new German government which accepted the treaty did so while protesting its injustice: 'Yielding to overpowering might, the government of the German republic declares itself ready to accept and to sign the peace treaty imposed by the Allied and Associated governments. But in so doing, the government of the German republic in no wise abandons its conviction that these conditions of peace represent injustice without example.'[80] This was the attitude, too, of much of the German population, including, most significantly for the future of the military clauses, the military leadership.

The military provisions of the Treaty of Versailles depended for their initial execution and even more for their continued enforcement on the co-operation not just of the German government but also of the German military. Even the system of Allied control assumed German co-operation.[81] While the treaty provided for Allied action if Germany failed to comply with the disarmament terms or, having complied, subsequently began to rearm, such action would be contingent upon continued Allied co-operation and a joint Allied determination to enforce the treaty provisions. The will to enforce would depend, in turn, upon each ally's commitment to the treaty, and in Britain there was to be no wholehearted, sustained commitment to enforcing the military clauses which British policy-makers had played such a crucial role in formulating.

Conclusion

Not only was the military disarmament of Germany not a British war aim, but, as we have seen, Britain's wartime governments had not seriously contemplated a significant permanent diminution of Germany's military power. Although they recognised the economic and territorial foundations of German military strength, their economic and territorial war aims did not have as their objective the undermining of these bases of German power. Rather, at the Paris Peace Conference British officials worked to thwart French designs for dismembering Germany and thus permanently debasing German power. During the pre-Armistice discussions when for a brief period British leaders supported the idea of demanding German disarmament as a condition of armistice, their goal was not to destroy Germany's long-term military potential but to deprive the German army of its immediate fighting capacity. Indeed, even before the signature of the Armistice they were considering the possibility of strengthening the German army as a bulwark against Bolshevism.

Most British policy-makers expected Germany to play a central strategic role in postwar Europe. They considered Bolshevism to be the greatest danger to European order and believed that Germany must be a barrier against its spread. Even a strategic realist like Amery became so preoccupied with the immediate danger of Bolshevism that he was willing to leave virtually intact the territorial, economic and military bases of Germany's power on the Continent.[1] It was not only imperialists like Amery who thought that Britain's interests, other than the containment of Bolshevism, lay outside Europe. Those who believed that it was essential to concentrate on domestic problems also wanted minimal involvement in European affairs. Hoping to withdraw from Europe, the British did not want to leave France dominant there, and Germany could be the only effective counterbalance to French military power. In addition, for many, the belief that another war between major powers was unthinkable had become a conviction that in the changed conditions resulting from the war it would be impossible. Thus, despite their uncertainty about Germany's political future, British statesmen ignored the reality of German power and disregarded the strategic lessons of 1914–18.

Britain's German disarmament policy, as it developed on the eve of the Paris Peace Conference and was implemented at the conference, was essentially Lloyd George's policy, and the Prime Minister had never thought in terms of unilateral German disarmament. Rather, he envisaged German disarmament as only part of a programme of general disarmament. In his view, general disarmament was the means of providing European security and assuring lasting peace in a way which best accorded with Britain's interests. In pursuing his policy, the Prime Minister had the wholehearted support of his Coalition partner Bonar Law, who shared his view of the centrality of disarmament to Britain's postwar policy. The Conservative leader told Churchill in the spring of 1919 that Lloyd George 'had gone to the root of the matter in pressing for disarmament and that he must be backed on that at all costs'.[2]

The idea of first demanding German disarmament was conceived not as a means of curbing German power but as part of a strategy for realising the long-term objective of general disarmament as well as for achieving more immediate political and diplomatic goals. While the disarmament of Germany was regarded as a security measure, it was to be only the first step in the creation of a general system of security based on arms reduction. The abolition of conscription in Germany was intended not just to prevent a revival of militarism there but to lead to the abolition of conscription and hence the destruction of militarism throughout Europe.

In the formulation of Britain's German disarmament policy and its implementation during the peace negotiations, political considerations took precedence over military and strategic ones, and wishful thinking replaced systematic analysis. Even when challenged by those who disagreed with them, Lloyd George and his closest advisers did not examine the assumptions upon which they based their policy. They occasionally acknowledged that Germany might not co-operate in fulfilling the treaty and that if it did not it would remain the strongest power in Europe, capable of, and perhaps determined to, 'attempt, within a few years, once more to establish . . . dominion over the world'.[3] But in the negotiation of postwar security arrangements, Lloyd George's faith in the peaceful nature of democratic governments and the efficacy of international conciliation, coupled with his recognition of the political and economic

constraints on British policy, overrode his doubts about the direction
of Germany's postwar policy.

When one considers the way in which German disarmament
became an object of British policy, the objectives which it was
intended to accomplish and the role which British policy-makers
expected Germany to play in postwar Europe, it is not surprising
that, despite British insistence at the Paris Peace Conference on the
necessity of disarming Germany, Britain adopted a more flexible
attitude than France towards the enforcement of the disarmament
clauses of the Treaty of Versailles. In Britain's post-Versailles policy
towards German disarmament political considerations continued to
take precedence over military ones.

British policy-makers regarded a stable Germany as essential to
European security, and they based their policy on the assumption
that Germany's participation as an equal partner in European affairs
would promote both its own internal stability and general European
order. In a 1921 review of foreign policy, Foreign Secretary Curzon,
describing the basis of Britain's German policy as 'the re-establish-
ment of Germany as a stable State in Europe', declared that
Germany was 'necessary, with her great population, with her natural
resources, with her prodigious strength of character . . . and any
idea of obliterating Germany from the comity of nations or treating
her as an outcast is not only ridiculous but is insane'.[4] Austen
Chamberlain, the British architect of Locarno, shared this outlook,
viewing Locarno as an opportunity for Germany to 'take her place as
an equal with the great nations'.[5] Reluctant to pursue a policy which
might foster a militarist reaction or a leftist revolution in Germany or
lead to Germany's alignment with Soviet Russia, Britain preferred to
disarm Germany by consent rather than by coercion and was willing
to overlook what it regarded as merely technical violations of the
disarmament clauses of the treaty. Even the anti-German Chamberlain was 'prepared to stretch a point here and there in favour of
Germany, provided she shows a reasonable spirit'.[6]

The British were reluctant to use force not only because of the
possible consequences in Germany and because of their desire,
especially after the Russo-German *rapprochement* at Rapallo, to win
Germany to the Western camp but also because of the limited
resources available to them and their wish not to become further
involved on the Continent. Although in the early post-Versailles
years they believed that British public opinion would countenance

military action to enforce disarmament,[7] British leaders themselves hesitated to act. Even more than when Churchill had rejected the idea of British participation in military action to force Germany to sign the treaty, Britain lacked sufficient forces both to act against Germany and to fulfil its other obligations. From the summer of 1919 the British army was steadily and drastically reduced in size. In 1921, unable to spare troops from trouble spots in the empire, Britain had to recall some of its forces from Europe in order to deal with a coal strike at home which threatened to become a general strike.[8] Well before a Foreign Office clerk noted in a 1926 minute that Britain was 'certainly not prepared' to use force to assure continuing German compliance with the disarmament provisions of the treaty,[9] British leaders had made clear their reluctance to use British troops to enforce complete fulfilment.[10]

Unwilling to commit British forces, the British also opposed French military action. Before the French occupation of the Ruhr in 1923 the British feared that if France occupied the Ruhr, the sanction favoured by the French, it would not withdraw and thus would become not only 'the mistress of Europe in respect of coal, iron and steel' but also 'the military monarch'.[11] This substitution of French for German hegemony would undermine Britain's policy of European reconciliation and pacification. Even after the collapse of French policy in the Ruhr, which, as Correlli Barnett has pointed out, 'marked a major shift in power from the victors towards Germany',[12] the British remained concerned about French military predominance.

Moreover, disarmament was only one aspect of the German problem and the problem of Germany only one of the major issues with which Britain's postwar governments had to deal. In June 1921 Lloyd George wrote to Bonar Law of 'crises chasing each other like the shadows of clouds across the landscape. Miners, Unemployment, Reparation, Silesia, and always Ireland.'[13] To these, one could add economic dislocation, emergent nationalism in Egypt and India and attempts to reach agreement on naval disarmament, all of which directly affected Britain's position as a world power as Britain's leaders believed European problems no longer did. Domestic, imperial and extra-European international pressures reinforced 'the escapist urge'[14] which characterised Britain's European policy between the wars. Lloyd George wanted Britain to return to its stance after Waterloo when the British 'obtained a predominant influence on the Continent without committing ourselves too deeply',[15] while the foreign policy principles enunciated by his successor Bonar Law included a 'resolute determination not to extend commitments: to curtail them should reasonable occasion arise'.[16] In 1919 George Saunders had asked whether Britain and France had 'sufficient moral force to spare from our own problems to keep Germany in leading-strings for ten, twenty, thirty or forty years'.[17] Britain's postwar policy towards Germany clearly demonstrated that Britain did not.

Only the economic aspects of the German problem seemed to British leaders to affect Britain's status as a world power. Consequently, the issue of reparation dominated Britain's postwar relations with Germany. Faced in 1920-1 with a depression at home, the British blamed their economic troubles on the failure to settle reparations. Lloyd George told an Allied conference in January 1921 that 'reparation was so very important a question that even disarmament must for a moment take a second place'.[18] Believing that Germany's economic recovery was necessary to British prosperity, Britain's political leaders overlooked the fact that Germany's economic revival would also provide the basis for its possible military resurgence. Rather, they divorced the question of reparations from that of European security. Hardinge expressed the predominant outlook when he wrote that once Germany was disarmed 'and the danger of militarism removed, there is no reason why we should not do our utmost to help them to improve their economic position, for their prosperity is essential for the whole of Europe as well as for themselves'.[19] Hence British policy-makers were eager to settle the disarmament question so that they could then take steps to assist Germany's – and their own – economic recovery. Even Crowe, who represented a minority viewpoint in his belief that Germany's recovery would foster the revival of the military spirit there and that 'the more normal and prosperous the German State, the stronger will become that feeling', nevertheless shared the prevalent belief that Germany's recovery was 'in itself most desirable for general political reasons'.[20]

The British continued to regard Germany's disarmament as only the first step towards general disarmament. The Lloyd George government early addressed itself to the problem of persuading France to reduce the size of its army,[21] while the Labour government came to power in 1924 committed to general disarmament as 'the only security for the nations'[22] and worked to secure the inclusion of a provision for a disarmament conference in the ill-fated Geneva Protocol. Britain's Conservative governments also embraced the concept of general disarmament. As Foreign Secretary in the second Baldwin government, Chamberlain asserted that only general disarmament could assure Germany's permanent disarmament.[23] The desire to turn attention to 'the Land Disarmament Problem'[24] was yet another pressure leading to a willingness to compromise in order to resolve the question of German compliance with the military clauses of the treaty.

Initially, the Lloyd George government insisted on Germany's strict compliance with the disarmament provisions of the treaty and even agreed to occupy the Ruhr if Germany failed to comply.[25] The Germans having failed to reduce their army to 100,000 by the extended deadline of 10 July 1920, at the Spa Conference of July 1920 Lloyd George 'stood up to the Germans about disarmament'.[26] Faced with the threat of coercion, the Germans pledged in the Spa Protocol to reduce their army to 100,000 by 1 January 1921 and to begin immediately to comply with the other disarmament provisions of the treaty.

After Spa, where the Allies had for the first time negotiated directly with the Germans, the British attitude began to change. Convinced that Germany intended to fulfil its pledges, Lloyd George returned from Spa declaring that it was 'easier to disarm Germany than France.'[27] Reports by the General Staff, by the chief British member of the Inter-Allied Military Control Commission, by Britain's diplomatic representatives in Berlin and by the Foreign Office[28] led members of the Cabinet to agree unanimously at the end of 1920 'that the disarmament of Germany had been carried out satisfactorily so far' and to oppose the dispatch by the Allies of a harsh note to Germany regarding its failure to disarm and disband the un-authorised military formations which remained active in some parts of the country. The Cabinet acknowledged that the existence of these irregular formations constituted a technical violation of the disarmament provisions of the treaty and of the Spa Protocol. But, adopting the position which was to characterise British policy until the withdrawal of the Control Commission in January 1927, it concluded that since this technical violation posed no danger to the Allies, Britain should try to convince its allies to abandon the idea of sanctions, 'which if carried out might precipitate a very serious crisis and involve consequences that it was impossible to foresee'.[29] Having achieved an agreement at Spa, with which they believed the German government had done its best to comply, the British wished to continue the process of disarmament by consent rather than by coercion.[30]

French policy prevented the implementation of this strategy and led, first, in March 1921 to the occupation of three German towns when Germany failed fully to comply with Allied demands regarding both reparations and disarmament and, then, in May to a threat to occupy the Ruhr if Germany continued in default. Despite their acquiescence in these actions, British policy-makers did not share France's concern about what they continued to regard as minor infractions of the treaty's disarmament clauses. Rather, after Germany pledged 'to carry out without reserve or delay the measures of . . . disarmament'[31] but before it had done so, Lloyd George, treating the German promise as tantamount to fulfilment, told the June 1921 Imperial Conference, 'The disarmament of Germany, I think, may be stated to be a settled problem'.[32]

So, too, Austen Chamberlain did not consider the more serious violations of the disarmament clauses reported by the Military Control Commission in December 1924 sufficient to warrant postponement of the evacuation of the first Rhineland zone, which had been scheduled for January 1925. Chamberlain, too, wanted to negotiate rather than to impose a disarmament arrangement, and he urged on the French the speedy conclusion of an evacuation-disarmament settlement in which the French would 'not insist on trifling matters of no military consequence'.[33] At Locarno he won acceptance of a compromise by which, in return for a German promise to carry out the most important remaining points, the Allies would promise to evacuate the Cologne zone by a specified date without waiting for the completion of disarmament. In accordance with this arrangement, British occupation forces completed their evacuation of the Cologne zone in January 1926. Thus, although the Rhineland Pact negotiated at Locarno in October 1925 committed Britain in principle to Europe, the negotiations at Locarno also made possible the end of the major component of its actual military involvement on the Continent.

It was also under the aegis of Chamberlain, ironically the most Francophile Foreign Secretary of the interwar period, that Britain intensified its efforts to end the Control Commission, the other component of its direct military involvement in Europe. From the end of 1920 British officials had regarded German compliance as sufficient to begin consideration of an end to military control.[34] When the Control Commission withdrew from Germany during the Ruhr occupation, a spokesman for the Bonar Law government told the House of Commons that its British member was 'satisfied that the reduction of the German Army contemplated by the Treaty, both in respect of men and material, have been so carried out as to constitute effective disarmament'.[35] The British government only reluctantly agreed to the Commission's return to Germany in 1924,[36] and MacDonald told his Cabinet colleagues in June that he intended to bring the Commission to an end.[37] Chamberlain accomplished what other British officials had worked towards.

Although he was justifiably suspicious of German Foreign Minister Stresemann's motives in seeking a Western security pact, believing quite correctly, for example, that the proposal was a subterfuge to escape full disarmament, Chamberlain nevertheless regarded the German overture as an opportunity not only for providing France with a sense of security and for ushering in a new era in European relations but also for negotiating a final settlement of the disarmament question and thus ending military control.[38] Chamberlain believed that the Locarno treaties 'fundamentally modified' the importance of 'the whole question of German disarmament',[39] and, especially after Germany entered the League of Nations in September 1926, intensified his efforts to end the Control Commission and transfer the question of Germany's disarmament to the league.[40] Under his direction, the Foreign Office in November and December 1926 worked for an Allied-German agreement to end control, and on 31 January 1927 the Military Control Commission was withdrawn, as the Cologne zone had been evacuated a year earlier, in exchange for German promises to fulfil the remaining disarmament clauses on whose execution the Allies insisted but before those promises had been fulfilled.

Much has been made of the fact that the withdrawal of the Control Commission deprived the Allies of direct means of enforcing the treaty's disarmament provisions.[41] But there is nothing in British policy in the 1930s to suggest that if the commission had remained in existence Britain would have agreed to take action against German rearmament. In 1931-2 when it became clear that Germany was secretly rearming, Britain interpreted the German violations of the disarmament clauses of the treaty as being defensive in nature and hence not warranting Allied action. In March 1935 after Hitler announced the reintroduction of conscription and proclaimed his intention of building an army of over half a million men, the British government postponed but did not cancel a diplomatic mission scheduled to meet with the German dictator. Soon after, Britain concluded a naval agreement with Germany, thereby itself renouncing the naval disarmament provisions of the Treaty of Versailles. In its policy towards German disarmament, as in the rest of its German policy, Britain continued to prefer conciliation to coercion.

When the framers of British foreign policy in the 1920s worked for an end to military control, they were, as we have seen, well aware of Germany's evasions of the treaty's disarmament provisions. Not only did the Military Control Commission, whose observations the British could more easily discount as biased because of its predominantly French membership, report in explicit detail the German violations, but from mid-1923 the War Office, too, expressed its concern at the German failure to comply.[42] Yet, while acknowledging the accuracy of the military reports, those responsible for Britain's German policy, convinced that Germany had been effectively disarmed and that its infractions of the treaty's disarmament provisions posed no threat to Britain's vital interests, dismissed the military's findings as unnecessarily meticulous. In September 1926 a Foreign Office official wrote that 'while agreeing that the Germans haven't got a leg to stand on . . . the time is surely past for haggling over these points of detail, however important they may appear to military eyes',[43] and in November at the height of Chamberlain's efforts to end military control the Foreign Secretary noted that Britain wanted to abolish the Control Commission 'even though the German Government have broken faith'.[44]

While this determination to end military control reflected the priority of political over military concerns in Britain's German disarmament policy, the authors of Britain's German policy were nevertheless correct in their assessment that, despite its failure fully to comply with the disarmament provisions of the Treaty of Versailles, Germany in 1926 was effectively disarmed. By 1926 the German army, which had been increased in size through the system of illegal recruitment instituted during the Ruhr crisis, had returned to treaty strength. In November a senior German staff officer noted in an internal memorandum that 'the Treaty of Versailles is observed in every point as far as our army is concerned'.[45] The new Chief of Army Command informed the German government in early 1927 that although the stockpiling of weapons in contravention of the treaty continued, stocks of ammunition were sufficient only for about one day of battle.[46] Both the British military attaché in Berlin and the CIGS agreed with Britain's civilian officials that despite the evasions of the treaty's disarmament provisions reported by their colleagues Germany was incapable of waging aggressive war.[47]

Yet Germany's disarmament did not produce the results intended by British policy-makers in 1919. It did not provide France with a sense of security. It did not lead to the abolition of conscription and the reduction of armaments throughout Europe. It did not inaugurate a new era of peaceful relations among the European powers.

Within Germany as well, the implementation of the treaty's major disarmament provisions did not have the anticipated effects. Contrary to Lloyd George's expectations, there was popular support in Germany not for disarmament but for repudiation of the restrictions of Versailles. Moreover, the army emerged from this period with its prestige undamaged and its position in German society and the German state enhanced. Not only did the old officer corps – the wellspring of Prussian militarism – survive, but the governments of the Weimar Republic were dependent upon it for the maintenance of their authority.

The disarmament provisions themselves worked to thwart British hopes for the permanent suppression of militarism in Germany and, as one historian has observed, 'made it hopeless to build up a democratic army'.[48] The new German army, created in conformity with the limitations of Versailles, was less democratic than its imperial predecessor. The necessity of reducing the army to 100,000 provided an opportunity for the officer corps to purge the army of all republican elements, while the stipulation that only 5 per cent of the officers could be replaced each year made it impossible for the government to purge the anti-republican officer corps. The requirement of long-term service made military service an un- attractive option for the working class and the liberal middle class, while the prohibition of conscription made it impossible to require their service. The ban on conscription and the requirement of long-term service, which had been adopted at Britain's insistence, resulted in the creation of the very type of professional army which the British believed had been responsible for the outbreak of war in 1914.

While the evasions of the disarmament provisions during the 1920s laid the groundwork for the expansion and modernisation of the army under Hitler and the Allied failure to implement the preamble to the disarmament section of the treaty gave Germany a moral justification for rearmament, the treaty requirements themselves created an atmosphere which facilitated Hitler's rise to power, and they fostered a spirit within the army which enabled him to become its master.

The tragic irony of Britain's German disarmament policy is that those provisions of the disarmament section of the Treaty of Versailles which were the specific achievements of British policy – the abolition of conscription and the requirement of a long-service army – contributed to the very revival of militarism which they were intended to prevent. British policy-makers' failure to examine the assumptions upon which they based their policy led them to pursue a course of action which undermined the European stability and peace which they were determined to preserve.

List of Abbreviations

AC	Austen Chamberlain Papers
Bbk	Beaverbrook Papers
BED	British Empire Delegation
BL	British Library
Cab.	Cabinet Records
DBFP	*Documents on British Foreign Policy*
FO	Foreign Office Records
HC Deb.	*Parliamentary Debates* (Commons)
HLRO	House of Lords Record Office
H-M	Headlam-Morley Papers
HNKY	Hankey Papers
HHW	Henry Wilson Papers
IOLR	India Office Library and Records
IWM	Imperial War Museum
LG	Lloyd George Papers
NLW	National Library of Wales
PRO	Public Record Office
SRO	Scottish Record Office
SWC	Supreme War Council
T	Treasury Records
TJ	Thomas Jones Papers
UB	Uncatalogued Bryce Papers
USFR	*Papers relating to the Foreign Relations of the United States*
USFR, PPC	*Papers relating to the Foreign Relations of the United States, the Paris Peace Conference, 1919*
WO	War Office Records

Notes

Introduction

1 V. H. Rothwell, *British War Aims and Peace Diplomacy, 1914–1918* (Oxford: Clarendon Press, 1971).

2 Michael Dockrill and Douglas Goold, *Peace without Promise: Britain and the Peace Conferences, 1919–1923* (London: Batsford, 1981), p. 43. See also Howard Elcock, *Portrait of a Decision: The Council of Four and the Treaty of Versailles* (London: Methuen, 1972), pp 130–1. These works apparently relied on David Lloyd George's account in *Memoirs of the Peace Conference*, 2 vols (New Haven, Conn.: Yale University Press, 1939), Vol. 1, pp. 183–4, 389.

3 John Keegan, 'The inter-war years', in Robin Higham (ed.), *A Guide to the Sources of British Military History* (Berkeley, Calif.: University of California Press, 1971), p. 452.

4 John P. Fox, 'Britain and the Inter-Allied Military Commission of Control, 1925–26', *Journal of Contemporary History*, vol. 4 (April 1969), pp. 143–64; Jon Jacobson, *Locarno Diplomacy: Germany and the West, 1925–1929* (Princeton, NJ: Princeton University Press, 1972), pp. 49–50, 62; Sally Marks, *The Illusion of Peace: International Relations in Europe, 1918–1933* (New York: St Martin's Press, 1976), p. 96.

5 The official records of the Paris Peace Conference discussions of German disarmament were published in 1943 in US, Department of State, *Papers relating to the Foreign Relations of the United States, the Paris Peace Conference, 1919*, 13 vols (Washington, DC: Government Printing Office, 1942–7), vols 3, 4. Cited hereafter as *USFR, PPC*. David Hunter Miller reproduced most of the records in 1925 in the documents section of his privately printed *My Diary at the Conference of Paris, with Documents* ([New York: for the author, Appeal Printing, 1925–8]), Vols 14, 15. In his study of the Paris Peace Conference, which appeared before the official publication of the conference's records, Paul Birdsall, who had had access to the House Collection, briefly discussed the British role in demanding German disarmament: *Versailles, Twenty Years After* (New York: Reynal & Hitchcock, 1941), pp. 148–9. See also F. S. Marston, *The Peace Conference of 1919: Organization and Procedure* (London: Oxford University Press, 1944), p. 126, and the narrative based on *USFR, PPC*, vols 3, 4, in Gerda Richards Crosby, *Disarmament and Peace in British Politics, 1914–1919* (Cambridge, Mass.: Harvard University Press, 1957), pp. 106–16, 120–30.

6 Frances Stevenson Diary, 1 February 1916, House of Lords Record Office (cited hereafter as HLRO), Historical Collection 195, Stevenson Papers.

Chapter 1

1 'The Anglo-German approach', *Nation*, vol. 12 (15 February 1913), p. 804.

2 R. C. K. Ensor, *England, 1870–1914* (Oxford: Clarendon Press, 1936), p. 472.

3 *Life, Journalism and Politics*, 2 vols (New York: Frederick A. Stokes, [1927]), Vol 2, p. 4.

4 ibid.
5 E. J. Dillon, 'Foreign affairs', *Contemporary Review*, vol. 106 (July 1914), p. 109.
6 House Diary V, 6 August 1914, House Papers, Yale University Library, New Haven, Conn., recalling his visit to London in June.
7 Bertie, Memorandum, 27 June 1914, Bertie Papers, Foreign Office records, class 800, vol. 171, Public Record Office, London (cited hereafter as PRO), recording his interview with Grey on 25 June. Foreign Office records cited hereafter using the form FO 800/171. All Foreign Office records are at the PRO.
8 Great Britain, Parliament, *Parliamentary Debates* (Commons), 5th ser., vol. 65 (1914), cols 727–8, 23 July. Cited hereafter as 5 *HC Deb*.
9 Resolution passed at a meeting held in London, 17 January 1912, *The Times*, 19 January 1912.
10 Speech at Nottingham, 21 November 1912, *The Times*, 22 November 1912. Much of Liberal thinking on Germany contained this admixture of Social Darwinist attitudes.
11 *Manchester Guardian*, 3 August 1914.
12 'Why we must not fight', *Daily News*, 1 August 1914.
13 ibid., 3 August 1914. Supporting letters from other Liberals also appeared that day.
14 5 *HC Deb.*, vol. 65 (1914), col. 1866, 3 August.
15 ibid., col. 1846.
16 Ensor, *England*, p. 475.
17 (New York: Macmillan, 1916), pp. 177–8.
18 'The character of the war', *Daily News*, 5 August 1914.
19 *Nation* vol. 15 (15 August 1914), p. 724; 'National character and the war', ibid., vol. 16 (24 October 1914), pp. 104–5.
20 'The objects of the war', *Manchester Guardian*, 20 August 1914.
21 'Neutral nations & the war', *Daily Chronicle*, 5 October 1914.
22 'The end of the balance of power', *Nation*, vol. 15 (8 August 1914), p. 694.
23 'In time of peril', *Daily News*, 8 August 1914.
24 Cromer to Dr von Hebentanz, 27 October 1914, Cromer Papers, FO 633/23.
25 'The war of fear', *Nation*, vol. 15 (8 August 1914), p. 692.
26 Cromer to J. St Loe Strachey, 30 August 1915, Cromer Papers, FO 633/24.
27 'Events of the week', *Nation*, vol. 15 (8 August 1914), p. 689.
28 ' "Roll up that map" ', *Daily News*, 22 August 1914.
29 Spender to Grey, 17 February 1915, Grey Papers, FO 800/111.
30 Wells, *Mr. Britling*, p. 177.
31 Haldane, Memorandum, 29 May 1915, reproduced in Sir Frederick Maurice, *Haldane: The Life of Viscount Haldane of Cloan*, 2 vols (London: Faber, 1937–9), Vol. 1, p. 365; Viscount Haldane, *Before the War* (New York: Funk & Wagnalls, 1920), pp. 15, 39, 71, 72, 81–2, 136, 144, 160.
32 Grey to Theodore Roosevelt, 20 October 1914, Grey Papers, FO 800/106.
33 Quoted in Maurice, *Haldane*, Vol. 1, p. 353.
34 Scott Diary, 3 August 1914, Scott Papers, Add. 50901, British Library, London (cited hereafter as BL).
35 Quoted in Burton J. Hendrick, *The Life and Letters of Walter H. Page*, 3 vols (Garden City, NY: Doubleday, Page, 1922–6), Vol. 1, p. 315.
36 Cromer to Strachey, 14 August 1914, Cromer Papers, FO 633/23.
37 Text of interview with William G. Shepherd of United Press Associates of America, *The Times*, 30 August 1914.
38 Grey to Roosevelt, 20 October 1914, Grey Papers, FO 800/106.

39   Read at Berwick, 4 September 1914, *The Times*, 5 September 1914.
40   *The Times*, 3 October 1914.
41   'Through terror to triumph!', speech at the Queen's Hall, London, 19 September 1914, in David Lloyd George, *Through Terror to Triumph*, ed. F. L. Stevenson (London: Hodder & Stoughton, 1915), p. 12.
42   *The Times*, 10 November 1914.
43   Speech at Lancaster House, 10 April 1916, ibid., 11 April 1916.
44   5 *HC Deb*, vol. 88 (1916), cols 1336–7, 19 December.
45   Rothwell, *British War Aims*, p. 18, so dismisses them.
46   11 August 1914, NLW MS 20433C, no. 1522, Lloyd George MSS, National Library of Wales, Aberystwyth (cited hereafter as NLW).
47   Grey to Oscar S. Straus, 10 November 1914, enclosed in Grey to Sir Cecil Spring Rice, 11 November 1914, Spring Rice Papers, FO 800/241.
48   Grey to Sir Francis Blake, 4 October 1914, reproduced in G. M. Trevelyan, *Grey of Fallodon* (London: Longmans, Green, 1937), p. 271.
49   'Note on the possible terms of peace', 12 October 1916, Cabinet Papers no. P 8, class 29, vol. 1, PRO. Cabinet Papers cited hereafter by series initials, paper number, class number and volume number, using the form P 8, Cab. 29/1. All Cabinet records are at the PRO.
50   'Suggested basis for a territorial settlement in Europe', 7 August 1916, G 78, Cab. 24/2.
51   'Views of the Foreign Office representatives on the question of the retention of the German colonies', 21 January 1917, TC 27, Cab. 16/36.
52   Mallet to Leopold Maxse, 15 October [1915], Maxse Papers, 469/560, West Sussex Record Office, Chichester. According to Mallet, the other two were Spring Rice and Eyre Crowe.
53   29 September 1916, ibid., 473/802–4.
54   'The peace settlement in Europe', 4 October 1916, P 7, Cab. 29/1.
55   Drummond to Bryce, 19 March 1916, Bryce Papers, UB 55, Bodleian Library, Oxford.
56   To Sir M. Findlay, 2 October 1916, Paget Papers, Add. 51256, BL.
57   Tyrrell to House, 3 January 1918, House Papers, box 111a, folder 3866. Cited hereafter as House 111a/3866.
58   G. P. Gooch and Harold Temperley (eds), *British Documents on the Origins of the War, 1898–1914*, 11 vols (London: HMSO, 1926–38), Vol. 11, no. 293, Minute, 30 July 1914 on Sir E. Goschen to Grey, 29 July 1914; ibid., no. 158, Minute, 29 July 1914 on Rumbold to Grey , 22 July 1914.
59   ibid., no. 144, 26 July 1914.
60   'Lord Bryce on the issues', *Daily Chronicle*, 5 October 1914.
61   *The Origins of the War* (Cambridge: Cambridge University Press, 1915), pp. 49, 67.
62   'Lord Esher and the war', *Glasgow Herald*, 28 April 1915, quoted in Peter Fraser, *Lord Esher: A Political Biography* (London: Hart-Davis, MacGibbon, 1973), p. 276.
63   Hewins Diary, 11 July 1917, Hewins Papers 196/26, Sheffield University Library.
64   'Notes on possible terms of peace', 11 April 1917, GT 448, Cab. 24/10.
65   25 May 1915, Amery Papers, box E 57, in the possession of the Rt Hon. Julian Amery, London.
66   'The prevention of war', June 1918, fragment, Amery E 72.
67   *Round Table*, vol. 4 (September 1914), p. 652.
68   (London: Heinemann, 1914).
69   'An Allied peace: V. – the destruction of Prussian militarism', *New Statesman*, vol. 8 (14 October 1916), p. 29.
70   Claud Schuster to John St Loe Strachey, 4 September 1914, HLRO, Historical Collection 196, Strachey Papers, S/18/1/5.

71 'Our financial position in America', 24 October 1916, HLRO, Historical Collection 192, Lloyd George Papers, E/9/2/21. Cited hereafter as LG.

72 'Report for the War Committee', 6 November 1916, ibid., E/9/2/3.

73 Report, 30 May 1916, Spring Rice Papers, FO 800/242.

74 'Memorandum on Anglo-American relations, August 1917', 20 August 1917, circulated by Cecil, 21 August, 739, FO 899/4.

75 For example, House to Grey, 3 September 1915, House 53/1664.

76 Viscount Grey of Fallodon, *Twenty-Five Years, 1892–1916*, 2 vols (New York: Stokes, 1925), Vol. 2, p. 124.

77 'Notes for speech, August 4', 30 July 1917, Lothian Papers, GD 40/17/644, Scottish Record Office, Edinburgh (cited hereafter as SRO).

78 Hankey Diary, 23 December 1917, HNKY 1/3, Hankey Papers, Archives Centre, Churchill College, Cambridge.

79 17 October 1917, LG F/17/6/10.

80 'The destruction of a false ideal', in David Lloyd George, *The Great Crusade* (New York: Doran, 1918), p. 195.

81 Minutes of a Meeting of the War Cabinet, 3 January 1918, 5.00 p.m., WC 313, Cab. 23/5. See also Ian Malcolm to Balfour, 5 January 1918, Balfour Papers, Add. 49748, BL, for concern about the effect of the speech on 'the German mind'.

82 *British War Aims* (New York: Doran, [1918]), p. 3.

83 Committee for Propaganda in Enemy Countries, No. 3, Minutes of the Third Meeting held at Crewe House, 31 May 1918, Northcliffe Papers, deposit 4890, vol. X, BL.

84 Henry Wickham Steed, Synopsis, 'Memorandum on war aims, prepared by a Select Committee of the Enemy Countries Propaganda for guidance in the Department of *Great Propaganda*', n.d. [submitted in advance for discussion by the Committee for Propaganda in Enemy Countries at its meeting 31 May 1918], ibid.

85 H. G. Wells, 'Memorandum on war aims, prepared by a Select Committee of the Enemy Countries Propaganda for guidance in the Department of *Great Propaganda*', n.d. [submitted in advance for discussion by the Committee for Propaganda in Enemy Countries at its meeting 31 May 1918], ibid.

86 *Northcliffe: An Intimate Biography* (New York: Macmillan, 1930), p. 251.

Chapter 2

1 23 May 1916, House 86/2989.

2 5 *HC Deb.*, vol. 82, col. 2194, 24 May.

3 House to Grey, 3 September 1915, House 53/1664; Grey to House, 22 September 1915, ibid.; House Diary VII, 8 October 1915; House to Grey, 17 October 1915, enclosed in House to President Wilson, 17 October 1915, House 120/4253; Grey to House, 11 November 1915, House 53/1665.

4 ' "British navalism": the attitude towards British naval policy in the U.S.A.', 34, Cab. 37/130.

5 To Brig.-Gen. Sir Hereward Wake, 9 August 1918, Amery E 61.

6 'The war aims of the Allies in the First World War', in Richard Pares and A. J. P. Taylor (eds), *Essays Presented to Sir Lewis Namier* (London: Macmillan, 1956), p. 479.

'7 Minutes of a Meeting of the War Council, 10 March 1915, 5, Cab. 42/2.

8 To J. W. Headlam, 6 June 1917, Amery E 59.

9 See, for example, Hankey Diary, 29 April 1916, HNKY 1/1, 6 August 1918, ibid., 1/5.

10 For example, Amery to [J. E.] Mackenzie, 19 April 1917, Amery E 60.

11 Speech at the City Carlton Club, 20 March 1916, *The Times*, 21 March 1916; speech at Conway, Wales, 6 May 1916, ibid., 8 May 1916.

12 'Once we can make Germany realize that after the war her opportunities for trade with Great Britain and the Allies are gone, we shall come nearer to victory than we should by the destruction of one of her armies.' Speech to British Imperial Council of Commerce, 8 June 1916, ibid., 9 June 1916.

13 'The future relations of the Great Powers', 8 April 1915, 17, Cab. 37/127.

14 'Memorandum on suggested possible terms of peace between the British Empire and Germany', n.d., enclosed in Aeneas O'Neill to Lloyd George, 29 December 1916, LG F/36/6/2.

15 G 78, Cab. 24/2.

16 Lady Algernon Gordon Lennox (ed.), *The Diary of Lord Bertie of Thame, 1914–1918*, 2 vols (New York: Doran, [1924]), Vol. 1, p. 149, Diary, 17 April 1915; Rumbold to Maxse, 27 September 1914, Maxse 469/548.

17 'Episodes of the month', *National Review*, vol. 66 (November 1915), p. 361.

18 London, 'A suggestion of peace terms to be imposed', ibid., vol. 68 (September 1916), pp. 42, 51.

19 'An Allied peace: I. – the disarming of Germany', *New Statesman*, vol. 7 (9 September 1916), p. 536.

20 *Memoirs of the Peace Conference*, Vol. 1, p. 11.

21 'The future relations of the Great Powers: observations on the Lord Chancellor's note', 21 April 1915, 34, Cab. 37/127.

22 5, Cab. 42/2.

23 In addition to the destruction of the military domination of Prussia, these were the restoration of Belgium, the security of France against aggression and the guaranteeing of the rights of small nations.

24 Viscount Cecil of Chelwood, *All the Way* (London: Hodder & Stoughton, 1949), p. 135.

25 'Note by Lady G. Cecil of a talk with A. J. B.', 14 August 1929, Balfour Add. 49833.

26 Grey, *Twenty-Five Years*, Vol. 2, p. 247.

27 Grey to Spring Rice, 2 January 1915, Grey Papers, FO 800/85; Grey to House, 12 May 1916, House 53/1667.

28 Minute by Grey, 18 September 1916, 180510, FO 371/2804.

29 Grey to Sir George Buchanan, 15 May 1916, 40, Cab. 37/147.

30 17, Cab. 37/127.

31 Grey to Howard Taylor, 2 August 1916, Grey Papers, FO 800/86. See also Grey to Spring Rice, 22 December 1914, ibid., FO 800/84, pt 3.

32 Text of statement made by Grey to the London representative of the *Chicago Daily News*, in *The Times*, 15 May 1916.

33 Grey, *Twenty-Five Years*, Vol. 2, p. 128.

34 Memorandum, 27 November 1916, 20, Cab. 37/160.

35 To Buchanan, 8 January 1915, Nicolson Papers, FO 800/377.

36 Nicolson to Buchanan, 3 May 1915, ibid.

37 Minute, 6 April 1916, on Bryce to Grey, 6 April 1916, Grey Papers, FO 800/105.

38 Hardinge to Sir Valentine Chirol, 9 August 1916, Hardinge Papers, vol. 24, Cambridge University Library. Cited hereafter as Hardinge 24.

39 Fraser, *Esher*, pp. 329–30.

40 Maurice V. Brett and Oliver Viscount Esher (eds), *Journals and Letters of Reginald Viscount Esher*, 4 vols (London: Nicholson & Watson, 1934–8), Vol. 4, p. 48, Journal, 11 August 1916.

41 Esher to Robertson, 11 August, 15 August 1916, Brett and Esher, *Journals*, Vol. 4, pp. 48–9, 50; Esher to Asquith, 13 August 1916, quoted in Fraser, *Esher*, p. 330.

42 Fraser, *Esher*, pp. 330–1; Robertson to Lloyd George, 17 August 1916, War Office records, class 106, vol. 1510, no. 1, PRO. War Office records cited hereafter using the form WO 106/1510/1. All War Office records are at the PRO.

43 H. A. L. Fisher, 'Memorandum of an interview with D. Lloyd George', 27 August 1916, Fisher Papers, box 24, Bodleian. Cited hereafter as Fisher 24.

44 Hankey Diary, 23 August 1916, HNKY 1/1.

45 Hankey Diary, 25 August 1916, ibid.

46 Hankey Diary, 23 August 1916, ibid.

47 'The problems of peace', 29 August 1916, G 76, Cab. 24/2.

48 Minutes of a Meeting of the War Committee, 30 August 1916, 8, Cab. 42/18.

49 *The Times*, 29 September 1916. Before publishing this interview Lord Northcliffe sent a copy to Lloyd George for his approval, and Lloyd George made several additions, including the sentence quoted above. LG E/2/21/3.

50 Fisher, Memorandum, 27 August 1916, Fisher 24.

51 24 May 1916, Curzon Papers, MSS Eur. F 112/116, India Office Library and Records, London (cited hereafter as IOLR).

52 Bertie, Memorandum, 15 August 1916, Bertie Papers, Mis/16/16, FO 800/175.

53 Curzon to Asquith, 24 May 1916, MSS Eur. F 112/116.

54 5 *HC Deb.*, vol. 86 (1916), cols 103–55, 240–4, 275, 324–44, 11 and 12 October.

55 William R. Robertson, 'General Staff memorandum submitted in accordance with the Prime Minister's instructions', 31 August 1916, P 4, Cab. 29/1.

56 P 8, ibid.

57 P 7, ibid.

58 ibid.

59 Esher Journal, 23 September 1916, Brett and Esher, *Journals*, Vol. 4, p. 54.

60 Minutes of a Meeting of the War Committee, 2, Cab. 42/21.

61 'The general review of the war', Memorandum by the Secretary of the War Committee, 31 October 1916, G 92, Cab. 63/15.

62 'Merchant shipping', Memorandum by Runciman, 24 October 1916, G 88, Cab. 24/2; 'Shipping', Note by Runciman, 9 November 1916, Annex to 11, Cab. 42/23; Grey, Memorandum, 20, Cab. 37/160.

63 Asquith Papers, vol. 17, fol. 129, Bodleian. Cited hereafter as Asquith 17/129.

64 'Memorandum by Lord Lansdowne respecting peace settlement', P 5, Cab. 29/1.

65 Memorandum, 27 November 1916, 21, Cab. 37/160.

66 *The Times*, 29 September 1916.

67 Memorandum, 24 November 1916, 15, Cab. 37/160.

68 Hankey Diary, 9 November 1916, HNKY 1/1.

69 Address to US Senate, 22 January 1917, in Ray Stannard Baker and William E. Dodd (eds), *The Public Papers of Woodrow Wilson*, 6 vols (New York: Harper, 1925–7), Vol. 4, pp. 407–14.

70 Speech at Carnarvon, *The Times*, 5 February 1917.

71 Lord Murray of Elibank, quoted in Esher, War Journals, 6 June 1917, quoted in Fraser, *Esher*, p. 366.

72 Wilson Diary, 1 March 1917, Henry Wilson Papers, HHW 26, microfilm, reel VII, Imperial War Museum, London (cited hereafter as IWM). Wilson Diaries and Notebooks cited hereafter by volume number only.

73 Letter to Hugh Glazebrook, 8 December 1914, quoted in John Marlowe, *Milner: Apostle of Empire* (London: Hamish Hamilton, 1976), p. 239.

74 Sidney Low, memorandum of an interview with Milner, 28 March 1917, reproduced in Desmond Chapman-Huston, *The Lost Historian: A Memoir of Sir Sidney Low* (London: John Murray, 1936), pp. 267–8.

75   Letter to the editor, *The Times*, 15 September 1914.
76   Letter to Charles Brumm, 24 November 1914, HLRO, Historical Collection 191, Law (Bonar Law) Papers, 37/4/30; Letter to Mr Strauss, 15 December 1914, ibid., 37/4/37; Robert Blake, *The Unknown Prime Minister: The Life and Times of Andrew Bonar Law, 1858–1923* (London: Eyre & Spottiswoode, 1955), p. 226.
77   Minutes of a Meeting of the Imperial War Cabinet, 23 March 1917, IWC 3, Cab. 23/40; Amery Diary, 23 March 1917; Minutes of a Meeting of the Imperial War Cabinet, 27 March 1917, IWC 4, Cab. 23/40; Report of the Imperial War Cabinet Committee on Territorial Changes, 28 April 1917, Cab. 21/77; 'The general strategic and military situation and particularly that on the western front', Memorandum by General Smuts, 29 April 1917, GT 597, Cab. 24/11.
78   Speech at Glasgow, 17 May 1918, in W. K. Hancock and Jean van der Poel (eds), *Selections from the Smuts Papers*, 6 vols. (Cambridge: Cambridge University Press, 1966–73), Vol. 3, p. 649, document 829 (Smuts Papers, box H, no. 21).
79   Amery to Fitz [Sir J. P. FitzPatrick], 7 April 1917, Amery E 59.
80   Balfour to Cecil, 29 December 1917, Balfour Add. 49738. See also Amery Diary, 23 March 1917.
81   Balfour to Cecil, 29 December 1917, Balfour Add. 49738.
82   Minutes of a Meeting of the War Cabinet, 18 December 1916, 38, Cab. 37/161; Minutes of Meetings of the War Cabinet, 21, 23, 26 December 1916, 3, 12, 17, Cab. 37/162.
83   Ambassador in France (Sharp) to Secretary of State, 10 January 1917, in US, Department of State, *Papers relating to the Foreign Relations of the United States, 1917*, supp. 1, *The World War* (Washington, DC: Government Printing Office, 1931), pp. 6–8.
84   Balfour to Spring Rice, 13 January 1917, ibid, pp. 17–21.
85   Minutes of a Meeting of the Imperial War Cabinet, 20 March 1917, IWC 1, Cab. 23/40.
86   Kerr to Lloyd George, n.d., Lothian GD 40/17/670/1.
87   IWC 1, Cab. 23/40.
88   Minutes of a Meeting of the Imperial War Cabinet, 12 April 1917, IWC 9, ibid.
89   Thomas Jones Diary, 20 April 1917, Jones Papers, Z 1917/58–9, NLW. Cited hereafter as TJ.
90   Minutes of Meetings of the Imperial War Cabinet, 26 April, 1 May 1917, IWC 12, 13, Cab. 23/40.
91   IWC 13, ibid.

Chapter 3

1   *The Times*, 21 March 1916.
2   ibid., 11 April 1916.
3   Harold I. Nelson, *Land and Power: British and Allied Policy on Germany's Frontiers, 1916–1919* (London: Routledge & Kegan Paul, 1963), p. 6.
4   TC 27, Cab. 16/36.
5   Report of Imperial War Cabinet Committee on Territorial Changes, Cab. 21/77.
6   GT 597, Cab. 24/11.
7   Letter to Theodore Roosevelt, 10 September 1914, Spring Rice Papers, CASR 9/1–2/9, Churchill College.

8   Minutes of a Meeting of the War Council, 19 March 1915, 14, Cab. 42/2.

9   GT 448, Cab. 24/10.

10 111th Meeting, CID, 11 May 1911, 3, Cab. 2/2, quoted in Michael Howard, *The Continental Commitment: The Dilemma of British Defence Policy in the Era of the Two World Wars* (London: Temple Smith, 1972), p. 51.

11 Notes, 2 August 1914, reproduced in Earl of Oxford and Asquith, *Memories and Reflections, 1852–1927*, 2 vols (Boston, Mass.: Little, Brown, 1928), Vol. 2, p. 12.

12 Reproduced in Grey, *Twenty-Five Years*, Vol. 2, app. D, p. 321.

13 22 September 1915, House 53/1664.

14 5, Cab. 42/2.

15 G 76, Cab. 24/2.

16 ibid.

17 Hancock and van der Poel, *Smuts Papers*, Vol. 3, pp. 503–4, document 748 (Smuts Papers, box N, no. 66).

18 'The geographical pivot of history', paper read at the Royal Geographical Society, 25 January 1904 (London: William Clowes, [1904]; reprinted from *Geographical Journal*, April 1904), pp. 3, 13–17, 23.

19 ibid., p. 16.

20 See Bernard Semmel, *Imperialism and Social Reform: English Social-Imperial Thought, 1895–1914* (Cambridge, Mass.: Harvard University Press, 1960), pp. 77, 173–4.

21 Bertie, Memorandum, 27 June 1914, FO 800/171.

22 *Manchester Guardian*, 1 August 1914.

23 Norman Angell, *After All: The Autobiography of Norman Angell* (New York: Farrar, Straus & Young, [1952]), p. 182.

24 3 August 1914.

25 [George Allardice Riddell], *Lord Riddell's War Diary, 1914–18* (London: Nicolson & Watson, 1933), p. 4, recounting a discussion of 2 August 1914.

26 Chirol to Hardinge, 4 August 1914, Hardinge 93; Cromer to Lady Alice Shaw Stewart, 20 August 1914, Cromer Papers, FO 633/23.

27 Nicolson to Buchanan, 15 March 1915, Nicolson Papers, FO 800/377.

28 Same to same, 8 January 1915, ibid.

29 ibid.

30 Spring Rice to Grey, 20 September 1914, reproduced in House Diary V. Spring Rice reached this conclusion after a conversation with House, who recorded that he 'made him see that if the Allies won and Germany was thoroughly crushed, there would be no holding Russia back'. ibid., 20 September 1914.

31 Letter to Margaret Lloyd George, 11 August 1914, NLW MS 20433C, no. 1522.

32 15 March 1915, FO 800/377.

33 14, Cab. 42/2.

34 Fisher, Memorandum, 27 August 1916, Fisher 24.

35 Lennox, *Diary of Lord Bertie*, Vol. 1, p. 149, Bertie Diary, 17 April 1915.

36 Wilson Notebook, 10 October 1916, HHW 25.

37 P 4, Cab. 29/1.

38 Angell, *After All*, p. 182.

39 'Committee on Territorial Changes, note by the General Staff as to the policy to be pursued in regard to the German colonies', 7 September 1916, TC 4, Cab. 16/36.

40 Robertson to Asquith, 6 November 1915, Robertson Papers, I 13/14, Liddell Hart Centre for Military Archives, King's College, University of London.

41 Esher Journal, 25 September 1916, Brett and Esher, *Journals*, Vol. 4, p. 54. This may have been the 7 September memorandum. I found no September memorandum authored solely by Macdonogh in the Macdonogh Papers in WO 106.

42 Amery Diary, 7 February 1917.

43 'German peace proposals', 14 December 1916, P 11, Cab. 29/1.

44 TC 4, Cab. 16/36.

45 P 11, Cab. 29/1.

46 Wilson Diary, 30 November 1914, HHW 23.

47 17, Cab. 37/127.

48 34, ibid.

49 'Notes by Sir Eyre Crowe on Lord R. Cecil's proposals for the maintenance of future peace', 12 October 1916, GT 484A, Cab. 24/10.

50 cf. 'A great and efficient population is the only firm source of great power', Halford J. Mackinder, *Money-Power and Man-Power: The Underlying Principles rather than the Statistics of Tariff Reform* (London: Simpkin, Marshall, Hamilton, Kent, 1906), p. 14, quoted in Semmel, *Imperialism*, p. 173. See also Halford J. Mackinder, 'Man-Power as a measure of national and imperial strength,' *National Review*, vol. 45 (March 1905), pp. 136–43.

51 GT 484A, Cab. 24/10.

52 'Anglo-German relations', reprinted in Arthur James Balfour, *Essays Speculative and Political* (New York: Doran, 1921), p. 182.

53 P 7, Cab. 29/1.

54 Minutes of a Meeting of the Imperial War Cabinet, 15 August 1918, IWC 32, Cab. 23/42.

55 *USFR, 1917*, supp. 1, pp. 19–20.

56 Montagu to Asquith, 18 March 1916, Asquith 16/95.

57 Minutes of a Meeting of the Imperial War Cabinet, 22 March 1917, IWC 2, Cab. 23/40.

58 'The Russian situation and its consequences', 20 May 1917, enclosed in Amery to Maj.-Gen. F. B. Maurice, 21 May 1917, Amery E 60. Amery sent the memorandum to Maurice for comment before submitting it to the War Cabinet.

59 'Notes on Allied strategy', n.d., WO 106/1514/15.

60 Scott Diary, 28 September 1917, Add. 50904.

61 Minutes of a Meeting of the War Cabinet, 24 September 1917, WC 238A, Cab. 23/16.

62 Milner to Glazebrook, 8 December 1914, quoted in Marlowe, *Milner*, p. 239.

63 WC 238A, Cab. 23/16; Minutes of a Meeting of the War Cabinet, 25 September 1917, WC 239A, ibid.; Hankey Diary, 24 September 1917, HNKY 1/3.

64 WC 239A, Cab. 23/16.

65 Scott Diary, 28 September 1917, Add. 50904. cf. Mackinder, 'Geographical pivot', p. 16.

66 Hankey Diary, 24 November 1917, HNKY 1/3.

67 Haig to Esher, 22 January 1918, quoted in Fraser, *Esher*, p. 398. See also Smuts to Lloyd George, 21 January 1918, LG F/45/9/9.

68 25 July 1918, quoted in Howard, *Continental Commitment*, p. 69.

69 'British interests at the peace conference', MS Milner dep. 359, box AD1, fol. 163, Bodleian. Cited hereafter as Milner 359/AD1/163.

Chapter 4

1 'Opportunity', *Nation*, vol. 15 (15 August 1914), p. 732.

2 ibid., p. 734.

3 'Utopia or hell?' ibid., p. 726.

4 1 September 1914, in H. A. L. Fisher, *The War: Its Causes and Issues* (London: Longmans, Green, 1914), p. 24.

5 Letter to the editor, 17 September 1914, signed by J. Ramsay MacDonald, Charles Trevelyan, Norman Angell, E. D. Morel, Arthur Ponsonby, *Nation*, vol. 15 (19 September 1914), p. 865.

6 *Nation*, vol. 15 (15 August 1914), p. 726.

7 Hobson published his proposals in July 1915 as *Towards International Government* (London: Allen & Unwin, 1915). Earlier he had submitted a draft to other members of the Bryce Group, a private group which Bryce had organised to discuss the problems of peace. ibid., p. 8.

8 'Memorandum on Mr J. A. Hobson's notes', 9 January 1915, UB 58.

9 Nicolson to Buchanan, 3 May 1915, Nicolson Papers, FO 800/377.

10 34, Cab. 37/127.

11 Grey to Spring Rice, 2 January 1915, FO 800/85; Grey to House, 22 September 1915, House 53/1664; 40, Cab. 37/147.

12 12 May 1916, House 53/1667.

13 G 78, Cab. 24/2.

14 Viscount Cecil of Chelwood, *A Great Experiment* (New York: Oxford University Press, 1941), p. 44. The Foreign Office files which contained Cecil's original memorandum have been destroyed. I found no record of this draft memorandum in the Cecil Papers or any other collection of private or official papers which I examined. 'Memorandum on proposals for diminishing the occasion of future wars', n.d. [indexed as both 30 March and 17 April 1917], GT 484, Cab. 24/10 is the revised memorandum which does not include the disarmament proposals but instead contains Cecil's explanation of why he withdrew them.

15 Cecil, *All the Way*, p. 141; Cecil to F. R. Coudert, 18 July 1916, Spring Rice Papers, FO 800/242.

16 GT 484, Cab. 24/10.

17 GT 484A, ibid.

18 Draft Minutes of a Meeting [the Fourth] of the Committee to Consider the Economic and Non-Territorial Desiderata in the Terms of Peace, 20 April 1917, Cab. 21/71. The minutes say nothing more about this discussion. The account in this paragraph is based upon Jones Diary, 20 April 1917, TJ Z 1917/58–60, supplemented by Henry Borden (ed.), *Robert Laird Borden: His Memoirs*, 2 vols (New York: Macmillan, 1938), Vol. 2, pp. 694–5. Jones served as the Milner Committee's secretary, and Canadian Prime Minister Borden was one of its members.

19 Jones Diary, 20 April 1917, TJ Z 1917/59.

20 Besides Milner and Borden, the members of the committee were Smuts; Arthur Henderson, Labour's representative in the War Cabinet; New Zealand's Prime Minister W. F. Massey, with Sir Joseph Ward representing New Zealand when Massey did not attend; Newfoundland's Prime Minister Sir Edwin Morris; Sir J. Meston, Lt.-Gov. of the United Province of India; the Maharaja of Bikaner; and H. A. L. Fisher. IWC 9, Cab. 23/40.

21 Speech at Sheffield, 2 September 1914, in Fisher, *The War*, p. 30.

22 Milner, 'Report of Committee on Terms of Peace (Economic and Non-Territorial Desiderata)', 24 April 1917, P 15, Cab. 21/70.

23 ibid.

24 IWC 13, Cab. 23/40.

25 'The objections to any attempt to limit armaments are very powerfully put.' Cecil, Minute on GT 484A, n.d., Balfour Papers, FO 800/214. See also GT

484, Cab. 24/10 and Cecil's remarks in IWC 12, 13, Cab. 23/40. Cecil later recounted that he had been so 'shaken' by Crowe's arguments he had omitted his proposal for international disarmament from the memorandum he circulated to the Cabinet. *A Great Experiment*, p. 61.

26 IWC 12, Cab. 23/40.
27 ibid.
28 Baker and Dodd, *Public Papers*, Vol. 4, pp. 414, 413.
29 IWC 12, IWC 13, Cab. 23/40. These minutes are inconsistent in attributing views to speakers. Some speakers are identified; others are not.
30 IWC 13, ibid.
31 IWC 12, IWC 13, ibid.
32 IWC 12, ibid.
33 ibid.
34 IWC 13, ibid.; Amery Diary, 1 May 1917.
35 IWC 13, Cab. 23/40.
36 Jones Diary, 24 April 1917, TJ Z 1917/63.
37 IWC 13, Cab. 23/40.
38 Quoted in Robert Craig Brown, 'Sir Robert Borden and Canada's war aims', in Barry Hunt and Adrian Preston (eds), *War Aims and Strategic Policy in the Great War, 1914–1918* (London: Croom Helm, 1977), p. 56.
39 IWC 13, Cab. 23/40.
40 W. K. Hancock, *Smuts: The Sanguine Years, 1870–1919* (Cambridge: Cambridge University Press, 1962), pp. 462–3; William H. Buckler to House, 7 June 1917, Buckler Papers 1/6, Yale.
41 Buckler to House, 7 June 1917, Buckler 1/6.
42 Scott Diary, 28 September 1917, Add. 50904.
43 GT 597, Cab. 24/11.
44 'A league of nations', in J. C. Smuts, *War-Time Speeches: A Compilation of Public Utterances in Great Britain* (New York: Doran, 1917), p. 58.
45 Smuts to Alice Clark, 24 May 1917, Hancock and van der Poel, *Smuts Papers*, Vol. 3, pp. 523–4, document 758 (Smuts Papers, vol, 98, no. 1026). See also Clark to Smuts, 19 May 1917, Smuts Papers, vol. 16, no. 35, microfilm, Cambridge University Library. Smuts Papers at Cambridge cited hereafter using the form Smuts 16/35.
46 1 June 1917, LG F/38/2/8.
47 26 May 1917.
48 Addison Diary, 8 May 1917, Addison Papers, box 98, file 55.6, Bodleian. Cited hereafter as Addison 98/55.6.
49 11 May 1917, Derby Papers, box 27, Liverpool Record Office, Liverpool City Library.
50 Minutes of a Meeting of the War Cabinet, 5 June 1917, WC 154, Cab. 3/3.
51 G. Wallace Carter, National War Aims Committee, Meetings, Department Reports, 25 September, 10 October 1917, Treasury records, class 102, vol. 16, PRO (cited hereafter as T 102/16); Addison Diary, 2 October 1917, Addison 98/55.7.
52 W. Athelstan Johnson to Bertie, 8 September 1917, Bertie Papers, Mis/17/19, FO 800/175; 'An annual balance sheet of the war', Report to House, 30 September 1917, Buckler 5/10.
53 *The Times*, 25 October 1917.
54 *The Morrow of the War*, reprinted in Peter Stansky (ed.), *The Left and War: The British Labour Party and World War I* (New York: Oxford University Press, 1969), p. 102.
55 1 August 1917, copy in LG F/160/1/1. The note was published on 15 August.

56 *The Times*, 25 October 1917.

57 *General Smuts's Message to South Wales* (London: Field & Queen, [1917]), p. 14.

58 Hancock and van der Poel, *Smuts Papers*, Vol. 3, p. 566. For Smuts's reception, see R. Wherry Anderson, 'Report on General Smuts's visit to South Wales, ibid., pp. 566–7, document 789 (Smuts Papers, box H, no. 15). Anderson was a local official, apparently a representative of the National War Aims Committee, who accompanied Smuts. Smuts's own account is in David Lloyd George, *War Memoirs*, 2 vols, 2nd edn (London: Odhams, 1938), Vol. 1, pp. 814–15. Interestingly, in his account to Lloyd George, Smuts did not mention his call for disarmament or, if he did, Lloyd George omitted that section of Smuts's report.

59 Amery to J.[ohn] Buchan, 22 May 1917, Amery E 59.

60 For example, *Daily News*, 15 May 1917; *Daily Mail*, 25 October, 30 October 1917; *Daily Chronicle*, 25 October 1917.

61 Buchan to Amery, 23 May 1917, Amery E 59. In 1917 Buchan was Director of Information. Schedule of Wellington House Literature, T 102/20, lists Smuts's speeches among the pamphlets issued by the National War Aims Committee's Department of Publicity.

62 Memorandum, Lansdowne to Balfour, November 1917, reproduced in Marquess of Lansdowne, 'The "peace letter" of 1917', *Nineteenth Century*, vol. 115 (March 1934), pp. 374–7.

63 Lansdowne to Balfour, 16 November 1917, Balfour Add. 49730; Balfour to Lansdowne, 22 November 1917, reproduced in Lansdowne, ' "Peace letter" ', p. 378. The letter appeared in the *Daily Telegraph*, 29 November.

64 *The Times*, 15 December 1917.

65 Lloyd George to C. W. Bowerman and Arthur Henderson, LG F/27/3/23. See also Bowerman and Henderson to Lloyd George, 20 December 1917, LG F/27/3/22.

66 'Report of General Smuts's mission', 20 December 1917, 27, Cab. 1/25.

67 28 December 1917.

68 Diary, 28 December 1917, Add. 50904.

69 Jones's account of a conversation with Hankey, Jones Diary, 7 January 1918, TJ Z 1918/9.

70 Draft Minutes of a Meeting of the War Cabinet, WC 307A, Cab. 23/13.

71 WC 313, Cab. 23/5.

72 Lloyd George to M. Lloyd George, 8 January 1917 [1918], NLW MS 20437C; Procès-verbal of the Sixth Meeting of the Third Session of the Supreme War Council, 2 February 1918, IC 44, Cab. 28/3.

73 Hankey Diary, 29 December 1917, HNKY 1/3.

74 WC 307A, Cab. 23/13.

75 Milner Diary, 28 December 1917, Milner 88.

76 WC 313, Cab. 23/5.

77 Hankey Diary, 1 January 1918, HNKY 1/3. Transmitting what he thought might be an apocryphal anecdote, Buckler reported a story circulating in the House of Commons in which Carson was quoted as having said, 'We are all pacifists now'. Report to House, 15 January 1918, Buckler 5/8.

78 Minutes of a Meeting of the War Cabinet, 31 December 1917, WC 308A, Cab. 23/13; Hankey Diary, 31 December 1917, HNKY 1/3; Addison Diary, 31 December 1917, Addison 98/55.7.

79 Jones Diary, 1 January 1918, TJ Z 1918/2.

80 Hankey to Lloyd George, 29 December 1917, and pencilled notes on same by Lloyd George or a member of his staff, LG F/23/1/38; Hankey Diary, 29 December 1917, HNKY 1/3; Jones Diary, 7 January 1918, TJ Z 1918/9.

81 'War aims', Draft Statement by General Smuts, 3 January 1918, GT 3180, Cab. 24/37.

82 Smuts to Mrs Hobhouse, 3 July 1917, Smuts 18/289. See also correspondence in Hancock and van der Poel, *Smuts Papers*, Vol. 3, pp. 459 ff.

83 Memorandum, 29 December 1917, enclosed in Minute, Kerr to Lloyd George, 30 December 1917, LG F/89/1/12.

84 ibid.

85 'Statement of war aims: draft statement based on General Smuts' draft', 3 January 1918, GT 3182, Cab. 24/37.

86 28 December 1917, Balfour Papers, FO 800/207.

87 'War aims', Draft Statement by Lord Robert Cecil, 3 January 1918, GT 3181, Cab. 24/37.

88 Cecil to Balfour, 28 December 1917, FO 800/207.

89 GT 3181, Cab. 24/37.

90 House Diary XII, 19 January 1918.

91 Minutes of a Meeting of the War Cabinet, 4 January 1918, WC 314, Cab. 23/13.

92 *British War Aims*, pp. 13–15.

93 In this speech Wilson called for 'adequate guarantees given and taken that national armaments will be reduced to the lowest point consistent with domestic safety'. Baker and Dodd, *Public Papers*, Vol. 5, p. 159.

Chapter 5

1 Procès-verbal of a Conference held at the Quai d'Orsay, Paris, 7 October 1918, 3.00 p.m., IC 79, Cab. 28/5.

2 Allied Military and Naval Representatives, 'Joint resolution regarding conditions of an armistice with Germany and Austria-Hungary', 8 October 1918, app. 2, Procès-verbal of a Conference held at the Quai d'Orsay, Paris, 8 October 1918, IC 80, ibid.

3 Wilson Diary, 8 October 1918, HHW 27.

4 Lt-Col. Cornwall, MI 3, War Office, 'Appreciation of the situation, 6th October, 1918', 7 October 1918, 4A, 26/E/24, SWC 330, Cab. 25/79.

5 Wilson Diary and Notebook, 8 October 1918, HHW 27.

6 Wilson Diary, 8 October 1918, ibid.

7 Hankey Diary, 8 October 1918, HNKY 1/5.

8 See Lloyd George's report on the Allied conferences in Paris in Minutes of a Meeting of the War Cabinet and the Imperial War Cabinet, 11 October 1918, IWC 35, Cab. 23/42.

9 'Conditions of an armistice with Germany', translation of a note by Marshal Foch, 8 October 1918, app. 1, IC 80, Cab. 28/5.

10 IC 80, ibid. See also Hankey Diary, 8 October 1918, HNKY 1/5, and Henry Wilson's record of a conversation with Hankey, Wilson Notebook, 8 October 1918, HHW 27.

11 Amery Diary, 6 October 1918.

12 'The peace note', *Daily News*, 7 October 1918.

13 Murray to Wiseman, 8 October 1918, Wiseman Papers, drawer 91, folder 87, Yale. Cited hereafter as Wiseman 91/87.

14 Copy Telegram, Prime Minister to Sir Eric Geddes, 12 October 1918, Lothian GD 40/1073/1. See also Lloyd George's remarks in Draft Notes of a Conference held at Danny, Sussex, 13 October 1918, GT 5967, Cab. 24/66.

15 IWC 35, Cab. 23/42.

16 Besides Lloyd George and Bonar Law, no War Cabinet members were present. Only three other members of the Cabinet attended: Balfour, Churchill and

Milner. Also attending were Hankey; Kerr; the ambassador to the United States, Lord Reading; Chief of the Naval Staff, Admiral Sir Rosslyn Wemyss; and General Wilson. GT 5967, Cab. 24/66.

17 ibid.
18 ibid.
19 ibid.
20 Wilson Notebook, 13 October 1918, HHW 27; GT 5967, Cab. 24/66; Riddell, *War Diary*, p. 372, Diary, 13 October 1918.
21 GT 5967, Cab. 24/66.
22 Milner to Sir Hugh Thornton, 31 October 1918, Milner Adds. 1; same to same, 31 October 1918, Milner 19.
23 GT 5967, Cab. 24/66.
24 Hankey to Lloyd George, 18 October 1918, reporting an informal Cabinet discussion that morning of which he was instructed to make no record. LG F/23/3/17.
25 'Conditions of armistice', 15 October 1918, GT 5980, Cab. 24/66.
26 Quoted in Riddell, *War Diary*, p. 372, Diary, 13 October 1918.
27 13 October 1918, LG F/18/2/23.
28 Jones Diary, 15 October 1918, TJ Z 1918/113.
29 Lloyd George to Geddes, 12 October 1918, Lothian GD 40/1073/1.
30 LG F/18/2/23.
31 On 18 October the CIGS commented on Lloyd George's changed mood. Wilson Notebook, HHW 27.
32 Quoted in Haig Diary, 19 October 1918, Haig Papers no. 132, Diary, vol. 34, National Library of Scotland, Edinburgh. Cited hereafter as Haig 132/34. See also 'Suggested military terms for an armistice with Germany and Austria-Hungary', Memorandum by General Wilson, 24 October 1918, GT 6087, Cab. 24/67. Wilson's only concession was his willingness to grant the withdrawing army the 'Honours of War', allowing the soldiers to retain their small arms.
33 General Staff, 'Summary of the military situation in the various theatres of war for the seven days ending 10th October, with comments by the General Staff', 11 October 1918, WO 106/319/124.
34 Fisher Diary, 16 October 1918, recounting a conversation with Bonar Law, Fisher 8A; Minutes of a Meeting of the War Cabinet, 16 October 1918, WC 487, Cab. 23/8.
35 Wilson Diary, 16 October 1918, HHW 27.
36 Wilson Notebook, 18 October 1918, ibid.
37 Wilson Notebook, 19 October 1918, HHW 27. See also Notes of a Conference of Ministers, 19 October 1918, X 29, Cab. 23/17.
38 Wilson Diary, 19 October 1918, HHW 27. See also Haig Diary, 19 October 1918, Haig 132/34.
39 Haig Diary, 19 October 1918, Haig 132/34.
40 In August 1917 during the Flanders offensive Esher described Haig's optimism as 'invulnerable'. War Journals, 19 August 1917, quoted in Fraser, *Esher*, p. 367. On 10 October 1918 Haig wrote in his diary: '*I assured him* [General Lawrence] *that the enemy has not the means, nor has the German High Command the will power,* to launch an attack strong enough to affect even our front line troops. We have got the enemy down, in fact he is a beaten Army, and my plan is to go on hitting him as hard as we possibly can, till he begs for mercy . . . The enemy is now in such a state that we can run all kinds of risks without any chance of the enemy hitting back in any force.' (Haig 132/34).
41 Haig Diary, 10 October, 17 October 1918, Haig 132/34.
42 Haig Diary, 19 October 1918, ibid.

43 X 29, Cab. 23/17; Minutes of a Meeting of the War Cabinet, 21 October 1918, WC 489A, Cab. 23/14; 'Memorandum by Field Marshal Sir Douglas Haig in regard to the military conditions of an armistice', 19 October 1918, app. 2, WC 489A, Cab. 23/14; Haig Diary, 19 October 1918, Haig 132/34; Wilson Diary and Notebook, 19 October 1918, HHW 27.

44 Haig to Lady Haig, 26 October 1918, Haig 152. See also same to same, 1 November 1918, ibid.

45 'Present situation of the German armies', Memorandum by Brig.-Gen. H. Wake, 'E' Branch, 8 October 1918, 26/E/24, SWC 330, Cab. 25/79.

46 'Summary of the military situation in the various theatres of war for the seven days ending 17th October, with comments by the General Staff', 18 October 1918, WO 106/319/125.

47 Cited in Cyril Falls and John W. Wheeler-Bennett, *Was Germany Defeated in 1918?* (Toronto: Oxford University Press, 1940), p. 19.

48 Sir Llewellyn Woodward, *Great Britain and the War of 1914–1918* (Boston, Mass.: Beacon Paperback, 1970), p. 417, n. 1.

49 'Summary of the military situation in the various theatres of war for the seven days ending 24th October, with comments by the General Staff', October 1918, WO 106/319/126.

50 Spears to Wilson, 2 November 1918, file 14/F/17, HHW 73/1/10.

51 After the 13 October conference Lloyd George's press secretary, William Sutherland, met individually with members of the press to 'impress upon them the absolute necessity of not assuming that the war is over & that indeed the best way to bring about the end is that all our papers should make it plain *that there can be no armistice unless the naval and military guarantees are such as to make it certain that Germany would not be in a position to* resume hostilities'. Kerr, Notes, Danny, Sussex, [13 October 1918], Lothian GD/40/17/61.

52 The jingo *John Bull* had already begun a campaign for harsh terms, publishing on 12 October a list of conditions which should be demanded of Germany. These did not, however, include land disarmament. Quoted in Raymond Postgate and Aylmer Vallance, *England Goes to Press: The English People's Opinion on Foreign Affairs as Reflected in their Newspapers since Waterloo (1815–1937)* (Indianapolis, Ind.: Bobbs-Merrill, 1937), pp. 289–90. Throughout October the *Daily Mail* demanded unconditional surrender; on 11 October it called for Germany to 'lead in disarmament' but specifically demanded only that Germany demonstrate its good faith 'by abandoning the submarine and the airship and the other cruel weapons which she has used so brutally'. 'Viscount Grey and free nations.'

53 'Parliament and peace', *Daily News*, 15 October 1918.

54 'Kaiserism must go', ibid., 16 October 1918.

55 16 October 1918, LG F/36/6/36.

56 Fisher Diary, Fisher 8A.

57 X 29, Cab. 23/17.

58 Draft Minutes of a Meeting held at 10 Downing Street, 25 October 1918, WC 491A, Cab. 23/14; Draft Minutes of a Meeting of the War Cabinet, 26 October 1918, WC 491B, ibid.

59 WC 491A, ibid.

60 WC 491B, ibid. See also 'Notes on armistice', Memorandum by A. J. Balfour, 20 October 1918, Amended Copy, GT 6045, Cab. 24/67.

61 Chamberlain to Ida Chamberlain, 26 October 1918, Austen Chamberlain Papers, AC 5/1/110, Birmingham University Library. Chamberlain, however, supported naval disarmament.

62 WC 491B, Cab. 23/14.

63 See also WC 491A, ibid.

64 WC 491B, ibid.

65 'Note on a general armistice', 23 October 1918, GT 6074, Cab. 24/67.

66 See Speech at Glasgow, 17 May 1918, Hancock and van der Poel, *Smuts Papers*, Vol. 3, pp. 649–50; Minutes of a Meeting held at 10 Downing Street, 14 August 1918, IWC 31, Cab. 23/42.

67 WC 491B, Cab. 23/14.

68 WC 491A, ibid.

69 Scott Diary, 26–28 September 1917, Add. 50904.

70 WC 491B, Cab. 23/14.

71 ibid. See also C. H. Harington, 'Appreciation of the situation', 26 October 1918, GT 6119, Cab. 24/68. Intelligence officers thought Harington's assessment was much too optimistic. Minutes on 'Appreciation of the situation, 26 October 1918', Enclosure 1A, 26/E/24, SWC 330, Cab. 25/79. Harington modified his position in his next appraisal: 'Appreciation of the situation', 30 October 1918, GT 6153, Cab. 24/68.

72 Although after meeting with Lloyd George on 26 October Scott received the impression that the military terms were 'completely to disarm Germany', he apparently misinterpreted the Prime Minister. Scott Diary, 28 October 1918, Add. 50905. Neither the War Cabinet's decision nor Lloyd George's initial position at the Supreme War Council reflect such an intention.

73 Account in Royal Archives of Lloyd George's conversation with the king, 18 October 1917, quoted in Harold Nicolson, *King George the Fifth: His Life and Reign* (London: Constable, 1952), p. 318.

74 Fisher Diary, 15 August 1918, Fisher 8A.

75 'A note on the early conclusion of peace', 24 October 1918, GT 6091, Cab. 24/67.

76 Amery to Smuts, 22 October 1918, Amery E 61.

77 'Our financial position in America', 24 October 1916, LG E/9/2/21.

78 Wiseman to Drummond, 14 March 1918, Wiseman 90/43.

79 Cambon to Xavier Charmes, 24 July 1918, in Paul Cambon, *Correspondance, 1870–1924*, 3 vols (Paris: Éditions Bernard Grasset, 1940–6), Vol. 3, p. 267.

80 Diary, Addison 99/55.9.

81 'United States naval policy', Memorandum for the War Cabinet, 7 November 1918, LG F/163/4/7.

82 'Note by Sir Maurice Hankey of a conversation between the Prime Minister and himself on Monday, October 15, 1917, at breakfast, at 9.30 a.m.', 15 October 1917, Cab. 1/42.

83 Minutes of a Meeting of the Imperial War Cabinet, 1 August 1918, IWC 27B, Cab. 23/44.

84 Diary, 11 October 1918, Addison 99/55.9.

85 WC 491B, Cab. 23/14.

86 Chamberlain to Ida Chamberlain, 24 October 1918, AC 5/1/110.

87 Draft Notes of a Meeting of the War Cabinet and Dominion Prime Ministers, 14 August 1918, IWC 31, Cab. 23/43.

88 GT 6091, Cab. 24/67.

89 WC 491B, Cab. 23/14.

90 GT 6091, Cab. 24/67.

91 Balfour to Bonar Law, 1 November 1918, HLRO, Historical Collection 187, Davidson Papers.

92 P 15, Cab. 21/70.

93 Nicolson, *King George*, p. 318.

94 Quoted in J. Martret, *Le Tigre* (Paris, 1930), p. 59, quoted in D. R. Watson,

'The making of the Treaty of Versailles', in Neville Waites (ed.), *Troubled Neighbours: Franco-British Relations in the Twentieth Century* (London: Weidenfeld & Nicolson, 1971), p. 67. Lloyd George's response was: 'Has that not always been the traditional policy of my country?' ibid.

95 Curzon to Amery, 20 October 1918, Amery E 61.

96 Quoted in Riddell, *War Diary*, p. 379, Diary, 20 October 1918.

97 Haig Diary, 19 October 1918, Haig 132/34.

98 'Armistice notes, notes by P. H. K.[err] taken to Paris', 28 October 1918, Lothian GD 40/17/1076.

99 Foch to the President of the Council, Minister of War [Clemenceau], 26 October 1918, reproduced in Charles Seymour, *The Intimate Papers of Colonel House*, 4 vols (Boston, Mass.: Houghton Mifflin, 1926–8), Vol. 4, pp. 143–5.

100 Hankey Diary, 1 November 1918, HNKY 1/5.

101 Notes of a Conversation at the Residence of Colonel House, Paris, 1 November 1918, 11.00 a.m., IC 87, Cab. 28/5.

102 Procès-verbal of the Second Meeting of the Eighth Session of the Supreme War Council, 1 November 1918, IC 88, ibid., and Procès-verbal of the Third Meeting of the Eighth Session of the Supreme War Council, 2 November 1918, IC 91, ibid.

103 Surrender of 5,000 guns, 25,000 machine guns, 3,000 trench mortars, 1,700 fighting and bombing airplanes. 'Conditions of an armistice with Germany', reprinted in Harry R. Rudin, *Armistice, 1918* (New Haven, Conn.: Yale University Press, 1944), app. G, p. 426. Originally Foch had called for the surrender of 30,000 machine guns. He made the small concession of reducing this number when the German representatives protested that unless the Allies permitted them the means of resistance, Germany would succumb to Bolshevism, which would then spread to the Allied countries. Integral Report of Interview between Marshal Foch and German Delegates, enclosed in Clemenceau to Lloyd George, 9 November 1918, LG F/50/3/46.

104 Kerr, 'Armistice notes', Lothian GD 40/17/1076.

105 Reading, Notes [27 or 28? October 1918], Reading Papers, MSS Eur. F 118/121, IOLR.

106 [Reading], 'Conversation with H.[ouse]', 28 October [1918], ibid.

107 Interception of House to Secretary of State Lansing, 29 October 1918, LG F/60/1/7.

108 Diary, 11 October 1918, Addison 99/55.9.

109 12 October 1918, Lothian GD 40/1073/1.

110 Reprinted in *Manchester Guardian*, 24 October 1918.

111 Maj. W. A. Greene, Memorandum, 24 October 1918, enclosed in 'The problem of peace, Oct. 1918', by Brig.-Gen. Wake, 25 October 1918, Milner 359/AD1.

112 Derby Diary, 18 October 1918, enclosed in Derby to Balfour, 20 October 1918, Balfour Add. 49744.

113 Wilson Notebook, 19 October 1918, HHW 27.

114 This series of reports, each of which was usually titled 'Fortnightly report on pacifism and revolutionary organisations in the United Kingdom', Report by the Home Secretary, is in Cab. 24.

115 GT 6091, Cab. 24/67.

116 To Ida Chamberlain, 9 November 1918, AC 5/1/112.

117 Gen. Tasker H. Bliss to House [29? October 1918], House 16/494.

118 Bliss to Secretary of War Baker, 10 November 1918, Tasker H. Bliss Papers, Library of Congress, Washington, DC, quoted in Paul Guinn, *British Strategy and Politics, 1914 to 1918* (Oxford: Clarendon Press, 1965), p. 321, n. 1.

119 Minutes of a Meeting of the War Cabinet, 29 October 1918, WC 492, Cab.

23/8; Draft Minutes of a Meeting held at 10 Downing Street, 6 November 1918, IWC 36A, Cab. 23/44; Minutes of a Meeting of the War Cabinet, 7 November 1918, WC 499, Cab. 23/8; Minutes of a Meeting of the War Cabinet, 8 November 1918, WC 500, Cab. 23/8; Minutes of a Meeting of the War Cabinet, 10 November 1918, WC 500A, Cab. 23/14.

120   WC 500A, Cab. 23/14.
121   Diary, 10 November 1918, Milner 89.
122   WC 500A, Cab. 23/14.
123   Wilson Notebook, 10 November 1918, HHW 27.
124   WC 500A, Cab. 23/14.
125   Diary and Notebook, HHW 27.
126   Chamberlain to Ivy Chamberlain, 2 November 1918, AC 6/1/330.
127   Cecil to Derby, 2 November [1918], Reading MSS Eur. F 118/121.

Chapter 6

1   'The eleventh hour', 9 November 1918.
2   Bryce to Dr Charles W. Eliot, 6 November 1918, reproduced in H. A. L. Fisher, *James Bryce*, 2 vols (New York: Macmillan, 1927), Vol. 2, p. 199.
3   Summary of London Morning Press, 11 November 1918, MI 7b, HLRO, Historical Collection 184, Beaverbrook Papers, Bbk E/16.
4   Hewins Diary, 4 April 1917, describing interview with Lloyd George, 3 April 1917, Hewins 196/26.
5   Speech at Manchester, 12 September 1918, *The Times*, 13 September 1918.
6   Speech to English Speaking Union, Criterion Club, London, 11 October 1918, *The Times*, 12 October 1918.
7   'Can Downing Street save Germany?' *National Review*, vol. 72 (November 1918), p. 332.
8   Speech to Meeting of National Democratic and Labour Party, Central Hall, London, 22 October 1918, *The Times*, 23 October 1918. See also Speech at York, 24 October 1918, ibid., 25 October 1918.
9   *Manchester Guardian*, 24 October 1918.
10   'Appreciation of the attached western and general report no. 94', 14 November 1918, Cab. 24/149.
11   Zimmern to Scott, 5 October 1918, Scott Add. 50909.
12   Same to same, [28 November 1918], ibid.
13   *Europe in Convalescence* (New York: Putnam's, 1922), p. 101.
14   J. W. Headlam, *The Issue* (London: Constable, 1917), p. 23.
15   ibid., p. 39.
16   To Rev. A. C. Headlam, 25 June 1919, Headlam-Morley Papers, photocopies, in the possession of Prof. Agnes Headlam-Morley, London. Cited hereafter as H-M.
17   To Ivy Chamberlain, 5 November 1918, AC 6/1/331. See also Chief of Naval Staff to First Lord, 11 November 1918, app. 2, WC 500B, Cab. 23/14.
18   To Lord Newton, 11 November 1918, Rumbold Papers, Rumbold dep. 25, Bodleian.
19   To Drummond, 11 November 1918, ibid.
20   'Social democratic parties and leaders in Germany', Memorandum by the Political Intelligence Department, GT 6264, Cab. 24/69.
21   Extracts from a Letter from Mr Harold Williams, 'Daily Chronicle' Correspondent in Geneva, n.d., Political Intelligence Department, Foreign Office, GT 6389, Cab. 24/70. Indexed as circulated 28 November 1918. This report

disagreed with Zimmern's and Headlam-Morley's assessments, declaring that the German 'revolution is not in any sense a real one. The German spirit is unchanged'.

22 'Memorandum on the prospects of order and ordered government in Berlin', GT 6551, Cab. 24/72.

23 Balfour Papers, FO 800/201.

24 See files in 14, HHW 73/1/10.

25 Minutes of a Meeting of the War Cabinet, WC 500B, Cab. 23/14.

26 [Frank] Cobb and [Admiral] Sims to House, 11 November 1918, House 81/2736.

27 Zimmern to Scott, 5 October 1918, Scott Add. 50909. See also same to same, [28 November 1918], ibid.; Zimmern to Jones, 18 December [1918], TJ W 20/204.

28 Smuts to A. B. G.[illett], 10 November 1918, reporting that night's conversation with Lloyd George, Smuts 20/254.

29 See, for example, Speech at the Australasian Club, Baltic Exchange, London, 7 November 1918, *The Times*, 8 November 1918.

30 App. 2, WC 500B, Cab. 23/14.

31 ibid.

32 Wiseman to House, 12 November 1918, House 123/4330.

33 Winston S. Churchill, *The World Crisis, 1918–1928: The Aftermath* (New York: Scribner's, 1929), p. 5.

34 To Hankey, 11 November 1918, HNKY 4/10.

35 To Lloyd George, 13 November 1918, Milner 355.

36 Fisher Diary, 21 November 1918, Fisher 8A.

37 'Fortnightly report on revolutionary organisations in the United Kingdom and morale in foreign countries', Report No. 26, 18 November 1918, GT 6328, Cab. 24/70.

38 *The Scene Changes* (Garden City, NY: Doubleday, Doran, 1937), p. 423.

39 Minutes of a Meeting of the War Cabinet, 14 November 1918, WC 502, Cab. 23/8.

40 Haig Diary, 27 November 1918, Haig 133/35.

41 *Manchester Guardian*, 24 October 1918.

42 Churchill, *Aftermath*, p. 5.

43 WC 500B, Cab. 23/14. Art. 26 of the Armistice, which called for the continuation of the blockade, provided also for 'the provisioning of Germany during the Armistice as shall be found necessary'. Rudin, *Armistice*, app. G, p. 431. However, French opposition prevented the providing of food until March.

44 'The ark of the covenant', *Daily News*, 16 November 1918.

45 Summary of London Evening Press, 12 November 1918, MI 7b, Bbk E/16.

46 WC 500B, Cab. 23/14.

47 1 November 1918, LG F/2/5/29.

48 WC 500B, Cab. 23/14. The War Cabinet met at 9.45 a.m. The Germans had signed the Armistice at 5.00 a.m.; it came into force at 11.00 a.m. Partial demobilisation did not actually begin until 9 December.

49 Wilson Diary, 12 November 1918, HHW 27.

50 8 November, 10 November, 12 November, 13 November, 14 November 1918, ibid.

51 'Note by Hankey', 15 October 1917, Cab. 1/42.

52 'Army demobilisation', Memorandum by the Secretary of State for War, 29 October 1918, GT 6151, Cab. 24/68.

53 Milner 355. Wilson had spoken to Milner about his concerns on 12 November. Wilson Diary, 12 November 1918, HHW 27.

54 Milner to Esher, 28 November 1918, cited in Stephen Roskill, *Hankey: Man of Secrets*, 3 vols (London: Collins, 1970–4), Vol. 2, p. 27; Wilson Diary, 8 November, 10 November, 25 November 1918, HHW 27.

55 HNKY 4/10.

56 'From war to work'.

57 'Message from the Chief through Price', Lord Northcliffe's Bulletins to the 'Daily Mail' Office, 1915–18, no. 228, MS Eng. hist. d. 303, Bodleian.

58 Stanley to Lloyd George, 21 November 1918, LG F/2/6/3; Wilson Diary, 6 December 1918, HHW 27.

59 LG F/3/3/49.

60 See Milner Diary, 9 December 1918, Milner 89.

61 'Military commitments remaining after peace has been signed', 5 December 1918, GT 6434, Cab. 24/71.

62 Minutes of a Meeting of the Imperial War Cabinet, 12 December 1918, IWC 42, Cab. 23/42.

63 Wilson Notebook, 31 December 1918, HHW 27.

64 13 November 1918, Milner 355.

65 To Lionel Curtis, 15 October 1918, quoted in J. R. M. Butler, *Lord Lothian (Philip Kerr), 1882–1940* (London: Macmillan, 1960), p. 68.

66 'Memorandum by the Chief of the Air Staff on air power requirements of the Empire', 9 December 1918, GT 6477, Cab. 24/71.

67 'Memorandum on the post-war functions of the Air Ministry and post-war strength of the Royal Air Force', GT 6478, ibid.

68 Copy Letter, General Seely to Churchill, 19 November 1918, LG F/8/2/41; Bliss to C.[harles] S.[eymour], 14 June 1928, quoted in Seymour, *Intimate Papers*, Vol. 4, p. 115.

69 'Appreciation of western & general report no. 94', Cab. 24/149.

70 'Memorandum on the settlement with Germany', 23 December 1918, PC 56, FO 371/4354. The memorandum was drafted 26 November; the revised draft of 23 December incorporated suggestions by Hardinge and Crowe.

71 15 December 1918, LG F/47/4/9.

72 Speech at Bristol, 11 December 1918, *The Times*, 12 December 1918.

73 IWC 42, Cab. 23/42.

Chapter 7

1 Speech at Dundee, *The Times*, 27 November 1918.

2 Quoted in Sir Charles Petrie, *The Life and Letters of the Right Hon. Sir Austen Chamberlain*, 2 vols (London: Cassell, 1939–40), Vol. 2, p. 129.

3 7 December 1918.

4 *The Times*, 3 December 1918; Hewins Diary, n.d., Hewins 196/13; Addison Diary, 6 January 1919, recounting 2 December 1918 discussion of election matters with Lloyd George, Addison 99/55.9; 'Synopsis of confidential reports from Lloyd George Liberal candidates', n.d., LG F/167/1/1; 'Summary of reports from Unionist agents indicating the subjects in which the electors are most interested', 4 December 1918, Law (Bonar Law) 95/2. See also the various 'Extracts from confidential reports by Unionist Central Office agents on subjects in which the electors are most interested', Law (Bonar Law) 95/2.

5 *National Opinion*, November 1918.

6 Croft, Letter to the editor, 18 November 1918, *Morning Post*, 19 November 1918; 'The National Party's 14 points for electors', *National Opinion*, December 1918; 'Drastic peace terms', ibid., November 1918, quoting Cooper's interview with the *Daily Graphic*.

7 *Morning Post* leading articles: 'Die Wacht am Rhein', 9 December 1918; 'The Suitors of Penelope', 12 December 1918; 'Asking for trouble', 13 December 1918.

8 ibid.: 'A candidates' catechism', 28 November 1918; 'Forgetting the enemy', 29 November 1918; 'Peace terms', 3 December 1918; 'The nominations', 5 December 1918.

9 'Germany must demobilise', *Daily Mail*, 13 December 1918.

10 13 November–14 December 1918, *passim*.

11 'An acid test of statesmanship', *National Review*, vol. 72 (December 1918), p. 495; 'Episodes of the month', ibid., p. 395.

12 ibid., p. 495.

13 'Report of the Committee on Indemnity', 2 December 1918, P 38, Cab. 29/2, 'Report of the Committee on Indemnity', 10 December 1918, P 39, Cab. 27/43, cited in Robert E. Bunselmeyer, *The Cost of the War, 1914–1919: British Economic War Aims and the Origins of Reparation* (Hamden, Conn.: Archon, 1975)), pp. 98, 103.

14 'From war to peace', *The Times*, 4 November 1918.

15 See leading articles in the *Observer:* 'President Wilson's visit', 24 November 1918; 'The President and Europe', 8 December 1918. See discussion on p. 124 for the *Nation's* position.

16 In addition to the articles cited in n. 7 above, see leading articles in the *Morning Post:* 'The peace of victory', 2 November 1918; 'The soldier in politics', 19 November 1918; 'The dead language', 21 November 1918.

17 'Peace for ever', *Nation*, vol. 24 (16 November 1918), p. 181.

18 *Daily News*, 2 November 1918.

19 Reprinted in Stansky, *The Left*, p. 319.

20 'Notes for Leeds speech', 6 December 1918, Lothian GD 40/17/654/1.

21 'A word to women, trustees for the silent', GES, No. 7, enclosed in sample of election literature prepared and sent by James Adam, Scottish Unionist whip's office, November 1918, Law (Bonar Law) 21/6/64(59).

22 22 November 1918, LG F/8/2/42(a).

23 Speech at Great Assembly Hall, Mile-End, 11 December 1918, *The Times*, 12 December 1918.

24 *Tribunal*, 31 October 1918.

25 Stansky, *The Left*, p. 98.

26 *The Times*, 2 December 1918.

27 'The one thing needful', *Nation*, vol. 24 (16 November 1918), p. 183.

28 ibid., pp. 180, 181.

29 Note by Montagu, 7 November 1918, in S. D. Waley, *Edwin Montagu: A Memoir and an Account of his Visits to India* (Bombay: Asia Publishing House, 1964), pp. 188, 190.

30 LG F/168/2/7.

31 Address to North Paddington Liberal and Radical Association at the Guardian Office, Harrow-road, 16 November 1918, *Observer*, 17 November 1918; Speech at Saltburn, 23 November 1918, *The Times*, 25 November 1918.

32 *Manchester Guardian*, 13 November 1918.

33 Revised copy of a draft letter from Lloyd George to Bonar Law, Lothian GD 40/17/1024.

34 Fisher Diary, 6 November 1918, Fisher 8A; Note by Montagu, 7 November 1918, in Waley, *Montagu*, pp. 186-8.

35 3 August 1918, LG F/21/2/30.

36 Copy Minutes of the Liberal Party Meeting held at 10 Downing Street, 12 November 1918, Lothian GD 40/17/1025.

37 ibid.
38 LG F/8/2/42(a).
39 H. A. L. Fisher, *An Unfinished Autobiography* (London: Oxford University Press, 1940), p. 92.
40 Addison 99/55.9.
41 'The League of Nations', Memorandum by Christopher Addison, enclosed in Addison to Balfour, 3 October 1918, Miscellaneous Correspondence respecting League of Nations, FO 800/400.
42 *The Campaign Guide: A Handbook for Unionist Speakers*, 13th edn (London: National Unionist Association of Conservative and Liberal Unionist Organisations, [1914]), pp. 175, 192, 176. According to the Conservative Research Department, London, no new guide was issued for the 1918 election. Although Amery's diary of 9 October 1918 refers to his working on 'the "Campaign Guide"' for the Unionist Literature Committee, I found no copy in his or Bonar Law's papers, and the Conservative Research Department has no record of its existence.
43 Speech at Drill Hall, Cambridge, 9 December 1918, *The Times*, 10 December 1918.
44 LG F/8/2/42(a).
45 Arnold Wolfers, *Britain and France between Two Wars: Conflicting Strategies of Peace from Versailles to World War II* (New York: Norton, 1966), p. 366.
46 *Politics from Within, 1911–1918*, 2 vols (London: Herbert Jenkins, 1924), Vol. 2, p. 241.
47 5 October 1918, Balfour Add. 49693.
48 Transcript of Stevenson's Shorthand Notes, Coalition Party Meeting, Report of Speeches Delivered at the Central Hall, Westminster, 16 November 1918, LG F/236.
49 Speech at Wolverhampton, 23 November 1918, *The Times*, 25 November 1918.
50 'Labour and the new social order', reproduced in Paul U. Kellogg and Arthur Gleason, *British Labor and the War: Reconstructors for a New World* (New York: Boni & Liveright, 1919), app. 4, pp. 388–9.
51 See Woodward, *Geat Britain and the War*, p. 515.
52 John Stubbs, 'The impact of the Great War on the Conservative Party', in Gillian Peele and Chris Cook (eds), *The Politics of Reappraisal, 1918–1939* (New York: St Martin's Press, 1975), p. 34.
53 *The Times*, 10 December 1918.
54 ibid.; Speech at Cambridge, 27 November 1918, *Manchester Guardian*, 28 November 1918.
55 House to Gordon Auchincloss, 5 March 1915, House 7/205.
56 *The Political Economy of War* (London: Dent, 1915), pp. 75–91, 303, and *passim*.
57 'The challenge', *Daily News*, 28 November 1918.
58 Adm. 116/1809, cited in J. Kenneth McDonald, 'Lloyd George and the search for a postwar naval policy, 1919', in A. J. P. Taylor (ed.), *Lloyd George: Twelve Essays* (New York: Atheneum, 1971), p. 193.
59 Leading article, 27 January 1919.
60 Haig Diary, 29 October 1918, Haig 132/34.
61 Alexander Murray of Elibank, 'Conversation with the Prime Minister and Mr Asquith', 2 October 1918, reproduced in Arthur C. Murray, *Master and Brother: Murrays of Elibank* (London: John Murray, 1945), pp. 175–8; Arthur Murray to Wiseman, 8 October 1918, Wiseman 91/87.
62 Fisher Diary, 6 November 1918, Fisher 8A; Waley, *Montagu*, p. 188.
63 Amery Diary, 8 November 1918 [apparently dictated 13 November].

64 Fisher Diary, 12 November 1918, Fisher 8A. Lloyd George's reply was that 'we can't tell before hand what we shall want but if we get a good peace we shan't want conscription'.

65 LG F/237.

66 Lothian GD 40/17/1025.

67 Diary, 8 [13] November 1918.

68 Partial lists of those attending appeared in *Daily News*, 13 November 1918, *Manchester Guardian*, 13 November 1918 and *The Times*, 13 November 1918.

69 Diary, 12 November 1918, Fisher 8A.

70 'The General Election', *Tribunal*, 14 November 1918.

71 *Tribunal*, 28 November 1918.

72 *The Times*, 27 November 1918.

73 Speech at Pontypool, ibid., 26 November 1918.

74 Speech at Oldham, 7 December 1918, *Manchester Guardian*, 9 December 1918.

75 Quoted in *The Times*, 9 December 1918.

76 ibid.

77 Excerpt from a speech, 11 December 1918, ibid., 12 December 1918.

78 Address to the Council of the London Liberal Federation, Caxton Hall, Westminster, 18 November 1918, ibid., 19 November 1918.

79 Speech at Albert Hall, Nottingham, 10 December 1918, *Manchester Guardian*, 11 December 1918.

80 'Labour's call to the people', *The Times*, 28 November 1918.

81 Published 1 December 1918, quoted in League of Nations Union, 'Weekly review of the British and foreign press on the question of the League of Nations', ser. 1, no. 5, 7 December 1918, TJ E 5/24/4.

82 See, for example, the questionnaire sent to Conservative candidate Arthur Steel-Maitland: Questions from Independent Labour Party, Edington Branch, Birmingham, Steel-Maitland Papers, GD 193/179/2, SRO.

83 Stansky, *The Left*, p. 319.

84 Unanimous resolution of a Labour meeting at Albert Hall, 30 November 1918, *The Times*, 2 December 1918.

85 First Batch of Reports, LG F/167/1/1; Fourth Batch of Reports, ibid. See also Third Batch of Reports, ibid.

86 12 December 1918, LG F/36/6/41.

87 See in the *Daily News*: 'The acid test', 4 December 1918; 'The blanks', 6 December 1918; A. G. G.[ardiner], 'What is it you seek?' 7 December 1918; 'Do they say "no conscription"?' 9 December 1918; 'Why conscription must be abolished', 'To the woman voter', 10 December 1918; 'Yes or no?' 11 December 1918; 'The conscriptionists', 12 December 1918; front-page news reports, 12, 13 December 1918; 'Conscription the issue', 'The plan of campaign', Gardiner, 'A letter to a voter', 14 December 1918.

88 'Memorandum by Edwin S. Montagu on his election', 16 December 1918, LG F/40/2/24.

89 LG F/21/2/57.

90 Vol. 49 (June 1919).

91 Denis Hayes, *Conscription Conflict: The Conflict of Ideas in the Struggle for and against Military Conscription in Britain between 1901 and 1939* (London: Sheppard Press, 1949; New York: Garland, 1973), p. 318.

92 Vol. 24 (14 December 1918).

93 'Notes for Newcastle speech', n.d., Lothian GD 40/17/655. Catalogued as '[?ca. 1918, Dec.].' However, Lloyd George delivered his Newcastle speech on 29 November.

94 'Notes for Leeds speech', ibid., GD 40/17/654/1.

95 *The Times*, 10 December 1918.
96 'Notes for Queen's Hall speech', 9 December 1918, LG F/237. Other handwritten notes for this speech are in NLW MS 20453E.
97 Transcript of Stevenson's Shorthand Notes, Report of Proceedings at a Meeting of Women's Associations, Queen's Hall, 9 December 1918, LG F/236.
98 'To the woman voter', *Daily News*, 10 December 1918.
99 *The Times*, 12 December 1918.
100 ibid.
101 10 December 1918, LG F/21/2/51.
102 T. J. Macnamara to Lloyd George, 10 December 1918, LG F/36/1/9.
103 10 December 1918, *The Times*, 11 December 1918.
104 *Morning Post*, 11 December 1918.
105 12 December 1918.
106 *The Times*, 12 December 1918. Italics mine.
107 ibid.
108 ibid.
109 *Manchester Guardian*, 14 December 1918.
110 LG F/36/6/41.
111 12 December 1918.
112 'Points for the peace conference', *Manchester Guardian*, 12 December 1918.
113 Speech at Camberwell, 13 December 1918, *The Times*, 14 December 1918.
114 'A diary and its moral', *Tribunal*, 19 December 1918.
115 Lloyd George reiterated his position in a 13 December interview. *Manchester Guardian*, 14 December 1918.

Chapter 8

1 'The attitude of the United States and of President Wilson towards the peace conference', Memorandum by Wiseman, [*c.* 20 October 1918], Balfour Papers, FO 800/214. See also Memorandum by Wiseman, 15 December 1918, enclosed in Wiseman to Reading, 15 December 1918, Reading MSS Eur. F/118/90.
2 Prothero to Lloyd George, 30 November 1918, Law (Bonar Law) 84/3/27. Minuted by Bonar Law for reply: 'All that you say is very much in our minds'.
3 Borden, *Borden*, Vol. 2, p. 874, Diary, 2 December 1918.
4 See, for example, Minutes of a Meeting held at 10 Downing Street, 8 June 1917, WC 159A, Cab. 23/16; Minutes of a Meeting of the War Cabinet, 11 October 1917, WC 247B, Cab. 23/13.
5 For example, Foreign Office, 'Europe', [December 1918], P 52, Cab. 29/2.
6 To Lloyd George, 29 November 1918, LG F/3/345.
7 'Note verbale', programme of work and principles suggested by the French government for the peace negotiations, French Embassy, Rome, 28 November 1918, communicated by Italian ambassador, 3 December 1918, 26, Cab. 1/27.
8 Notes of Allied Conversations in London, 1 December-3 December 1918, IC 97-IC 102, Cab. 28/5.
9 Wilson Notebook, 1 December 1918, HHW 27.
10 Wilson Diary, 13 November 1918, ibid.
11 Borden, *Borden*, Vol. 2, p. 874.
12 Minutes of a Meeting of the Imperial War Cabinet, 30 December 1918, IWC 47, Cab. 23/42.
13 Minutes of a Meeting of the Imperial War Cabinet, 24 December 1918, IWC 46, ibid.
14 Eastern Committee Minutes, Secret, 2 December 1918, Cab. 27/24.

15 IWC 47, Cab. 23/42.

16 Eastern Committee Minutes, 2 December 1918, Cab. 27/24.

17 'Our policy at the peace conference', Note by General Smuts, 3 December 1918, P 39, Cab. 29/2.

18 'United States and the occupied enemy territories', Memorandum by Amery, enclosed in Amery to Smuts, 12 December 1918, Smuts 19/19.

19 IWC 47, Cab. 23/42. On 4 December Cecil wrote to Smuts to express his agreement with Smuts's recommendation. Cecil Papers, Add. 51076, BL.

20 Address at Birmingham University, 12 November 1918, *The Times*, 13 November 1918.

21 Minutes of a Meeting of the Imperial War Cabinet, 18 December 1918, IWC 43, Cab. 23/42.

22 'Limitation of armaments', 23 December 1918, P 78, Cab. 29/2.

23 'Some principles and problems of the settlement', *Round Table*, vol. 9 (December 1918), pp. 94–5.

24 A. E. Z.[immern] to T. J.[ones], 27 October 1918, TJ E 5/20/2. See also Zimmern, 'Some principles', p. 95.

25 Jones to Zimmern, 29 October 1918, TJ E 5/21.

26 Zimmern to Jones, 30 October 1918, TJ W 20/202.

27 'The League of Nations', November 1918, P 68, Cab. 29/2.

28 'The League of Nations', November 1918, P 69, ibid.

29 The members were Lord Walter Phillimore, the historians A. F. Pollard, Sir Julian Corbett and J. Holland Rose and from the Foreign Office Crowe, Tyrrell and Cecil Hurst, the Foreign Office's legal adviser.

30 Henry R. Winkler, *The League of Nations Movement in Great Britain, 1914–1918* (New Brunswick, NJ: Rutgers University Press, 1952), p. 57.

31 League of Nations Committee: Minutes of Proceedings, Meetings 1–14, 30 January–3 July 1918, 214189, FO 371/3483.

32 The Committee on the League of Nations, Minutes of the 11th Meeting, 29 May 1918, ibid.

33 The Committee on the League of Nations (Phillimore), Final Report, 3 July 1918, P 26, Cab. 29/2.

34 'The League of Nations: a programme for the peace conference', 16 December 1918, P 44, ibid. This memorandum is the source of the quotations on pp. 153–5.

35 IWC 46, Cab. 23/42.

36 ibid.

37 Letter to a constituent, 9 December 1918, reproduced in Churchill, *Aftermath*, p. 36.

38 IWC 46, Cab. 23/42.

39 ibid.

40 ibid.

41 See Stansky, *The Left*, pp. 99–101, for the complete statement of the UDC view of the relationship between profit-making in armaments production and the outbreak of war.

42 IWC 46, Cab. 23/42.

43 *The Times*, 13 November 1918.

44 'League of Nations', Memorandum by Lord R. Cecil, 5 October 1918, P 29, Cab. 29/1.

45 Cecil to J. H. Thomas, 23 December 1918, Cecil Add. 51162; IWC 46, Cab. 23/42.

46 Cecil to Lloyd George, 21 November 1918, LG F/6/5/47.

47 Cecil to the Electors of North Herts., 26 November 1918, Cecil Add. 51162.

48 Report of his speech at Letchworth, 5 December 1918, *The Times*, 6 December 1918.
49 IWC 46, Cab. 23/42.
50 ibid.
51 ibid.
52 ibid.
53 Minutes of a Meeting of the Imperial War Cabinet, 31 December 1918, IWC 48, Cab. 23/42.
54 See Hughes, Speech to Australian and New Zealand Luncheon Club, Holborn Restaurant, London, 9 January 1919, *The Times*, 10 January 1919.
55 'Note on General Smuts's memo.', 24 December 1918, Cecil Add. 51076. Instead of charging the League of Nations at its inception with responsibility for disarmament, Cecil recommended the appointment of a league commission to study the disarmament problem in order to resolve the difficulties he saw in Smuts's proposals.
56 ibid.
57 The meeting with President Wilson was an informal conversation, and the President refused to allow any record to be made. Hankey, who had accompanied Lloyd George and Balfour, was not admitted. Hankey Diary, 27 December 1918, HNKY 1/5. The only record is Lloyd George's report to the Imperial War Cabinet in IWC 47, Cab. 23/42, reproduced in Lloyd George, *Memoirs of the Peace Conference*, Vol. 1, pp. 115–16.
58 IWC 47, Cab. 23/42.
59 In notes and a book written over forty years later Hankey, who had not been present at this meeting, maintained that it was President Wilson who suggested the abolition of conscription in Germany. 'President and Peace Conference', notes used at talk with Mr Walworth, USA at US Club lunch, 14 October 1959, HNKY 24/2; *The Supreme Control at the Paris Peace Conference, 1919: A Commentary* (London: Allen & Unwin, 1963), p. 16. However, in *Supreme Control*, p. 15, he says that his account derives from his contemporary notes of the Imperial War Cabinet discussion. Although the minutes of this meeting use the indefinite 'he' in recording this portion of Lloyd George's report of his talk with Wilson, it seems from the context as well as from Lloyd George's previous position that it was Lloyd George who recommended abolishing conscription in Germany: 'They had not overlooked the question of reserves and system of training, and he himself had reminded the President of what Prussia had done when her forces were limited to a fixed figure by Napoleon. He had suggested that Germany should not be allowed to impose conscription in any shape or form until she had entirely failed by voluntary means to raise the army provisionally assigned to her . . . In answer to a question by Sir J. Cook, Mr Lloyd George said that what he contemplated would prevent Germany from enforcing even the compulsory training of the young such as they had in Australia.' (IWC 47, Cab. 23/42) Thomas Jones, *Lloyd George* (Cambridge, Mass.: Harvard University Press, 1951), p. 170, notes of the Anglo-American discussion, 'President Wilson was perhaps as eager to abolish compulsory military service as Lloyd George'.
60 IWC 32, Cab. 23/42.
61 IWC 47, ibid.

Chapter 9

1 'Note on the forces to be maintained by the Allies confronting Germany', n.d., translation, enclosed in Milner to Lloyd George, 1 January 1919, LG F/39/1/1.

2   Milner to Lloyd George, 1 January 1919, ibid.
3   'Recent reports regarding the situation in Germany', n.d., GT 6617, Cab. 24/73. Indexed as circulated 29 April 1919, but volume number and location in volume indicate that the paper was circulated to the War Cabinet in early January.
4   6 January 1919, LG F/16/1/26.
5   Wilson Notebook, 5 January 1919, HHW 28.
6   Minutes of a Meeting of the War Cabinet, 8 January 1919, WC 514, Cab. 23/9.
7   Memorandum, 24 December 1918, Milner 374.
8   'Report of conference held in the room of the Secretary of State, War Office', 5 January 1919, ibid.
9   LG F/16/1/26.
10 Macdonogh, 'Report of a committee on demobilisation, armies of occupation and home and overseas garrisons', circulated by Churchill, 17 January 1919, GT 6674, Cab. 24/73. These forces were to serve in all of Britain's occupation forces, not just the army in Germany.
11 Wilson Notebook, 21 January 1919, HHW 28.
12 Lloyd George to Churchill, 18 January 1919, LG F/8/3/2; J. T. Davies to Churchill, 21 January 1919, telephone message communicating message from Lloyd George, in Randolph S. Churchill and Martin Gilbert, *Winston S. Churchill*, 5 vols with companion vols (London: Heinemann, 1966–), Vol. 4, companion, pt 1, p. 474.
13 Haig Diary, 22 January 1919, Haig 135/37. Since no secretary was present, there are no minutes of this meeting.
14 Bonar Law to Lloyd George, [22 January 1919], LG F/30/3/2; Wilson Notebook, 22 January 1919, HHW 28.
15 Wilson Notebook, 22 January 1919, HHW 28.
16 See, for example, Minutes of a Meeting held at 10 Downing Street, 26 February 1919, WC 537, Cab. 23/9.
17 Haig Diary, 24 January 1919, Haig 135/37; Wilson Diary, 24 January 1919, HHW 28.
18 Notes of Conferences held in Paris, 24 January 1919, 18/B/57, Cab. 21/149; Haig Diary, 24 January 1919, Haig 135/37; Wilson Diary and Notebook, 24 January 1919, HHW 28.
19 Minutes of a Meeting of the War Cabinet, 28 January 1919, WC 521, Cab. 23/9.
20 ibid.
21 26 January 1919, *The Times*, 27 January 1919. For the assumption that the new army scheme would include the extension of conscription, see 'The new army', *Daily News*, 30 January 1919.
22 5 *HC Deb.*, vol. 113 (1919), cols 667–782, 6 March; vol. 114 (1919), cols 921–94, 31 March.
23 'Impressions from lobby on Hull election', in Guest to Lloyd George, 11 April 1919, LG F/21/3/16; J. W. P.[ratt], 'Notes on Central Aberdeenshire', 1 May 1919, in Guest to Lloyd George, 1 May 1919, ibid., F/21/3/19; Wiseman to Reading, 18 April 1919, Wiseman 90/29; Percy to Maxse, 3 April 1919, Maxse 476/40; Eustace Percy, *Some Memories* (London: Eyre & Spottiswoode, 1958), p. 74. Percy was the unsuccessful candidate for Central Hull.
24 'The new military service bill', annex to short notes for Coalition MPs to be circulated by 50 Parliament Street, n.d. [after 29 March 1919], LG F/238.
25 Blanche E. C. Dugdale, *Arthur James Balfour*, 2 vols (New York: Putnam's, 1937), Vol. 2, pp. 194–5.
26 Kenneth Young, *Arthur James Balfour: The Happy Life of the Politician, Prime Minister, Statesman, and Philosopher, 1848–1930* (London: Bell, 1963), p. 406.
27 Notes on Conversations held in the Office of M. Pichon at the Quai d'Orsay, 21

January 1919, 10.30 a.m., *USFR, PPC*, vol. 3, p. 669. See also Secretary's Notes of a Conversation held in M. Pichon's Room at the Quai d'Orsay, 21 January 1919, 15 hours, ibid., p. 654.

28 Secretary's Notes of a Conversation held in M. Pichon's Room at the Quai d'Orsay, 23 January 1919, 10.30 a.m., ibid., pp. 694–5, and app. A, ibid., p. 702. In *Memoirs of the Peace Conference*, written in the 1930s when he had become increasingly hostile to France and sympathetic to Germany, Lloyd George cited this resolution as a proposal merely for a general reduction in armaments and omitted his role in demanding additional German disarmament as a condition of Armistice renewal, dated the demand in February and attributed it to Foch (Vol. 1, pp. 183–4, 389). Although in February Foch did present to a Supreme Council sub-committee demands for the imposition of additional disarmament as a condition of Armistice renewal, Lloyd George's demand came almost three weeks before.

29 Davies to Churchill, 21 January 1919, Churchill and Gilbert, *Churchill*, Vol. 4, companion pt 1, p. 474.

30 Notes of Conversation in Pichon's Room, 23 January 1919, *USFR, PPC*, vol. 3, p. 694.

31 ibid.

32 See 'The appeal to the workshop (I)', speech delivered at Manchester, 3 June 1915, in Lloyd George, *Through Terror to Triumph*, p. 98; 'The Munitions Bill', speech delivered in the House of Commons, 23 June 1915, ibid., p. 134; 'A safe investment', extracts from a speech delivered at the Guildhall, 11 January 1917, in Lloyd George, *The Great Crusade*, p. 94.

33 Notes of Conversation in Pichon's Room, 23 January 1919, *USFR, PPC*, vol. 3, p. 694.

34 ibid., p. 695.

35 House Diary XV, 3 January 1919.

36 Spears to Wilson, 23 January 1919, 14/L/34, HHW 73/1/10.

37 Quoted in [George Allardice Riddell], *Lord Riddell's Intimate Diary of the Peace Conference and After, 1918–1923* (New York: Reynal & Hitchcock, 1934), pp. 11–12, Diary, 21 January 1919.

38 ibid., p. 12.

39 Procès-verbal of the Twelfth Session of the Supreme War Council, 24 January 1919, 10.30 a.m., *USFR, PPC*, vol. 3, p. 709. Cited hereafter as SWC. The rest of this paragraph is based upon ibid., pp. 705–13.

40 Minutes of the First Meeting of the Thirteenth Session of the Supreme War Council, 7 February 1919, 3.30 p.m., *USFR, PPC*, vol. 3, p. 897; 'Report by the committee appointed by the Supreme War Council at the meeting of the 24th January 1919 (morning)', app. B, ibid., pp. 910–12.

41 SWC 13, 1, ibid., pp. 897, 898–900.

42 ibid., p. 901.

43 First Meeting of the Technical Sub-Committee on the Limitation of Armaments, 27 January 1919, 3.00 p.m., 2136/314/1110, FO 608/267; 'Report to main committee – conclusions of the sub-committee on the limitation of German armaments (naval armaments excluded)', SWC 13, 1, app. B, annex 2, *USFR, PPC*, vol. 3, pp. 916–20.

44 SWC 13, 1, *USFR, PPC*, vol. 3, p. 907.

45 On 7 February the Supreme War Council appointed the Tardieu Committee, composed of André Tardieu, Clemenceau's foreign policy adviser, Milner and American Secretary of State Robert Lansing (ibid., p. 908). The committee submitted its report 8 February. Minutes of the 2nd Meeting of the 13th Session of the Supreme War Council, 8 February 1919, 3.00 p.m., ibid., pp. 929–33, and app. 'C', pp. 937–8.

46 Minutes of the Meeting of the Five Great Powers at 3.00 p.m., and of the Meeting of the Supreme War Council at 5.00 p.m., 12 February 1919, ibid., p. 1002.

47 See, for example, SWC 12, ibid., p. 709.

48 SWC 13, 1, ibid., pp. 903–7.

49 SWC 13, 2, ibid., p. 933.

50 House Diary XV, 9 February 1919. Haig's and Hankey's accounts of events cast some doubts on whether Balfour, who was notoriously indecisive, had at this stage actually agreed to this proposal. Haig to Wilson, 14 February 1919, HHW 73/1/21; Hankey to Jones, 14 February 1919, TJ W 9/131.

51 Francis Bullitt Lowry, 'The generals, the Armistice, and the Treaty of Versailles, 1919' (PhD dissertation, Duke University, 1963), p. 232; Cecil Diary, 11 February 1919, Add. 51131.

52 Cecil Diary, 11 February 1919, Add. 51131.

53 Conclusions of a Committee Assembled in Accordance with the Decision of the Supreme War Council on 10th February 1919, 2121/1/1/1933, FO 608/249.

54 Haig Diary, 11 February 1919, Haig 136/38; Hankey to Jones, 14 February 1919, TJ W 9/131; Haig to Wilson, 14 February 1919, HHW 73/1/21.

55 Lloyd George to Kerr, 12 February 1919, Lothian GD 40/17/1217.

56 Dugdale, *Balfour*, Vol. 2, p. 198.

57 Minutes of the Meeting of the Supreme War Council, 11.00 a.m., 12 February 1919, *USFR, PPC*, vol. 3, p. 972.

58 Meeting of the Five Great Powers and Meeting of SWC, 12 February 1919, ibid., p. 1005.

59 Wilson Notebook, 19 February 1919, HHW 28.

60 Kerr to Lloyd George, [19? February 1919], Lothian GD 40/17/1223.

61 IWC 47, Cab. 23/42.

62 Notes of Conferences in Paris, 24 January 1919, 18/B/57, Cab. 21/49.

63 Wilson Notebook, 26 January 1919, HHW 28. See also Wilson Notebook, 7 March 1919, ibid.

64 Haig Diary, 16 February 1919, Haig 136/38.

65 ibid.; Haig, 'Military considerations for preliminary treaty of peace', 16 February 1919, Haig 220m; Haig Diary, 17 February, 18 February 1919, Haig 136/38; 'Draft regulations concerning a definite military status of Germany', [17 February 1919], WCP 154, Cab. 29/8; Wilson Notebook, 17 February 1919, HHW 28.

66 For the maintenance of internal order, they proposed the retention of ten divisions.

67 H. Wilson, 'Memorandum on our present and future military policy in Russia', 13 November 1918, GT 6311, Cab. 24/70.

68 Wilson Diary and Notebook, 19 February 1919, HHW 28; Haig Diary, 19 February 1919, Haig 136/38.

69 *Versailles*, p. 161.

70 Haig Diary, 19 February 1919, Haig 136/38.

71 ibid.; Haig Diary, 20 February, 21 February 1919, ibid.

72 Gen. P. P. de B. Radcliffe to General Degoutte, 28 February 1919, Annex, MS 114, 2136/3/4/3152, FO 608/267.

73 See, for example, the memorandum by Edwyn Bevan, 'Memorandum on the inner change in Germany', 4 February 1919, PID, Foreign Office, GT 6770, Cab. 24/74; Bevan to Headlam-Morley, 5 February 1919, Headlam-Morley to Bevan, 7 February 1919, Bevan to Headlam-Morley, 6 March 1919, H-M.

74 Minutes of a Meeting of the British Empire Delegation, BED 7th Minutes, 7 February 1919, Cab. 29/28/1; Kerr to Lloyd George [19? February 1919], Lothian GD 40/17/1223.

75 Colonel Beadon to General Cowans, 12 February 1919, Cowans Papers, IWM.

76 'The present state of the German army', British [*sic*] [Military] Section, British Delegation, 2129/1/1/4227, FO 608/265.

77 'Combined report on food conditions in Germany during the period 12th January–12th February 1919', Military Section, British Delegation, 16 February 1919, GT 6921, Cab. 24/76.

78 Headlam-Morley to Kerr, 5 March 1919, H-M. Wilson to Lloyd George, 5 March 1919, LG F/47/8/6.

79 'Bolshevism in Germany', report by Thornely Gibson, Lieutenant, Irish Guards, on journey through Germany lasting from February 1–24, 1919, and including visits to Munich, Berlin, Cassel, Frankfurt, Mannheim, Heidelberg, Karlsruhe, Baden-Baden and Offenburg, Military Section, British Delegation, 6 March 1919, WCP 203, Cab. 29/9.

80 'Report on visit to Leipzig, 13th to 14th February 1919, by Capt. Stewart Roddie', in 'Further reports on visits to Germany, 13th to 15th February 1919,' n.d., GT 6936, Cab. 24/76. Indexed as circulated February 1919.

81 See 'Food conditions in Germany', Military Section, British Delegation, 5 March 1919, WCP 200, 29/8.

82 Lieut.-Col. Twiss to DMI, 24 February 1919, ibid.

83 Brig.-Gen. W. Bartholomew to DMI, 28 February 1919, ibid.

84 Saunders to Headlam-Morley, 22 April 1919, same to same, 16 May 1919, H-M.

85 See, for example, Saunders to Maggie Saunders, 20 August 1914, GS/2/50, same to same, 29 August 1914, GS/2/51, SAUN 3, Saunders Papers, Churchill College.

86 Saunders to Headlam-Morley, 10 June 1919, H-M.

87 Fragment, same to same, 28 February 1919, ibid.

88 Wilson Diary, 26 February, 28 February, 2 March 1919, HHW 28.

89 GT 6921, GT 6936, Cab. 24/76; 'Extract from a report by an agent just returned from Berlin, who is considered particularly reliable', c. mid-February 1919, WCP 200, Cab. 29/8; WCP 203, Cab. 29/9.

90 Derby to Curzon, 1 March 1919, Curzon MSS Eur. F 112/196.

91 Headlam-Morley to Esme Howard, H-M.

92 Hankey to Jones, 5 March 1919, TJ W 9/133.

93 Minutes of a Meeting of the British Empire Delegation, BED 9th Minutes, Cab. 29/28/1.

94 'Why we want peace quickly'; TJ Z 1919/29.

95 Borden, *Borden*, Vol. 2, p. 909; Borden to Lloyd George, 13 February 1919, LG F/5/3/7.

96 BED 9, Cab. 29/28/1.

97 *The Times*, 28 February 1919.

98 'Note by Marshal Foch', 18 February 1919, WCP 129, Cab. 29/8; General Du Cane to General Wilson, 18 February 1919, reporting a conversation with Foch, enclosed in Kerr to Lloyd George, 19 February 1919, LG F/89/2/24; Balfour to Davies, 20 February 1919, enclosed in [Davies to Lloyd George, 21 February 1919], LG F/3/4/13.

99 Balfour to Davies, 20 February 1919, LG F/3/4/13.

100 BED 9, Cab. 29/28/1; Balfour to Davies, 20 February 1919, LG F/3/4/13.

101 Balfour to Davies, 20 February 1919, [Davies to Lloyd George, 21 February 1919]; Handwritten draft, Lloyd George to Davies [21 February 1919], LG F/3/4/13; Secretary's Notes of a Conversation held in M. Pichon's Room at the Quai d'Orsay, 22 February 1919, 3.00 p.m., *USFR, PPC*, vol. 4, pp. 85–97; Secretary's Notes of a Conversation held in M. Pichon's Room at the Quai d'Orsay, 24 February 1919, 3.00 p.m., *USFR, PPC*, vol. 4, pp. 102–3.

102 Notes of Conversation in Pichon's Room, 22 February 1919, *USFR, PPC,* vol. 4, pp. 85–97.
103 Lothian GD 40/17/1233.
104 Minutes of the Meeting of the Supreme War Council, 3 March 1919, 3.00 p.m., *USFR, PPC,* vol. 4, pp. 183–4.
105 LG F/23/4/28.
106 Kerr to Lloyd George, 3 March 1919, Lothian GD 40/17/1240.
107 'Notes on the military peace proposals', 5 March 1919, enclosed in Malcolm to Lloyd George, 5 March 1919, LG F/3/4/15.
108 Haig Diary, 26 January 1919, Haig 135/37.
109 See Minutes on 'Disarmament in France and Germany', [14 March 1919], 461/2/1/4211, FO 608/128.
110 *The Times,* 10 January 1919.
111 GT 6551, Cab. 24/72.
112 Haig Diary, 11 February 1919, Haig 136/38.
113 Haig Diary, 12 February 1919, ibid.
114 Derby to Curzon, 7 March 1919, Curzon MSS Eur. F 112/196.
115 Extract from Derby Diary, 27 January 1919, enclosed in Derby to Balfour, 28 January 1919, Balfour Add. 49744.
116 House Diary XV, 6 March 1919.
117 Wilson Diary, 27 February, 5 March 1919, HHW 28.
118 Draft Minutes of a Meeting, 4 March 1919, 12.00 m., WC 541A, Cab. 23/15.
119 3 March 1919, Lothian GD 40/17/1240.
120 In addition to Foch's memorandum, see Tardieu's 25 February memorandum, 'Short note for Mr A. J. Balfour on the subject of the left bank of the Rhine', WCP 135, Cab. 29/8.
121 WC 541A, Cab. 23/15.
122 Lloyd George to Kerr, 12 February 1919, Lothian GD 40/17/1217.
123 Draft Minutes of a Meeting, 28 February 1919, 11.30 a.m., WC 538A, Cab. 23/15.
124 WC 541A, ibid.
125 BED 9, Cab. 29/28/1.
126 House Diary XV, 6 March 1919. See also ibid., 10 March 1919.
127 WC 538A, Cab. 23/15.
128 Kerr to Lloyd George, 18 February 1919, Lothian GD 40/17/1222, reporting his explanation of Lloyd George's policy to House.
129 ibid.
130 Unsigned handwritten note in box of peace conference notes, n.d., LG F/99.
131 'On conscription and militarism', 4 January 1919, PC 176, FO 371/4356. Headlam-Morley wrote to Zimmern, 'My paper was a direct criticism of Lloyd George's speeches and Smuts's Memorandum on the point, but of course the reference to them had to be cut out before it was printed'. 17 January 1919, H-M.
132 Minutes on PC 176, 4 January 1919 and n.d., FO 371/4356; 6 January 1919, PC/020, Davidson Papers. In circulating the memorandum Cecil did not identify its author and did not fully endorse its conclusions.
133 See Wilson's accounts of discussions of the military proposals among himself, Lloyd George, Balfour, Milner, Chamberlain, Hankey, Kerr and Cecil. Wilson Diary and Notebook, 5 March 1919, Diary, 6 March 1919, HHW 28.
134 'Notes on the military peace proposals', LG F/3/4/15.
135 WC 541A, Cab. 23/15; Wilson Diary and Notebook, 5 March 1919, Diary, 6 March 1919, HHW 28.
136 Wilson Diary and Notebook, 5 March 1919, Diary, 6 March 1919, HHW 28.

137 Minutes of the 17th Session, Supreme War Council, 6 March 1919, 3.00 p.m., *USFR, PPC*, vol. 4, p. 216.

138 Wilson Diary and Notebook, 6 March 1919, HHW 28; SWC 17, *USFR, PPC*, vol. 4, pp. 216–19; House Diary XV, 6 March 1919: 'I was amused at the adroit way in which he [Lloyd George] has led Clemenceau into believing that he, George, was objecting to the military terms because they were not drastic enough. As a matter of fact, his whole purpose was to get "Conscription" struck out because he knows that England will not stand for future conscription [;] therefore they will not look with favor upon terms which leave conscription in Germany.'

139 SWC 17, *USFR, PPC*, vol. 4, pp. 217–18. General Wilson did not submit his letter, which included the same argument, until after this meeting. Wilson Notebook, 6 March 1919, HHW 28.

140 SWC 17, *USFR, PPC*, vol. 4, p. 219.

141 ibid.

142 Lloyd George, 'Notes on an interview between M. Clemenceau, Colonel House and myself, held at the Ministry of War, Rue Dominicq, at 10.30 a.m., 7th March 1919', 7 March 1919, LG F/147/1; House Diary XV, 6 March 1919; House to W. Wilson, 7 March 1919, House 121/4297.

143 Minutes of the 2nd Meeting of the 17th Session, Supreme War Council, 7 March 1919, 3.00 p.m., *USFR, PPC*, vol. 4, pp. 263–6.

144 'Conscription "verboten"', *Daily Mail*, 12 March 1919; 'A great decision', *Daily News*, 11 March 1919.

145 Quoted in Stevenson Diary, 7 March 1919. See also House to Wilson, 7 March 1919, House 121/4297.

146 Wilson Diary, 8 March 1919, HHW 28.

147 Wilson Diary, 10 March 1919, ibid.

148 Minutes of the Meeting of the Supreme War Council, 10 March 1919, 3.00 p.m., *USFR, PPC*, vol. 4, pp. 295–9.

149 According to General Wilson, President Wilson on his return threatened to reopen the question of conscription but backed off when Lloyd George countered with a threat to reopen the question of the league. Wilson Diary and Notebook, 14 March 1919, Diary, 17 March 1919, HHW 28; Wilson to Churchill, 18 March 1919, 18A/16, ibid., 73/1/11.

150 SWC, 10 March 1919, *USFR, PPC*, vol. 4, pp. 299–304 and app. 'A', 'Draft regulations concerning a definite military status of Germany', ibid., pp. 305-13. These provisions were embodied in pt V, sec. I of Great Britain, Parliament, *Parliamentary Papers, 1919*, vol. 53 (*Accounts and Papers*, vol. 22), Cmnd 153, July 1919, 'Treaty of peace between the Allied and Associated Powers and Germany, signed at Versailles, 28th June 1919'. Cited hereafter as 'Treaty'. Since the future of the Rhineland was still under discussion, the proposal for its demilitarisation was removed from the military conditions.

151 Minutes of a Meeting of the Supreme War Council, 17 March 1919, 3.00 p.m., *USFR, PPC*, vol. 4, pp. 375–6. This became 'Treaty', art. 203: 'All the military, naval and air clauses contained in the present Treaty, for the execution of which a time-limit is prescribed, shall be executed by Germany under the control of Inter-Allied Commissions specially appointed for this purpose by the Principal Allied and Associated Powers.'

152 Diary, 17 March 1919, HHW 28. Wilson told Churchill that the numbers had been 'dangerously cut down'. 11 March 1919, ibid., 73/1/21.

153 Minute, 14 March 1919, 461/2/1/4211, FO 608/128.

154 House Diary XV, 10 March 1919. The members of the committee were Kerr, Tardieu and Sidney Mezes of the American delegation.

155 In his discussions with Tardieu and Mezes, Kerr argued against Tardieu's demand for separation and occupation of the Rhine that as long as the military terms were observed, 'there was no menace to France'. Kerr, 'Notes of discussion with M. Tardieu and Dr Mezes', 12 March 1919, LG F/89/2/40.
156 'Notes on the suggestion made on March 14th', [17 March 1919], Lothian GD 40/17/60.

Chapter 10

1   'Memorandum on the disorders in Germany', 19 March 1919, GT 7038, Cab. 24/77.
2   Lloyd George to Bonar Law, 19 March 1919, LG F/30/3/31.
3   Lloyd George to Jones, 17 March 1919, LG F/23/4/37.
4   Wiseman 90/31.
5   SWC, 10 March 1919, 3.00 p.m., *USFR, PPC*, vol. 4, p. 298.
6   Notes, 18 March 1919, LG F/3/4/19.
7   Wilson thought that French designs on the Rhine were 'mad'. Diary, 27 February 1919, HHW 28.
8   Wilson Notebook, 13 March 1919, ibid.
9   Wilson Diary, 19 March 1919, ibid.
10   Wilson Notebook, 18 March 1919, ibid.; Wilson to Churchill, 18 March 1919, 18A/16, ibid. 73/1/11.
11   19 March 1919, LG F/23/4/39.
12   ibid.
13   ibid.
14   Kerr to Lloyd George [19? February 1919], Lothian GD 40/17/1223.
15   LG F/23/4/39.
16   On 23 March Lords Cunliffe and Sumner of the British Reparations Delegation joined them briefly to discuss indemnities. Wilson Diary, 22 March, 23 March 1919, HHW 28. When he informed Bonar Law of the conference, Lloyd George did not include Montagu in the group, and in his memoirs he omitted Montagu and incorrectly included Smuts. Lloyd George to Bonar Law, 30 March 1919, Law (Bonar Law) 97/1/17; *Memoirs of the Peace Conference*, Vol. 1, p. 266. However, Wilson recorded the details of Montagu's participation, and Smuts was ill in London that weekend. Wilson Diary and Notebook, 22 March, 23 March 1919, HHW 28; Smuts to A. Clark, 28 March 1919, Smuts 98/70.
17   Diary, 22 March 1919.
18   See Lloyd George to Lord Birkenhead, 15 March 1919, LG F/4/7/9.
19   Quoted in Stevenson Diary, 27 March 1919.
20   'Some considerations for the Peace Conference before they finally draft their terms', Final, 25 March 1919, Lothian GD 40/17/61. Lloyd George's first draft expressed this idea more strongly: 'You may strip Germany of her colonies, reduce her armies to a mere police force, and her Navy to the position of the Argentine; all the same, in the end, if she concentrates her mind upon it, she will find means of returning the blow.' 'Some considerations for the Peace Conference before they finally draft their terms', Draft, 23 March 1919, Lothian GD 40/17/60.
21   'Some considerations', Final, 25 March 1919, Lothian GD 40/17/61.
22   'General remarks on Mr Lloyd George's note of 26th March', Translation of French reply, [31 March 1919], ibid. See also Cecil Diary, 26 March 1919, Add. 51131: 'The French will say that all the moderation is to come from them,

while we get everything we want, in which there is some truth.'

23 [23 March 1919], Lothian GD 40/17/61.

24 'Outline of peace terms', 23 March 1919, ibid.

25 Wilson Notebook, 23 March 1919, HHW 28. Marginal notes on the draft of 23 March, Lothian GD 40/17/61 listed the abolition of conscription as a condition of joining the league. In addition to the drafts already cited, see the one of 24 March 1919 and [Lloyd George?], Notes, [23? March 1919], Lothian GD 40/17/60.

26 'Some considerations', Final, 25 March 1919, Lothian GD 40/17/61.

27 ibid.

28 Wilson Diary and Notebook, 5 April 1919, HHW 28.

29 House Diary XV, 27 March 1919; Wiseman to Reading, 6 April 1919, Wiseman 90/29.

30 Hankey Diary, 26 April 1919, HNKY 1/5; Notes of a Meeting held at President Wilson's House, 26 April 1919, 3.00 p.m., *USFR, PPC*, vol. 5, p. 299.

31 'Treaty', pt V, preamble.

32 'Draft agreement of UK and USA on German disarmament', minuted by Hankey as approved by Lloyd George and Wilson, 5 April 1919, HNKY 8/14. The Anglo-American agreement to league control was not communicated to the French until 17 April. This control provision of the agreement became 'Treaty', art. 213.

33 These Rhineland provisions were embodied in 'Treaty', arts 42–4, 428–9, 431. Art. 430 provided for reoccupation if Germany defaulted on its reparations obligations.

34 Notes of a Meeting held at President Wilson's House, 22 April 1919, 11.00 a.m., *USFR, PPC*, vol. 5, p. 113. The arrangement was for France to provide most of the troops, which would serve as an international force.

35 Minutes of a Meeting of the British Empire Delegation, 5 May 1919, BED 30, Cab. 29/28/1.

36 Wilson Diary, 16 April 1919, Diary and Notebook, 23 April 1919, HHW 28; 'The military situation throughout the British Empire with special reference to the inadequacy of the numbers of troops available', Memorandum by CIGS, 26 April 1919, circulated 3 May 1919, GT 7182, Cab. 24/78.

37 Wiseman to Reading, 18 April 1919, Wiseman 90/29.

38 Smuts to Lloyd George, 14 May 1919, LG F/45/9/34.

39 Smuts to Lloyd George, 5 May 1919, LG F/45/9/33; same to same, 14 May 1919, LG F/45/9/34; same to same, 22 May 1919; LG F/45/9/35; Smuts to Wilson, 14 May 1919, Smuts 101/88; same to same, 30 May 1919, Smuts 101/97; 'Negotiations for the peace treaty', Memorandum by General Smuts, 17 May 1919, WCP 799, Cab. 29/14; Smuts to Margaret Gillett, 18 May 1919, Smuts 122/38; Smuts to A. Clark, 23 May 1919, Smuts 98/84; Cecil Diary, 20 May 1919, Add. 51131.

40 Smuts to Lloyd George, 26 March 1919, LG F/45/9/29; Smuts to Margaret Gillett, 27 March 1919, Smuts 22/215; Smuts to A. Clark, 28 March 1919, Smuts 98/70.

41 Stevenson Diary, 7 May 1919: 'He [Lloyd George] says it [Brockdorff-Rantzau's behaviour] has made him more angry than any incident of the war, & if the Germans do not sign, he will have no mercy on them.' Headlam-Morley to Percy A. Koppel, 8 May 1919, H-M: 'I saw the Prime Minister . . . last night and he was full of indignation . . . He said that he had never been so angry with the Germans through out the war.'

42 Notes of a Meeting held at President Wilson's House, 9 May 1919, 4.00 p.m.,

USFR, PPC, vol. 5, p. 527; Notes of a Meeting held at President Wilson's House, 10 May 1919, 11.00 a.m., ibid., p. 539; Notes of a Meeting held at President Wilson's House, 14 May 1919, 11.45 a.m., ibid., p. 600.

43 Barnes to Lloyd George, 6 May 1919, LG F/4/3/14; same to same, 6 May 1919, LG F/4/3/15; 'Negotiations for the peace treaty', Memorandum by Mr Barnes, 19 May 1919, WCP 807, Cab. 29/15.

44 Barnes to Lloyd George, 6 May 1919, LG F/4/3/14; same to same, 16 May 1919, LG F/4/3/15.

45 Cecil to Lloyd George, 27 May 1919, LG F/6/6/47. See also same to same, 30 May 1919, LG F/6/6/48.

46 Wilson Notebook, 13 March 1919, HHW 28; Cecil to Bryce, 22 March 1919, UB 55.

47 LG F/6/6/47.

48 Notes of a Meeting held at President Wilson's House, 19 May 1919, 11.00 a.m., *USFR, PPC*, vol. 5, p. 703.

49 20 May [1919], LG F/8/3/55. Also 'Negotiations for the peace treaty', Memorandum by Mr Churchill, 21 May 1919, WCP 825, Cab. 29/15, in which there is an added paragraph stating that the CIGS concurred.

50 To Davies, 23 May 1919, LG F/23/4/69.

51 28 May 1919, LG F/16/7/39.

52 Minutes of a Meeting of the British Empire Delegation, 30 May 1919, BED 32, Cab. 29/28/1; Minutes of a Meeting of the British Empire Delegation, 1 June 1919, 11.00 a.m., BED 33, ibid.; Minutes of a Meeting of the British Empire Delegation, 1 June 1919, 5.30 p.m., BED 34, ibid.; Cecil Diary, 30 May, 31 May 1919, Add. 51131; Note by Montagu, 4 June 1919, in Waley, *Montagu*, pp. 211–14; Wilson Diary and Notebook, 30 May, 31 May 1919, Diary, 1 June 1919, HHW 28.

53 BED 33, Cab. 29/28/1.

54 To Lloyd George, 2 June 1919, LG F/36/4/17.

55 BED 34, Cab. 29/28/1.

56 'German counterproposals of May 29, 1919', doc. 57, in Alma Luckau, *The German Delegation at the Paris Peace Conference* (New York: Columbia University Press, 1941), p. 374.

57 BED 33, BED 34, Cab. 29/28/1.

58 Notes of a Meeting held at President Wilson's House, 29 May 1919, 11.00 a.m., *USFR, PPC*, vol. 6, pp. 108–11.

59 Notes of a Meeting held at Mr Lloyd George's Flat, 2 June 1919, 4.00 p.m., ibid., pp. 141, 143–5.

60 Notes of a Meeting held at President Wilson's House, 12 June 1919, 11.00 a.m., ibid., p. 328; Lloyd George, *Memoirs of the Peace Conference*, Vol. 1, p. 486; Report Presented to the Council of the Principal Allied and Associated Powers by the Inter-Allied Commission on the Left Bank of the Rhine, app. I to Notes of a Meeting held at President Wilson's House, 13 June 1919, 12.00 m., *USFR, PPC*, vol. 6, p. 381.

61 Luckau, *German Delegation*, doc. 57. pp. 322–3. They also proposed oral negotiations on these demands.

62 BED 33, Cab. 29/28/1.

63 BED 34, ibid.

64 BED 32, ibid.

65 'Memorandum on the military aspect of the German peace proposals', 31 May 1919, WCP 897, Cab. 29/15.

66 'The League of Nations and the German counter-proposals', 3 June 1919, WCP 916, Cab. 29/16.

67 Cecil Diary, 7 June 1919, Add. 51131; Report to the Council of the Allied and Associated Powers: 'Proposed reply to the German proposals with regard to the League of Nations', 7 June 1919, M 242, Cab. 29/25.

68 House Diary XVI, 8 June, 9 June 1919; 'The League of Nations – proposed reply to the German proposals', 11 June 1919, WCP 970, Cab. 29/16; Notes of a Meeting held at President Wilson's House, 12 June 1919, 11.00 a.m., *USFR, PPC*, vol. 6, p. 328; 'The League of Nations: reply to the German proposals', approved by the Council of the Principal Allied and Associated Powers, 12 June 1919, WCP 970 (Revised), Cab. 29/16.

69 WCP 970 (Revised), Cab. 29/16.

70 WCP 897, Cab. 29/15; Committee on Military Clauses, 'Suggested answers to the German counter-proposals', 7 June 1919, WCP 945, Cab. 29/16. General Wilson also recommended a change in the terms of service and was willing to reduce the German army to 100,000 if the European situation improved 'sufficiently'.

71 Notes of a Meeting held at President Wilson's House, 3 June 1919, 4.00 p.m., *USFR, PPC*, vol. 6, p. 157.

72 Notes of a Meeting held at President Wilson's House, 12 June 1919, 4.00 p.m., ibid., p. 354.

73 WCP 945, Cab. 29/16.

74 *Memoirs of the Peace Conference*, Vol. 1, p. 484.

75 Notes of a Meeting held at President Wilson's House, 12 June 1919, 4.00 p.m., *USFR, PPC*, vol. 6, p. 354.

76 ibid.

77 Committee on Military Clauses, 'Reply to the German counter-proposals', approved by the Council of the Principal Allied and Associated Powers, 12 June 1919, WCP 945 Revise, Cab. 29/16.

78 Allied reply to the German counterproposals', 16 June 1919, doc. 60, Luckau, *German Delegation*, pp. 411–19.

79 ibid., p. 412.

80 Quoted in S. William Halperin, *Germany Tried Democracy: A Political History of the Reich from 1918 to 1933* (New York: Norton, 1965), p. 152.

81 See 'Treaty', arts 204, 206, 208.

Conclusion

1 Amery Diary, 24 March 1919.

2 Jones to Hankey, 26 March 1919, TJ Z 1919/35.

3 Lloyd George to General Botha, 26 June 1919, Smuts 101/101.

4 Stenographic Notes of a Meeting of Representatives of the United Kingdom, the Dominions and India, 22 June 1921, 11.30 a.m., E 4th Meeting, Cab. 32/2.

5 Quoted in Jacobson, *Locarno*, p. 24.

6 Lord Crewe to Chamberlain, 13 May 1925, describing Chamberlain's disarmament policy, AC 52/212, quoted in ibid., p. 50.

7 See, for example, Kerr to Lloyd George, [20 September 1920], LG F/90/1/18.

8 Conclusions of a Meeting of the Cabinet, 4 April 1921, C 17(21), Cab. 23/25.

9 M. W. Lampson, 30 January 1926, on H. Knatchbull-Hugessen to Lampson, 23 January 1926, no. 201, in E. L. Woodward *et al.* (eds), *Documents on British Foreign Policy*, 56 vols in 4 series (London: HMSO, 1946–), ser. 1A, Vol. 1, p. 349, n. 2. Cited hereafter as *DBFP*. The minute was approved by Tyrrell, then Permanent Under-Secretary, and Chamberlain 1 February. ibid., p. 350.

10 See, for example, Conclusions of a Meeting of the Cabinet, 20 January 1921, C 3(21), Cab. 23/24.

11 Curzon in E 4, Cab. 32/2.
12 *The Collapse of British Power* (London: Methuen, 1972), p. 327.
13 7 June 1921, LG F/31/1/58.
14 W. N. Medlicott, *British Foreign Policy since Versailles, 1919–1963* (London: Methuen, 1968), p. 45.
15 Fisher Diary, 30 December 1920, Fisher 8.
16 'Principles of Unionist foreign policy', [November 1922], Law (Bonar Law) 113/10/1.
17 To Headlam-Morley, 8 March 1919, H-M.
18 British Secretary's Notes of an Allied Conference, Paris, 29 January 1921, 11.00 a.m., ICP 156, Cab. 29/90.
19 To Sir Harcourt Butler, 22 June 1920, Hardinge 42.
20 Minute, 13 November 1920, on 'Progress of disarmament (3)', 13 November 1920, C 11056/113/18, FO 371/4757.
21 See, for example, Fisher Diary, 20 July 1920, Fisher 8; Drummond to Lloyd George, 17 December 1921, LG F/42/7/13.
22 Labour Party Election Manifesto, 17 November 1923, *The Times*, 19 November 1923, quoted in Wolfers, *Britain and France*, p. 350.
23 Jacobson, *Locarno*, p. 95.
24 Drummond to Lloyd George, 17 December 1921, LG F/42/7/13.
25 'German request to maintain an army of 200,000: Allied declaration in answer to German note', approved by Supreme Council, San Remo, 26 April 1920, CP 1184, Cab. 24/104; British Secretary's Notes of a Meeting, Spa, 8 July 1920, 11.15 a.m., ICP 123, no. 50, in *DBFP*, ser. 1, vol. 8, pp. 470–81.
26 [Kerr?], 'Notes for speech in House of Commons after Prime Minister's return from Spa', 21 July 1920, LG F/243/8. See also British Secretary's Notes of an International Conference, Spa, 6 July 1920, 4.30 p.m., ICP 119, no. 45, in *DBFP*, ser. 1, vol. 8, pp. 431–41; Kerr to Bonar Law, 6 July 1920, Law (Bonar Law) 99/3/6; British Secretary's Notes of an International Conference, Spa, 7 July 1920, 3.30 p.m., ICP 121, no. 48 in *DBFP*, ser. 1, vol. 8, pp. 455–64.
27 Quoted in Fisher Diary, 20 July 1920, Fisher 8.
28 General Staff, War Office, 'Memorandum on the execution by Germany of the military articles of the Peace Treaty of Versailles', 5 November 1920, BED 49, Cab. 29/100; Conclusions of a Meeting of the Cabinet, 28 December 1920, C 78(20), Cab. 23/23.
29 C 78(20), Cab. 23/23.
30 [R. F. Wigram], 'Draft memorandum prepared in Central European Department on the position as regards disarmament', 12 January 1921, and Minutes by Wigram, S. Waterlow, Crowe and Curzon, 12 January 1921, in 'Disarmament of Germany: memorandum on questions to be considered by Supreme Council', 12 January 1921, C 1118/13/18, FO 371/5854; Conclusions of a Meeting of the Cabinet, 20 January 1921, 3(21), Cab. 23/24; Fisher Diary, 18 [20?] January 1921, Fisher 8; Minutes by Wigram, Waterlow, Crowe, 18 January 1921 and 'Memorandum no. 1: disarmament', 19 January 1921, in 'Papers submitted 18 January', 21 January 1921, C 1553/13/18, FO 371/5854; British Secretary's Notes of an Allied Conference, Paris, 24 January 1921, 4.00 p.m., ICP 150 (Revise), Cab. 29/90.
31 Quoted in Wigram, Minute, 20 September 1921, on Sir C. Hurst to Wigram, 15 September 1921, C 18727/37/18, FO 371/5864.
32 Stenographic Notes of a Meeting of Representatives of the United Kingdom, the Dominions and India, 10 Downing Street, 20 June 1921, 12.00 m., E 1st Meeting, Cab. 32/2.
33 Quoted in Jacobson, *Locarno*, p. 49.

34 Fox, 'Britain and Commission of Control', p. 163.
35 Quoted in Arnold J. Toynbee, *Survey of International Affairs, 1920–1923* (London: Humphrey Milford, Oxford University Press, 1925), p. 112.
36 Thomas E. Boyle, 'France, Great Britain, and German disarmament, 1919–1927' (PhD dissertation, State University of New York at Stony Brook, 1972), pp. 135, 143.
37 Fox, 'Britain and Commission of Control', pp. 147–8.
38 Jacobson, *Locarno*, pp. 22–6, 49–50, 97.
39 Quoted in Boyle, 'France, Great Britain, and German disarmament,' p. 177.
40 Fox, 'Britain and Commission of Control', p. 156; Jacobson, *Locarno*, p. 95.
41 For example, Hans W. Gatzke, *Stresemann and the Rearmament of Germany* (Baltimore, Md: Johns Hopkins Press, 1954), p. 72; Jacobson, *Locarno*, pp. 134, 366.
42 Boyle, 'France, Great Britain, and German disarmament', p. 135. See also Fox, 'Britain and Commission of Control', p. 149.
43 Orme Sargent, 16 September 1926, quoted in Fox, 'Britain and Commission of Control', p. 156.
44 18 November 1926, quoted in ibid., p. 258.
45 Quoted in F. L. Carsten, *The Reichswehr and Politics, 1918 to 1933* (Oxford: Clarendon Press, 1966), p. 259.
46 ibid., p. 221.
47 Jacobson, *Locarno*, p. 110, n. 19.
48 Carsten, *Reichswehr*, pp. 73–4.

Select Bibliography

Unpublished Documents at the Public Record Office, London

Cabinet Records

Cab. 1   Miscellaneous records.

Cab. 16   Records of *ad hoc* sub-committees of the Committee of Imperial Defence: Sub-Committee on Territorial Changes.

Cab. 17   Committee of Imperial Defence. Correspondence and miscellaneous papers.

Cab. 21   Registered files.

Cab. 23   Minutes of the War Cabinet and Conclusions of the Cabinet.

Cab. 24   Memoranda. G series: War Council, Dardanelles Committee, War Committee and Cabinet papers; GT series: Cabinet papers, December 1916–November 1919; Western and General Reports; CP series: Cabinet papers after November 1919.

Cab. 25   Supreme War Council.

Cab. 27   Committees. General series.

Cab. 28   Allied conferences. IC series. Minutes.

Cab. 29   Peace Conference and other conferences. P series: Cabinet papers concerned with war aims, peace terms and the peace conference and treaty; WCP and M series: Cabinet papers circulated at the peace conference; BED series: minutes of meetings of the British Empire Delegation; ICP series: minutes of international conferences.

Cab. 32   Imperial conferences. Minutes and memoranda.

Cab. 37   Photographic copies of Cabinet papers.

Cab. 41   Photographic copies of Cabinet letters in the Royal Archives.

Cab. 42   Photographic copies of papers of the War Council, Dardanelles Committee and War Committee. Minutes of the War Council and Dardanelles Committee, minutes and papers of the War Committee.

Cab. 63   Hankey Papers.

Foreign Office Records

FO 371   General correspondence. Political: Germany, Political Intelligence Department, the War.

FO 373   Peace conference handbooks prepared by Historical Section.

FO 374   Peace conference papers and minutes.

FO 608   Peace conference correspondence.

FO 800   Private collections. Ministers and officials: Earl of Balfour, Sir Francis Bertie, Viscount Cecil, Marquess Curzon of Kedleston, Sir Edward Grey, Sir Arthur Nicolson, Marquess of Reading, Sir C. A. Spring Rice. Private Office: General. League of Nations.

FO 899   Papers circulated directly to the Cabinet.

Treasury Records
   T 102   National War Aims Committee. Minutes and reports.

War Office Records
WO 106   Directorate of Military Operations and Intelligence: Papers.

Private Papers in the United Kingdom

Aberystwyth
National Library of Wales
   Dr Thomas Jones Collection.
   Lloyd George Manuscripts.

Birmingham
Birmingham University Library
   Papers and Letters of Sir Austen Chamberlain.

Cambridge
Cambridge University Library
   Papers of Charles Hardinge, 1st Baron Hardinge of Penshurst.
   Private Papers of Gen. Jan C. Smuts (microfilm).

Churchill College, Archives Centre
   Archives of Lord Croft of Bournemouth (Sir Henry Page Croft).
   Archives of Lord Hankey of the Chart (Maurice Hankey).
   Archives of the Rt Hon. Reginald McKenna.
   George Saunders Papers.
   Sir Cecil Spring Rice Collection.

Chichester
West Sussex Record Office
   Leopold James Maxse Papers.

Edinburgh
National Library of Scotland
   Papers of Field Marshal the Earl Haig.
   Correspondence and Papers of Richard Burdon Haldane, Viscount
      Haldane of Cloan.

Scottish Record Office
   Papers of Philip Kerr, 11th Marquis of Lothian.
   Papers of Sir Arthur Herbert Drummond Ramsay Steel-Maitland.

Liverpool
Liverpool Record Office, Liverpool City Library
   Papers of 17th Earl of Derby.

London
In the Possession of the Rt Hon. Julian Amery
  Leopold S. Amery Papers.

British Library
  Papers of Arthur James Balfour, Lord Balfour.
  Papers of Lord Robert Cecil, Viscount Cecil of Chelwood.
  Papers of Alfred Charles William Harmsworth, Viscount Northcliffe.
  Sir Ralph Spencer Paget Papers.
  C. P. Scott Papers.

In the Possession of Prof. Agnes Headlam-Morley
  Sir James Headlam-Morley Papers (photocopies).

House of Lords Record Office (formerly in the Beaverbrook Library)
  Papers of Max Aitken, Lord Beaverbrook.
  Papers of John Colin Campbell Davidson, 1st Viscount Davidson.
  Andrew Bonar Law Papers.
  David Lloyd George Papers.
  Frances Stevenson Papers.
  John St Loe Strachey Papers.

Imperial War Museum
  Papers of Gen. Sir John Cowans.
  Journal of Lord Thomson of Cardington.
  Diaries and Papers of Field Marshal Sir Henry Wilson.

India Office Library and Records
  Viscount Curzon of Kedleston Collection, part 2: British Political Papers.
  Marquess of Reading (Private) Collection.

Liddell Hart Centre for Military Archives, King's College, University of
    London
  Field Marshal Sir William Robertson Papers.

Public Record Office
  Earl Cromer Papers – FO 633.

Oxford
Bodleian Library
  Dr Christopher Addison Papers.
  Papers of Herbert Henry Asquith, 1st Earl of Oxford and Asquith.
  Uncatalogued Papers of James Viscount Bryce.
  H. A. L. Fisher Papers.
  Papers of Alfred Milner, Viscount Milner.
  Alfred Charles William Harmsworth, Viscount Northcliffe, Lord
    Northcliffe's Bulletins to the 'Daily Mail' Office, 1915–22.
  Papers of Sir Horace George Montagu Rumbold, 9th Bt.
  Sir Alfred Zimmern Papers.

Sheffield
Sheffield University Library
  William Albert Samuel Hewins Papers.

Private Papers at Yale University Library

William H. Buckler Papers.
Edward M. House Papers.
William Wiseman Papers.

Published Documents

Gooch, G. P., and Temperley, Harold (eds), *British Documents on the Origins of the War, 1898–1914*, 11 vols (London: HMSO, 1926–38).
Great Britain, Parliament, *Parliamentary Debates* (Commons), 5th ser., vols 65 (1914)–118 (1919).
Great Britain, Parliament, *Parliamentary Debates* (Lords), 5th ser., vols 17 (1914)–35 (1919).
Great Britain, Parliament, *Parliamentary Papers, 1919*, vol. 53 (*Accounts and Papers*, vol. 22), Cmnd 153, July 1919, 'Treaty of Peace between the Allied and Associated Powers and Germany, signed at Versailles, 28th June 1919'.
Mantoux, Paul, *Les Délibérations du Conseil des Quatres (14 Mars–28 Juin 1919)*, 2 vols (Paris: Éditions du Centre National de la Recherche Scientifique, 1955).
US, Department of State, *Papers relating to the Foreign Relations of the United States, 1917 and 1918*, supp. 1, *The World War* (Washington, DC: Government Printing Office, 1931–3).
US, Department of State, *Papers relating to the Foreign Relations of the United States, the Paris Peace Conference, 1919*, 13 vols (Washington, DC: Government Printing Office, 1942–7).
Woodward, E. L., *et al.* (eds), *Documents on British Foreign Policy*, 56 vols in 4 ser. (London: HMSO, 1946–), ser. 1, vols 1–3, 7–11, 15–16, 19–20; ser. 1A, vols 1–7.

Newspapers and Periodicals

Contemporary Review.
Daily Mail.
Daily News.
Gleanings and Memoranda.
Herald.
Manchester Guardian.
Morning Post.
Nation.

National Opinion.
National Review.
New Statesman.
Observer.
Round Table.
Spectator.
The Times.
Tribunal.
Westminster Gazette.

Speeches and Contemporary Publications

Angell, Norman, *Prussianism and its Destruction* (London: Heinemann, 1914).

Baker, Ray Stannard, and Dodd, William E. (eds), *The Public Papers of Woodrow Wilson*, 6 vols (New York: Harper, 1925–7), Vols 3–5.

Balfour, Arthur James, 'Anglo-German relations', in Arthur James Balfour, *Essays Speculative and Political* (New York: Doran, 1921), pp. 177–86.

Campaign Guide: A Handbook for Unionist Speakers, The, 13th edn (London: National Unionist Association of Conservative and Liberal Unionist Organisations [1914]).

Fisher, H. A. L., *The War: Its Causes and Issues* (London: Longmans, Green, 1914).

Headlam, James Wycliffe, *England, Germany, and Europe* (London: Macmillan, 1914).

Headlam, James Wycliffe, *The Issue* (London: Constable, 1917).

Headlam, James Wycliffe, *The Peace Terms of the Allies* (London: Richard Clay, 1917).

Hirst, Francis W., *The Political Economy of War* (London: Dent, 1915).

Hobson, J. A., *Towards International Government* (London: Allen & Unwin, 1915).

Labour Party, 'Labour and the new social order', reproduced in Paul U. Kellogg and Arthur Gleason, *British Labor and the War: Reconstructors for a New World* (New York: Boni & Liveright, 1919), app. 4.

Labour Party, 'Statement of war aims of the Labour Party', reproduced in Peter Stansky (ed.), *The Left and War: The British Labour Party and World War I* (New York: Oxford University Press, 1969), pp. 318–26.

Lloyd George, David, *British War Aims* (New York: Doran, [1918]).

Lloyd George, David, *The Great Crusade* (New York: Doran, 1918).

Lloyd George, David, *Through Terror to Triumph*, ed. F. L. Stevenson (London: Hodder & Stoughton, 1915).

Mackinder, Halford J., 'The geographical pivot of history' (London: William Clowes, [1904]; reprinted from *Geographical Journal*, April 1904).

Mackinder, Halford J., 'Manpower as a measure of national and imperial strength', *National Review*, vol. 45 (March 1905), pp. 136–43.

Morel, E. D., *The Morrow of the War*, reprinted in Peter Stansky (ed.), *The Left and War: The British Labour Party and World War I* (New York: Oxford University Press, 1969), pp. 88–103.

Morgan, J. H., 'The disarmament of Germany and after', *Quarterly Review*, vol. 242 (October 1924), pp. 415–57.

Rose, J. Holland, *The Origins of the War* (Cambridge: Cambridge University Press, 1915).

[Smuts, J. C.], *General Smuts's Message to South Wales* (London: Field & Queen, [1917]).

Smuts, J. C., *War-Time Speeches: A Compilation of Public Utterances in Great Britain* (New York: Doran, 1917).

Wells, H. G., *Mr. Britling Sees It Through* (New York: Macmillan, 1916).

Wells, H. G., *The War that Will End War* (New York: Duffield, 1914).

Edited Collections of Private Papers, Letters and Diaries

Brett, Maurice V., and Esher, Oliver Viscount (eds). *Journals and Letters of Reginald Viscount Esher*, 4 vols (London: Nicholson & Watson, 1934–8), Vol. 4.

Cambon, Paul, *Correspondance, 1870–1924*, 3 vols (Paris: Editions Bernard Grasset, 1940–6), Vol. 3.

Churchill, Randolph S., and Gilbert, Martin, *Winston S. Churchill*, 5 vols with companion vols (London: Heinemann, 1966–), companion vols 1–4.

Hancock, W. K., and van der Poel, Jean (eds), *Selections from the Smuts Papers*, 6 vols (Cambridge: Cambridge University Press, 1966–73), Vols 3–4.

Lennox, Lady Algernon Gordon (ed.), *The Diary of Lord Bertie of Thame, 1914–1918*, 2 vols (New York: Doran, [1924]).

[Riddell, George Allardice], *Lord Riddell's Intimate Diary of the Peace Conference and After, 1918–1923* (New York: Reynal & Hitchcock, 1934).

[Riddell, George Allardice], *Lord Riddell's War Diary, 1914–1918* (London: Nicholson & Watson, 1933).

Seymour, Charles, *The Intimate Papers of Colonel House*, 4 vols (Boston, Mass.: Houghton Mifflin, 1926–8), Vols. 3–4.

Biographies, Autobiographies and Memoirs

Addison, Christopher, *Politics from Within, 1911–1918*, 2 vols (London: Herbert Jenkins, 1924).

Amery, L. S., *My Political Life*, 3 vols (London: Hutchinson, 1953), Vol. 2.

Angell, Norman, *After All: The Autobiography of Norman Angell* (New York: Farrar, Straus & Young, [1952]).

Asquith, H. H., *The Genesis of the War* (London: Cassell, 1923).

Blake, Robert, *The Unknown Prime Minister: The Life and Times of Andrew Bonar Law, 1858–1923* (London: Eyre & Spottiswoode, 1955).

Bonham-Carter, Victor, *The Strategy of Victory, 1914–1918: The Life and Times of the Master Strategist of World War I, Field-Marshal Sir William Robertson* (New York: Holt, Rinehart & Winston, 1963).

Borden, Henry (ed.), *Robert Laird Borden: His Memoirs*, 2 vols (New York: Macmillan, 1938), Vol. 2.

Callwell, Sir C. E., *Field-Marshal Sir Henry Wilson: His Life and Diaries*, 2 vols (New York: Scribner's, 1927).

Cecil of Chelwood, Viscount, *All the Way* (London: Hodder & Stoughton, 1949).

Cecil of Chelwood, Viscount, *A Great Experiment* (New York: Oxford University Press, 1941).

Chamberlain, Austen, *Down the Years* (London: Cassell, 1935).

Chapman-Huston, Desmond, *The Lost Historian: A Memoir of Sir Sidney Low* (London: John Murray, 1936).

Churchill, Winston S., *The World Crisis, 1918–1928: The Aftermath* (New York: Scribner's, 1929).

Collier, Basil, *Brasshat: A Biography of Field-Marshal Sir Henry Wilson* (London: Secker & Warburg, 1961).

Conwell-Evans, T. P., *Foreign Policy from a Back Bench, 1904–1918: A Study Based on the Papers of Lord Noel-Buxton* (London: Oxford University Press, 1932).

Cooper, Duff, *Haig*, 2 vols (London: Faber, 1935–6).

Dugdale, Blanche E. C., *Arthur James Balfour*, 2 vols (New York: Putnam's, 1937).

Fisher, H. A. L., *An Unfinished Autobiography* (London: Oxford University Press, 1940).

Fraser, Peter, *Lord Esher: A Political Biography* (London: Hart-Davis, MacGibbon, 1973).

Fyfe, Hamilton, *Northcliffe: An Intimate Biography* (New York: Macmillan, 1930).

Gilbert, Martin, *Sir Horace Rumbold: Portrait of a Diplomatist, 1869–1941* (London: Heinemann, 1973).

Gollin, A. M., *Proconsul in Politics: A Study of Lord Milner in Opposition and in Power* (New York: Macmillan, 1964).

Grey of Fallodon, Viscount, *Twenty-Five Years, 1892–1916*, 2 vols (New York: Stokes, 1925), Vol. 2.

Haldane, Viscount, *Before the War* (New York: Funk & Wagnalls, 1920).

Hancock, W. K., *Smuts: The Sanguine Years, 1870–1919* (Cambridge: Cambridge University Press, 1962).

Hankey, Lord, *The Supreme Command, 1914–1918*, 2 vols (London: Allen & Unwin, 1961).

Hankey, Lord, *The Supreme Control at the Paris Peace Conference, 1919: A Commentary* (London: Allen & Unwin, 1963).

Havinghurst, Alfred F., *Radical Journalist: H. W. Massingham* (Cambridge: Cambridge University Press, 1974).

Hendrick, Burton J., *The Life and Letters of Walter H. Page*, 3 vols (Garden City, NY: Doubleday, Page, 1922–6), Vols 1–2.

Jenkins, Roy, *Asquith: Portrait of a Man and an Era* (New York: Dutton Paperback, 1966).

Jones, Thomas, *Lloyd George* (Cambridge, Mass.: Harvard University Press, 1951).

Koss, Stephen, *Fleet Street Radical: A. G. Gardiner and the Daily News* (London: Allen Lane, 1973).

Koss, Stephen, *Sir John Brunner: Radical Plutocrat, 1842–1919* (Cambridge: Cambridge University Press, 1970).

Lloyd George, David, *Memoirs of the Peace Conference*, 2 vols (New Haven, Conn.: Yale University Press, 1939).

Lloyd George, David, *War Memoirs*, 2 vols, 2nd edn (London: Odhams, 1938).

Marlowe, John, *Milner: Apostle of Empire* (London: Hamish Hamilton, 1976).

Maurice, Sir Frederick, *Haldane: The Life of Viscount Haldane of Cloan*, 2 vols (London: Faber, 1937–9).

Morley, John Viscount, *Memorandum on Resignation, August 1914* (London: Macmillan, 1928).

Murray, Arthur C., *Master and Brother: Murrays of Elibank* (London: John Murray, 1945).

Nicolson, Harold, *Curzon: The Last Phase, 1919–1925 – a Study in Post-War Diplomacy* (New York: Harcourt, Brace, 1939).

Nicolson, Harold, *King George the Fifth: His Life and Reign* (London: Constable, 1952).

Nicolson, Harold, *Sir Arthur Nicolson, Bart, First Lord Carnock: A Study in the Old Diplomacy* (London: Constable, 1930).

Owen, Frank, *Tempestuous Journey: Lloyd George, his Life and Times* (London: Hutchinson, 1954).

Oxford and Asquith, Earl of, *Memories and Reflections, 1852–1927*, 2 vols (Boston, Mass.: Little, Brown, 1928), Vol. 2.

Percy, Eustace, *Some Memories* (London: Eyre & Spottiswoode, 1958).

Petrie, Sir Charles, *The Life and Letters of the Right Hon. Sir Austen Chamberlain*, 2 vols (London: Cassell, 1939–40), Vol. 2.

Robbins, Keith, *Sir Edward Grey: A Biography of Lord Grey of Fallodon* (London: Cassell, 1971).

Robertson, Sir William, *From Private to Field-Marshal* (Boston, Mass.: Houghton Mifflin, 1921).

Robertson, Sir William, *Soldiers and Statesmen, 1914–1918*, 2 vols (New York: Scribner's, 1926).

Roskill, Stephen, *Hankey: Man of Secrets*, 3 vols (London: Collins, 1970–4), Vols 1 and 2.

Rowland, Peter, *Lloyd George* (London: Barrie & Jenkins, 1975).

Spender, J. A., *Life, Journalism and Politics*, 2 vols (New York: Stokes, [1927]).

Stuart, Sir Campbell, *Secrets of Crewe House* (London: Hodder & Stoughton, [1920]).

Thomson, Basil, *My Experiences at Scotland Yard* (Garden City, NY: Doubleday, Page, 1923).

Thomson, Basil, *The Scene Changes* (Garden City, NY: Doubleday, Doran, 1937).

Thomson, Malcolm, *David Lloyd George: The Official Biography* (London: Hutchinson, [1948]).

Trevelyan, G. M., *Grey of Fallodon* (London: Longmans, Green, 1937).

Waley, S. D., *Edwin Montagu: A Memoir and an Account of his Visits to India* (Bombay: Asia Publishing House, 1964).

Young, Kenneth, *Arthur James Balfour: The Happy Life of the Politician, Prime Minister, Statesman, and Philosopher, 1848–1930* (London: Bell, 1963).

General Histories and Special Studies

Barnett, Correlli, *Britain and her Army, 1509–1970: A Military, Political, and Social Survey* (New York: Morrow, 1970).

Barnett, Correlli, *The Collapse of British Power* (London: Methuen, 1972).

Beloff, Max, *Imperial Sunset*, Vol. 1: *Britain's Liberal Empire, 1897–1921* (London: Methuen, 1969).

Bertram-Libal, Gisela, *Aspekte der britischen Deutschlandpolitik, 1919–1922* (Göppingen: Alfred Kümmerle, 1972).

Birdsall, Paul, *Versailles, Twenty Years After* (New York: Reynal & Hitchcock, 1941).

Bowley, Arthur L., *Some Economic Consequences of the Great War* (London: Butterworth, 1930).

Boyle, Thomas E., 'France, Great Britain, and German disarmament, 1919–1927' (PhD dissertation, State University of New York at Stony Brook, 1972).

Bunselmeyer, Robert E., *The Cost of the War, 1914–1919: British Economic War Aims and the Origins of Reparation* (Hamden, Conn.: Archon, 1975).

Butterfield, Herbert, 'Sir Edward Grey in July 1914', *Historical Studies*, vol. 5 (1965), pp. 1–25.

Calleo, David, *The German Problem Reconsidered: Germany and the World Order, 1870 to the Present* (Cambridge: Cambridge University Press, 1978).

Carsten, F. L., *The Reichswehr and Politics, 1918 to 1933* (Oxford: Clarendon Press, 1966).

Collier, Basil, *The Defence of the United Kingdom* (London: HMSO, 1957).

Collins, Doreen, *Aspects of British Politics, 1904–1919* (Oxford: Pergamon, 1965).

Craig, Gordon A., *The Politics of the Prussian Army, 1640–1945* (New York: Oxford University Press, Galaxy Book, 1964).

Crosby, Gerda Richards, *Disarmament and Peace in British Politics, 1914–1919* (Cambridge, Mass.: Harvard University Press, 1957).

Cruttwell, C. R. M. F., *A History of the Great War, 1914–1918* (Oxford: Clarendon Press, 1934).

Dahlin, Ebba, *French and German Public Opinion on Declared War Aims, 1914–1918* (Stanford, Calif.: Stanford University Press, 1933).

Davis, Rodney Oliver, 'British policy and opinion on war aims and peace proposals, 1914–1918' (PhD dissertation, Duke University, Durham, NC, 1958).

Davis, Rodney Oliver, 'Lloyd George: leader or led in British war aims', in Lillian Parker Wallace and William C. Askew (eds), *Power, Public Opinion, and Diplomacy: Essays in Honor of Eber Malcolm Carroll by his Former Students* (Durham, NC: Duke University Press, 1959), pp. 222–43.

Dockrill, Michael, and Goold, Douglas, *Peace without Promise: Britain and the Peace Conferences, 1919–1923* (London: Batsford, 1981).

Egerton, George W., *Great Britain and the Creation of the League of Nations: Strategy, Politics, and International Organization, 1914–1919* (Chapel Hill, NC: University of North Carolina Press, 1978).

Ekstein, Michael, 'Sir Edward Grey and imperial Germany in 1914', *Journal of Contemporary History*, vol. 6 (July 1971), pp. 121–31.

Ekstein, Michael, 'Some notes on Sir Edward Grey's policy in July 1914', *Historical Journal*, vol. 15 (June 1972), pp. 321–4.

Ekstein-Frankl, Michael, 'The development of British war aims, August 1914–March 1915' (PhD thesis, University of London, 1969).

Elcock, Howard, *Portrait of a Decision: The Council of Four and the Treaty of Versailles* (London: Methuen, 1972).

Ensor, R. C. K., *England, 1870–1914* (Oxford: Clarendon Press, 1936).

Eyck, Erich, *A History of the Weimar Republic*, trans. Harlan P. Hanson and Robert G. L. Waite, 2 vols (New York: Atheneum, 1970).

Falls, Cyril, and Wheeler-Bennett, John W., *Was Germany Defeated in 1918?* (Toronto: Oxford University Press, 1940).

Fest, W. B., 'British war aims and German peace feelers during the First World War (December 1916–November 1918)', *Historical Journal*, vol. 15 (June 1972), pp. 285–308.

Fischer, Fritz, *Germany's Aims in the First World War* (New York: Norton, 1967).

Fischer, Fritz, *War of Illusions: German Policies from 1911 to 1914*, trans. Marian Jackson (New York: Norton, 1975).

Fowler, W. B., *British-American Relations, 1917–1918: The Role of Sir William Wiseman* (Princeton, NJ: Princeton University Press, 1969).

Fox, John P., 'Britain and the Inter-Allied Military Commission of Control, 1925–26', *Journal of Contemporary History*, vol. 4 (April 1969), pp. 143–64.

Fry, Michael G., *Lloyd George and Foreign Policy*, Vol. 1: *The Education of a Statesman: 1890–1916* (Montreal: McGill–Queen's University Press, 1977).

Gatzke, Hans W., *Germany's Drive to the West (Drang nach Westen): A Study of Germany's Western War Aims during the First World War* (Baltimore, Md: Johns Hopkins University Press, 1950).

Gatzke, Hans W., *Stresemann and the Rearmament of Germany* (Baltimore, Md: Johns Hopkins University Press, 1954).

Gilbert, Martin, *The Roots of Appeasement* (London: Weidenfeld & Nicolson, 1966).

Gordon, Harold J., *The Reichswehr and the German Republic, 1919–1926* (Princeton, NJ: Princeton University Press, 1957).

Grady, Henry F., *British War Finance, 1914–1919* (1927; reprint edn, New York: Ams Press, 1968).

Graham, John W., *Conscription and Conscience: A History, 1916–1919* (London: Allen & Unwin, 1922).

Graubard, Stephen Richards, 'Military demobilization in Great Britain following the First World War', *Journal of Modern History*, vol. 19 (December 1947), pp. 297–311.

Guinn, Paul, *British Strategy and Politics, 1914 to 1918* (Oxford: Clarendon Press, 1965).

Halperin, S. William, *Germany Tried Democracy: A Political History of the Reich from 1918 to 1933* (New York: Norton, 1965).

Hayes, Denis, *Conscription Conflict: The Conflict of Ideas in the Struggle for and against Military Conscription in Britain between 1901 and 1939* (London: Sheppard Press, 1949; New York: Garland, 1973).

Higham, Robin, *Armed Forces in Peacetime: Britain, 1918–1940 – a Case Study* (Hamden, Conn.: Archon, 1962).

Hinsley, F. H. (ed.), *British Foreign Policy under Sir Edward Grey* (Cambridge: Cambridge University Press, 1977).

Hirst, Francis W., *The Consequences of the War to Great Britain* (London: Oxford University Press, 1934).

Holborn, Hajo, *A History of Modern Germany, 1840–1945* (New York: Knopf, 1969).

Howard, Michael, *The Continental Commitment: The Dilemma of British Defence Policy in the Era of the Two World Wars* (London: Temple Smith, 1972).

Howard, Michael, *War and the Liberal Conscience* (New Brunswick, NJ: Rutgers University Press, 1978).

Hunt, Barry, and Preston, Adrian (eds), *War Aims and Strategic Policy in the Great War, 1914–1918* (London: Croom Helm, 1977).

Hutchison, Keith, *The Decline and Fall of British Capitalism* (New York: Scribner's, 1950).

Jacobson, Jon, *Locarno Diplomacy: Germany and the West, 1925–1929* (Princeton, NJ: Princeton University Press, 1972).

Jordan, W. M., *Great Britain, France, and the German Problem, 1918–1939* (London: Oxford University Press, 1943).

Kennedy, Paul M., 'Idealists and realists: British views of Germany, 1864–1939', *Transactions of the Royal Historical Society*, ser. 5, vol. 25 (1975), pp. 137–56.

Kennedy, Paul M., *The Rise and Fall of British Naval Mastery* (New York: Scribner's, 1976).

Kennedy, Paul M., *The Rise of the Anglo-German Antagonism, 1860–1914* (London: Allen & Unwin, 1980).

Kennedy, Paul M. (ed.), *The War Plans of the Great Powers, 1880–1914* (London: Allen & Unwin, 1979).

Kernek, Sterling J., 'The British government's reactions to President

Wilson's "peace" note of December 1916', *Historical Journal*, vol. 13 (December 1970), pp. 721–66.

Kernek, Sterling J., *Distractions of Peace during War: The Lloyd George Government's Reactions to Woodrow Wilson, December, 1916–November, 1918* (Philadelphia, Pa: American Philosophical Society, 1975).

Koss, Stephen, *Nonconformity in Modern British Politics* (Hamden, Conn.: Archon, 1975).

Lansdowne, Marquess of, 'The "peace letter" of 1917', *Nineteenth Century*, vol. 115 (March 1934), pp. 370–84.

Louis, William Roger, *Great Britain and Germany's Lost Colonies, 1914–1919* (Oxford: Clarendon Press, 1967).

Lowry, Francis Bullitt, 'The generals, the Armistice, and the Treaty of Versailles, 1919' (PhD dissertation, Duke University, Durham, NC, 1963).

Luckau, Alma, *The German Delegation at the Paris Peace Conference* (New York: Columbia University Press, 1941).

Marks, Sally, *The Illusion of Peace: International Relations in Europe, 1918–1933* (New York: St Martin's Press, 1976).

Marston, F. S., *The Peace Conference of 1919: Organization and Procedure* (London: Oxford University Press, 1944).

Martin, Laurence W., *Peace without Victory: Woodrow Wilson and the British Liberals* (New Haven, Conn.: Yale University Press, 1958).

Marwick, Arthur, *The Deluge: British Society and the First World War* (Harmondsworth, Middx: Penguin, 1967).

Mayer, Arno J., *Politics and Diplomacy of Peacemaking: Containment and Counterrevolution at Versailles, 1918–1919* (New York: Vintage, 1969).

Mayer, Arno J., *Wilson vs. Lenin: Political Origins of the New Diplomacy, 1917–1918* (Cleveland, Ohio: World Publishing, 1964).

Medlicott, W. N., *British Foreign Policy since Versailles, 1919–1963* (London: Methuen, 1968).

Medlicott, W. N., *Contemporary England, 1914–1964* (New York: McKay, 1967).

Morgan, J. H., *Assize of Arms: The Disarmament of Germany and her Rearmament (1919–1939)* (New York: Oxford University Press, 1946).

Morgan, Kenneth O., *David Lloyd George: Welsh Radical as World Statesman* (Cardiff: University of Wales Press, 1963).

Morris, A. J. Anthony, *Radicalism against War, 1906–1914: The Advocacy of Peace and Retrenchment* (Totowa, NJ: Rowman & Littlefield, 1972).

Mowat, Charles Loch, *Britain between the Wars, 1918–1940* (Chicago: University of Chicago Press, 1955).

McDougall, Walter A., *France's Rhineland Diplomacy, 1914–1924* (Princeton, NJ: Princeton University Press, 1978).

Nelson, Harold I., *Land and Power: British and Allied Policy on Germany's Frontiers, 1916–1919* (London: Routledge & Kegan Paul, 1963).

Northedge, F. S., '1917–1919: the implications for Britain', *Journal of Contemporary History*, vol. 3 (October 1968), pp. 191–210.

Northedge, F. S., *The Troubled Giant: Britain among the Great Powers, 1916–1919* (New York: Praeger, 1966).

Postgate, Raymond, and Vallance, Aylmer, *England Goes to Press: The English People's Opinion on Foreign Affairs as Reflected in their Newspapers since Waterloo (1815–1937)* (Indianapolis, Ind.: Bobbs-Merrill, 1937).

Renouvin, Pierre, 'Les buts de guerre du gouvernement français (1914–1918)', *Revue historique*, vol. 235 (January–March 1966), pp. 1–38.

Robbins, Keith, *The Abolition of War: The 'Peace Movement' in Britain, 1914–1919* (Cardiff: University of Wales Press, 1976).

Robbins, Keith, 'Lord Bryce and the First World War', *Historical Journal*, vol. 10 (June 1967), pp. 255–78.

Rosenberg, Arthur, *Imperial Germany: The Birth of the German Republic, 1871–1918*, trans. Ian F. D. Morrow (Boston, Mass.: Beacon Paperback, 1964).

Rothwell, V. H., *British War Aims and Peace Diplomacy, 1914–1918* (Oxford: Clarendon Press, 1971).

Rudin, Harry R., *Armistice, 1918* (New Haven, Conn.: Yale University Press, 1944).

Scally, Robert J., *The Origins of the Lloyd George Coalition: The Politics of Social-Imperialism, 1900–1918* (Princeton, NJ: Princeton University Press, 1975).

Schmidt, Gustav, 'Wozu noch "politische Geschichte"?: zum Verhältnis von Innen- und Aussen politik am Beispiel der englischen Friedenstrategie 1918/1919', *Aus Politik und Zeit Geschichte*, vol. 17 (April 1975), pp. 21–45.

Semmel, Bernard, *Imperialism and Social Reform: English Social-Imperial Thought, 1895–1914* (Cambridge, Mass.: Harvard University Press, 1960).

Stansky, Peter (ed.), *The Left and War: The British Labour Party and World War I* (New York: Oxford University Press, 1969).

Steiner, Zara, *Britain and the Origins of the First World War* (New York: St Martin's Press, 1977).

Steiner, Zara, *The Foreign Office and Foreign Policy, 1898–1914* (Cambridge: Cambridge University Press, 1969).

Stubbs, John, 'The impact of the Great War on the Conservative Party', in Gillian Peele and Chris Cook (eds), *The Politics of Reappraisal, 1918–1939* (New York: St Martin's Press, 1975), pp. 14–38.

Swartz, Marvin, *The Union of Democratic Control in British Politics during the First World War* (Oxford: Clarendon Press, 1971).

Taylor, A. J. P., *English History, 1914–1945* (New York: Oxford University Press, 1965).

Taylor, A. J. P., 'The war aims of the Allies in the First World War', in Richard Pares and A. J. P. Taylor (eds), *Essays Presented to Sir Lewis Namier* (London: Macmillan, 1956), pp. 475–505.

Taylor, A. J. P. (ed.), *Lloyd George: Twelve Essays* (New York: Atheneum, 1971).

Thompson, John M., *Russia, Bolshevism, and the Versailles Peace* (Princeton, NJ: Princeton University Press, 1966).

Tillman, Seth P., *Anglo-American Relations at the Paris Peace Conference of 1919* (Princeton, NJ: Princeton University Press, 1961).

Trachtenberg, Marc, *Reparation in World Politics: France and European Economic Diplomacy, 1916–1923* (New York: Columbia University Press, 1980).

Ullman, Richard H., *Anglo-Soviet Relations, 1917–1921*, 3 vols (Princeton, NJ: Princeton University Press, 1961–72).

Waite, Robert G. L., *Vanguard of Nazism: The Free Corps Movement in Postwar Germany, 1918–1923* (Cambridge, Mass: Harvard University Press, 1952).

Waites, Neville (ed.), *Troubled Neighbours: Franco-British Relations in the Twentieth Century* (London: Weidenfeld & Nicolson, 1971).

Walworth, Arthur, *America's Moment, 1918: American Diplomacy at the End of World War I* (New York: Norton, 1977).

Ward, Stephen R., 'Intelligence surveillance of British ex-servicemen, 1918–1920', *Historical Journal*, vol. 16 (March 1973), pp. 179–88.

Warman, Roberta M., 'The erosion of Foreign Office influence in the making of foreign policy, 1916–1918', *Historical Journal*, vol. 15 (March 1972), pp. 133–59.

Wheeler-Bennett, *The Nemesis of Power: The German Army in Politics, 1918–1945* (New York: St Martin's Press, 1954).

Willis, Irene Cooper, *England's Holy War: A Study of English Liberal Idealism during the Great War* (New York: Knopf, 1938).

Wilson, Trevor, *The Downfall of the Liberal Party, 1914–1935* (London: Collins, 1966).

Winkler, Henry R., *The League of Nations Movement in Great Britain, 1914–1919* (New Brunswick, NJ: Rutgers University Press, 1952).

Wolfers, Arnold, *Britain and France between Two Wars: Conflicting Strategies of Peace from Versailles to World War II* (New York: Norton, 1966).

Woodward, David R., 'David Lloyd George, a negotiated peace with Germany, and the Kühlmann peace kite of September, 1917', *Canadian Journal of History*, vol. 6 (March 1971), pp. 75–93.

Woodward, David R., 'The origins and intent of David Lloyd George's January 5 war aims speech', *Historian*, vol. 34 (November 1971), pp. 22–39.

Woodward, Sir Llewellyn, *Great Britain and the War of 1914–1918* (Boston, Mass.: Beacon Paperback, 1970).

Wrigley, Chris, *David Lloyd George and the British Labour Movement: Peace and War* (Hassocks, Sussex: Harvester, 1976).

Index

Addison, Christopher 74, 97, 104, 127-8

Admiralty: memorandum on arms limitation 150; recommendations for peace terms 12, 31

Agadir crisis 3, 9, 46

Alsace-Lorraine 146, 163, 196

Amery, Leopold S. 14, 15, 22, 37, 38, 43, 49, 55, 110, 118, 133, 149, 214

Anderson, R. W. 237

Angell, Norman 5, 15, 46

Anglo-American:
co-operation 82, 144, 148, 156, 175–6; economic relations 16, 97; effort to check France 164; guarantee to France 193, 195, 202; naval rivalry 97, 103, 201; peace strategy 162–3; tension over mediation 17

Anglo-French: conference 39; conflict over treaty 208; differences on conscription 160–2, on disarmament 72, 176–7, on postwar security 63, 173–4, 184–6; economic relations 100; Entente 4, 7; rivalry for German compensation 100; tensions over Rhineland agreement 204; territorial rivalry 45, 100, 101

Anglo-Russian Entente 4, 45

armaments 24, 25, 26, 63, 85, 128, 186–7, 211; definition 70, 151, 154–5; limitation 24–5, 26, 61–8, 123, 124–8, 151

Armistice:
Foch's proposals 86, 101–2; German overture 60, 84, 109; Haig's recommendations 84, 91–2; military and naval staff recommendations 85, 87–8; Pres. Wilson's note 89–90, 93–4; renewal 118, 176; signature 112, 244; terms discussed by Allies 85–6, 101–3

army, armies: Canadian 182; conscript 153, 160, 178; demobilisation 115; German postwar 179, 181, 189–93, 223; of occupation 118, 139, 147, 168, 173, 177, 204, 208, 220; police function of 162, 196; professional 191, 224; recruiting 115, 191–2; standing 75, 132; volunteer 154, 190

Asquith, Herbert Henry 2, 10–11; advocates abolition of conscription 135; offered Lord Chancellorship 132–3; reluctant to define war aims 31; speech at Guildhall (1914) 10, 26; speech (April 1916) 10–11; statements on war aims 10–11, 26; suspicions of French 100

Australia 156, 182, 183, 251

Austria (-Hungary) 9, 14, 18, 51, 77, 89

Balfour, Arthur J.: accepts need for preliminary military terms 176; advises co-operation with USA 146; article in *Nord und Sud* 53; concern at possible Russian victory 46; First Lord of the Admiralty 13; Foreign Secretary 38, 54, 56, 111–12; meets French at London conference 146; memorandum on peace terms 30, 33, 38, 53–4, 69; note to US 39–40, 54; opposes drastic treatment of Germany 196–7; present at Congress of Berlin (1878) 53; views on armistice and treaty terms 88, 94, 182–3, 184, 192; on Foch's proposals 189–90, 192; on French naval power 100

Balkan War, First 3, 9

Barnes, George 56, 183, 205

Barnett, Correlli 217

Bartholomew, Brig.-Gen. W. 180

Belgium 5, 7, 10, 14, 64, 193, 196, 230

Berlin:
general strike 180; House's prewar visit 4; Spartacist rising 179; threat of occupation 205, 206; war party in control 9

Bertie, Sir Francis 4, 26, 27, 31, 46, 48, 75

Bikaner, Maharaja of 235

Birdsall, Paul 178, 226

Bliss, Gen. Tasker 105–6

blockade of Germany 17, 22, 205
Bolsheviks, Bolshevism: British fears
104–6, 107, 110, 112, 113–14, 117,
154, 159, 195, 197–9; containment
107, 165, 178, 180; German 104–6,
179–81; Hungarian 202; Russian
77, 159, 178–9, 197–8
Borden, Sir Robert 71, 144, 146–7, 158,
182, 235
Bourgeois Committee 152
Brest-Litovsk 77, 78. *See also* Treaties
Briand, Aristide 33
British Empire 36, 37, 38, 146–7; colonial ambitions 147; consultation
40; Delegation 182, 204, 206; effect
of Rhineland agreement on 204–5;
German territorial challenge to 42,
49, 55, 56; postwar security 96; sea
power 97; tactics at peace confer-
ence 147–8; threats to 43–4, 58. *See
also* Great Britain
Brockdorff-Rantzau, U. von 205, 212,
259
Brunner, Sir John 5, 6
Bryce, Lord 7, 14, 62–3, 235; Bryce
Group 235
Buchanan, Sir George 47
Buckler, William H. 72, 75
Buxton, Francis Noel 4

Cambon, Paul 97, 145
Canada 147, 158,,,,, 182
Carson, Sir Edward 31, 35, 79
Cecil, Lord Robert 27, 34, 64–5, 66, 69,
70, 79, 81–2, 149, 158–9, 161–2,
176, 189, 190, 205
Central Aberdeenshire by-election 169
Central Hull by-election 169
Central Powers 33, 77, 79, 80
Chamberlain, Sir Austen 55, 69, 94, 98–
9, 105, 107, 111, 120, 168, 207, 209,
216, 220–1
Chamberlain, Joseph 37
Churchill, Winston L. S.: anti-
Bolshevism 106–7; declares German
people guilty 120; doubts defensive
value of league 156; expects Russian
resurgence 57, 59; First Lord of
Admiralty 9, 23, 44–5; Minister of
Munitions 57; shares Lloyd
George's anxiety over Germany 113;
supports disarmament recom-
mendations 88; suspicious of France

and Russia 44; urges conciliatory
line on treaty 205–6; views on conscription 134–5; (mentioned) 215
Civil Liberties, National Council for 169
Clemenceau, Georges 101, 147, 175,
191, 192, 193, 195, 200–1, 203, 204,
208, 209, 210
Clerk, George 12, 42
coal (-mines) 76; industry 129; shortage
67, 115; release of miners 115, 116;
strike 195, 217
Coalition, Lloyd George: campaign
pledges 122–3, 137, 138, 141, 169;
candidates 136; conscription plans
138–40; demobilisation plans 166;
disarmament policy 142, 159–64;
domestic aims 128, 130, 166; election manifesto 125, 128, 134
Coefficients, the 51
Cologne zone 220
command of the sea 43–4, 97, 201
Committee of Imperial Defence: Grey's
address to 43–4; Sub-committee on
Territorial Changes 12, 49
conscription: abolition of 80, 122, 126–7,
153–4, 160, 191; election issue 132–
41, 179; German (*see* Germany);
Liberal opponents 126–7; proposed
extension to Ireland 133; seen as
source of militarism 153–4, 188–9
Conservative(s): businessmen 129;
imperialists 38; malcontents 35;
MPs 185; moderate 34; newspapers
121, 191; prewar defence stance
128; reactions to disarmament 128–
9, to Fontainebleau Memorandum
203
Contemporary Review 3
Cook, Sir Joseph 182–3, 251
Cooper, Sir Richard 121
Corbett, Sir Julian 250
Council: of Three 203, 208; of Four 210,
212; of Five 211; of Ten 170–1
Crewe House 19, 20, 122
Croft, Gen. Henry Page 121
Cromer, Lord 7–8, 42
Crowe, Sir Eyre 13–14, 52–3, 54, 56, 65–
6, 69, 82, 118, 151, 154, 218
Curzon, Lord 31, 37, 43, 56, 78–9, 89,
94–5, 216

Daily Chronicle 7, 14, 111
Daily Mail 16, 116, 121, 182, 191, 240